The panorama of baseball is unfolded in
this book's sprightly words and lively
photos — many published for the first
time — against a background of historical turning points. From primitive stick-
ball games played in village squares
during the American Revolution to the
refined professional sport of the
mid-1980s, baseball has continually mirrored the American scene.

Baseball's triumphant moments are
featured here: the high spots of every
season from the 1858 contest between
the New York Knickerbockers and the
Brooklyn Atlantics, to the 1985 world
championship campaign of the Kansas
City Royals; the constant setting of new
records, including Hank Aaron's overtaking of Babe Ruth and Pete Rose's
outnumbering of Ty Cobb; and the brilliant leadership of the game's statesmen
such as Ban Johnson and Branch
Rickey. But baseball's headaches and
coping strategies, successful or un-
successful, get due attention. The game
has weathered wars, depressions, and
such social changes as immigration, urbanization, unionization, and integration that have called for agonizing
but finally effective adjustments. Technological changes like floodlighting and
astroturf have required even tougher
adjustments by players, and the staggering riches brought by television are a
bonanza that players, managers, and
owners are still learning to live with.

Unlike some pessimistic observers,
Voigt remains convinced that organized
baseball will meet its current challenges
with its historic fortitude. In this book
he offers entertainment and food for
thought to both new and seasoned fans.

David Quentin Voigt, who
is on the faculty of Albright College,
earned an M.A. in American history at
Columbia and a Ph.D. in social science
at Syracuse.

Baseball: An Illustrated History

BASEBALL
An Illustrated History

DAVID QUENTIN VOIGT

92-804

THE PENNSYLVANIA STATE UNIVERSITY PRESS
UNIVERSITY PARK AND LONDON

FOR MY BATTERY MATE,
VIRGINIA,
AND FOR MY COACHES,
SONS DAVE AND MARK.

The team logos depicted herein are the property and trademarks of their respective Major League Clubs and have been reproduced with the permission of Major League Baseball.

Library of Congress Cataloging-in-Publication Data
Voigt, David Quentin.
Baseball, an illustrated history.
Bibliography: p.
Includes index.
1. Baseball—United States—History. I. Title.
GV863.A1V654 1987   796.357'0973   85-43558
ISBN 0-271-00434-7

9 # CONTENTS

FEW LOVE AFFAIRS ENDURE FOR SEVEN SCORE YEARS, BUT # PREFACE
America's passion for baseball has so endured, and there are no signs of
diminishing ardor. Indeed, recent years have seen a vast outpouring of
words and pictures touching on all forms and aspects of the game.

As a veteran historian of major league baseball, I have been profoundly gratified by the reception given to my three-volume history.
Favorable reactions to *American Baseball* have been received from fellow
historians, fans, players, and students in college-level courses about
baseball's impact on American society. From such respondents have
come encouraging suggestions that I undertake the task of writing a
concise, single-volume history of American baseball. Certainly, such a
work is sorely needed.

Baseball: An Illustrated History strives to meet the need for a comprehensive overview of the American game. The book condenses the
highlights of baseball's evolution from colonial village greens to the
elaborate stadiums of the Electronic Age. While mainly concerned with
the major league game, which has always influenced the growth of
other forms of the game, my coverage also embraces the Negro major
leagues, the minor leagues and semi-pro action, and amateur forms of
the game, including collegiate competition. To vivify the narrative,
more than four hundred pictures are integrated into the historical
flow.

Happily, the task of writing *Baseball: An Illustrated History* was no
solitary effort. In acknowledging the support of baseball fans and fellow
scholars, I am especially mindful of members of the Society for American Baseball Research and of the North American Society for Sports
History. With a membership now grown to seven thousand persons,
SABR provided not only forums for testing my ideas, but also individual critical suggestions and valuable assistance. Among many SABR
benefactors, several deserve special thanks: Cliff Kachline, W. Lloyd
Johnson, John Holway, John Pardon, Verne Luse, Kit Crissey, and
Tom Heitz, the last of whom also functions as the efficient librarian of
the Baseball Library at Cooperstown.

Like SABR, NASSH, with its membership of academic sports scholars, provided a useful forum at its annual Symposium on Baseball.
Among my NASSH colleagues, Richard Crepeau served as the Penn
State Press's outside reader. Ronald Smith generously allowed me to
read the manuscript of his forthcoming history of intercollegiate athletics. Special thanks for encouragement and suggestions go also to Dick
Crepeau, Jim Harper, Harry Jebsen, Tony Papalas, Sam Regalado,

Steve Riess, and Lyle Olson; these and other perennial NASSH baseball symposium contributors supplied invaluable and continuing support.

Meanwhile, the formidable task of obtaining the more than four hundred photographs, drawings, and cartoons that enliven this history could not have been surmounted without the generous assistance of corporate and individual collectors. Among the former, I gratefully acknowledge the assistance of directors of the National Baseball Library and Museum at Cooperstown, the Goulston and Schomburg collections of the New York Public Library, the Boston Public Library, the Temple University School of Photojournalism Library, and the public relations departments of all of the major league clubs, as well as those of Little League Baseball and the University of Miami. I am also heavily indebted to a number of individual collectors, whose generosity is much treasured. Among them, Dennis Goldstein opened up his dazzling collection of rare photos of players and events. Special thanks also go to Mike Mumby for making available lively action photos from his fine collection, and to John Thorn for providing dramatic photos from his outstanding collection. Other providers of great illustrations include Charles Burkhardt, Herman Seid, Mike Anderson, George Brace, Gordon Miller, and Ron Smith. By their kindly assistance, the awesome task of collecting such a variety of illustrative material became a true labor of love.

Finally, deep appreciation for professional acumen and sympathetic criticism and advice goes to my editor, John M. Pickering, who assisted with both the architecture and the carpentry of this work. The director, Chris W. Kentera, and staff of Penn State Press also provided valuable help and support.

THE FORMATIVE YEARS, COLONIAL DAYS TO 1900

MAJOR LEAGUE BASEBALL HAD ITS ORIGINS IN BRITISH *stick-ball games, notably one called rounders; an American version of rounders, called "base ball," was played as far back as Revolutionary War times. A popular pastime of youngsters and adults in northeastern American towns and villages, differing versions of base ball competed until 1845, when the New York Knickerbocker Club's formal version of base ball was generally adopted.*

By the 1850s the proliferation of men's baseball clubs ushered in the "Gentlemen's Era" of organized baseball. Baseball clubs, located mainly in northern and midwestern towns and cities, served the recreational interests of America's growing centers of commerce and industry. By the late 1850s baseball enthusiasts were touting the game as America's national pastime, and dozens of clubs enrolled under the National Association of Base Ball Players. Loosely organized championship competition among clubs stirred competitive spirits and attracted paying crowds that kindled interest in the game's commercial possibilities. The onslaught of the Civil War failed to dampen baseball's popularity; indeed, the game gained adherents among Civil War soldiers, and the nationalistic sentiments stirred by the Union victory enhanced baseball's mythic claim to being "America's national game."

In the late 1860s the game's booming popularity paved the way for the professionalization of baseball. Although some players were paid for playing ball years earlier, the Cincinnati Red Stockings of 1869 became the first openly professional team. When others followed, the National Association of Professional Base Ball Players was organized and commenced play in 1871 as the first professional major league. After five seasons of play, the player-run National Association was succeeded by the National League of Professional Base Ball Clubs. Organized in 1876 by entrepreneurial club owners, the National League became a permanent major league; it has endured for more than a century as the first "officially" credited major league.

Under National League leadership, major league baseball entered upon a "Golden Age" during the decade of the 1880s. In those years cash and glory rained on the game and its principals. Attendance soared, new parks were built, technological innovations were introduced, rules were rewritten, and newspapers and weeklies, such as The Sporting News *and* Sporting Life, *popularized the game and its player-heroes. Although the National League predominated, the American Association won recognition as a second major league; dual major league competition allowed for popular World Series competition between the two leagues. Moreover, baseball's surging popularity was enhanced by books, songs, and theatrical skits; among the latter, Ernest Thayer's poem "Casey at the Bat" was performed thousands of times by monologist De Wolfe Hopper before a generation of vaudeville audiences. Enthusiasm for baseball reached new heights when Albert G. Spalding sponsored a world tour of professional baseball teams in 1888–89.*

Baseball's Golden Age ended in 1890 when organized players challenged club owners over such issues as the reserve clause and the salary limitation plan. The defiant players organized a rival major league that year, but they were compelled by financial losses to surrender. Skill on the diamond, they found, does not guarantee business acumen. In the wake of the Players League war, the National League owners battled the American Association and forced the surrender of that rival in 1891. In 1892 four franchises from the vanquished Association were enrolled under the "National League and American Association" to form a single twelve-club "big league," which lasted until 1900. Emulating the monopolists in business and industry, major league owners hoped to profit by their baseball monopoly, forgetting that most American investors and sports fans relish competition.

The "big league" venture proved to be both unprofitable and unpopular, however. Instead of attaining new uplands of prosperity, major league baseball during the 1890s entered a dismal "Feudal Age." In those years assertive owners fought one another like medieval robber barons. To add to the disharmony, some owners embarked on divisive "syndicate" ventures; one owner, Andrew Freedman, led a faction with the quixotic goal of pooling players and resources under a "baseball trust." In 1900 National League owners abandoned the twelve-club format and returned to eight teams. By then the new American League had challenged the National League monopoly. When the National League conferred major league status upon the American League in 1903, restoration of the dual major league system headed the game on a popular and successful course.

1

IN THE BEGINNING WERE THE PLAYERS

BASEBALL'S PLACE IN AMERICAN SOCIETY WAS DE-bated in *Harper's Weekly* in the fall of 1859. One observer saw the game as chiefly a spectator sport for city dwellers, whereas another testified he had seen baseball played throughout rural America at barn raisings and during school recesses "and often enjoyed by youths of both sexes." Both reporters were partly right, as events of the Civil War era were to prove.

On the one hand, baseball was widely played in both town and country as the young nation moved toward the War Between the States. On the other hand, many city dwellers gained the habit of rooting for their favorite clubs, sometimes even paying for admission to games. Then—between Confederate bombardment of Fort Sumter in 1861 and Union victory at Appomattox in 1865—Billy Yank and Johnny Reb kept baseball alive on drill fields and parade grounds and even in prison stockades.

Baseball's evolution mirrored the nation's progress. The number of players and spectators grew as the U.S. population exploded, from

Base ball as played on Boston Common, depicted in the 1834 *Book of Sports.* (Courtesy John A. Lucas and Ronald A. Smith)

Union soldiers with baseball bats in a Civil War camp. (Courtesy Dennis Goldstein)

Abner Doubleday in his general's uniform. (Courtesy National Baseball Library, Cooperstown, New York)

thirty-one million to fifty million, in the generation between 1860 and 1880. This population explosion came partly from a vigorous birthrate and partly from a flood of immigration—a constant source of new baseball talent. The emergence of the United States as an industrial giant—from a global fourth place in factory output in 1860 to first place before the end of the century—expedited baseball's rise to national prominence. An expanding railroad network facilitated competition among clubs in widely scattered cities; telegraphy kept fans' interest high through speedy journalistic reports; streetcars moved fans to and from ballparks; and increasing purchasing power and decreasing working hours created a market for recreational activity.

Progress brings its problems. America's transformation from a mostly rural-agricultural society to a largely urban-industrial one—a process that moved with breathtaking speed from 1860 to 1880—caused many social dislocations, most of them reflected in organized baseball. Many captains of industry and finance were brilliant innovators and organizers, while some were greedy and ruthless "robber barons." Most Americans adapted their lives to the discipline of factory or office, but many took to loafing, drunkenness, gambling, or crime. Although workers' purchasing power rose by an estimated 40 percent between 1850 and 1880, many workers failed to get a fair share, and many others felt they were shortchanged—including some professional ball players. Reform movements thrived as always in the United States. Many reformers were dedicated crusaders for constructive change, like the elimination of slums and the abolition of child labor, whereas some were spoilsports obsessed with the prohibition of beer and Sunday baseball.

A new brand of reformers, labor leaders, was spawned by industrial growth. Some labor leaders simply urged workers to organize and bargain collectively, while others—notably the Knights of Labor—were convinced that workers could cooperatively finance and manage their own businesses. This "knightly" dream was pursued briefly by the player-controlled National Association of Professional Base Ball Players from 1871 to 1875. Then came the modern National League, organized by skilled entrepreneurs, managers, and marketers. Among the marketing strategies that evolved in the new league was the concoction of a myth about baseball's origins.

How easy it would be to begin a history of baseball by announcing that the game began in 1839 as the inspired invention of that young West Point cadet Abner Doubleday!

But historical realities seldom allow such easy explanations. Indeed, more than the lore of any other team sport, baseball folklore is studded with fanciful myths like the Doubleday legend. Factual accounts are rarely as satisfying as tall stories of heroic deeds. Yet, even as tough-minded Americans sense the phoniness of such yarns, they usually resent historians who shoot them down. Like messengers bearing bad news, historians who try to set the record straight are about as welcome as fathers telling children there is no Santa Claus.

In truth, major league baseball was thirty-five years old by the time the Doubleday legend surfaced. When the story came to light, telling of Doubleday's invention in the summer of 1839 at Cooperstown, New York, the tale was the solemn conclusion of a committee commissioned by major league owners of 1905 to inquire into the origins of "the national game." Dominated by Albert Goodwill Spalding, the former star pitcher turned millionaire sporting-goods tycoon, the committee met several times and claimed to have amassed impressive data. But when the time came for the committee's report, Spalding explained that a fire had destroyed the records. Hence, the final report drew mostly on the testimony of Abner Graves, an aged mining engineer, who vaguely recalled seeing Doubleday design the game during that far-off summer of 1839. With Doubleday long in his grave—he died in 1893—no disclaimer from him was heard, so major league officials dutifully accepted the signed report in December of 1907.

That the story was patently false has been demonstrated time and again by historians. An inveterate diarist, Abner Doubleday made no mention of baseball, nor did he depart West Point for Cooperstown in 1839. Moreover, printed references to "base ball" date back as early as 1700 in America, and various forms of the game were played in America long before 1839. Indeed, Doubleday was credited with inventing a modernized version of the game unknown in 1839 and closely resembling the game as played in 1907. Still, Doubleday was an ideal hero for a legend; a small-town boy, he had risen to the rank of major-general and commanded a Union corps at Gettysburg. Clearly, the acceptance and propagation of the Doubleday myth require a childlike faith, which apparently was in plentiful supply among sportswriters and baseball propagandists in 1939 when the major leagues solemnly celebrated the centennial of the game's mythic invention.

Perhaps Spalding doubted his own legend, since his celebrated history book contains records of games played earlier than the magical year of 1839. Nevertheless, Spalding deliberately fostered a myth. An ardent nationalist, proclaiming baseball as "America's National Game," Spalding stubbornly rejected baseball's mundane evolution from English bat-

Albert G. Spalding as a Boston Red Stocking pitcher in the early 1870s. (Courtesy New York Public Library)

Alexander Jay Cartwright with his fireman's trumpet. (Courtesy National Baseball Library, Cooperstown, New York)

and-ball games, arguing that baseball owed nothing to "English traditions, customs and conventionalities."

But the weight of scholarly opinion is on the side of baseball's evolution from stick-and-ball games played by generations of ordinary Englishmen and American colonists. Among baseball's ancestors were varieties of "old cat" games, rounders, and town ball. Town ball was an American version of rounders played by children and adults. Writing in his *Book of Sports* in 1827, British author Robin Carver noted that Americans called their form of rounders "base ball" because they used bases instead of stakes as in cricket.

Carver admitted regretfully that base ball was choking off cricket in America. Nevertheless, the British game of cricket played its part in baseball's evolution. From cricket came umpires and innings; also, early baseball writers used cricket lingo to describe baseball games, using idioms like "excellent field," "batsmen," "punishing loose bowling," and "playing for the side." And pioneer baseball innovators like William Henry ("Harry") Wright, a cricket pro turned baseball manager, resourcefully used cricket savvy to professionalize and promote American baseball.

As an evolving blend of informal rounders games and formalized cricket, baseball needed no sudden invention to burst forth as a popular American sport. That grown men played baseball in rural villages of New York as early as the 1820s was vouchsafed by the grandfather of historian Samuel Hopkins Adams, who played the game as a boy "in Mumford's Pasture Lot."

What grandfather Adams played was a crude version of the modern game. In his day informal versions competed until a survival-of-the-fittest process narrowed contending versions of baseball to two rivals. One version, the "Massachusetts game," employed a rectangular field of play, with the three bases located asymmetrically from each other and with home base located behind the batter's position. Fielders called "scouts" could put a batter out by hitting him with a thrown ball or catching a hit ball on the first bounce as well as in the air.

The sprightly Massachusetts game lasted until the 1840s, when the rival "New York game" won the struggle for existence. This triumph owed much to a human catalyst, the urbane New Yorker Alexander Joy Cartwright, whose claim to fathering baseball as we know it is mostly forgotten. In 1845 Cartwright persuaded his young friends to try a symmetrical version of the game that he devised. In quick time his plan

New York Knickerbockers playing on Elysian Fields in Hoboken, New Jersey, as seen by an artist for *Harper's Weekly* in 1859. (Courtesy John A. Lucas and Ronald A. Smith)

of using a diamond-shaped infield, with bases set ninety feet apart, was accepted along with other suggestions, like playing nine men on a side, limiting team batting to three outs, setting the pitching distance at forty-five feet, requiring the pitcher to "pitch" the ball in a stiff-armed, underhanded manner, establishing the three-strikes-and-out rule, and limiting outs to catches or balls thrown to the first baseman before the runner arrived.

To some extent, Cartwright's rules prevailed because he wrote them down, formalized them, and propagated them. Moreover, Cartwright's own Knickerbocker Base Ball Club was one of the first organized clubs, a fact that enhanced its influence as a baseball propagating force. Still, it must not be supposed that the game suddenly became the game we now know. Missing from Cartwright's scheme were umpires, bases on balls, the nine-inning rule, and, above all, the tactical and strategic byplay of teamwork.

As other baseball clubs organized, the Knickerbocker example was widely imitated by the 1850s. Mostly these clubs sprang up in New York City and its hinterlands and in the cities of nearby states, such as New Jersey, Pennsylvania, Maryland, and the District of Columbia. Thus, organized baseball appeared as an urban innovation, not the rustic creation of arcadian myths.

Nor did the gentlemen of the Knickerbocker Club succeed in establishing themselves as baseball's social arbiters, because Americans, then as now, recognized no elite class. Certainly not the Knickerbockers, with their written rules, formal etiquette, and flannel uniforms topped by straw hats! In truth, the Knickerbockers were only a pretentious band of local merchants, clerks, and white-collar workers. Nor were bona fide gentlemen to be found in the ranks of the other baseball clubs that sprang up and ignited a baseball boomlet in the 1850s. In the New York area, games were played "on every available green plot within a ten mile circuit of the city." But the players were gentlemen only by egalitarian customs that "sirred" and "mistered" every adult male. Some clubs, like the Brooklyn Atlantics, housed local Democratic politicians, while the Brooklyn Eckfords' roster ran to shipwrights and mechanics, the Morrisania Unions to members of the Workingmen's Party, and the Mutuals to city firemen and Tammany Hall boss William Marcy Tweed.

If these rivals refused to accept the suzerainty of the Knickerbockers, at least they accepted the amateur code prescribed by them. Under threat of being frozen out of games, the Knickerbocker code demanded gentlemanly behavior and no hint of any pay for play. Since no leagues or regular schedules existed, games had to be arranged through formal correspondence between club secretaries, and refusals to play lent force to the code. Nevertheless, like the notion of gentlemanly players, amateurism was a shaky ideal in American sport. Both were aristocratic British imports that generally ran against the egalitarian and competitive themes of American society. Nor were American baseball clubs tardy about demonstrating a preference for victories over aristocratic niceties.

The dethroning of the Knickerbockers as baseball's would-be fashion dictators came with shocking suddenness. In 1858 some twenty-five

Al Reach, Philadelphia Athletics star, as a young player. (Courtesy National Baseball Library, Cooperstown, New York)

Left:
Brooklyn Atlantics in 1865. (Author's Collection)

Right:
Baseball Day in 1865, in New York City's Central Park, attracted players of all ages. (Courtesy Dennis Goldstein)

fessionals" to retain memberships. But hints of a coming purge came at the 1864 meeting when the Association defined a "professional player" as one who "plays base ball for money, place or emolument."

The threatened purge of professionals never came off, perhaps because the professionals had strong grass-roots support. Fans seemed to worship stars like Harry Wright, who, with other stars, was honored in 1863 with a benefit game where admission was charged and souvenir pictures of professionals sold for a quarter apiece. After the game the honorees split the receipts, each man getting $29.65.

Nor did peacetime stay creeping commercialism. As new clubs sprang up like dandelions, good players were courted and rewarded. Some clubs, including the Mutuals and Atlantics, gave good men easy jobs with good pay. At Washington the National stars got cushy government jobs and shares of receipts from games. And clubs like the Athletics and half a dozen others reportedly paid stars straight salaries. This mercenary trend was so far gone by 1868 that Henry Chadwick, the influential baseball journalist and pundit, wrote matter-of-factly of entire teams being paid for play. In January, Chadwick casually noted that the Atlantics "will have their regular professional ten," along with "their amateur first nine and their muffins."

Such easy acceptance testified to other changes affecting American baseball. In the short span of a single decade, clubs were transformed from amateur organizations—with gentlemanly members playing for the sport—into highly competitive organizations whose skilled players were paid to win. To finance such clubs, admissions were charged, talented players courted and coddled, and less talented club members relegated to the status of "muffins," a derisive term from which the familiar term "muff," meaning a misplayed ball, derives.

And yet clubs of the late 1860s stubbornly clung to gentlemanly codes. Muffins and professionals co-existed, with no invidious distinctions between management and players. On the contrary, professional players and member-owners seemed to enjoy an artist-patron relationship, and as yet dues-paying club members did not view baseball as a business. The spirit of the gentlemanly amateur and the patron-owner was dying, but the myth that club owners should be regarded as "sportsmen" even today is a holdover from this early era. The gap between professionals and amateurs widened for other reasons. Offensively and defensively the game was changing, demanding more skill and strategy. Indeed, old-time Knickerbockers of 1845 would hardly recognize the game as played in 1869.

For one thing, pitching styles were changing. In 1860 Jim Creighton, a young fastball pitcher, revolutionized the art of underhand pitching by augmenting his speed with a baffling twisting delivery. Landing Creighton, who reportedly was paid for his services, made a formidable contender of the Excelsiors, a team composed of merchants and clerks with aristocratic pretensions. The team's reputation soared in the wake of its unprecedented road tour that covered four states, attracting large crowds and producing a string of victories. Touted as the nation's best team, the Excelsiors were challenged by the rival Brooklyn Atlantics, a blue-collar team of hard-hitters with a large and vocal following. The three games between these contenders drew crowds of 10,000, 12,000, and more than 15,000. With Creighton in the box, the Excelsiors won the first match, but the Atlantics took the second by a 15-14 score. The third game played at the Atlantics' home grounds resulted in so many hostile incidents by the pro-Atlantic crowd that the Excelsior captain ordered his team off the field. The match was declared a tie, and ever after the gentlemanly Excelsiors refused to play the Atlantics. The Excelsiors' descent from the top rank was speeded by the tragic death of Creighton in 1862. While batting, he strained himself and died from internal injuries. His saddened mates thereupon immortalized him, erecting a garish monument with carvings of crossed bats, a baseball cap, a base, and a scorebook, topped off with a giant baseball.

Henry Chadwick, whose unflagging zeal as baseball reporter, historian, critic, and rule maker won him the title "Father of the Game." (Courtesy National Baseball Library, Cooperstown, New York)

Creighton's death liberated hitters for a time, although hitters then could wait for a desirable pitch with no penalty of called strikes. But in 1863 the Association introduced umpires instructed to call balls or strikes and to penalize "poor form" in pitching, or game-delaying tactics. Also, iron plates were introduced to mark the pitcher's box and home plate. And the new rules demanded more skilled fielding by requiring fair balls to be caught on the fly instead of on the first bounce, although foul balls caught on the first bounce still counted as outs.

Until the 1880s batters enjoyed the advantage of requesting high or low strikes, forcing pitchers to throw to a hitter's strength. But pitchers, then as now, were adaptive. In 1865 young Arthur Cummings observed how clam shells could be made to curve to the right when hurled underhanded with a wrist twist. Thus inspired, he learned to curve a baseball. Although such pitching once dislocated his wrist, Cummings's curve and "drop ball" made for a baffling mix and catapulted him to stardom with the New York Mutuals in 1872.

To see such stars, fans flocked to games, taking partisan delight in cheering local teams against outlanders. A strong gambling fever added excitement. "So common has betting become at base ball matches," complained a *Harper's* editor, "that the most respectable clubs . . . indulge in it," and he warned that "games have been sold for the benefit of gamblers." Nevertheless, fans braved such threats and flocked to Association matches. In 1861 the Brooklyn Atlantics dominated, followed by the Brooklyn Eckfords, who ruled in 1862 and went undefeated in 1863. But then the Atlantics regained the heights, going undefeated in 1864 and 1865.

In modern parlance these teams were not champions, nor was the Association a league. In those freewheeling years no system of recognized franchises or formal schedules of games existed. It was a time when any club might play, provided rivals agreed to schedule them. And there was the rub. Written challenges passed between clubs, but decisions to play depended on the whims of club members. Frequently, requests were turned down because a challenger was deemed "unworthy" or, worse, "ungentlemanly." For this reason claims to national honors were disputed. For example, in 1867 the Washington Nationals, captained by George Wright, a star shortstop and brother of Harry Wright, toured the East and Midwest, beating all contenders until losing 29-23 to the lightly regarded Forest City Club of Rockford, Illinois, whose ranks included Albert Spalding and Ross Barnes. That defeat, coming amidst charges that the Nationals had thrown the game, marred Washington's otherwise glorious season.

To clarify the question of national champs, editor Frank Queen of

Cincinnati Reds parade on their opening day in 1869. (Courtesy National Baseball Library, Cooperstown, New York)

Cincinnati Reds pose for a group portrait in 1869. (Courtesy John Thorn)

the *New York Clipper* in 1868 offered a gold ball to the best team and an individual medal to the star player at each position. That year five medals went to members of the Philadelphia Athletics, but no gold ball was awarded because of arguments among the top claimants.

Plagued by such disputes, the Association's credibility was marred further by accusations of gambling, revolving, and hippodroming. "Hippodroming" referred to fixing games in advance, and "revolving" was applied to contract jumping by players. Vainly, journalist Henry Chadwick urged clubs to refuse to sign jumpers, but an Association rule merely demanded that a player give sixty days' notice before quitting. Not for a decade would the revolving problem be resolved—via the reserve clause binding a player to his parent club.

But the major problem vexing the Association was the growing tension between amateur and professional players. As the 1869 season dawned, Chadwick conceded that baseball was fast becoming a commercialized spectacle. Surveying the leading contenders, Chadwick counted nine professional teams, including the newly reorganized Red Stocking Club of Cincinnati. Managed by Harry Wright, the Reds styled themselves as the first all-salaried team, with each player contracted for a season's service at a stated rate of pay. They were not, as legend would have it, the first paid players, or even the first all-salaried team. But they were the first frankly admitted professional team. And if successful under this banner in competition with rivals, they would advance the cause of professional baseball and pave the way for the first commercialized major league.

MR. CHAMPION'S CHAMPIONS

Rival skippers of the 1870 season are pictured here and on the opposite page. Above is Robert Ferguson, captain and catcher for the Brooklyn Atlantics, as seen by an artist in the *New York Clipper*. (Author's Collection)

Among the handful of baseball pundits of 1869, a *Clipper* writer warned "contestants . . . to keep one eye turned towards Porkopolis." That meant Cincinnati, the hog-butchering capital of America, whose citizens were just being exposed to big-time baseball. Only four years earlier, Aaron B. Champion, a young lawyer and merchant, had organized the Union Cricket Club, but the baseball mania of the times persuaded him to add baseball to the club's agenda. A zealous local booster, Champion viewed baseball as a gimmick for stimulating local business and glorifying his beloved "Queen City."

Early in 1868 Champion persuaded his fellow club directors to spend $11,000 to refit the Union Grounds for baseball. The results were encouraging, as the club's new Red Stocking team unexpectedly beat their local rivals, the Buckeye Club. Thus inspired, Champion called for a $15,000 stock issue to strengthen the Reds for an all-out 1869 assault on the nation's best teams. Notwithstanding financial losses from 1868, Champion's appeal carried. With new money pledged, Champion set out to obtain the nation's top pro players. A two-man committee headed by George Ellard, a local sporting-goods merchant, was entrusted with the ivory hunt. But the committee's ham-handed approach was simply to try to sign the nine *Clipper* gold-medal winners. Although this was feasible, rival clubs were forewarned and took countermeasures, while the courted stars used the Cincinnati bids as wedges to pry more money from their parent clubs. Thus, just when it appeared as if five medalists were in the Cincinnati fold, two reneged. Outraged, Champion screamed "revolvers" and "ungentlemanly conduct," but his protests failed to land the pair.

Chastened by his education in the ways of baseball, Champion turned the recruiting project over to Harry Wright. As the manager of the 1868 Reds, Wright had a reputation in baseball circles that was enviable—and astonishing, too, considering that prior to 1867 he had been a part-time baseball player and a full-time professional cricketer for Champion's Union Club. But the handsome, bewhiskered Wright easily switched from cricket to baseball. Already a first-rate player, Wright benefited from the similarities between cricket and baseball. So did his brother George, a *Clipper* gold-medal shortstop, and to a lesser extent his brother Sam. Indeed, the three Wrights were British-born sons of a professional cricketer who plied his skills in America and imbued his sons with his dedication to training and endless practice.

Actually, baseball was so new that a man of Wright's athletic skills could speedily master the game. As a player, manager, league organizer, and promoter of the professional game, Wright successfully applied cricket ways to baseball, earning him the accolade of "Father of Professional Baseball." In 1868 Wright's success as playing manager of the Reds won the admiration of Chadwick, also British-born, who noted that the Reds were "better trained and more practiced" than other teams. He might have added that Wright was a shrewd judge of playing talent and a confirmed believer that ball fans, like cricket devotees, would pay to see well-disciplined teams in action. Wright's previous experience served him well in handling such matters as grounds maintenance, scheduling games, and even uniforming his men. In 1868 local fans saw a well-tailored team, outfitted in flashy uniforms of the finest white cricket-flannel, with bright red stockings, spiked Oxford shoes, and natty caps. Admiring their cut, Chadwick credited the Reds with inspiring "comfortably cool, tasteful" baseball dress.

Handed the job of recruiting a paid team equal to Champion's dreams, Wright completed the task within a few weeks. In his judgment only a few changes were needed, since the 1868 team already had six good men. To supplement his own skills as pitcher and outfielder, Wright retained catcher Doug Allison, first baseman Charles Gould (dubbed "Bushel Basket" for his sure hands), third baseman Fred Waterman, outfielder Cal McVey, and his bearded pitching ace, Asa Brainard. For added strength, Wright raided the rival Buckeyes, snaring outfielder Andy Leonard, second baseman Charles Sweasy, and utility man Dick Hurley. Then Wright plucked brother George from the Morrisania Unions, along with outfielder Dave Birdsall.

Player contracts ran from March till November, and individual salaries ranged from $600 for substitute Hurley to $1,400 for George Wright. But George later declared that he collected $1,800, with brother Harry getting $2,000. Whatever the true rate, it was good money for the time. The average annual wage for all manufacturing workers, skilled and unskilled, was less than $400 in 1868; professors at the University of Michigan earned $1,500. Ever the optimist, Champion boasted that the Reds' $15,000 stock issue would meet the payroll; actually, the team was a barebones operation, heavily dependent on shares of gate receipts from road games and vulnerable to shifting local support, which so far had been hardly overwhelming.

To bolster the Red Stocking image, Wright imposed a spartan training regimen in the spring of 1869. A tireless drillmaster and inventive tactician, Wright molded his men into an efficient machine, one that Chadwick urged as a model for others who expected "a similar degree of success." Prophetic words those, and they were echoed by Harry M. Millar, who covered the Reds for the *Cincinnati Commercial* and who fed local fans with gossipy items on the team's movements. An effective publicity man, Millar glorified Wright and his team, creating the legend of a freshly minted super-team, which now he brashly described as "so well regulated that it should avail itself of its capabilities of defeating every club with which it contests."

Coming on the eve of the team's departure on an extended eastern swing that would match the Reds against the best teams in the land, Millar's prophecy seemed well founded. At that point the Reds owned a seven-game winning streak, compiled at the expense of regional rivals and local "picked nines." Heading east, the Reds extended their winning streak to seventeen straight games before invading metropolitan New York for the acid test of their strength. On June 14 at Brooklyn's Union Grounds, a crowd of eight thousand gathered to see the Reds battle the New York Mutuals. That day, in a hard-fought contest, the Reds won 4-2. It was the victory Champion had dreamed of, and his telegraphed announcement brought joy to Cincinnati, where cheering fans filled the streets. "Go on with your noble work," rang a congratulatory reply from Cincinnati, "Our expectations have been met."

Emboldened by victory, the invaders continued their assault on eastern clubs. In Washington the Reds met with President Grant, "who

Harry Wright, captain and player for the 1870 Cincinnati Reds.

Four stalwarts of the Atlantic team that beat the Reds in 1870: left to right, Dicky Pearce, Joe Start, Charles Smith, and John Chapman. (Courtesy John Thorn)

treated them cordially and complimented them on their play." And well he might, as the Reds defeated the Nationals 24-8 and the Olympics 16-5 before what Chadwick called the "most aristocratic assemblage . . . that ever [appeared] . . . at a baseball match." As the undefeated tally mounted, the Reds' reputation grew. Now *Harper's Weekly* took note and published likenesses of the great "picked nine," including a group drawing showing grim young faces bordered by formidable beards and sideburns. On the team's returning home, local fans welcomed them as conquerors bearing shields. The love feast lasted for days, and its glow lingered for weeks. But nothing matched the first day's festivities, marked by a serial round of fetes and parties, highlighted by the presentation of a twenty-seven-foot bat with all the heroic names carved on it, and climaxed by a gala ball extending into the wee hours of the morning. Then, relaxing under the "Welcome Red Stockings" banner, Champion declared that he held the highest office in America.

A long home stand followed, the Reds continuing their winning ways, although once tied by the visiting Troy Haymakers. This single blot on the team's 1869 escutcheon was locally denounced as a dirty deal pulled off by the New Yorkers. With the game tied 17-all after five innings, the Troy captain challenged an umpire's decision and refused to play any longer. This put Cincinnati fans in a menacing mood, but the umpire cooled tempers by forfeiting the game to the Reds. Afterwards the *Commercial* blamed New York Congressman John Morrisey, accusing him of stirring the incident to escape losing a $17,000 bet he had laid on the Haymakers. The umpire's decision was later overruled by an Association committee, and the game was declared a tie.

The Reds notched a record of fifty-seven wins, a tie, and no losses for

1869. But if the performance was Olympian, the men who achieved it were human. Reading Wright's diary accounts of the campaign enables one to share the mixed joys and distresses of managing this "super-team." At times the team drew well, including crowds of 15,000 at two Philadelphia games and 23,217 for six games in New York. Those were good paydays for Wright, but other times the Reds' share was depressingly small. Thus, when the Reds arrived in Syracuse for a scheduled game, Wright was horrified to find a pigeon shoot taking place on the field. Nobody knew of any scheduled ball game, so the Reds were losers. Hard after this jolt, the team arrived in Rochester, where a freak cloudburst soaked the field. Determined to save receipts, Wright's men "swept the water off, put sawdust in the muddy places," and commenced play.

At times Wright's pros defied his authority by straggling, missing trains, or cutting practices. Even brother George was guilty occasionally, but pitcher Brainard was the worst offender. A hypochondriac, Brainard needed constant coddling, and there were days when he refused to pitch, forcing Wright to toe the slab. Moreover, Brainard liked to roam the streets at night, thus defying Wright's rules. And while he could pitch superbly, the flaky Brainard's "odd notions" set him to loafing behind good leads, and on one occasion he gave up two runs that scored after he playfully flung the ball at a wild rabbit. Usually, player hijinks could be held in check by fines. But booze was a knotty problem, so vexing that Wright set a policy for 1870 that read, "No player will be accepted . . . who will not contract to abstain from intoxicating beverages at all times unless prescribed by a physician in good standing."

More than stern discipline was needed to cope with the anti-Red resentment stirred by Wright's victorious team. Over the winter New York sportswriters attacked Wright's mercenaries, some advising respectable teams not to play them. Arguing that respectable teams ought only to use local amateur talent was absurd, however, as most of Wright's rivals now used paid outsiders. Indeed, jealousy of Red successes was the prime motive behind attacks. Wright knew that his team was marked for humiliation, and his best hope was that his rivals would be hard put to catch up to his innovations.

Alas, he was wrong. After winning their first twenty-seven games in 1870, the Reds found themselves back in Brooklyn on the 14th of June. It was a year to the day since the Reds bested the Mutuals in Brooklyn and climbed atop the baseball world. Now they were back as indomi-

Atlantics beat the Reds in an eleven-inning game in Brooklyn on June 14, 1870, as depicted in *Harper's Weekly*. (Courtesy John Thorn)

table conquerors matched against the Atlantics. Playing at the Capito-line Grounds, the Reds suffered their first loss since late in 1868 (having won either 81, 84, 87, or 92 games without a defeat, depending on which games were counted), by an 8-7 count. Ironically, Wright could have settled for a tie. It was 5-5 after nine innings, but Wright and Champion gambled on an extra-inning win. It looked like a good decision, as the Reds rallied for two in the top of the eleventh, but the Atlantics' last at-bats was a crusher. To begin, Brainard let down, yielding a single and a long fly ball that fell for extra bases because a fan interfered with McVey's attempt to catch it. With one run in, captain Bob Ferguson tied the game on another hit, and then infield errors sent Ferguson home with the winner.

Departing the grounds in open carriages, the distraught Reds ran a gauntlet of jeering fans. Afterwards a weeping Champion wired home the result: "The finest game ever played. Our boys did nobly, but fortune was against us . . . Though defeated, not disgraced." He might have added that the vast publicity surrounding this game boosted big-time baseball's stock. But Cincinnati would not be part of the next stage of baseball's evolution. Falling attendance and another loss to Chicago precipitated a stockholder revolt that ousted Champion and inaugurated austerities. When the new leaders voted to discontinue the professional experiment, the Wrights quit Cincinnati in 1871 for Boston, where their services were much sought.

In Boston the Red Stockings were reborn, and the proud name would last to this day. So too, after a time, did Cincinnati restore the "Reds" totem. But two extant major league teams bearing the Red Stocking totem are only a small part of Wright's legacy. Still strong in baseball folklore is the legend of the spontaneous creation of major league baseball credited to the Reds of 1869–70. That the professional game really arose by evolutionary processes much earlier is well established historically. But such is the power of myths that many fans still credit the Reds with giving birth to major league baseball.

THE PLAYERS' MAJOR LEAGUE, 1871–1875

In 1871 the first professional major league was launched, and it lasted for five seasons, during which time fans saw a brand of ballplaying as good as would be seen until the early 1880s. Yet, official accounts of major league records, such as the authoritative Macmillan *Baseball Encyclopedia*, refuse to recognize this National Association of Professional Base Ball Players as a major league.

Nonetheless, the Players Association was the first major league; it was organized by professional players who granted themselves complete freedom of contract and movement. True, clubs sponsored and financed teams, but ownership of clubs was in the hands of members, who as stockholders willingly passed up income for the prestige of being seen as gentlemen who could afford such conspicuous consumption. The gentlemen who enjoyed winning more than preserving amateur purity belonged to clubs that hired players—much as Renaissance princes hired artists and musicians. By 1870 the intimidating presence of professional players in the once purely amateur Association erupted into a

An artist for the *New York Daily Graphic* uses baseball clichés as pegs for his action sketches in order to whet the appetites of fans for the forthcoming 1874 season. The sketches depict the action in a National Association game between the Philadelphia Club (now the Phillies) and the Philadelphia Athletics on opening day. (Courtesy Goulston Baseball Collection, New York Public Library)

Scorecard of the New York Mutuals in August 1874, the month they became the first club accused of "throwing" a game. (Courtesy Dennis Goldstein)

confrontation between amateur and professional interests. At a stormy meeting late that year, the outnumbered professionals walked out, leaving the amateurs smugly confident of victory to come just as soon as the professionals slunk back and submitted to terms.

The amateurs never expected the professionals to embark upon a league of their own. Yet this was the goal of the defiant professionals who met on a stormy St. Patrick's night in 1871 at the Colliers Rooms in New York City. With the baseball season soon to begin, there was no time to spare. With western clubs from Chicago, Cleveland, Rockford, and Fort Wayne and eastern clubs from Boston, Washington, Philadelphia, New York, and Troy backing the idea of a professional league, the player delegates had a secure power base. Representing the interests of more than a hundred professional players, the delegates determined to organize a league in one night. And they did, by burying animosities and moving fast. With little drama, they simply reworked the constitution of the amateur Association, inserting the word "professional" in the right places, then voting to adopt the established playing rules of the amateurs. Once this was done, they voted to name the new league the National Association of Professional Base Ball Players. If aping the amateur Association was a conservative move, the commitment to professional players was a radical departure. It was all done up in a few hours, and a *Clipper* reporter in attendance was impressed: "In fact, we have never attended any convention of the fraternity which reflected so much credit on the delegates and the clubs they so ably represented."

In their determination to float the new league, the rebels allowed easy entrance. To join, all a club needed to do was petition the steering committee and pay a ten-dollar entrance fee. By comparison, one must now spend millions and undergo careful scrutiny to acquire a major league franchise, but the 1871 delegates apologized for the fee, explaining that it was needed to purchase championship pennants. Such easy entrance would plague the new league, as would annual attrition from dropout teams. Moreover, like the amateur Association, this one lacked a fixed schedule of games. Instead, each club was required to play each rival five times, with dates to be arranged by club secretaries. The pennant would go to the team with the most victories, and in the event of a tie, the steering committee must decide the winner. The only strict rule required each team to play its games by the first of November.

Once the rules were decided, the meeting lapsed into chaos, as delegates milled about, buttonholing each other for choice playing dates. The western clubs quickly set up a three-week eastern tour, while the Washington Olympics arranged a fortnight's northern road swing. Small wonder, then, that most clubs never got around to playing all their games, but this was the way of old-time baseball. Not until the National League introduced a fixed playing schedule would the job be done efficiently.

George Hall, an outfielder who moved from Baltimore to the Boston Red Stockings in 1874. In 1877 he became one of the four Louisville Grays expelled for throwing games. (Courtesy John Thorn)

Other omissions shortened the life of the new league. A longer life might have ensued had delegates created a professional staff of umpires, but it was decided to use gentlemanly volunteers who must be "acknowledged as competent." Thus, the home team selected the umpire, and if he failed to show, the rival captains were to agree on a substitute. Equally damaging was the delegates' inability to agree on uniform ticket prices. Most favored a fifty-cent basic admission, with two-thirds of the gate going to the home club. Harry Wright, the Boston delegate, pressed for this rate and kept pushing it for the life of the league, but no standard admission price was then achieved, nor does one now exist. Still another stumbling block was the league's inability to bar gamblers, who were to continue their bribery and game-fixing. Indeed, when the National League overthrew this league in 1876, one of their founders' most damaging attacks was the gambling menace.

In retrospect, we see that the delegates sowed the seeds of their league's destruction, but harmony was urgently needed to get the league going. Had the delegates shaped a lasting major league in a single evening, it would have been miraculous. It was no night of miracles, though the players' league delighted fans with five years of first-rate baseball. The amateur Association was too stunned to counterattack. Faced with the secession of their most powerful clubs, that group died by 1874. Thus, by default, all changes in baseball's rules and style of play have come from professional councils, and to this day the main course of the game's evolution has been charted by professional major leaguers.

Having pulled off their coup, the professionals faced a free-for-all fight for cash and glory. Within weeks, nine clubs joined the players' league, all from the northeastern and northwestern sections of the land. This regionalism was understandable, since the South was prostrated by the war and the trans-Mississippian West was too remote for the transportation of the time. Hence, circumstances forced an east-west alignment upon this first major league. Time would hallow the arrangement,

Boston Red Stockings, 1874 Players Association champions: seated (left to right), James O'Rourke (first base), Andrew Leonard (left field), George Wright (shortstop), Harry Wright (captain, center field), George Hall (outfield), Harry Schafer (third base), Tommy Beals (outfield); standing, Cal McVey (right field), Al Spalding (pitcher), James White (catcher), Roscoe Barnes (second base). Drawn from a photograph for *Harper's Weekly*. (Courtesy John A. Lucas and Ronald A. Smith)

and eighty years would pass before succeeding major leagues broke this geographical alignment.

Hopes ran high among contenders girding for battle in 1871. The Chicago White Stockings, ensconced in their new 7,000-capacity Lake Front Park and boasting a $4,500-salaried star, headed the western division, which included Rockford, Fort Wayne, and Cleveland. But baseball writers, based mainly in the East, touted the New York Mutuals, Philadelphia Athletics, and Boston Red Stockings above the westerners or the remaining eastern outposts of Troy and Washington.

The first major league campaign furnished action and drama enough to please any fan. In Boston, Wright fielded a formidable squad, having snagged pitcher Al Spalding and infielder Ross Barnes from Rockford and teamed them with brother George, McVey, Leonard, Birdsall, and Gould of Cincinnati, plus rookie Harry Schafer. With Philadelphia and Chicago equally strong, a three-way race ensued that was curbed when the disastrous Chicago fire destroyed the White Stockings' physical assets. Left homeless and penniless, the White Stockings took to the road, cadging free railroad tickets and borrowing equipment from rivals. A sympathetic reporter lamented their motley appearance: "none were dressed alike"; those "who could get white stockings did so, but they were not many." Nevertheless, this wandering team stayed in contention till the last day, losing to the Athletics before a sparse crowd. Boston, meanwhile, hampered by injuries much of the season, came on strong in the stretch, finishing at 22-10. According to league rules, which counted only victories, that tied the Athletics' record of 22-7. Forced to choose the champion, the championship committee logically awarded the Athletics the pennant. Wright protested the decision, alleging tainted Athletic victories and arguing that Boston alone came close to playing its required forty games.

When Wright's protest was disallowed, the A's were touted as the first champions of the Players Association. As pictured in the *Clipper*, the A's looked formidable indeed. All wore blazers and sported facial hair. The first champions included stars like pitcher Dick McBride and catcher Fergus Malone. The infield had Wes Fisler at first, veteran Al Reach at second, Levi Meyerle at third, and John Radcliff at short. Outfielders John Sensenderfer, George Heubel, and Ed Cuthbert rounded out the roster. Hicks Hayhurst managed the young team, whose average age was twenty-five. Moreover, the team was a financial success; after expenses of $22,457.14 were paid, a dividend of $200 was split by stockholders.

All things considered, 1871 was a good beginning. Only one team quit the race, but a substitute was found to shoulder the dropout's poor record. Like the controversial decision over the championship, that awkward decision indicated more problems to come, but no remedial legislation was enacted at the annual meeting. Indeed, the players moved to strengthen their control by electing one of their own, Bob Ferguson, as president and declaring that a player would always serve as president. So for a time the players called the tune, but theirs was to be a short-lived paradise. By failing to cure obvious weaknesses like dropouts, by putting their interests above those of club sponsors, the players

hitting to fielders during batting practice, are standard practices now. They are so because the records support the wisdom of Wright's tactics. Thus, in 1875, six Boston men topped all rivals in fielding their positions, and notwithstanding their still gloveless state, their fielding approached modern standards. Wright's own self-image was that of a persistent teacher. When jealous rivals sneered that anyone could win with his team's talent, Wright retorted that every player was a special case, a bundle of promises and problems requiring personal handling. And Wright repeatedly proved his point and demonstrated his skill by redeeming castoffs from other teams.

Certainly Wright deserved the accolade of "Father of the Professional Game." Convinced that players were motivated by money, he paid well. His 1875 payroll was major league baseball's best till the 'Eighties. Measured by standards of pennants and profits, Wright's club was in a class by itself. Wright zealously handled such administrative details as scheduling, grounds-keeping, and park supervision, in addition to such tasks as recruiting, drilling, and disciplining his men and masterminding their play; he shouldered tasks that now occupy a dozen specialists. In 1875 he directed the spending of a $35,000 annual budget, the largest so far in the new world of major league baseball. He also pioneered in uncharted areas like advertising, equipment design and procurement, and salary negotiations.

THE NATIONAL LEAGUE COUP

Given a dozen managers like Wright, the Players Association might have survived and profited well enough to keep gentlemanly club investors interested. In most clubs, however, mismanagement and losses discouraged backers. As club-sponsored stock companies failed, more business-minded individuals took control; of these, some envisioned a major league controlled by independent owners. By 1875 enough men of this view had emerged to plan replacement of the Players Association with an owner-dominated league. Their ranks included Spalding, Wright's ace pitcher, whose driving ambition eventually prodded him to become a millionaire sporting-goods entrepreneur. Although only in his mid-twenties, Spalding now chose to make his move. Thus, before the 1875 season ended, he persuaded three Boston superstars to join the Chicago White Stockings for the upcoming season. Spalding had more in mind with this move than a change of scenery. With William Hulbert, president of the Chicago club, Spalding worked quietly to overturn the Association and supplant it with an owners' league, to be called the National League of Professional Base Ball *Clubs*. Indeed, Spalding had Wright's blessing. As Wright advised Hulbert: "Professional clubs, to keep in existence, must have gate money, to receive gate money they must play games, and to enable them to play games, their opponents must have faith that such games will prove remunerative."

With such support, masterminds Hulbert and Spalding brushed aside the weak Players Association as easily as that association had outmaneuvered the amateurs. With like-minded owners from St. Louis, Cincinnati, and Louisville in fold, Hulbert called eastern clubs to a meeting in February 1876 in New York, where he persuaded the assemblage to adopt his ready-made thirteen-point plan for a new major league. With minor changes, Hulbert's thirteen points became the constitution of the new National League of Professional Base Ball Clubs. Frankly designed to increase the power of the club owners, its major thrusts were to seize control from players, to initiate uniform contracts designed to stop contract jumping, and to lay down strict disciplinary rules backed by threats of expulsion.

To attract serious investors, League admission rules were tightened. Henceforth all franchise petitions were to be strictly screened and membership in the League limited to towns with populations of at least 75,000. Moreover, the territorial integrity of each franchise was to be protected from interlopers; only one club would represent a city. Overall League membership was thus limited to eight clubs based on east-west alignments. And to regulate interclub doings, a central organization was created under a paid secretary-treasurer and an elected president and board of directors, all charged with maintaining records, adjudicating disputes, deciding rule changes, and overseeing umpires, who were to be paid five dollars a game.

Professionalizing umpires was a necessary reform, but no more vital than establishing a schedule of fixed playing dates, which the new League promised to introduce in 1877. Meanwhile, for 1876, clubs were warned that failure to meet schedule obligations would result in expulsion, with reinstatement virtually impossible. Finally, to gain public support for their coup and to block any counterattack by the Players Association, the delegates mounted a moral crusade. Grandiose promises were aimed against gambling, Sunday ball, rowdyism at the parks, and drunkenness and insubordination among players. To enhance the League's moral image, Morgan Bulkeley, a noted Connecticut politician, was named president, with Nicholas Young chosen as the secretary-treasurer.

The National League coup proved to be astonishingly successful. To be sure, the Players Association tried to regroup, but its March meeting failed to attract clubs from sizable cities, forcing the delegates to throw in the sponge. Nor did outraged voices from excluded clubs, including the Philadelphia Phillies, who were denied membership in favor of the A's, or that of Chadwick, who was not invited to the proceedings, halt the National League steamroller. After registering vigorous protests over the methods employed by the conspirators, Chadwick trimmed his sails, and in due course this accomplished writer was welcomed aboard and rewarded with such plums as the editorship of the official league guide.

The League was a personal triumph for Spalding, who now became playing manager of Hulbert's well-financed Chicago White Stockings. As manager, team captain, pitcher, and fledgling sporting-goods merchant, Spalding was on his way to wealth and power. In 1876 he led his White Stockings to the first National League pennant, his team's 52-14 record easily outdistancing Hartford. Nor did his team's loss to St. Louis in a postseason match, which was a harbinger of the coming World Series, tarnish Spalding's image. To Chicagoans Spalding was a winner. His sporting-goods store was thriving, thanks to getting the contract for supplying official balls and the right to publish official records. Thus

Harry Wright, "Father of the Professional Game," as an elder statesman off the playing field. (Courtesy John Thorn)

established, young Spalding soon retired from active play, but not from owner councils.

But Spalding's success was not shared by the new League. Growing pains plagued the circuit. Pleading financial losses, the A's and Mutuals refused to play their late-season road games. It was a direct challenge to the constitution, and newly elected President Hulbert met it squarely by ousting the pair, despite tearful pleas from their leaders. That remorseless decision cut the League to six teams in 1877, the year the new uniform playing schedule went into effect. But the new plan failed to arrest declining income. Thus, belt-tightening measures were employed, forcing players to pay for their uniforms and part of their road expenses. Naturally, such measures brought howls, and they may have contributed to the great scandal of 1877.

That season Louisville looked like a sure winner. With Jim Devlin pitching brilliantly and backed by hitters like George Hall, captain William Craver, and Al Nichols, the Louisville Grays needed but seven wins in their last fifteen games to land the pennant. They never did. Instead they frittered away games, with Devlin, Hall, Craver, and Nichols displaying suspicious ineptitude. In the end Wright's Reds won, but most observers smelled a rat. Indeed, the fix was in, and its blatant crudity made it obvious to all. An investigation by Louisville directors wrung confessions from the above quartet, who were expelled from baseball that fall by an angry Hulbert. Moreover, Hulbert beefed up his holy war against sinful players and empowered umpires to fine abusive players. For failure to meet the League's fiscal standards, the Hartford club was dropped, while Cincinnati was ousted for nonpayment of dues.

By banishing the Louisville "crooks" and dropping mavericks, Hulbert's crusade won much public sympathy during this time of troubles. Indeed, Hulbert emerged as the militant prophet whose righteous wrath preserved the integrity of the League and hence of the professional game. But almost unnoticed amidst his punitive acts, Hulbert moved to strengthen National League control over organized baseball. By boldly creating the "League Alliance," the National League agreed to protect the interests of all professional clubs, including a club's territorial rights, player contracts, and player blacklists. By modern standards this proposal smacks of a protection racket, with minor pro clubs asked to pay ten dollars each for protection. Yet some did, and the bold act established National League suzerainty over some minor professional leagues and clubs—pointing directly to the later devised National Agreement, whereby major leagues would wield power over all professional baseball organizations.

Although the way was cleared for the dominance of the National League, there were dark days ahead before the Nationals moved into the bright and profitable uplands of the 1880s. The business depression that gripped the land in 1873 lingered through 1878, the year Wright led his Reds to the pennant that would be his last major league championship. Once again six teams made up the League, and while none profited, at least each team played its full schedule. It was a hollow victory for Wright and a trying year for the National League, whose major league claim was ridiculed by writers from big cities like Philadelphia, New York, and Washington that were unrepresented. Indeed, some claimed that the rival International Association was stronger.

Nevertheless, Hulbert stuck to his moralistic stance. Refusing to lift his banishment of Philadelphia and New York, his League dropped Milwaukee and Indianapolis as unremunerative and voted in Troy, Syracuse, Cleveland, and Buffalo. While this restored the eight-club circuit, the League's lofty claim to baseball preeminence had a hollow ring. But the National League's ordeal was coming to an end. Although the 1879 campaign was profitless, the pennant victory by the Providence Grays stirred public interest. With George Wright managing the team and John Montgomery Ward pitching stoutly, the Grays captured the imagination of fans. Along with returning prosperity, the promise of more sprightly campaigns like this one held promise for a brighter future for the beleaguered National League.

2

THE GOLDEN 'EIGHTIES

DISMAL WERE THE PROSPECTS OF THE NATIONAL League as the 1880s dawned. By then, four seasons of major league baseball under this banner had produced a murky record: the Louisville scandal, the exclusion of New York and Philadelphia teams, and, worse still, profitless performances by nearly all clubs. Small wonder that doomsayers predicted the League's death. Even President Hulbert had harbored gloomy thoughts, having confided to Spalding in 1876 that "the wit of man cannot devise a plan . . . that will control the game of Base Ball for over five years."

To be fair one would have to blame a lingering seven-year business depression for the woeful financial performance. So far the National League hadn't even matched the profits of its player-run predecessor. Nowhere was the disparity more apparent than in the belt-tightening austerities adopted by the League. Despite economizing, even Boston, winner of two consecutive pennants under manager Harry Wright, failed to earn anything close to the $3,261 profit tallied by the 1875 Boston Reds. Baseball clubs were not attractive investment opportunities in early 1880.

No one should be surprised to find the players suffering most under the austerities. Now their salaries averaged a bit more than $1,000, no matter if one played for a winner or loser. At Boston, the 1879 payroll totaled $14,007.96, down from $20,685 in 1875 and hardly more than the 1869 Cincinnati pioneers received with fewer men. And how the Reds of 1880 must have envied the freedom of those old-timers to change clubs! The reserve clause, newly adopted in 1879, compelled a good player to stay with his club and accept what was offered, or else quit the profession. As proof that players lost bargaining power, Boston records show five reserved players taking annual salary cuts from 1879 through 1881.

Such were the new restrictions on players that National Leaguers of 1880 could neither fight back nor take extended consolation in drink. President Hulbert saw to that, ordering dismissals, backed by blacklists, for mutinous behavior or acts of "drunkenness and bummerism." And Hulbert wielded his club; by 1882 at least three dozen players were expelled, and some injured ones lost pay "for no services rendered." Even able players were exploited. Boston's 1880 travel budget totaled a mere $2,813, a chintzy one-third of the 1875 allotment. Everywhere it was the same, as players were dunned for uniforms, laundry, part-payment for food on the road, and the like. Small wonder that players groused, and when low morale contributed to

Boston's sixth-place finish in 1880 and 1881, manager Wright was sacked.

Not surprisingly, weaker teams folded under the financial pressure. In 1879 Syracuse quit and was replaced by Worcester. The following year last-place Cincinnati tried to lure fans with beer sales and Sunday ball, innovations for which they were expelled by the moralizing Hulbert and replaced by Detroit.

Under such grim circumstances only a cockeyed optimist might have predicted a turnabout in League fortunes. Yet he'd have been right, since 1880 saw the national depression bottoming and prosperity returning. And as baseball fortunes brightened, Hulbert was cast as the hero; his stubborn moral stance and his insistence that clubs stick to the basic fifty-cent admission price were interpreted as wisdom. The sainting of Hulbert also gained from the coincidental demise of the International Association. For three years that rival league pressed the Nationals hard with its good play, open admissions policy for clubs, and cheaper admission prices for fans. Luckily for Hulbert, the Association died in 1879, the victim of small parks, haphazard membership and scheduling practices, and brutal opposition from the National League. In attacking this rival, Hulbert used the League Alliance as an effective boycott. By banning exhibition games with Association teams, the Nationals weakened their enemy's finances. But the Nationals scored a more telling blow by luring Association powers Troy, Buffalo, and Worcester into their ranks. By this signal victory over the Association, the National League in 1880 stood as the chief claimant to major league status.

William A. Hulbert, president of the National League from 1876 until his death in 1882. (Courtesy National Baseball Library, Cooperstown, New York)

THE CHICAGO DYNASTY

If belonging to the National League in 1880 served as a status symbol for members, events unfolding in Chicago soon added lustre to the distinction. Blessed with the League's only profitable franchise in these early years, Hulbert and Spalding resolutely built the White Stockings into a formidable contender. In addition to his League presidential duties, Hulbert headed this team, assisted by Spalding. Overshadowed for the moment by Hulbert, ex-pitcher Spalding was learning much from his mentor, enough to become the League's most powerful figure when Hulbert died in 1882. At the same time, Spalding waxed wealthy by the success of his thriving sporting-goods firm. Thus armed with wealth and influence, Spalding soon was summoned to guide the National League through trying times, and when he succeeded with Machiavellian brilliance, he joined Harry Wright, Henry Chadwick, Adrian Anson, and Mike ("King") Kelly in the quintet of outstanding innovators who shaped the major league game in the nineteenth century.

Personal contacts bound these five men together. At Boston, Spalding had been Wright's star pitcher and learned much of baseball promotion from Wright. Then, when Spalding quit Boston for Chicago, he soon chose the venerable sportswriter Chadwick to edit the official *Spalding Guide*, along with other journals that poured from his American Sports Publishing Company presses. Acting as Spalding's mouthpiece also benefited Chadwick, as bylines added lustre to his reputation as "Father of Baseball."

In the spring of 1880, at Chicago, the White Stockings fielded two other members of the influential quintet. One, Adrian Anson, was the star first baseman of the team, and Hulbert's recent choice to succeed bluff Bob Ferguson as the team's playing manager. Handed the post in 1879, Anson led the team to a respectable finish, which won him free rein to shape the team in his own way for the 1880 campaign. Big and burly, Anson was a fixture at first base, where he fielded well despite limited range. No matter that he lacked mobility, because hitting was his forte. In Anson's twenty-two seasons of League play, he captured four batting titles and only twice fell below the .300 mark. As the driving force behind the Chicago team, Anson became the first nationally popular baseball hero. Tough, gruff, and outspoken, this mustachioed hero proudly swaggered onto fields at the head of his team. In uniform he was formidable, and his rugged durability had fans everywhere hooting nicknames like "Babe" in his younger days; then as he aged they switched to "Unk," "Pop," "Pappy," or "the Old Man." Such was the force of his personality that his team came to be known as "Anson's Colts," and by 1889, as the poet Vachel Lindsay later recalled, "Pop Anson was our darling, pet and pride."

A baseball Hercules, Anson shared some of that god's strength and naiveté; a natural showman, he titillated fans with clever stunts and enraged some by his brawling and bullying style of umpire-baiting. Both admired and resented, he gave newsmen colorful copy and inspired a

Popular enthusiasm for baseball in the 1880s is reflected in this sketch of a game played on ice skates in New York's Central Park during the winter of 1884, as recorded in *Harper's Weekly*. (Author's Collection)

raft of articles describing his real and imaginary feats. A Chicago hero, Anson rode the crest of public adulation, returning a full measure of loyalty to his employers and to the League. Sadly for him, this counted for little in his waning days. Abandoned by Spalding and cut loose in 1898, he spent his last years bitterly criticizing the game that had unceremonially discarded him.

In 1880, however, the curtain of vigorous youth shielded Anson from this bleak prospect. That year he practiced his talented young team hard and revolutionized team play by insisting that infielders and outfielders back each other up defensively, by going with a two-man pitching rotation to meet the challenge of the expanded eighty-four-game schedule, and by adopting a daring running attack. That year his team's stunning total of stolen bases was owed to six men whose running speed matched any rival's.

Among the speedsters, Michael ("King") Kelly soon rivaled Anson in popularity, and before his career ended in untimely death, Kelly shouldered his way into the immortal quintet as the superstar of the nineteenth century. Only twenty-two in 1880, Kelly was a newcomer plucked from the roster of the ousted Cincinnati team. A proven hitter, the handsome, dark-haired Kelly was incredibly versatile. A good outfielder, Kelly also caught, played every infield position, and even pitched on occasion. Throughout his career Kelly filled in wherever help was needed. A stinging heckler and needler, Kelly sparked the

Slide, Kelly, Slide, the popular painting by Frank O. Small, shows the "King" stealing second base during the 1880s. (Courtesy MacGreevy Collection, Boston Public Library)

Mike Kelly, after being sold to Boston in 1887. (Author's Collection)

White Stockings. As a base runner, he upset defenses with his base stealing. An opportunistic runner, Kelly took advantage of the League's single-umpire system; when an ump's back was turned, Kelly sometimes sprinted from first to third without bothering to touch second. The tactic infuriated opponents but endeared Kelly to local fans, already used to chanting "Slide, Kelly, Slide." Soon that battlecry became the title of a famous print that hung in many saloons.

Alas, saloons undid Kelly. Despite fines and prying detectives hired by Spalding, Kelly bottled on; his boozing did little to hurt his image or his performance. Over sixteen seasons he won two batting titles and managed a pennant winner, credentials enough to land him a later niche in the Hall of Fame. His untimely death in the early 1890s was laid to his dissipation, however.

In the 1880s Kelly's impact went much further than statistics. In his prime he was a dazzling figure. Fans acclaimed him "king" of ball players, and when Chicago sold him to Boston in 1887 for the unprecedented sum of $10,000, fans and writers gasped in awe. At Boston, Irish-American fans worshipped him, and Kelly wore his fame with rakish wit. Fully aware of his glamour, Kelly advised other players to court the press: "I am 'the only player'. . . . Why don't some of you dubs break a window and get yourselves talked about?" As the superstar of the decade, Kelly cashed in with vaudeville performances and a sprightly autobiography that told of a time when he squeezed President Grover Cleveland's glad hand and made that portly official wince. These and other capers fed the Kelly mystique, and when he died in 1894, the thirty-six-year-old star became an enduring baseball legend.

In 1880 Kelly was one of four White Stocking newcomers. Two others were pitchers: Fred Goldsmith, who had played briefly with Troy the year before, and little Larry Corcoran, a twenty-year-old rookie. Handling these men was catcher Frank ("Silver") Flint, himself a yearling, whose steadfast refusal to wear gloves soon had his fingers pointing in directions never intended by Mother Nature. Another newcomer, Tom Burns, played shortstop alongside Ed Williamson at third and Joe Quest at second. With Anson at first, Chicago had a sound infield, and when Fred Pfeffer replaced Quest in 1883, the quartet won fame as Chicago's "stonewall infield." Equally strong was the outfield, where Kelly joined George Gore and young Abner Dalrymple. At twenty-seven, Gore's fulfillment as a hitter was nigh, and his .360 batting won the title in 1880. Backed by Dalrymple's .330, Anson's .337, and Kelly's .294 hitting, Chicago led the League with a .279 team batting mark.

Once unleashed, Anson's team rolled up the League; its 67-17 record distanced second-place Providence by 15 games. Proof of Chicago's dominance showed as the team outdid rivals in hitting, fielding (.910), and pitching. In the pitching box Corcoran justified Anson's faith by posting a 43-14 record, while Goldsmith's 21-3 effort was the best winning percentage among League pitchers.

Indeed, 1880 was an awesome year for pitchers. Corcoran's victory total included a no-hitter, but two others hurled perfect games. One was spun by Lee Richmond, a young collegian pitching for Worcester; and hard after his gem, John Ward of Providence threw another.

Alarmed at such pitching dominance, League officials that fall voted to increase the pitching distance from forty-five to fifty feet. But pitching domination also owed to the fact that pitchers were throwing hard underhanded, instead of "pitching." Still, changing the hallowed pitching distance was a radical departure; but rule makers of this decade were radical tinkerers, despite the conservatism of League officials about such matters as Sunday games. Before the decade ended, more radical changes were effected in hopes of balancing batting and pitching.

Chicago stormed to another championship in 1881. The race was a mite closer, as Anson's men won by nine games over runner-up Providence. As expected, pitchers suffered when League batting soared to .260. While Chicago's pitching suffered too, Corcoran slackening to 31-14 and Goldsmith to 24-13, the hitters batted a collective .295. Anson led the League with a .399 mark. The team's .916 fielding tied Troy for the lead.

That fall the annual League meeting produced no major changes in team alignments or rules, but troubles were brewing. For one, Hulbert was to die in the spring of 1882, at the very time the new American Association posed a major challenge to National League suzerainty. Had he lived, Hulbert might have waged an all-out war against these interlopers. Certainly he would have fretted over the spectacle of his Chicago team staggering to a tainted 1882 victory over Harry Wright's Providence Grays. Although Chicago won a third straight pennant, the triumph was blighted by a ruling that allowed the financially crippled Buffalo team to transfer its three home games with the White Stockings to the Windy City. It was done to give the Buffalos more gate money, but the home field advantage helped Chicago to thrash the Buffalos three times. Since that was Chicago's winning margin, Wright rightly protested, demanding that the championship be settled by a postseason series. This was granted, and Chicago's victory dispelled some of the stench.

A. G. Mills, president of the National League from 1882 to 1885, displaying his Civil War honors. (Courtesy National Baseball Library, Cooperstown, New York)

In retrospect, Hulbert's passing was a boon for the National League. The American Association challenge demanded shrewd diplomacy rather than his stubborn moralizing. Indeed, just before his fatal seizure, Hulbert unwittingly helped stock the invaders by banishing ten hard-drinking players, who then promptly joined Association teams. The ousted Cincinnati club became a charter member of the new organization. Moreover, it was time to rethink Hulbert's quixotic boycott of New York and Philadelphia, for teams were needed in these populous sites if the League was to fend off its rival. Mindful of the limitations of Hulbert's personal rule, the owners never again invested a National League president with his powers. Meanwhile, the times demanded Machiavellian tactics, which the owners employed, ousting Troy and Worcester and consoling them with honorary memberships, and admitting teams from Philadelphia and New York, who were permitted to sign players from Hulbert's blacklist.

Indeed, the League leaders now displayed an aptitude for devious politicking. At Spalding's suggestion, Abraham G. Mills was named

COMPETITION FROM INTERLOPERS

president and charged with the task of outmaneuvering the Association men. With statesmanlike aplomb, he succeeded; over the winter of 1883 he negotiated with representatives of the Association and the fledgling Northwestern League and hammered out major league baseball's first National Agreement. Its cornerstone was the reserve rule, which Mills foisted upon these interlopers. Arguing that, if they did not accept, contract-jumping players would boost salaries, Mills prevailed; then he magnanimously granted the Association major league status and bestowed the rank of high minor league upon the Northwestern League.

Surely, the Association men should have recalled the hazards of accepting a Trojan horse. Granting major league status cost the Nationals little, while the terms damaged the Association's player relations. After all, the Association clubs began life by damning the reserve clause; in reneging they faced threats of organized action by their irate players. Although this threat subsided, the Association received another jolt when it learned that the owners of the National League's New York team, the Giants, also owned that city's Association team, the Mets. That scary revelation put Association leaders on full alert.

Over the next two seasons the two major leagues eyed each other suspiciously. Fearing duplicity, the Association refused to meet the

St. Louis Browns of 1888, the year they won their fourth consecutive American Association pennant. The champs are wearing formal blazers, the early equivalent of warm-up jackets. Thus clad, the Browns would march across the field before the start of a game. Players as numbered by the photographer: (1) Handsome Harry Boyle, (2) Bill White, (3) Nat Hudson, (4) Jim H. Devlin, (5) Elton ("Ice Box") Chamberlain, (6) Yank Robinson, (7) Arlie Latham, (8) Charles Comiskey, (9) Mascot, (10) Tom McCarthy, (11) Tip O'Neill, (12) Denny Lyons, (13) Jocko Milligan, (14) Silver King, (15) Tom Dolan, (16) Ed Herr. (Courtesy John Thorn)

Providence Grays, managed by Frank Bancroft, who won the first World Series for the National League in 1884 against the American Association's New York Mets. (Courtesy John Thorn)

National League champion in a World Series match in 1883. Had the Series been played, Boston would have represented the Nationals. In a surprise victory Boston had ended Chicago's pennant monopoly through beating Anson's men by four games over the extended ninety-eight-game season. Managed by first baseman John Morrill, who took over from teammate Jack Burdock in midseason, Boston got good pitching from Jim Whitney and Charley Buffinton. Offensively, Boston posted the second-best batting average and set new standards by slugging a record eighty-six triples and thirty-four homers. Yet fielding made the difference, as Boston's .900 mark far exceeded the error-prone Chicagoans.

That year the Nationals prospered, enough so that all eight members stayed to face a second interloper's challenge. This latest threat came from a third major league pretender, the newly organized Union Association, brainchild of a wealthy St. Louis sportsman, Henry V. Lucas. Arguing that Americans needed more first-rate baseball, Lucas proposed to serve it up without the evils of the reserve clause. By now, attacking the reserve clause was a familiar ploy for luring discontented players from the established majors; at the same time, Lucas pledged to embrace the National Agreement if the majors would afford his circuit major league status. Obviously, the Union promoters simply wanted a piece of big-time baseball action. But the established majors spurned the olive branch; if the Unions wanted in, they would have to fight all the way. In girding for war, the Nationals and Americans tightened the reserve rule, allowing each club to reserve fourteen men; moreover, blacklists were imposed on contract-jumping players, territorial bounda-

A New York Giant sliding home in a game against the Chicago White Stockings in August 1885, as depicted by an artist for *Harper's Weekly*. (Courtesy Ronald A. Smith)

ries of each club were tightly defined, and games played with Union teams were forbidden.

Although the existing majors made common cause, the Nationals slyly undercut their ally by encouraging the Association's idea of expanding to twelve clubs in hopes of denying favorable locations to the Unions. Association teams were thus saddled with expensive travel costs and lessened income from fewer home games. Hence, the Nationals smugly watched their ally suffer financial losses. Still, the Unions were crushed. Despite Lucas's strong leadership, his generous subsidies, and his bold stand against the reserve clause, he watched in agony as his fellow promoters buckled under financial stress. Five of the original eight Union teams, including Lucas's own lavishly financed St. Louis Maroons, were in costly direct competition with established Association teams. Moreover, the Unions' Boston and Chicago teams battled the best entrenched National clubs, while the remaining Union entry, Altoona, Pennsylvania, lacked a viable population base.

To add to Union woes, Lucas personally fielded an invincible team. So good were his Maroons that they ended the Union race at the start by winning their first twenty-one games (a record breakaway win streak unsurpassed by any "major team" since 1884). Off and running, the Maroons coasted, posting a gargantuan 94-19 won-lost record—twenty-one games better than second-place Cincinnati. Such crushing dominance killed public interest, so that only five Union charter members finished, after dropout succeeded dropout in confusing fashion until a total of twelve clubs participated. In the end the Union Association sank in a sea of red ink, with losses estimated as high as $250,000.

But the allies too were bloodied, since the surfeit of baseball cut profits everywhere. For its part the American Association deeply regretted its ill-advised expansion, which included Richmond, the first city from the war-battered South to host a major league team and the last for another eighty years. Having paid dearly for National cajolery, the Association retreated to an eight-team format. This retreat was humiliating, but more so was the defeat of its 1884 champs, the New York Mets, who fell to the National League's Providence winners in the first official World Series. It was no contest, as the Mets lost in three straight games.

Hard after that setback, the Association saw the Mets become a virtual farm club of the National League's New York Giants, who announced that in 1885 the Mets' star pitcher and champion batter would join the Giants. This latest lesson in National League duplicity alerted Association men. For the next five years the Association played a lone hand, seldom relaxing vigilance. The result was a spirited rivalry for cash and glory between the two rivals that produced unprecedented public interest in major league baseball.

In 1884, however, the Nationals had strengthened their dominant position. Although profits fell, the League benefited from one of the most colorful pennant races in major league history. That year the National schedule expanded to 112 games, with the added attraction of allowing pitchers to throw overhand. This rule change set the stage for the pitching heroics of Charley ("Hoss") Radbourn of Providence. Blessed with tremendous stamina and a baffling curve ball, Radbourn was a hot-tempered, driven man. Having spurned a $2,000 bonus offer from the Unions, Radbourn hotly attacked his Providence manager, Frank Bancroft, for naming Charles Sweeney as the ace pitcher. Radbourn was suspended for his outburst, but when Sweeney's boozing incurred fines, Sweeney jumped to the Unions. Now Radbourn was in position to dictate terms, so he offered to pitch every game until Providence clinched the pennant, provided his suspension be lifted and that he be granted his release at the season's end. When his terms were met, Radbourn pitched every game from July 23 till late September. In one of the most dazzling pitching feats in baseball history, he won 62 of 74 games to lead the Grays to the championship. Astonishingly, Radbourn's splendid performance attracted disappointing home crowds, with seldom more than a thousand turning out for even the crucial games. Nevertheless, Radbourn received a bonus for his feats, which also included the three World Series victories over the Mets. Thus consoled, the hero condescended to stay with the Grays.

In retrospect, Providence's triumph was the last hurrah for struggling National League outposts. With the Union Association threat removed, the League faced an economic question that loomed as a perennial dilemma in big-time professional athletics: Should membership be granted to clubs without adequate fan support? The answer seemed obvious where the population base was too small, as in Providence. But what about a club that was simply unable, perhaps temporarily, to draw

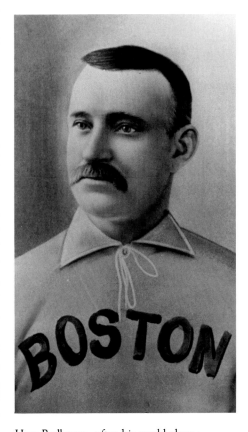

Hoss Radbourn, after his world champion Providence club was bought by Boston in 1885. His pitching prodigies won him early election to the Hall of Fame. (Courtesy MacGreevy Collection, Boston Public Library)

big crowds? Spalding favored a ruthless policy of targeting the healthiest baseball markets. Thus, in the fall of 1884, Cleveland was dropped in favor of Lucas's St. Louis Maroons. This switch was Spalding's idea, which cost Lucas $6,000 and the ignominy of accepting the reserve clause. Such cold-blooded diplomacy was too much for President Mills to stomach, and he resigned in protest. The colorless secretary, Nicholas Young, was elevated as his replacement, but Spalding was known to be the power behind the throne.

THE NATIONALS' CASH AND GLORY YEARS

Double-play action at the Polo Grounds, as depicted by a *Harper's Weekly* artist, W. P. Snyder, during a game between the New York Giants and Boston in late April 1886. (Courtesy The New-York Historical Society, New York City)

As president of the elite Chicago team, Spalding built a new park, capable of seating ten thousand in its wooden stands. Other powerful clubs in Philadelphia, Boston, and New York followed suit. Such edifices marked these clubs as the aristocrats of the League and widened the gap between the haves and have-nots. Luckily for Spalding, a resurgence of Chicago's baseball fortunes coincided with the 1885 opening of his new park. The year before, Anson's men finished a dismal fourth, despite pounding an unprecedented 142 homers, a feat attributed partly to the shortened fences at the old ballpark.

Chicago's two-year fall from grace stemmed from the failure of Corcoran and Goldsmith to adjust to the increased pitching distance, so Anson now replaced them with John Clarkson and big Jim McCormick. Now a

Action at the Polo Grounds, as caught by R. Hoe Lawrence in one of the earliest extant baseball action photographs, during a game between the New York Giants and Boston in early May 1886. (Courtesy The New-York Historical Society, New York City)

sophomore, Clarkson pitched well in limited action in 1884 and was destined to become one of baseball's all-time star pitchers. For his part, McCormick was a proven winner, snagged from the defunct Cleveland team, but he carried a reputation for hard-drinking and hard-headedness. Along with these, Fred Pfeffer and Billy Sunday were the only additions to the team that won three consecutive pennants early in the decade. Since 1883, Pfeffer had played second base, where his brilliant fielding lent lustre to the "stonewall infield." While Sunday still carries a storied reputation because of his later career as an evangelist, he was a minor factor in the Chicago lineup. A speedy base-stealer, he was a weak hitter, and then as now the rules barred him from stealing first base.

In a tense, close race Chicago regained the championship heights by edging the Giants. In 1885 these rivals left all others behind, with the Giants threatening to treat Chicago the same way. By winning nine of the first twelve games played against Chicago, the Giants were confident of dispatching Anson's team in a final four-game set at Chicago. Needing three of these games to tie Anson's team, the invading Giants were backed by trainloads of New York rooters, who watched in stunned horror as Chicago posted 7-4, 2-1, and 8-3 victories to clinch the flag. A glorious Chicago victory, it was blighted in the World Series (or U.S. Championship as it was called in 1885) when the Association champion St. Louis Browns deadlocked the White Stockings at three games apiece.

Still, 1885 was a profitable year for the League's elite clubs; not so for financially strapped Buffalo, which late in the season sold its vaunted "big four" slugging quartet of Dan Brouthers, Dave Rowe, Jim White, and Hardie Richardson to Detroit for $7,000. A stunning and unprecedented sale, it was within the rules but okayed by President Young only with the stipulation that Detroit refrain from playing these acquisitions against the contending Giants and White Stockings. On the heels of this deal, Boston purchased the Providence franchise for $6,600. Thus, Buffalo and Providence passed from the major league scene and were replaced by Kansas City and Washington.

Along with the hated reserve clause, such player sales incited a number of players to form their Brotherhood of Professional Base Ball Players. Although announced as a fraternal, self-help organization at its

Three stars of Harry Wright's Phillies in the 1880s: *above,* Sid Farrar, first baseman; *opposite top,* Jack Clements, left-handed catcher (photos courtesy John Thorn); and *opposite bottom,* Arthur Irwin, captain and shortstop (Courtesy Spalding Baseball Collection, New York Public Library). Posed photos testify to the slow pace of action photography.

inception in 1885, the Brotherhood soon clamored for reforms in personnel practices. By the late 1880s ball players, like workers at most other crafts, had given up the idea of business ownership in favor of collective bargaining for "bread-and-butter" gains. (A coalition of such craft unions, the American Federation of Labor, was founded in 1886.) Meanwhile, favorable public reaction to the trades lulled owners into ignoring player protests. Understandably, fans viewed such deals as power restoratives; if so, Boston fans were disappointed when the team gained no ground in 1886. Not so at Detroit, however; there the Wolverines became a formidable contender, an offensive wrecking crew that led the League in batting and fielding.

Sadly, Detroit lacked an extra pitcher, an aid sorely needed over the extended 124-game season. Shrewdly spotting this deficiency, Spalding checkmated frantic Detroit moves to acquire pitching help. As a result Chicago won again, albeit by only 2½ games over the thundering Detroits. In the end Chicago's pitching advantage told; Clarkson won 36, down from his 53 victories of 1885, but McCormick upped his wins to 29, and young John ("Jocko") Flynn, in his only stint as a major league pitcher, turned in a sparkling 24-6 effort. Backing this staff, Kelly batted a league-leading .388, and Anson weighed in at .371. But Chicago fell hard in the World Series when the feisty Browns won four of the six games. Defeat cost the Chicagoans $15,000, since the winner-take-all purse went to the Browns. In the stormy aftermath Spalding angrily leveled charges of drunkenness against Kelly and McCormick.

After brooding over these hard cases, Spalding unleashed a bombshell announcement in Chicago by selling "King" Kelly to Boston. While player sales had occurred before, Kelly was a superstar who fetched a super price. Boston, with its huge Irish-American contingent in mind, paid Spalding $10,000 for the man they wanted as team captain. What's more, any scruples Kelly harbored about being sold like a chattel vanished when he signed for a salary of $5,000.

This mind-boggling deal stunned the baseball world of 1887, then trying to digest an astonishing recipe served up by the rules committee. In an effort to balance the puzzling pitching and hitting equation, the committee's latest formula radically departed from tradition. The complicated plan favored pitchers by replacing the traditional dual (high and low) strike zone with a single one (from a batter's shoulders to his knees). While this freed pitchers from throwing to a batter's strength, a batter was compensated by getting four strikes (an extra one if the third was called), a base on five balls, and the added sweetener of counting a walk as a base hit. Such periodic baseball rule changes have resulted in never-ending disputes over historical statistics like Anson's batting records and the batting records compiled by hitters under the 1887 rules.

These twin bombshells added zest to the 1887 season. Kelly, idolized at Boston as the "$10,000 beauty," hit .394 and stole 87 bases. Boston remained becalmed in its fifth-place doldrums, however. Chicago fared worse; despite Anson's league-leading .424 batting, the Whites finished third behind Wright's rising Phillies. Mercifully, Chicago fans were shielded from knowledge of the future that would show no Anson team again scaling the heights. When the smoke of 1887 battles cleared, championship honors went to Detroit's hard-hitting crew, which posted a .343 team batting average. This was power enough to bolster a shaky five-man pitching staff and to win by 3½ games. Then the Wolverines easily thrashed the Browns in the World Series, winning 10 of the 15 games. Only one team, the 1894 Phillies, ever matched Detroit's gargantuan hitting. The rule makers saw to that by rescinding both the four-strike rule and the one that counted walks as hits. Such a reversal brought a sense of normalcy to baseball that not even another blockbuster deal by Spalding disturbed much. This time Spalding sold ace pitcher Clarkson to Boston for another $10,000, but the city's love affair with Kelly made this sale anticlimactic.

Clarkson gave better return than Kelly in 1888, leading the League in pitching victories, but Boston managed only fourth place. Ironically, Chicago did better, but its second-place finish was a remote nine games back. For Detroit, 1888 was a crusher for lack of pitching strength. Home attendance, modest enough when the team was winning, fell off badly as the Wolverines sank to fifth. This prompted owner Fred Stearns to throw in his hand; up for sale, the club fetched $55,000, and three stars went to Boston to beef up that city's 1889 team.

While lack of pitching crippled Chicago and Detroit, the New York Giants used a quartet of talented hurlers, Tim Keefe, Mickey Welch, Ledell Titcomb, and Ned Crane, to win easily in 1888. Managed by flamboyant Jim Mutrie, the well-financed and enthusiastically supported Giants made up for weak hitting by pitching virtuosity that yielded fewer runs than any rival staff. Strong defense was led by catcher Buck Ewing and shortstop John M. Ward. A former pitching ace whose arm gave out, Ward shifted to infield play and ranked among the best—as did slugging first baseman Roger Connor, who pounded fourteen homers. Thus, the black-clad Giants brought the pennant to the Polo Grounds and for good measure drubbed the Browns in the World Series.

In 1889 the Giants' bid for a repeat performance was frustrated by local authorities who preempted the Polo Grounds site, forcing the team to seek temporary quarters at Staten Island while awaiting construction of a new Polo Grounds. Torrential spring rains made life miserable for the Giants as they slogged through twenty-five games on their tight little isle. Once ensconced in their new grounds, they found life better till September, when more rains flooded the Harlem River and inundated the new park. Naturally, other teams suffered as well, but Boston's powerful team kept playing and winning. Weather permitting, the Giants kept pace, and the two teams dueled till the last day. Then the Giants won by beating Cleveland, while Pittsburgh downed Boston. Had Boston won that day, the pennant would have been theirs. It was the closest race in League history, and the Giants' winning momentum carried into the World Series as they downed the Association's Brooklyn team six games to three.

This latest demonstration of National League superiority marked the coming end to baseball's Golden Age. Just over the horizon loomed a grim struggle between aroused players and assertive owners. In that conflict the two majors would be allies, but soon afterwards the Nationals and Americans would fight against each other. While ultimate victory went to the Nationals, their leaders rued the day that they destroyed the popular American Association.

THE BEER BALL LEAGUE

The gilding of this decade in baseball owed much to the American Association, whose brash appearance in 1882 had detractors calling it "the beer ball league." Granted that four brewmasters numbered among the founders and that they forthrightly sold their foamy product at ballparks, even on Sundays where local laws permitted; still, it must be said that this offering, along with twenty-five-cent admissions, brought major league baseball to hordes of working-class fans. Indeed, Association baseball was people's baseball, and this approach was anathema to the powers behind the National League. Even more offensive to moralizers like Hulbert were the Association's return of major league ball to excluded cities such as Philadelphia and New York and hiring of players off the National's blacklists. Finally, the Association invaders took a shot at the League's reserve clause by inviting players to sign up under a slogan of "Liberty for All."

Boldly defying the National monopoly, six teams took the field in 1882, representing Cincinnati, Philadelphia, Louisville, Pittsburgh, St. Louis, and Baltimore. Using League rules, the American Association profitably played an eighty-game schedule, with income flowing from Sunday games and ballpark saloons in those cities where the Continental European customs were accepted. The Association's success was an astonishing demonstration of the public's appetite for more and cheaper major league ball; nor could the Nationals dismiss the circuit's claim to major league status.

By a hefty margin the Cincinnati Reds won the 1882 Association pennant over the Philadelphia Athletics. Pitcher Will White won forty games for the Reds, and young "Bid" McPhee began his long career as a slick-fielding, bare-handed second baseman. Elsewhere, too, unheralded players blossomed into stardom, including Pete Browning of Louisville, the batting king, and first baseman Charles Comiskey of the St. Louis Browns. Such stars furnished ample proof for Chadwick's contention that the Nationals often overlooked promising young talent.

That fall the Association struck telling blows against its rival; in October Association President Denny McKnight ordered Cincinnati to cease playing a postseason series with Anson's Chicagos, and later raids on League rosters lured some established players to Association ranks. The raids constituted an attack on the reserve clause, and alarmed League leaders turned to shrewd diplomacy. Summoning a peace conference, as noted previously, League President Mills persuaded Association owners to accept the reserve clause in return for major league recognition. The Association's joy over gaining status recognition was dampened by accusations from players who charged a sell-out.

Ignoring this warning of troubles to come, the Association leaders now expanded to eight clubs, adding Columbus and New York. Thus enlarged, the Association enjoyed an even more profitable 1883 season, which saw the Philadelphia A's win the pennant by five games over

Cincinnati. However, the champion A's, who outdrew the League's new Phillies team, suffered embarrassing postseason losses to their local rivals, prompting the A's to cancel a "World Series" test of strength with the National Boston champions. The cancellation was humiliating, but more so was the revelation that the Association's New York Mets entry was a satellite of the League's Giants.

The Mets proved to be a major embarrassment to the Association in 1884. With the Union Association fighting for major league recognition, the Association faced troubles enough fending off challenges in many of its cities. Unwisely, the Association expanded to twelve clubs, adding to the baseball glut of 1884 and resulting in financial losses all around. Meanwhile, the Mets, whose shoddy park nested atop a layer of decaying garbage, proceeded to win the Association pennant. It was a well-earned victory by a team that batted .262 and received excellent pitching from a pair of thirty-seven-game winners, Tim Keefe and Jack Lynch. But no sooner did the Mets' victory parade end, when the shocking news came of Keefe and third baseman Tom Esterbrook joining the League's Giants for 1885. Shocked Association leaders could only gasp at this example of National League cunning. In the 1890s similar cases of dual ownership would be scornfully labeled "syndicate baseball," but for now the practice was legal and no Association sanctions could stop it. Forced to take defensive countermeasures, the Association returned to eight clubs and stole a march on the League by opening its season two weeks earlier.

But the Association sorely needed a Samson to battle the League Philistines. Happily, such a man was at hand; his ass's jawbone was his powerful St. Louis Browns. The man was Christopher Von der Ahe, "boss president" of the Browns. Part-genius and part-clown, he was a tragic figure who saw his team reach the heights of cash and glory and then collapse ignominiously. A portly, bulbous-nosed German-American beer garden owner, Von der Ahe viewed baseball partly as a medium for hyping beer sales. Alert to the thirsts of St. Louis's large German-American population, he bought Sportsman's Park and outfitted it for baseball. When the Association surfaced, Von der Ahe became a charter member, pushing his formula of twenty-five-cent admissions, Sunday games, and a raft of promotional enticements that included sideshows like fireworks and horse races. It worked well, as St. Louis speedily became baseball's most profitable site.

Over the years Von der Ahe's detractors mocked him for invincible ignorance of the game and its stratagems. This unfair judgment was accompanied by gibes at his outlandish appearance, his guttural German accent, and his many malapropic utterances. Yet the "funny Dutchman" was smart enough to select Charles Comiskey to captain and manage his Browns. A superb first baseman, Comiskey revolutionized play at that position by his mobility, and his defensive and offensive insights added new dimensions to team play. Moreover, Comiskey encouraged his team's aggressive heckling and umpire-baiting style. It worked well, but suffering rivals quickly made Comiskey's cocky "monarchs of the diamond" their favorite hate objects.

Astonishingly, four seasons passed before the Browns got their comeuppance. Like a young tree, Comiskey's team was sturdily resilient. Its

Christopher Von der Ahe, "boss president" of St. Louis Browns in the Golden 'Eighties. (Author's Collection)

Toledo Club of the American Association in 1884. Manager Charlie Morton is seated in the middle, and Tony Mullane holds the ball. Moses Fleetwood ("Fleet") Walker, the first black major league player (for one season), is not shown. (Courtesy Dennis Goldstein)

trunk was the infield, where Comiskey played next to Sam Barkley at second, with Bill Gleason at short and brawling Arlie Latham at third. The main branch was the outfield, where center fielder Curt Welch and left fielder Tip O'Neill roamed; among outfielders, none bettered Welch's fielding or the hitting of converted pitcher O'Neill. Indeed, pitching was the root strength of the Browns, and ex-pitcher Comiskey kept coming up with skilled young arms. These newcomers at times replaced established pitchers whose hitting abilities prompted "Commy" to turn them into daily regulars. Thus, in 1885 the Browns got 73 victories from Dave Foutz and Bob Caruthers, but three years later Commy used Nat Hudson, "Silver" King, and Elton Chamberlain as pitching mainstays. The pitchers' rapid development owed much to the effective catchers Doc Bushong and Jocko Milligan.

In 1885 the Browns stormed to the top, their 79-33 mark lapping second-place Cincinnati by 16 games. Next time out, with the playing schedule upped by 20 games, the Browns won 93 and distanced Pittsburgh by 12 games. And in the radically innovative year of 1887, Comiskey's terrors won 95, besting Cincinnati by 14. These were the salad years of the Browns. Over this time Caruthers and Foutz each notched 99 pitching victories, and in 1887 each batted .357 while playing other positions. As Yank Robinson took over at second base, the team's inner defense average improved, and outfielder Tip O'Neill weighed in with awesome hitting. In the inflated year of 1887, O'Neill batted .492, the like of which has never been approached, even when discounted for base-on-balls hits. Glory also rained on the Browns in World Series competition. In 1885 they tied Anson's haughty White Stockings, then beat them in the winner-take-all money struggle of

1886 on Curt Welch's famous steal of home. Welch's "$15,000 slide" was the apogee of Brownie glory, however; in 1887 the Detroit Wolverines crushed them in Series play.

After that the Browns' dynasty tottered. Harried by salary demands that shot his 1887 payroll over $40,000, Von der Ahe sold Caruthers and Foutz to Brooklyn, an intense competitor also strengthened by their purchase of the hated Trojan Horse Mets. Thus bolstered, the 1888 Brooklyns eyed the pennant, but once more Comiskey barred the way. Combing through some thirty rookies, Commy came up with pitcher Charles ("Silver") King, who hurled the Browns to a fourth consecutive title. But Brooklyn dogged their tracks, and the bitter rivalry between these clubs turned into a vendetta. Brooklyn charged Von der Ahe with manipulating Association councils, and this year's Brownie triumph was marred by a crushing World Series defeat laid on by the League's New York Giants.

In 1889 the Brooklyn–St. Louis vendetta blazed, as manager Bill McGunnigle's Brooklyns defeated the Browns by two games to end their pennant monopoly. Relentlessly pursued by the Browns, the "Bridegrooms," so called because of the newlyweds in their ranks, voted to abstain from connubial bliss during the September stretch drive. While this may have invigorated the Brooklyns, a three-day sit-down strike staged by Yank Robinson of the Browns hurt his team. Ironically, a pair of pants stirred Robinson's ire; with a ladies'-day crowd on hand, he wanted a clean pair, but a testy gatekeeper refused to cooperate. Incensed, Robinson cursed the gatekeeper and drew a $25 fine from Von der Ahe. Outraged, Robinson sat out three games—games that the Browns lost—before winning his point. While this may have decided the Browns' fate, the Bridegrooms soon met their match by falling to the Giants in the World Series. In retrospect, Robinson's solo strike heralded the coming, devastating player walkout of 1890. That strike stunned the Association, already crippled by the secession of Brooklyn and Cincinnati to the National League. Prompted by resentment over the Browns and their leader, the defection of two key teams struck a body blow at the Association, whose imminent demise was to bring down the curtain on the Golden Age.

While rhapsodizing over baseball's supposedly timeless and enduring qualities, present-day pundits should study the game in the 1880s. Indeed, that dynamic decade welcomed change and profited from it. Inspired perhaps by the feverish social climate, officials launched bold experiments based on plentiful ideas from insiders and outsiders. Although some innovations failed miserably, others succeeded brilliantly, and fans in unprecedented numbers stormed the parks, while even more devoured newspapers, journals, and books devoted to the game. For a brief period professional baseball in this decade flourished, growing to seventeen major and minor leagues, including two black leagues. But too soon the noonday sun declined, and from the sobering vantage point of the 1890s owners and players sadly contemplated the Golden 'Eighties as a lost Camelot.

NUGGETS FROM THE GOLDEN AGE

Of all the blessings enjoyed by the major leagues, money was the most welcomed. After the profitless early years following 1876, a turn-about came in 1883, when nearly every Association team profited, with the A's banking $75,000. By then National League teams shared in the cornucopia, as $20,000 annual profits became an expected standard. Coveting a share of the new wealth, Union Association promoters caused a baseball glut in 1884, but soon that league expired, and the two surviving majors recovered momentum. From 1885 through 1889 profits spiraled; dazzled by personal gains, St. Louis promoter Von der Ahe boasted that he'd not sell his Browns for $200,000, while the profits of the National's Chicago, Boston, and New York owners approached $100,000 each during these years. But then as now, wide financial divides existed between have and have-not clubs; some failed enterprises dropped out each year, including the well-financed Detroit Wolverines, who were unable to draw adequate home crowds and became too dependent upon shares of gate receipts from road trips to survive.

As club profits swelled by 300 percent in the late 'Eighties, player salaries grew by 30 percent, but again disparities existed between rich and poor clubs. By 1886 most able players earned $2,000 a year, good pay by prevailing wage standards and nearly double the average player salary of 1880. In comparison, the average salary of all college faculty members, as late as 1893, was $1,470. Moreover, stars earned $3,000 and more, among them Mike Kelly, Fred Dunlap, and Bob Caruthers at $5,000, and player-manager Comiskey at $8,000. Von der Ahe's fourteen-man payroll of 1887 topped $40,000. Alarmed by soaring salaries, owners in 1885 tried to impose a $2,000 limit, which was widely evaded. But owners pressed on, and in 1889 they voted for a sternly enforced $2,500 ceiling. When it was estimated that fewer than thirty players would qualify for the maximum, the players, who after the 1885 attempted limitation had retaliated by organizing the Brotherhood of Professional Base Ball Players, were in no mood to submit and geared for a strike.

The appearance of the Brotherhood coincided with the acceptance of the ballplaying profession. Players were not only established professionals, but also established folk heroes. The 240 major leaguers now plied glamorous careers that hundreds of struggling aspirants sought to attain. Alas, black aspirants were counted out; after brief appearances of black players in the majors—notably the Walker brothers (Fleet and Welday), Vincent ("Sandy") Nava, and George Treadway—they were harried out by segregationists, including the venomous Anson. To accommodate black players, two black leagues now took the field; later, a black major league system would emerge, with players fully equal to the best white major leaguers. Meanwhile, each passing year saw a fresh crop of white youths vying for major league positions. Most came from minor leagues, shaky operations at this time. While the minors nurtured most future major leaguers, a steady flowering of talent blossomed from sandlots, schools, colleges, and amateur leagues. Since few rival sports matched baseball's grass-roots popularity, major and minor leagues enjoyed a bounteous talent surplus.

Too much competition pot-holed the road to the majors, toppling

Charles Comiskey, first baseman, captain, and manager of the 1880s Browns. (Courtesy Charles Burkhardt)

the hopes of many aspirants. Moreover, life in the majors proved no bed of roses. Besides the rigors of the game, it demanded conformity to strict rules, and failure to perform for any reason, including injury, typically resulted in swift, uncompensated dismissal. Nevertheless, those who made the majors found team life intensely tribalizing, marked by unique language, nicknames, customs, and rituals, along with shared hopes and fears and off-the-field adventuring. Such was the impact of this communalizing experience, and so intense was a player's commitment to the game, that once his short career ended, he tended to regard it as the high point of his life. Certainly, being bathed by mass cheers was hard to forget. The popular idolization of players was seen in the growing crowds, whose numbers totaled 20,000 and more for big games. Now, indeed, baseball enthusiasts came to be called "fans," a likely corruption of "fanatics" that outlasted the older term "kranks" and soon became a vital word in the language.

To accommodate burgeoning numbers of fans, old parks were refurbished and new wooden double-decked grandstands were built. Easily and cheaply built, new parks sprang up at most Association sites, while the National's Chicago fans were accommodated at a new West Side Park, Giant fans crowded another new Polo Grounds in uptown Manhattan, and Phillies fans jammed the Baker Bowl from its 1887 opening until its long overdue abandonment in 1938. Sometimes the hordes of fans frightened owners. To be sure, fans' money was welcomed, and canny concessionaires like Harry M. Stevens showed owners how to profit from scorecard sales and by hawking the popular baseball lunch of hot dogs and soda pop. On the other hand, crowds were volatile; at times they rioted, hurled bottles and seat cushions, mobbed umps and players, and offended decorous patrons by foul language. To cope with unrulies, clubs hired cops, provided aloof seating for aristocratic patrons, and even offered vantage points where well-heeled fans could watch games from the privacy of parked carriages.

As ever, the fans were a diverse lot. Some, like Boston's Arthur Dixwell, headed formally organized rooting sections and regaled their team and its opponents with theme songs; others affected individual cheering styles; and some banded together into fan clubs to honor favorite players. When pennants were landed, organized victory marches were staged by joyous fans. At the Association's western sites beer sales and Sunday games swelled attendance and revenue but raised hackles of Sabbatarians, who fought a fifty-year battle against Sunday ball. Meanwhile, ladies'-day games caught on; at Philadelphia Harry Wright lowered admission rates for escorted ladies on the hopeless assumption that the presence of more women would upgrade ballpark decorum. However, Wright's idea of staging pregame batting and fielding drills proved enormously popular with fans and was widely imitated.

Umpire-baiting by fans now became an established ballpark ritual. Newly professionalized, umpires were contracted and controlled by league officials, but their job security was low. Easily fired from their $1,500-per-year jobs, the blue-clad umps also became scapegoats and hate symbols. Assigned singly to games, umpires could hardly cover all aspects of play, and often players took advantage of this weakness. Players routinely stirred emotions by arguing decisions, and not seldom

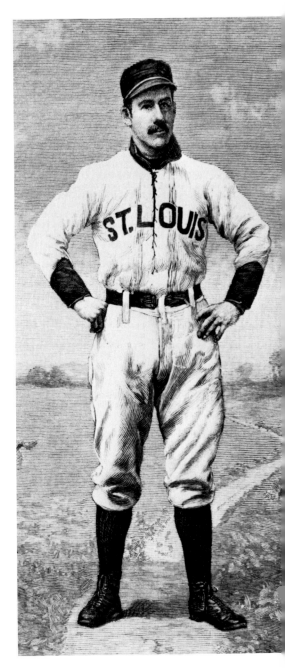

Arlie Latham, third baseman for the Browns in the 1880s. (Courtesy Charles Burkhardt)

umps were mobbed and beaten. Allowing umps to fine and expel players did little to help, as shrewd owners, noting that fans enjoyed ump-baiting, encouraged more of the same by paying player fines. Thus, owners, players, and sportswriters conspired to turn umps into universal hate symbols. While a few stalwart umps like Bob Ferguson, Ben Young, and John Gaffney prevailed by devising their own systems, many were harried out of the profession. As manufactured folk villains, umps suffered for nearly a century, until safety in numbers and the support of a strong union forced a measure of long overdue dignity and respect.

The presence of sportswriters among umpire-baiters testified to the potent impact of this baseball constituency. In the Golden 'Eighties baseball's surging popularity was boosted by massive free coverage of games in leading newspapers and journals. This was by no means an altruistic act on the part of publishers; on the contrary, baseball sold newspapers as much as the press helped the game by developing fans. Thus, publisher Joseph Pulitzer stole a march on his New York competitors when in 1882 he organized a separate sports department for his *New York World.* Its success quickly inspired others to imitate him as they observed readers turning first to sports pages. As baseball sold papers, so papers sold baseball, converting untold numbers to the game by dint of printed accounts of games, served with box scores and statistical records. Luckily for baseball, no other sport so benefited from the linear form of newspaper coverage or wedded fans so assiduously to its records. With no exaggeration one could say that newspaper coverage created a second form of baseball, a vicarious type that allowed readers who never saw a major league game to become rabid fans.

While major dailies hired baseball writers to cover baseball all year long, weekly journals devoted to the game appeared. Of these, the *New York Clipper* was a pioneer, but its interests included theatrical and popular arts, and eventually it concentrated on these and became *Variety,* the organ of show business. Without doubt this decision was hastened by crowding from competitive weeklies, including Frank Richter's Philadelphia-based *Sporting Life* and the St. Louis newcomer *The Sporting News,* which the Spink brothers, Alfred and Charles, launched in 1886 and eventually raised to become the declared "Bible of Baseball."

When baseball writers emerged as a peculiar journalistic species, recognized stylists appeared. With twenty years of experience behind him, Henry Chadwick towered above all others. To many, this bearded dean of baseball writers was the "Father of the Game," an appellation he never disclaimed. Immodest or not, Chadwick's shaping impact on baseball writing is undeniable. As the game's leading historian, he devised a box-scoring system, and as editor of *Spalding's Official Base Ball Guide,* his imprimatur was on the seasonal records. As the pioneer statistician, he inspired such worthy successors as Clarence Dow and, later on, Jacob Morse. By their zealous squirreling, annual statistical compilations linked each passing baseball season into a marvelous chain of continuity, of incalculable importance in popularizing the "national game."

Reflecting the lively personal journalism of this era, baseball writers affected sprightly personal styles. Indeed, for a time it appeared as if

Opposite:

Top left: John Gaffney, dubbed "King of Umpires" in the 1880s for his "system": keeping an eye on the ball, studying rules and playing styles, and handling players with calm firmness. By 1888 he was the highest-paid umpire, with an annual salary of $2,500 plus expenses. (Author's Collection)

Top right: William E. ("Dummy") Hoy, mute outfielder, who began his fourteen-year major league career with the Washington Nationals in 1888. (Courtesy John Thorn)

Bottom: "Scorecard Harry" Stevens, who built a concessions empire on scorecards, hot dogs, and soda pop. (Author's Collection)

writers might emerge as shapers of the game rather than as its chroniclers. For one, Chadwick urged writers to uplift the game; while others agreed, they departed from Chadwick's gentlemanly strictures. Thus, Richter battled for players' rights and trumpeted his "millennium plan," urging annual player drafts for competitive balance and fixed salary schedules for players. If that latter proposal soured players, Richter sweetened it by suggesting incentive bonuses. When his plan got nowhere, Richter supported the cause of organized players along with Spink and others. But baseball scribes soon learned the limits of their role. While writers, including Chadwick, Richter, and O. P. Caylor, briefly served on inner councils of major leagues, their influence was slight. For one reason, their energies were dissipated by reportorial duties; for another, like other spirited journalists, they lost credibility by lambasting each other and by excessive editorializing. Moreover, baseball writing rapidly became stylized; by the decade's end, most of the well-known clichés were already trite. Still, fans doted on their favorite reportage and clucked over witticisms and tall tales that soon became more than twice told. As writers' dreams of becoming baseball shapers died, at least they found a permanent niche in baseball by serving as tireless chroniclers and yarn-spinners.

Meanwhile, there were hints of a dawning day when baseball information would be carried by new media. At this time urban fans crowded around telegraph office boards to watch electric displays of telegraphed game accounts. Yet another signal of a coming Electronic Age in baseball came in 1883 when teams in Fort Wayne demonstrated the feasibility of night baseball. Though repeated at the minor league level that same year, its adoption by the majors lay far in the future. If innovations like these heralded a bright new future for baseball, an ominous threat to the game's dominance showed in the rise of football. Though limited to eastern colleges at this time, the rival game benefited from young Walter Camp's innovations. This Yale coach's scheme of allowing three downs to gain five yards and introducing the four- and then six-point touchdown scoring system invigorated football. Just as the game ceased being a dull possession spectacle, however, the popularity of the brutal flying-wedge offense stirred heated controversy by its frequent injuries to players.

Important as these trends were to baseball's future, they were presently overshadowed by constant tinkering with the playing rules. At this time hardly a year passed without the rules committee effecting a drastic change in the game. Mostly the new rules aimed at striking a balance between pitching and batting. In 1881 batters benefited when the pitching distance was upped to 50 feet, and again in 1887 when the pitcher's box was reduced to 4 feet by 5½ feet, thus limiting a pitcher's tactic of delivering a ball on the run. Moreover, the steady reduction of errant throws allowed to pitchers forced them to become more accurate. In 1880 a pitcher could throw eight balls before walking a batter, but this number was steadily reduced until in 1889 it became the present four balls. This trend was a gain for batters, who were never more blessed than in 1887, when a base on balls was scored as a hit and when batters were allowed four strikes (if the third one was called). This radical innovation lasted only that year, however. For their part, har-

Pitcher Tim Keefe of the New York Giants in the Golden 'Eighties. (Courtesy Charles Burkhardt)

ried pitchers gained some advantages. After 1884 overhand pitching was permitted, and after 1887 batters no longer could call for a low or a high strike zone. Thenceforth, a constant strike zone was employed, fixed that year from the top of a batter's shoulder to the bottom of his knee.

Drastic as these experiments and changes seemed, they resulted in greater balance and consistency. By the decade's end, no longer was a batter put out by a hit ball caught on a bounce; a batter's sacrifice bunt was recognized; a batter hit by a pitcher's toss was awarded first base; base runners hit by batted balls were out, with the hitter awarded a safe hit; and fences had to be set at least 210 feet from home plate.

These years also saw new equipment improve fielding and otherwise alter the style of play. Armed with protective masks, catchers positioned themselves behind hitters to greater advantage. But inadequate gloves, resembling dress gloves and worn on both hands by many receivers, failed to protect them from mangled fingers. Mercifully, by 1890 relief came with the appearance of outsized, padded mitts, including the popular "decker," designed by ex-catcher Harry Decker and later marketed by Spalding. By now other fielders wore small gloves on one hand. Spalding's firm—grown now to oligopolistic proportions by absorbing competitors like Al Reach and Wright & Ditson—sold these along with spiked shoes, colorful uniforms, bats, balls, and other accoutrements. Yet many players bought custom-made bats from the Louisville-based Hillerich & Bradsby Company, bats which they then honed and bone-rubbed with tireless, superstitious zeal. As for balls, which varied from year to year in liveliness, old-timers, recalling games when one ball sufficed, marveled over 1889 reports of eight teams consuming eighty dozen just in spring training.

So many changes stamped the decade as the most dynamic of baseball history. With astonishing speed the major leagues surmounted shaky beginnings to become the elite of the nation's favorite field sport. More than just a game on playing fields, major league baseball was touted in books, journals, songs, and theatres, where patrons listened to De Wolfe Hopper declaim "Casey at the Bat." Promoters and players profited, with lionized players finding their pictures used to promote products, and stars becoming folk heroes. Among the touted heroes were superstars like King Kelly; doughty veterans like Pop Anson and "old reliable" Joe Start; ladies'-day idols like pitcher Tony Mullane; sluggers like Dan Brouthers, Roger Connor, and Dave Orr; adversity defiers like one-armed pitcher Hugh Daly and the mute "Dummy" Hoy; base stealers like Harry Stovey and Arlie Latham; slick fielders like Fred Dunlap, Fred Pfeffer, and Jack Glasscock; dominating pitchers like Charles Radbourn, John Clarkson, and Tim Keefe; and sturdy catchers like Buck Ewing and Charley Bennett. Heroes like these glorified the Golden Age and prompted the ebullient Spalding to promote another world baseball tour in 1888–89. To spread the American game and to advertise his firm, this baseball missionary took two teams to far-off places, including Australia, Hawaii, Egypt, and Italy. His aim was to convert the world to American baseball, but the format of staging games played by American professionals stirred little interest. On balance, the plan ignored baseball's complexities or the ingrained tradi-

Catcher William ("Buck") Ewing, who with Tim Keefe (pictured opposite) made up the outstanding battery of the New York Giants in the 1880s. (Courtesy Charles Burkhardt)

HARPER'S WEEKLY.

JOURNAL OF CIVILIZATION.

Vol. XXXII.—No. 1649.
Copyright, 1888, by HARPER & BROTHERS.
All Rights Reserved.

NEW YORK, SATURDAY, JULY 28, 1888.

TEN CENTS A COPY.
WITH A SUPPLEMENT.

Albert Spalding and his 1888–89 world-tour teams: nine White Stocking stars versus nine stars from other clubs. Spalding, wearing Ascot tie, is seated in the middle, with Pop Anson on his right and John Ward on his left. George Wright is kneeling in front, holding straw hat and cricket bat; Ned Hanlon is seated in front of Spalding. (Courtesy John A. Lucas and Ronald A. Smith)

Opposite:
Baseball was featured on the cover of *Harper's Weekly,* a self-styled "Journal of Civilization," in July 1888. (Courtesy John A. Lucas and Ronald A. Smith)

Spalding's all-stars on the Sphinx in February 1889, after playing an exhibition game in the nearby Sahara. (Courtesy National Baseball Library, Cooperstown, New York)

tions and customs of the natives, and hindsight wisdom must judge it to have been anthropologically hopeless. But Americans liked the idea, and the venture boosted baseball's stock at home.

Sad to say, that stock plummeted in the wake of the quixotic mission. In 1889, soon after the missionaries returned, the smoldering conflict between owners and players burst into flame. Igniting the fires of conflict were issues like the reserve clause, salary limitations, and resentments over player sales. When unresolved, these issues erupted into war in 1890, followed by internecine warfare between the two majors a year later. Thus, with the inevitability of a Greek tragedy, a drab and profitless Feudal Age descended upon the major league scene, raising wistful memories of a lost Golden Age that lingered so briefly in the 1880s.

NATIONAL LEAGUE OWNERS MIGHT HAVE CHOSEN TO
make the 1890s an "era of good feeling." The rival major league,
the American Association, had accepted National League domination after vainly resisting the reserve clause and other restrictive policies. The players had abandoned the idea of controlling their
own league, and the 107 National Leaguers who by 1886 had joined the
Brotherhood of Professional Base Ball Players seemed inclined to bargain in a friendly fashion. Instead, the National League owners chose to
behave as self-styled "magnates" determined to crush both the union
and the competition. The baseball magnates thus emulated the "robber
barons" of American industry and finance, whose shenanigans of the
Gay 'Nineties led to the Progressive Era at the turn of the century.
Even the business-minded Spalding, in his 1911 history, denounced the
magnates' behavior as one of the great evils in major league annals.
Business leaders do not normally aspire to be magnates.

The developing conflict between owners and players in the late 1880s
reflected differing views of baseball's newfound prosperity. After seven
years of financial losses since National League hegemony was established in 1876, owners wanted the lion's share of their new profits for
various standard business purposes: retiring debt, declaring dividends,
retaining for growth, or reserving for contingencies. Players, having
endured seven years of short rations, wanted a larger share in the
bonanza. Average players, especially those on the less profitable teams,
typically earned less than $2,000 a year—considerably more than a
factory worker and somewhat more than a state university professor, but
less than a civil engineer. Outstanding players earned as much as
$3,000 to $5,000, putting them in a class with mechanical engineers
and Harvard professors. Most players seemed to want to bargain, either
individually or collectively through their Brotherhood, for higher pay.
But they faced two obstacles: salary ceilings and the reserve clause.

The reserve clause had been devised to stop "revolving," the movement of players from club to club, which Chadwick had deplored as
early as 1869. Owners, as well as many fans and sportswriters, credited
the clause with maintaining some degree of competitive balance among
clubs. Inconsistently, however, most owners asserted their right to sell
and trade players. The feistier players contended that they and they
alone should enjoy the benefits of a free market for their services.

Such were the issues that led the Brotherhood of Professional Base
Ball Players to act more like a trade union than a benevolent association in 1887, two years after its founding. By now the 107 Brotherhood

3
THE
WAYWARD
'NINETIES

members had chapters in every National League club. They also had an astute and eloquent spokesman, John M. Ward, captain and shortstop of the New York Giants.

JOHN WARD'S LEADERSHIP

Even before the Brotherhood movement began, owners faced individual challenges, like that of Pittsburgh catcher Charley Bennett's attack against the reserve clause. Indeed, Bennett won his point in a state court in 1882, but his victory was limited to his case. More menacing was Ward's 1884 attack because of its class-action possibilities. In an open letter to the *New York Clipper,* Ward argued with impressive logic that players suspended that year for jumping reservations were being punished for a crime that had no standing under civil law. In short, he argued that the reserve clause was a peculiar baseball rule, intimidating to players, but lacking legal or moral standing. Here was a man to be reckoned with, and it was astonishing to see a man of Ward's stature casting his lot with his fellow players. A former Penn State college athlete, Ward had starred as a Providence pitcher; then, when his arm gave out, he switched to shortstopping and starred with the Giants. Off the field, the handsome Ward earned a law degree from Columbia University, penned a popular book on baseball, hobnobbed with New York socialites, and married and divorced a celebrated actress. Coming in 1890, his divorce strained relations with his teammate and co-leader in the Brotherhood, Tim Keefe, whose wife was the sister of Ward's former wife.

Had Ward chosen otherwise, he could have risen high in National League councils, but he spurned offers from Spalding and Giant officials. Indeed, one searches in vain for some ulterior motive behind Ward's decision to serve his fellow players. Finding none, one must credit him with a deep sense of mission. While players respected and trusted him, they did not fully understand him, and some resented his affectations, like reporting late to practices, which soon earned ordinary latecomers the jeering epithet of "a Johnny Ward."

Led by men like Ward, Keefe, and Dan Brouthers, the Brotherhood impressed writers and fans by its clear-cut presentation of player grievances. So persuasive were Ward's words that only four well-known writers opposed the movement, and three of those were in the pay of owners. Among many Brotherhood supporters, Richter's *Sporting Life,* Spink's *Sporting News,* and Tim Murnane of the *Boston Globe* gave strong backing. Given access to these organs, Ward used his pen tellingly; in a series of letters and articles, he blasted the lack of equity in player contracts. So effective were his words that they were studied anew some sixty years later by a congressional committee looking into possible antitrust violations by major league officials.

Up against an ably led, solid array of players, the owners seemed ready to compromise in 1887. At the annual League meeting, they listened as Ward proposed a model player contract. Such a pact would be formally issued to players, would set no limits to salaries, and would take account of player wishes in sales or transfers. In return, Ward promised that the players would accept a fair-minded disciplinary code.

When Ward's proposal was taken under advisement by the owners, who offered a vague promise to study the reserve clause for possible reform, hopes for a peaceful settlement soared, and the 1888 playing season was marked by cordial relations between players and owners.

Fully expecting a compromise, Ward sailed in the fall of 1888 with Spalding's overseas baseball mission. His absence left the Brotherhood without its top leader, and the owners took advantage, voting to impose their dreaded salary limit scheme. Ward was in Egypt when informed of this sneak attack, and he laid plans for an all-out war in 1890 unless the owners recanted. Returning home in 1889, Ward found the opposition stonewalling on all issues. Hence, gauntlets were flung down, and the profitable 1889 season rang with martial preparations as the two sides girded for war to follow.

THE PLAYERS LEAGUE

In July of 1889 the Brotherhood resoundingly approved Ward's plan for a Players League. Given this green light, Ward labored to build a rival major league even as he captained his Giants to another pennant. Lining up investors, managers, players, and even white-clad umpires, Ward boldly raised the standard of the Players National League. By fall the League was afoot. Players were distributed among its eight teams, whose backers invested an average of $50,000 per club for park construction, guarantees, and League operations. Since player interests came first, each player was guaranteed a salary equal to his 1888 figure. While the first $10,000 of a team's profits were to go to its financial backers, the players were to divide the next $10,000 of profits. Should a team profit more than $20,000, any excess was to be shared among poorer clubs or divided among all the League's players. Thus, it was a players league in fact as well as name, as Ward made abundantly clear by placing players on the League's board of directors and seeing that players held a majority of the League's stock shares.

Planning extended to playing rules, which called for two umpires to work each game and extended the pitching distance by a foot (to fifty-one feet). Spalding was cut out of equipment sales, and Keefe's firm got the contract for the official ball. Overall it was an impressive organization; with the best players in fold, the Players League confronted owners with their most fearsome rival to date. In his keynote address to the Brotherhood that fall, Ward blamed the owners for the coming war, saying that they perverted major league baseball into an "instrument for wrong" by their "dollars and cents" mentality.

Thoroughly alarmed, the National owners rallied around Spalding, their kingmaker and elder statesman. Shunting aside the figurehead president Nick Young, Spalding headed a three-man war committee; joined by John Day and John Rogers, he formed a tough-minded, realistic trio. In shoring up defenses, Spalding welcomed two malcontent Association teams, Cincinnati and Brooklyn, into National ranks. That this blow at the Association destined that circuit to minor status apparently bothered Spalding not at all. Using a $250,000 war fund wrung from tremulous colleagues, Spalding bribed fourteen players, including star pitcher John Clarkson, who reportedly accepted $10,000, to jump

Opposite:
John Montgomery ("Monte") Ward, star player for seventeen years, leader of the Brotherhood of Professional Base Ball Players in the 1880s, and head of the Players League in the 1890 season. (Courtesy John A. Lucas and Ronald A. Smith)

Dennis Joseph ("Big Dan") Brouthers, a leader of the Players Brotherhood in the 1880s and a star first baseman for nineteen years with a lifetime batting average of .343. (Courtesy MacGreevy Collection, Boston Public Library)

the Players League. When the Brotherhood denounced these "scabs," Spalding accused the Brotherhood of being in cahoots with controversial labor organizations, perhaps even harboring socialistic and anarchistic sentiments. This was dirty propaganda but effective in neutralizing the players' powerful newspaper support. Eventually, by threatening to withdraw advertising, Spalding turned many papers away from the players' cause.

On the legal front Spalding retained lawyer John Rogers to file breach-of-contract suits against selected players. Two suits were lost in Pennsylvania and New York courts, however, when judges held the reserve clause to be lacking in equity. Still, these were costly victories for the players, as the suits drained money from the vulnerable Players League. Having invested much, the Players' promoters were skittish; should they fail to recoup at the turnstiles, Spalding counted on defections. Certainly, National owners were advantaged; being unfettered with new capital outlays, they could better absorb losses from a head-to-head clash with their rivals.

That the two rivals would clash head-on was certain, since both fielded teams in the same seven cities. Noting this, Spalding withheld publishing the National League schedule until the Players League released theirs; then the National schedule listed games on the same dates as the Players. Forced to choose between them, fans were confused, sometimes intimidated by hired thugs, and constantly bombarded by shrill propaganda from both sides. Ironically, the two biggest financial failures, Buffalo of the Players League and Cincinnati of the National, faced no direct opposition. Elsewhere, despite intimidation, fans were treated to many free tickets dispensed by both sides, along with numerous ladies' days and other cut-rate enticements. It was a costly battle aimed at showing which side could outdraw the other. At the end of the 1890 season authorities had the Players League winning, outdrawing the Nationals by more than 100,000 admissions. Moreover, one authority claimed that the Nationals lost $300,000.

Yet the fledgling Players League could not stand the financial drain. As disappointing profits and dreaded deficits were piled atop its heavy capital outlays, winning the attendance battle was a Pyrrhic victory. Realistically, player hopes centered on denuding the Nationals of star players, as they did, but baseball's talent surplus favored the Nationals. Also, by retaining able and loyal field managers like Anson and Wright, the Nationals had men who were gifted at filling vacant ranks with credible young players. Indeed, Wright was the unsung hero of the National cause; such was his magnetism that his Phillies suffered the fewest desertions of regulars.

Surprisingly, neither Wright nor Anson captured the National League pennant. The turncoat Brooklyns won, making the Bridegrooms the only team in major league history to win back-to-back pennants in different major leagues. Just as astounding was Louisville's turnabout in the moribund Association. After losing 111 games in 1889, manager Jack Chapman's rookie-studded team won handily in 1890 and even deadlocked the Bridegrooms in a poorly attended World Series. Reporting these results serves mainly to keep the records straight. Actually, the eyes of most fans were on the Players League, where most of the

Nicholas E. ("Nick") Young, president of the National League in the 1880s and of the merged National League and American Association in the 1890s, as depicted by a *New York Clipper* artist. (Author's Collection)

Liberty passing her torch to a White Stocking, as the players launch their own league; depicted on a scorecard from the period. (Courtesy Dennis Goldstein)

"Magnates" of the 1890s attending a schedule meeting of the National League and American Association of Base Ball Clubs: seated (left to right), J. T. Brush, A. J. Reach, F. A. Abell, N. E. Young, I. E. Wagner, S. Robison, C. H. Byrne; standing, E. F. Becker, C. Von der Ahe, E. Hanlon, F. D. Robison, H. R. Von der Horst, J. A. Hart, J. W. Spalding, H. M. Pulliam, Dr. T. H. Stucky, Col. J. I. Rogers. (Author's Collection)

New York Giant fans of the 'Nineties enjoying a free look at action on the Polo Grounds from Coogan's Bluff in upper Manhattan. (Courtesy Dennis Goldstein)

stars played. Indeed, the Players League vitalized baseball with its homer barrages. Meanwhile, the Boston Players—managed, captained, and joshed along by the charismatic King Kelly—won the league title by beating off a determined charge by Ward's "Wonders," as his lightly regarded Brooklyn entry was dubbed. Sadly, even this sprightly race was half-buried amidst the confusion and uncertainties of the war.

At the season's end both sides were exhausted. The National League Giants faced bankruptcy until financed by Spalding, and only last-minute financial aid spared the Players' Philadelphia team from a similar fate. Would the war drag on? For the moment it seemed likely when the Players purchased the National's Cincinnati club for $40,000. But this incursion was the high tide for the player cause. As resentful promoters carped over financial losses and poor discipline, players brooded over salary cuts and shattered dreams of bonuses. Rumors of treason marred the annual meeting of the Players League, some reports telling of investors closeting themselves with Spalding. A crushing blow fell when Pittsburgh and New York resigned, and a heavier tremor struck when the financial report showed only Boston profiting, while the others lost a total of $125,000. The news touched off hostile recriminations between players and promoters, prompting Ward to admit that the cause was lost.

On the face of it, the victorious Spalding seemed too willing to forgive and forget. Such was his magnanimity that all players were welcomed back, Ward included. Also, the revised National Agreement, which followed the Players League surrender, glossed over the hated reserve clause and salary issues with weasel words. As prodigal players returned for good salaries under "option to renew" contracts, it all sounded too good to be true—and it was. What Spalding wanted and needed was player backing for a coming showdown with the American Association. Once that organization was trashed, the National League would hold a monopoly. Then rebel players would pay the piper; most would soon be harried out of baseball, and those hanging on would play for low fixed salaries.

Bled by financial losses in 1890, American Association leaders were heartened by the Players League's collapse. Earlier that year, thirty Association players had joined the Brotherhood. Still, hopes for resurgence hinged on the orderly return of prodigal players. However, after Spalding conceded that all rebels must rejoin their former teams, the Nationals reneged. In a provocative incident the Boston Nationals refused to return two former Athletics, a refusal that touched off the 1891 war between the two major leagues.

Battling back, the Association reorganized, strengthened all its teams, and planted competing teams in the National territories of Cincinnati and Boston. With new financial backing, hopes soared, but Von der Ahe and other Association leaders were outmatched by "baseball's Bismarck," as Spalding was dubbed. In the 1891 campaign the Association's fragile Cincinnati team folded quickly and was replaced by Milwaukee. That freed the great Mike Kelly, whom Von der Ahe had installed as Cincinnati manager. When the popular Kelly chose to manage the Association's Boston Red Stockings, National owners quaked. But after one joyous week of good crowds, the smiling Irishman suddenly resigned and accepted an offer to manage the Boston Nationals. Kelly's defection was a crusher; now fickle fans flocked to the League grounds to see the star, and Kelly responded by sparking an

THE SINKING OF THE ASSOCIATION

Boston Beaneaters of 1892, champions of the magnates' one big league: on ground (left to right), Tommy McCarthy, Bobby Lowe, Hugh Duffy; seated, Harry Staley, Herman Long, Mike Kelly, manager Frank Selee, captain Billy Nash, Tom Tucker, Joe Quinn, John Clarkson; standing, Jack Stivetts, Charlie Ganzel, Kid Nichols, Harry Stovey, Dan Brouthers. (Author's Collection)

Edward Hugh ("Ned") Hanlon, who managed the Baltimore Orioles in the 1890s after thirteen years as a big league outfielder. (Author's Collection)

eighteen-game winning streak that carried the "Beaneaters" to the National League pennant.

Little did it matter that the Association's Red Stockings also won, as Boston fans virtually ignored the team. Hard after this crushing blow, at the Association's fall meeting, Columbus and Louisville resigned, opening the floodgates for others. Smelling victory, Spalding moved in with cash and a peace plan. His proposal called for a merger of the two leagues, resulting in a single twelve-club major league, to be named the National League and American Association of Professional Base Ball Clubs. When Von der Ahe of St. Louis accepted and persuaded Louisville, Washington, and Baltimore to throw in with him, the sellout was complete.

On December 7, 1891, the Association died, and the new combined League spent $131,000 buying out the remnants. For the moment Von der Ahe basked in self-congratulation for his diplomatic skill. Pleased with forging a monopolistic league, he and the other eleven owners saw themselves as baseball equivalents of the prevailing captains of industry. Alas for Von der Ahe; his joy turned to ashes when his weakened Browns faltered and failed to draw fans. Mired deep in the loser's bracket of the twelve-club League, he saw his losses mount, and he left baseball a ruined man. For him it was small consolation that his fellow monopolists also lived to regret the day they sank the American Association.

THE BASEBALL MAGNATES

Smugly proud of their new baseball trust, club owners now took to styling themselves as baseball magnates, as horsehide imitators of reigning economic royalists. As such, they enjoyed considerable coverage from admiring sportswriters—whose ranks, however, included a few Cassandras warning of disaster to follow such "commercial Jesuitism." In the magnates' folly, they ignored those warnings, preferring to preen over newspaper accounts extolling their million-dollar "big league," its $420,000 annual payroll and $140,000 travel budget, and its network of minor league satellites.

Lionized by most of the press, these chieftains were well known to fans. Ostensibly, President Nick Young was their ruler, but in fact he was a mere caretaker. While Spalding was the architect of the superleague, pressing outside business concerns now forced him into the background. It was well they did, for it is likely that he would have spent much energy vainly trying to control the egocentricities of his prideful colleagues. Among these new magnates, Spalding's Chicago partner, Jim Hart, emerged as a strong leader, along with A. H. Soden of Boston, "the Dean of the National League." Others included Charles Byrne of Brooklyn, "the Napoleon of Base Ball"; John Rogers of Philadelphia, the league's lawyer; and that puritanic scourge of misbehaving players, John T. Brush of Cincinnati. Zealously, Brush pushed his resolution calling for fines against rowdy and swearing players. Then, in 1894, the sinister Andrew Freedman imposed his colossal ego. A Tammany politician who gained control of the Giants, Freedman brashly determined to restore the team's glory days; by openly bidding for other teams' stars, he insulted his colleagues for rejecting his bids. Real or fancied slights stirred his ire, and his angry utterances turned fans, players, and owners against him.

Freedman fed on controversy and stubbornly pushed his favorite scheme, to run the twelve-club league as a genuine trust. Essentially his plan aimed at curbing the rampant individualism of his colleagues. It called for each team to submit to an overall control that would regulate salaries, discipline, and profits, while calling for the annual redistribution of playing talent. Since populous cities like New York drew better than others, Freedman expected his Giants to get the pick of the players. Indeed, based on his assumption that baseball was strictly a business, Freedman's plan made sense. But others would have none of it. Scoring the plan as "Freedmanism," his colleagues argued that the plan ignored the sporting aspects of baseball. Above all, the other magnates were unwilling to surrender their rights to run their clubs as they chose. Seemingly, most were proud to be part of a monopolistic league but wanted to run their individual fiefs in dog-eat-dog fashion, like robber barons of yore.

Divided by ideologies served up by Brush and Freedman, the baseball magnates scrapped among themselves. Because the unwieldy "big league" each year fielded many economic losers, the rich and the poor franchises formed embattled factions that wrangled over matters like the division of gate receipts and the payment of league debts. In this decade the "little seven" faction, composed of the profit-poor teams at Baltimore, Brooklyn, Cincinnati, St. Louis, Cleveland, Washington, and Louisville, managed to soak the wealthy "big five" by forcing a 50-50 split of gate receipts and making the rich pay a bigger share of the debt. Moreover, the "little seven" favored Sunday baseball where permitted. This caused hot debate, and so did the issues of the league presidency, appointment of umpires, rule changes, and other matters.

Such divisiveness testified to the grim fact that monopoly baseball did not pay off. As profitless years mounted, even the wealthy clubs admitted to making less than they did in the palmy 1880s. For proof, Rogers of the Phillies, who won permission to charge a twenty-five-cent basic admission price, declared that his 1898 gross receipts of $49,000 amounted to only $2,000 more than the club took in during the profitless conflict-ridden year of 1891. Elsewhere, the same bleak picture appeared; in 1897 the league attracted 2,883,631 paying fans, but only six clubs profited and all modestly. In retrospect, 1897 seemed a good year, since attendance plummeted in 1898–99. While much blame for the decline in league fortunes centered on the unwieldy twelve-club league, the decade was a depression-wracked era. To cope, some magnates imposed rigorous austerities. Cheap clubs, like the 1899 Cleveland Wanderers, cost $45,000 a year to operate; an average club like the Phillies cost $66,500, while the elite Bostons cost $95,000. To cut costs, clubs cut corners by slashing salaries, administrative costs, and travel and grounds-keeping expenses. Players were assigned to fill vacant posts at ticket counters and gates. Widely damned as niggardly practices, these ploys at least were honest; some were not, as when owners friendly to Jim Hart, the league's schedule maker, received favoritistic schedules that cut costs and upped profits.

But the most controversial profit-making scheme of this decade was

Wilbert Robinson, catcher for the Baltimore Orioles in the 1890s, wearing regalia of the late 'Nineties. He was elected to the Hall of Fame for his prowess. (Courtesy Charles Burkhardt)

"syndicate baseball." It was not a new idea: In 1883 the Giants controlled the Mets and soon took to stripping that team of its better players; in the 1890 struggle, Spalding and other outsiders controlled the financially embarrassed Giants; in the Association war of 1891, Von der Ahe controlled the Browns and Cincinnati teams. Except for the Giants-Mets connection, however, these were non-exploitive rescue operations. Not so with the syndicates of the 1890s by which magnates tried to profit by their dual ownerships. Since no rule barred double ownerships, some owners openly acquired two teams and took to shunting the better players to one of them. Thus, in 1898, Harry Von der Horst and Ned Hanlon of Baltimore joined with Ferdinand Abell of Brooklyn in an openly announced merger that created an interlocking board of directors and sent the better players to Brooklyn to play for the elite "Superbas." Later, ugly charges of corruption were leveled when Hanlon's midseason efforts to move other players from Baltimore to Brooklyn were publicized.

As Hanlon's brazen moves discredited syndicatism, a western version added to the stench of pooling. That same year owner Fred Robison of Cleveland acquired Von der Ahe's bankrupt St. Louis Browns. Disgusted at poor attendance in Cleveland, Robison dispatched his best players to St. Louis to play for the renamed and highly touted "Perfectos." Robison confidently expected to match the Superbas, but his loaded Perfectos faded, and his emasculated Cleveland team lost so often that attendance in that city fell to mere handfuls. So badly was the Cleveland team snubbed that after July they played the remainder of the season on the road, where they were jeeringly labeled "the Wanderers." And they won only twenty games. Despite this ludicrous failure, syndicate baseball frightened rival owners into taking countermeasures, including a shady deal between Boston and New York whereby the latter dispatched a pitcher to Boston. Determined to cripple his hated Brooklyn rival, Giant owner Freedman also used his

Giants versus Orioles in the 1894 Temple Cup Series, in which the New Yorkers defeated the league-champion Baltimoreans. (Courtesy MacGreevy Collection, Boston Public Library)

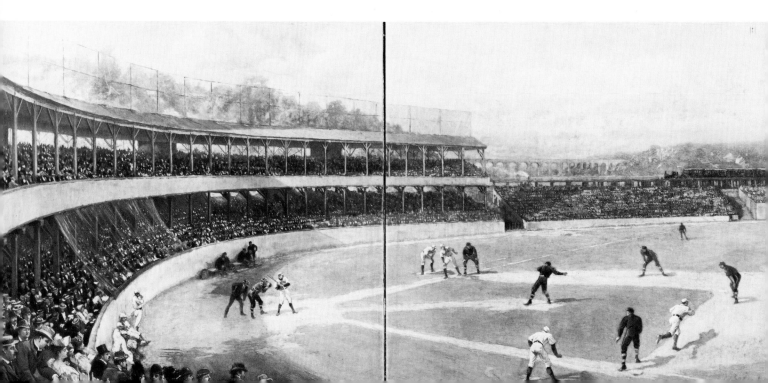

local political clout to deny the Superbas a convenient subway stop near their park.

Along with such controversial empire-building as syndicate baseball, magnates sought control of minor league clubs. To be sure, in the past major league clubs had purchased minor league "farms" for the purpose of developing young talent. Moreover, the National Agreement provided for the systematic drafting of minor league players by the majors. Thus, minor league promoters were used to being exploited, but at this time owner Brush's blatant efforts to control a network of minor leagues stirred Western League President Byron ("Ban") Johnson's ire. To defend his league from Brush's incursions, he waged a campaign to win major league recognition for his league. As a start, in 1899 Johnson won an annual deadline for all player drafts.

Not surprisingly, overbearing actions cast major league owners as villains. So did their treatment of umps and players. Harshly disciplined, ill paid, and much fined, players could only rage as their masters spent money accumulated from fines for annual gargantuan banquets. But baseball writers took note and skewered the owners, who came to know the mixed blessings of public exposure. Much vilified, and pressured by steady financial losses, the owners learned how damaging were their syndicates and trusts and their constant preening as magnates. Forced to refurbish tarnished images, in 1900 they lopped off the four weakest clubs and returned once more to an eight-club league. By then the chastened magnates were saddled with a new debt; at $110,000 this was almost equal to what they had to pay in 1892 to launch their twelve-club league. If some owners now pondered the wisdom of that venture, they had to admit the harsh truth—born in debt, their monopoly league died in debt. In retrospect, the major league era of 1892–

Giants of 1894, winners of the Temple Cup. Monte Ward, numbered 11 by the photographer, is seated in the middle behind the catcher's mask, with Jack Doyle (10) on his right and Hall of Famer Roger Connor (4) standing behind him; talented catcher Charlie Farrell (2) is standing second from left. (Courtesy Dennis Goldstein)

1900 looms as a misbegotten Feudal Age. Baseball men who lived through those times recalled with a shudder the arrogance of its robber-baron owners. Recalling the posturing and greed of the magnates, Spalding, in his 1911 history, marveled that the game was strong enough to survive such excesses.

THE BIG LEAGUE CAMPAIGNS

In straining to recall the big league pennant winners of the 1890s, students of baseball history can lean on a helpful crutch if they bear in mind the letter B. With one minor exception (the split season of 1892), all championships were won by Boston, Baltimore, or Brooklyn teams, all victors being managed either by Frank Selee of Boston or by Ned Hanlon of Baltimore and, later, Brooklyn.

The "big league," as fans dubbed the twelve-club National League, opened play in 1892. Louisville, Washington, St. Louis, and Baltimore were the four newcomers, all Association refugees; they joined with Boston, Chicago, New York, Philadelphia, Cleveland, Brooklyn, Cincinnati, and Pittsburgh. As the price of victory over the Association, each club had to pay a share of the National's $130,000 war debt. That burden, plus hefty salary obligations, demanded a profitable season, which the owners sought to insure by upping the playing schedule to 154 games and splitting the championship season into halves. The first half-season race would end July 15, to be followed by a second race ending October 15; then the two winners would square off in a playoff series to decide the league championship. It was a gamble, heavily dependent on good weather since each half jammed 77 games into only 80 playing dates.

Quite likely, the officials devised this radical format in hopes of preventing the Boston Beaneaters from running away with honors. After all, the 1892 Bostons included stars who took the Players League title in 1890 and who won the National League pennant in 1891. Now they were stronger, having snagged pitcher Jack Stivetts and outfielder Hugh Duffy as spoils of the Association war. Thus fortified, manager Frank Selee fielded a formidable lineup, including catchers Mike Kelly, Charles Bennett, and Charles Ganzel; pitchers John Clarkson, Charles ("Kid") Nichols, Harry Staley, and Stivetts; infielders Tom Tucker, Joe Quinn, Bill Nash, and Herman Long; and outfielders Tom McCarthy, Bob Lowe, and Duffy. The leader, manager Selee, was an enigmatic figure; taciturn, colorless, and with little playing experience, he still commanded five champions during the 'Nineties and left baseball as one of the winningest managers of all time.

Certainly, Selee and his charges wanted to win the 1892 flag in order to wipe away charges that their 1891 victory was tainted by games that the Giants allegedly threw. Thus dedicated, Selee trained his men hard in a southern camp, imposing strict rules against carousing and staying up late. Responding heroically, the Beaneaters won 11 of their first 13 and stormed through the first half-season, playing at a .700 clip and beating second-place Brooklyn by 2½ games. Alas for the players' purses, the spirited race failed to lure droves of fans. Pleading poverty, owners took the drastic midseason step of slashing salaries and dropping fading stars. At Boston, Kelly and Harry Stovey were dropped, and when Clarkson balked at taking a pay cut, he too was cut. Understandably demoralized, Boston played sluggishly in the second half. To "ginger up" the team, Kelly was recalled as captain—a good move, as Kelly worked his inspirational magic for the last time; though batting poorly, he stole twenty-four bases and spurred the Beaneaters to a 50-26 second-half finish. While this fell short of catching the Cleveland Spiders, Boston owned the best overall record.

Cleveland's ascension from a fifth-place finish in the first half owed much to the fiery leadership of playing manager Oliver ("Pat") Tebeau. A fierce gamecock, Tebeau battled umps and opponents; disdaining "goody-goody" players, he demanded "aggressive hustlers." As opponents marked the success of his controversial formula, Tebeau's brand of scrappy baseball became the hallmark of the era. Tebeau also had a brilliant pitching staff, including Cy Young, George Cuppy, George Davis, and the recently acquired prodigal Clarkson. Backing the staff were sturdy catcher Charles ("Chief") Zimmer; an infield of Jake Virtue, Charles ("Cupid") Childs, Ed McKean, and Tebeau; and an outfield of Jess Burkett, Jim McAleer, and Ed O'Connor. Off to a fast start, the Spiders mounted a commanding lead, too much for Boston's late drive to surmount.

With two claimants for the 1892 league title, after hot debate it was decided that a nine-game playoff series would settle matters. Staged amidst widespread charges that Boston had deliberately dragged its feet just to force such a playoff, the outcome hardly allayed the accusations.

An overflow crowd at Baltimore watching the Orioles in the big league playoffs of September 1897, which the Boston Beaneaters won. (Courtesy Library of Congress and Ronald A. Smith)

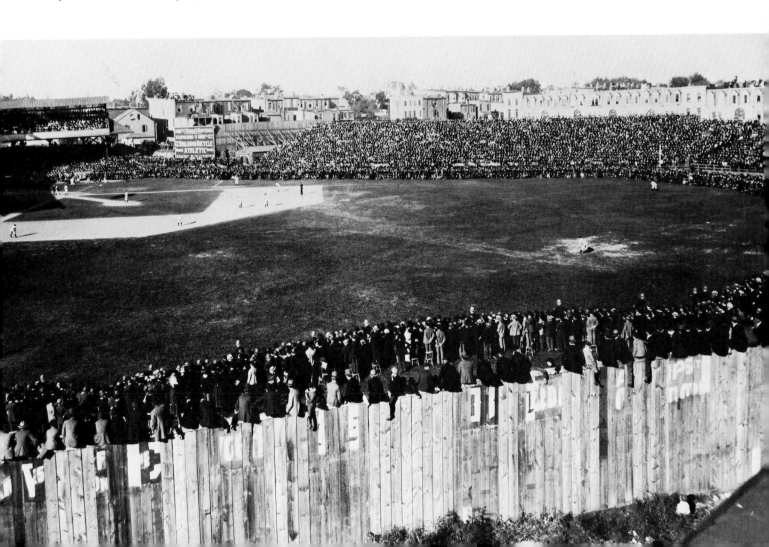

After the opening game ended in a tie, Boston scored five straight victories to win the championship. Not surprisingly, the series was a financial bust, and since the second half was too, the magnates decided to scrap the split-season plan. At the same time, players were handed another round of salary cuts aimed heavily at veterans. Indeed, 1893 rosters showed only fifty-four holdovers from the 1890 Brotherhood teams. Cut loose, these disgruntled veterans were easily replaced by hungry, ill-paid rookies whose presence lowered payrolls to the $30,000 level.

To improve the attendance picture, the magnates decided to inject more hitting into games. In 1892 the league batting average hovered around .245, and the Boston champs batted only .250. Overpowering pitching was the cause, as Cleveland's Cy Young notched 36 wins and Boston fielded two 35-game winners in Stivetts and Nichols. Some drastic remedy was needed to balance the pitching-hitting equation. Brushing aside suggestions like employing livelier balls or forcing pitchers to throw only fastballs, rule makers opted to increase the pitching distance; this time they extended it ten and a half feet, to the present mark of sixty feet, six inches. A traumatic blow to pitchers, it took most of them several years to adjust. Moreover, a pitcher was now confined to a mound marked by a twelve-by-four-inch rubber slab, which was enlarged to twenty-four by six inches in 1895. For batters these were welcomed blessings, and hitters' averages also benefited from a rule decreeing that a sacrifice hit not be counted as a time at bat. Finally, to quash criticisms of "hippodroming," rule makers voted to cut the 1893 playing schedule from 154 to 132 games and to award the pennant to the team with the best overall record.

To most observers this meant Boston. After a slow start, the Beaneaters took charge in July, dashing the hopes of Wright's Phillies. By September they led by twelve, then coasted to a five-game win over Pittsburgh. In winning a third straight National pennant, Boston retired the Dauvray Cup but otherwise gained little cash or glory. Combined with the business panic that swept the land, Boston's easy victory hurt attendance. In winning, Boston pitchers adapted better than most to the increased distance. That year all pitching staffs yielded at least four runs a game, as batting averages soared to .280. The official *Spalding Guide* had Pittsburgh batters leading all others at .319, but Boston hit well, paced by Duffy, McCarthy, and catcher Bill Merritt, and topped by Lowe's slugging. Though bested in particular areas by other teams, the Beaneaters were the best-balanced entry. Yet, for winning so easily, they were taunted by rivals, some crying "Break up the Bostons" and some criticizing Boston's sissified "scientific" bunting game. Still, there must have been some spice to Boston's play, since Chadwick chided their noisy, aggressive behavior. In the main Boston learned that the price of excellence was envy.

In 1894 a pair of tragedies portended Boston's fall. In January veteran catcher Bennett lost a leg in a railroad accident, and early in the playing season fire destroyed the team's park and equipment. Forced to do battle at the old Congress Street Grounds, the Beaneaters suffered financially and psychologically. Meanwhile, the fire of determination sparked the hapless Baltimore Orioles.

Dead-last finishers in their maiden National League season of 1892, the Birds under manager Ned Hanlon rose to fifth place in 1893. Few expected them now to rise higher, but Hanlon, an ex-player who owned a share of the team, swung some shrewd trades. From Louisville he acquired fiery shortstop Hugh Jennings, and from Brooklyn he landed the aging first baseman Dan Brouthers and rookie outfielder Willie Keeler. Then, scanning the latest list of cast-off veterans, Hanlon snared outfielders Walt Brodie and Joe Kelley and pitchers Tony Mullane, Duke Esper, and George Hemming. These were fitted to a nucleus of tested players, including pitchers Bill Hawke and John McMahon, catchers Wilbert Robinson and Bill Clarke, and infielders John McGraw and Henry Reitz. Pitching was the weak spot, but team captain Robinson was a talented receiver. Although burly Robinson and his flock spun a lasting legend of toughness and of spartan disdain for injury, the team was no more rugged than contemporaries and less so than some of the 1880s. Indeed, at various times stalwarts like Robinson, Jennings, and McGraw yielded to injuries, and pitcher McMahon displayed hypochondriacal propensities. Likewise, the image of these Orioles as hell-for-leather scrappers is exaggerated; indeed, the contemporary Browns, Beaneaters, and Spiders matched their reputation.

Even the storied Oriole bad boy, John McGraw, seemed at first like a carbon copy of Arlie Latham of the Browns. As a runaway youth, McGraw had supported himself by odd jobs and spent spare moments playing ball. When Hanlon eyed him in the minors, McGraw's determination proved decisive in winning a draft. Surpassing Latham's devious tricks, McGraw bent rules to Oriole advantage, employing tactics like inciting beered-up crowds, berating umps, sporting sharp spikes, or slapping balls out of an infielder's hands. Such tactics earned McGraw the derogatory nickname of "Muggsy," but local fans and writers loved their "young scrapper." Even McGraw's detractors had to recognize his skill and mastery of fundamentals.

In the spring of 1894, at a Georgia training camp, Hanlon welded his acquisitions into a strong team that stressed base-stealing and hit-and-run offensive tactics. His ambitious players were eager learners; indeed, half a dozen later became noted managers and coaches—Robinson, Jennings, Gleason, Kelley, Clark, and, above all, McGraw. Meanwhile, envious observers like Giant captain John Ward marked the Birds as contenders, and Ward regretted sending outfielder Keeler to Hanlon. Ward's premonition about Keeler was on target; already the youngster impressed reporters with his succinct hitting philosophy: "Keep your eye clear and hit 'em where they ain't; that's all!" Later in that depression-wracked spring, which saw "General" Jake Coxey lead his unemployed army towards Washington, Hanlon unleashed his hungry team in the pennant chase. Opening at home, the Orioles swept four from Ward's Giants. Thereafter, despite shaky pitching, they hovered near the top. Still contending in August, the team got a decisive boost when Hanlon bought pitcher Bert Inks from Louisville. Still, the stretch drive against Ward's Giants was tense, and Oriole tempers were frayed when the race finally ended with their narrow 2½-game victory.

Unwisely, the Orioles let down, succumbing to rounds of victory

Big league umpires of 1895 included (*opposite page*) Harry Wright (supervising chief of staff, not an active umpire), William Betts, T. J. Lynch, John McQuaid, and (*this page*) R. D. Emslie, John McDonald, and Timothy Keefe. Wright and Keefe were playing stars at one time; Emslie and Lynch were former major leaguers. (Author's Collection)

celebrations at home. Thus, the victory was soured by defeat at the hands of the Giants in the first Temple Cup Series. That series, hatched by Pittsburgh sportsman William Temple, called for the league champs to defend their honors against the runner-up. At stake was a $500 trophy and 65 percent of the net profits from the games played. Such rewards went to the Giants, as they swept the Birds in four straight games. On top of the humiliation, Gotham papers trumpeted the Giant victory as climactic, and Ward chose this moment of glory to retire from baseball. Yet the Orioles were league champs, and the passing of time soon showed the Temple Cup Series to be a passing fad that was little remembered.

Hard after the Orioles' pennant year, a costly fire early in the 1895 season destroyed their wooden park. Since this was the league's fourth destructive fire in a single year, suspicions of arson were rife. As insurance rates for wooden stands rose, Baltimore's new park used concrete and steel for its main seating. An expensive outlay, it led management to make a second round of salary cuts on the heels of one prompted by the depression. This infuriated the players, who already chafed over a league policy condemning their scrappy play and threatening $100 fines for "indecent language." Disgruntled, the Birds fell seven games back in May. Worse, McMahon refused to pitch because his arm hurt. Not till August did the temperamental ace return, but then he won ten straight to enable the Orioles to close in on Cleveland. In another nail-biting stretch drive, the Orioles clinched the pennant with a home victory, one of a fantastic 54 against only 14 losses. On the road the Orioles were all too mortal. Cleveland took advantage of this vulnerability to hang another Temple Cup loss on the Birds. Fortunately for Oriole morale, the cup matches failed to stir much interest; mostly, fans recalled the Orioles' 1895 offensive in which they led all others in batting, stolen bases, and sacrifice hits. That six Oriole batters topped the .350 mark was proof aplenty that league hitters enjoyed their biggest feast-year against hurlers still struggling to master the increased pitching distance.

With poor attendance and financial losses besetting owners, more players were up for sale. From the hard-up Giants, Hanlon purchased first baseman Jack Doyle, who joined a pair of rookie pitchers, Arlie Pond and Joe Corbett. With McGraw sidelined by typhoid fever, the Birds needed such strength in 1896. That year's race saw the Orioles trail Cincinnati until August. Then McGraw returned, sparking a spate of wins that winged the team into first. In September the Orioles thrice thrashed Cincinnati, knocking them out of contention. From then on the Orioles coasted to an easy nine-game victory over the runner-up Spiders. And this time the Orioles added a Temple Cup victory to their honors. Although this postseason win was done in fine fettle, by a four-game sweep, the games drew poorly. So did the Orioles' seasonal home games, prompting critics to ask why "dead rabbit towns" like Baltimore and Cleveland should remain in the majors. To such charges, Hanlon responded by acquiring hard-hitting outfielder Jake Stenzel from Pittsburgh, while his Cleveland counterpart Tebeau unleashed a flashy Penobscot Indian ball player, Lou Sockalexis.

Neither of these 1897 additives matched Boston's rebuilding efforts.

Earlier, a brilliant trade with the Phils put speedy outfielder Bill Hamilton in a Boston uniform; now rookie Chick Stahl joined Hamilton and veteran Hugh Duffy to give the Beaneaters an awesome outfield. At the same time, third baseman Jimmy Collins defended against Oriole bunting; moody Marty Bergen provided skillful catching; and recently acquired hurlers Fred Klobedanz, Jim Sullivan, and Ed Lewis joined star pitchers Kid Nichols and Jack Stivetts. Still, not many expected this team to down the Orioles, especially after the Birds beat Boston three straight at the outset. In June, however, Selee's team turned tartars, and in July a seventeen-game winning streak astonished the league. From then on it was a struggle between Boston and Baltimore; whenever they clashed, fists flew, insults purpled the air, and umpires quaked. Such was the intensity of the struggle that sportswriters portrayed it as a battle between good and evil. In the end, by taking two of three in the Orioles' home park, the touted Boston good guys won by two games. Nor did a loss in the Temple Cup Series wipe the sheen off Boston's triumph. Indeed, the banquet following the 1897 Temple Cup Series proved to be the last supper for that contrived affair; one owner denounced the series as no more resembling the old World Series than "a crabapple does a pippin."

Boston's resurgence did little to allay the problems of the unwieldy National League. While Boston counted $100,000 profits, losing teams like the Browns brooded over losses and blamed the Boston-Baltimore pennant monopoly. Disenchantment reached epidemic proportions in 1898 as America's war with Spain upstaged major league baseball. With cruel coincidence, that "splendid little war" paralleled the baseball season almost exactly. Naturally, war news robbed baseball of press coverage, and empty stands and mounting losses made the season a financial nightmare. Although the war was a major cause of distress, few owners were ready to admit that the unwieldy league was as much to blame. Instead, some fixed on Boston's domination, and some cited the bad weather and the imprudently extended playing schedule; one, John Brush, blamed immoral players; and a *New York Clipper* writer cited the popularity of bicycling and motion pictures as distractions. For the record, Boston repeated in 1898, beating the Orioles by six games. Strong pitching boosted the Beaneaters, while the hard-hitting Orioles might have won if pitchers Pond and Corbett had not quit the game for more lucrative outside careers.

It would have been wise had owners addressed these symptoms of baseball's malaise, but instead they welcomed the war's end in August 1898 and chose to muddle along with the one big league. All but a few blamed the Boston-Baltimore pennant monopoly, and the Robison brothers of Cleveland hatched a syndicate plan to counter this. To meet the threat, Baltimore owners Hanlon and Von der Horst erected a rival syndicate. Thus, as the Robisons built up the St. Louis Perfectos, Hanlon and Von der Horst dispatched Oriole stars to the newly named Brooklyn Superbas. Syndicate baseball was disastrous; instead of solving the league's imbalance it exacerbated the problem. Small wonder that other teams protested these behemoth rivals. Such paranoia was a natural reaction, and it stirred shady countermeasures, like a midseason Boston-Giant deal that dispatched a pitcher to the Beaneaters—to no

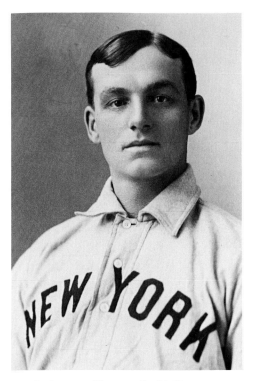

Joseph Jerome ("Ironman") McGinnity, after he joined the Giants in 1902. He was elected to the Hall of Fame for his phenomenal ten-year pitching record of 247 wins against 145 losses. (Courtesy Dennis Goldstein)

avail, as Boston finished a distant second to the star-studded Superbas.

In stacking his Brooklyn entry, which fans dubbed the "Trolley Dodgers," Hanlon screened forty men, ransacking the Orioles of out-fielders Kelley and Keeler, infielders Dan McGann and Hugh Jennings, and pitchers Jim McJames, Jim Hughes, and Al Maul. Blended with Brooklyn holdovers like outfielder Fielder Jones, infielders Tom Daly and Bill Dahlen, and pitchers Jack Dunn and Bill Kennedy, by July the Superbas outdistanced the St. Louis Perfectos, and they clung to first place for twenty-one weeks. This was a crushing blow to the Perfectos, who fell to fifth and drew poorly. The Cleveland arm of Robison's syndicate was a disaster. Unmatched since by any major league team, Cleveland's 20-134 record stands starkly in baseball's annals of futility. So bad was this team that they were forced out of town; playing on the road they were dubbed "Exiles" or "Wanderers." If the Cleveland fiasco made mockery of the syndicate system, Hanlon's Brooklyn victory exposed its dark side. Determined to win big with his dream team, Hanlon fretted over a midseason slump and unexpected competition from his own Baltimore satellite, ably managed by McGraw. To boost his Superbas and damp down the Orioles, Hanlon tried to draft two Oriole stars but backed down amidst volleys of criticism.

Hurt by such manipulations, the 1899 season was a flop. Again attendance lagged, leaving eight teams in the red. Bereft of fresh ideas for propping up the "melancholy wreck" of the twelve-club league, owners voted in 1900 to cut back to eight teams. For poor attendance Louisville and Washington were dropped, along with Baltimore and Cleveland, who also bore the onus of syndicatism. This radical surgery left eight clubs that were saddled with a $110,000 debt incurred from buying out the rejects. It was a case of bite the bullet or suffer a worse calamity, such as the threat from interlopers who sought to revive the American Association. To head off this threat, the Nationals allowed an established minor circuit, President Ban Johnson's Western League, now named the American League, to invade Chicago and Cleveland. In another year this upstart circuit would demand and win major league recognition. National owners could hardly reject the notion of returning to the old dual major league system; certainly, monopoly baseball was a proven loser. Nevertheless, when the American League raised its major league standard, the Nationals waged a face-saving war in 1901. While that brief struggle ended the monopoly era of baseball, the old order lingered through the 1900 season. Once again Hanlon drove his "Dodgers" to a pennant, although the race was close. A rising Pittsburgh team battled all the way, and only herculean pitching by "Iron-man" Joe McGinnity, who pitched and won six games in as many September days, saved Hanlon. Brooklyn followed with a postseason "world series" win over the Pirates, but there was little cash from the matches. Indeed, only Pittsburgh, Boston, and Philadelphia profited in 1900, and Brooklyn's financial losses and Boston's fall from power signaled the end of the pennant monopoly. Now, rising newcomers like Pittsburgh, Chicago, and New York ushered in a new era in National League baseball as the American League entered the scene.

Charles Augustus ("Kid") Nichols, who pitched seven straight seasons of 30 or more victories for the Beaneaters in the 'Nineties. He was elected to the Hall of Fame for his incredible fifteen-year tally of 360 wins, 202 losses. (Courtesy John Thorn)

Truly, a player had to love baseball to play in the one big league of the 'Nineties, for the monetary rewards were modest. Salaries were slashed midway in the 1892 season, and thereafter the best players were paid a maximum of $2,400, a figure sometimes augmented by small bonuses for outstanding play or by piddling shares of postseason cup game receipts. While some protested and a few quit, most players submitted. It was a time when submission was dictated by the harsh reality of a talent surplus. Highly favorable to owners, the surplus had hundreds of aspirants bucking for big league positions. Not included were black players; at this time baseball segregation was institutionalized. Hence, black players formed a "Negro National League," where stars earned $460 a season, well below the $570 earned by a good white minor leaguer. For perspective it should be noted that in 1890 an estimated 90 percent of all American families earned less than $380 a year.

As surviving stars from 1889 now discovered, they could be replaced; thus, by 1897 an estimated 137 new faces appeared. Such talent competition explains in part why owners of 1893 pared team payrolls to an average of $30,000. Another reason was the business depression; manufacturing wages in the United States declined for seven years starting in 1893. The monopoly position of the National League was a two-edged factor; it blunted fan interest and cut attendance, and it led owners to undervalue players. President Young compared players with dollar-a-day laborers, indicating that reduced salaries were here to stay. So they stood until 1901, when the rival American League bid salaries upward. A year before, players had flexed their muscles and organized a short-lived Players Protective Association, which requested that the maximum salary be raised to $3,000. The Association's no-strike pledge encouraged owners to refuse, however. Worse, Cincinnati owner John Brush's 1898 resolution calling for stiff fines and firings for boozing, brawling, and swearing forced players to defend themselves on another front.

Brush's quixotic but forceful crusade struck at a popular aspect of the big league's playing style. Inspired by the Orioles and quickly imitated by others, a "scrappy," crowd-pleasing brand of fighting baseball "short of physical violence" was rife. Defended by some writers as "manly," tactics included aiming abusive language at opponents and umpires, intimidating rival base runners, doctoring playing fields, and otherwise bending or flouting rules. Such tactics caused umpire resignations, incurred fines, and prompted Brush's moral war. Although Brush's resolution became a dead letter after 1899, when the alleged offender in the first disciplinary case drew only a rebuke, the issue of player decorum remained to be solved in a less nice-nellyish way.

Not seldom, the scrappy play issue overshadowed the contest between two styles of play. Teams like Boston and Baltimore stressed the "scientific" style, a blend of offensive tactics like bunting, stealing, and the hit and run, and intricate defensive tactics such as rally-busting infield double plays. Against this style teams like Philadelphia and Washington mounted a "manly slugging" offense—epitomized in Sam Thompson's career total of 127 homers for the Phillies and Buck Freeman's 1899 seasonal mark of 29 for the Senators.

While controversy raged over the merits of these playing styles, pitchers struggled to master a revolutionary change. Because "cyclone" pitching blew away the offense in 1892, owners extended the pitching distance from fifty feet to the present sixty feet, six inches. This rule delighted hitters but traumatized hurlers. From an average of just over three runs per game yielded by pitchers in 1892, the figure climbed to 4.6 in 1893, soared to five-plus in 1895, and held at four-plus in 1897. In the years 1893–97 batters clobbered pitchers; in 1894 the league batting average was .309, and the slugging Phillies posted an astronomical .349 team average. But that year was the high-water mark for batters. Although league batting averages topped .290 in the years 1895–97, pitchers were adapting to the change. From 1898 to 1900 pitchers yielded fewer than four runs per game.

That pitchers survived such assaults testifies to the hardihood of the species. Although the added distance forced each club to carry at least five pitchers, durable throwers like Young, Nichols, McGinnity, Amos Rusie, and Ted Breitenstine started and finished as many as fifty-six games a season. The lengthened distance militated against such feats, however. In the performance of trickster pitchers like Clark Griffith, a fan could glimpse the pitching style of the future. It called for a pitcher to make fewer starts and to augment his fastball with off-speed deliveries, breaking balls, and experiments with spit and foreign substances to make the ball do tricks.

As old heroes like Clarkson and Radbourn passed on, the pitchers just named became new heroes. Fans of this era also warmed to catchers like Robinson, Zimmer, and Bergen. As the decade unraveled, old infield stars like Brouthers, Pfeffer, Williamson, and Latham yielded to newcomers like first baseman Joe Kelley, the graceful Nap Lajoie at second, John Peter ("Honus") Wagner at short, and Jim Collins at third. In outfields a surfeit of brilliant players roamed, including Bill Hamilton, Jess Burkett, Willie Keeler, Hugh Duffy, Ed Delehanty, and Sam Thompson. These were all-round hitters and fielders, the stuff of hero worship. Fittingly, fans embraced them, cheered them on, devoured newspaper accounts of their prowess, and collected their portrait cards from packages of cigarettes.

By now fans were used to swapping old heroes for new. In like fashion fans adjusted to new concrete-and-steel parks, an innovation speeded by fires that consumed wooden structures. Yet fans of this time were less buffeted by change than those of the 1880s. If accepting a single big league, an increased pitching distance, and scrappy ball was bewildering, rule changes like the pentagon-shaped home plate, the pitching slab, the banning of squared bats, and free substitution of players were easier to absorb than the fundamental changes of the 1880s that established the modern game. Fans also adapted to Sunday ball, although Sabbatarians still pushed restrictive laws; but where the law permitted, fans swarmed in great numbers to Sunday games.

While baseball fans have shown their adaptability to change since the game began, the lesson of the "Wayward 'Nineties" is that fans stay away in droves when they are bored or deeply offended. Fans by their absences served notice on the would-be magnates of the National

League that improvements were sorely needed. If the owners failed to heed the message of empty seats, then the popularity of rival sports like biking and football underscored the warning. Indeed, football caused such a scare that a few owners tried to promote a professional football league using their ballparks in the off-season; at a cost of $2,000 they learned that this move was premature. By the end of the 1890s astute owners could see that monopoly and syndicate baseball was a failure. What fans wanted was competition among truly independent clubs, culminating in a genuine World Series between the pennant winners of equally matched major leagues.

BENEATH THE MAJORS: THE PROFESSIONAL MINOR LEAGUES AND SEMI-PROS

THE EVOLUTION OF MAJOR LEAGUE BASEBALL IN AMERica would have taken a different course without the co-evolution of minor professional leagues, which began to flourish soon after the majors were established and grew to function as talent suppliers for the majors. The first circuits in this subcategory of professional baseball evolved soon after the National League began in 1876, and until the 1950s minor leagues flourished in all sections of the land. Although ubiquitous and plentiful for almost seventy-five years, the minors proved exceedingly vulnerable to changing economic and social conditions. Among these vicissitudes, television's impact dealt the minors a crushing blow. Consequently, by the 1960s the once thriving minor leagues had diminished to the point where their survival required hefty subsidies from the majors. Belatedly by that time, the majors recognized how important the minor leagues were to their own continuing success. For one thing, in the major leagues' formative years the minors had fanned public interest in professional baseball in localities remote from major league cities. Serving as nurseries of playing talent, moreover, minor league teams recruited and trained many, often most, of the players who replaced flagging major league veterans. Finally, the minor leagues have contributed to the evolution of professional baseball families. As reported in Chapter 9, an estimated 68 percent of all major leaguers in 1980 were the sons of minor leaguers, according to a book by Laband and Lentz.

Notwithstanding their historical importance, the minor leagues and their players have received only scant attention from baseball historians dazzled by the deeds of major leaguers. Of course, justifications exist for this scholarly myopia. After all, the major leagues appeared first, and major league innovators shaped the course of the game's growth and adaptation in a fast-changing American society. Moreover, major leagues themselves assigned the minor leagues to subordinate ranking and often exploited them.

The cavalier treatment of lesser baseball organizations by major league circuits was evident at the time of the founding of the first major league in 1871. During its five-year history the National Association of Professional Base Ball Players operated as the nation's only professional baseball league. As such, the National Association basked in its elite status atop a thousand organized amateur teams. As a *New York Times* writer characterized the American baseball world of the early 1870s, the National Association ranked above organized amateur teams and far above semi-organized pickup teams.

When the National League dethroned the Players Association in 1876, its leaders determined to maintain and embellish this elite status. To this end National League leaders William Hulbert and Albert Spalding sought to limit membership to well-financed clubs located in cities with populations of at least 75,000. By admitting only one team from any city, these innovators established the principle of a sports franchise based on a team's monopoly over a defined urban territory; over the years such franchises appreciated in value. Moreover, Spalding and Hulbert added such innovations as a fixed playing schedule and the reserve clause in players' contracts. Besides these features, the National League clubs erected classy ballparks and maintained relatively high admission prices in order to buttress the big league's preeminent position.

When confronted by competing professional organizations, the National League's superior organization consigned such rivals to minor league status because they lacked the clout of the National League. In the early going, however, rival leagues did not readily concede National League superiority. A strong challenge came from the International Association, the strongest of three professional leagues organized in 1877. The loose-knit International Association lasted only three seasons, but at times it threatened to overshadow its lordly rival. In its first

The Syracuse Stars of the 1888 International Association fielded two black players, pitcher Bob Higgins (seated left) and catcher Fleet Walker (standing left in the top row). At the time, a controversy over the playing of black players divided the International Association and later led to the exclusion of black players. (Courtesy John Thorn)

Ballpark at a Pennsylvania Railroad resort, developed to encourage train travel. (Courtesy Library of Congress and Ronald A. Smith)

season the Association fielded teams in some fairly populous cities, and that year the Lowell team, champions of the Association, defeated the National League's Boston champs in a postseason series that foreshadowed future World Series matches. In addition, Association teams frequently defeated National League teams in exhibition games.

Poor organization, however, doomed the International Association. The circuit's easy admission policy permitted teams from smaller cities, such as Allentown, Pennsylvania, or Holyoke, Massachusetts, to compete with nines from cities as large as Pittsburgh, Brooklyn, and Washington. Moreover, most Association teams were poorly financed "cooperative nines" that depended on gate receipts to pay their players, a policy that hurt small-town teams. The Association also lacked a fixed playing schedule, and its unwieldy subdivisions complicated the determination of a seasonal championship. On top of these woes, the Association leadership, which included a player-president, was out-generaled by National League leaders. In the crucial infighting the National League scored coups by persuading strong Association teams, such as Providence, Buffalo, and Cleveland, to desert to the National League. These and other tactics—like pirating Association playing rosters, refusing to play exhibition games with Association clubs, and advancing the interests of rival minor leagues—enabled the National League to crush this rival in 1879.

In surveying the brief history of the International Association, most baseball historians regard it as the first minor league. By spawning professional teams in small towns in the Northeast, the Association fostered the growth of successor minor leagues. And by planting teams in larger cities that the National League had abandoned or ignored, the Association forced National League leaders to occupy such centers, lest some new rival league beat them to it.

Such a prospect came to pass in 1882 when the American Association bid for major league status. Shocked by this upstart rival's success, the National League took action to occupy sites in New York and Philadelphia and also mounted a diplomatic campaign. Over the winter

the National League president met with leaders of the American Association and the Northwestern League, the latter being a reorganized midwestern circuit that also had posted a profitable season in 1882. From this summit meeting came the Tripartite Agreement of March 1883. The historic agreement conceded major league status to the American Association and a slightly lower status to the Northwestern League. The territorial rights of each of the three leagues were recognized, and teams from the three leagues each were allowed to reserve as many as eleven players a season. This extension of the reserve clause was intended to halt roster raids by any of the three signatories.

Because all other professional leagues were excluded from the agreement, the effective division between major and minor professional baseball leagues dates from this agreement. The major-minor divide was recognized anew under the first National Agreement promulgated by the major leagues in 1884. Although frequently revised, this National Agreement lasted until 1901. Not until 1888 did the major leagues (under a revision of the National Agreement) concede the right of player reservations to minor leagues; by then the ranks of the minors included the defunct Northwestern League, reorganized as the Western Association. Prior to 1888 the two majors raided minor league rosters, seldom compensating owners for losses. Mercifully for the minors, the 1888 concession granted a compensation schedule for players drafted by the majors; depending on the status of its minor league, a club received from $250 to $1,000 in payment for a player. Thus, it was evident that a ranking of pro baseball leagues had come to pass.

By the year 1888 there were plenty of minor leagues to be graded. Indeed, the decade of the 1880s was a fertile time for pro baseball ventures in America. In 1883 two minor leagues were launched, followed by seven more in 1884—the year that also saw the Union Association make its abortive bid for major league recognition. By 1890 an estimated 160 professional baseball teams were operating, including some integrated clubs and a few all-black teams. Although encroaching segregation patterns were forcing black teams out of the mainstream of

John Thoney on his way to first base for Toronto in a 1907 season opener. "Bullet Jack" won the International League batting championship that year, while Toronto was the top team in the league. Thoney played three years in the majors before going to Toronto and three years afterwards. (Courtesy Ron Menchine)

pro ball, in 1885 one famous team, the Cuban Giants, declined an invitation to join the Eastern League, believing they could do better independently. During the Golden 'Eighties minor league baseball's sturdy growth produced nearly twenty leagues, located in every region but mostly in the Northeast. America's continuing urbanization fueled the baseball boom, as did low costs of playing fields and equipment, subsidies from industries, and expanding newspaper coverage of games; the decade saw the founding of two successful baseball weeklies, *The Sporting News* and *Sporting Life*. The baseball boom of the 1880s inspired a host of hopeful young players. Mostly they came from the sandlots of towns and cities. Not until the next century would high school and public recreational programs swell the numbers with their organized leagues. At this time college baseball programs provided a trickle of talent, and during the 1890s a larger flow came from industry-sponsored leagues.

The distinction between amateur and professional players was not always clear in the early years of baseball—as is evident in the opening chapter of this book and the vignette on collegiate and other amateur forms of the national pastime—and this distinction remains a vexing issue throughout the world of sport. Because of the large number of Americans who have "played for pay" while holding down jobs off the diamond, the role of the semi-pro has been significant in the history of baseball. Well-heeled fans often have been disposed to slip a few banknotes, either openly or on the sly, to talented players who seem likely to tip the scale of victory toward the team sponsored by a favored town, commercial enterprise, or college.

Also blurred at times is the distinction between sport and entertainment. While the major leagues always have frowned on "grandstanding," and even take a dim view of "sideshows" like those staged by Chris Von der Ahe or Bill Veeck, some of the "minor minors" have felt

Charley Hickman rounds the bases after homering for Toledo in the Mud Hens' 1909 opening game at Swayne Field. Although Toledo belonged to the second American Association from its start in 1902 until 1952, the Mud Hens never won a league championship until 1927, when Casey Stengel was their manager. "Piano Legs" Hickman had played in the majors for twelve years before going to Toledo. (Courtesy Ron Menchine)

compelled to put on a good show. Deliberate emphasis on entertainment values, even "clowning," has not necessarily produced bad baseball. "Show biz" teams have survived by barnstorming throughout the continent, mostly but not exclusively in small towns. In their gypsy lifestyle, barnstormers resemble teams described in the vignette on the black majors. Some barnstorming teams are racially integrated, notably the Indianapolis Clowns, self-described as the "Harlem Globetrotters of Baseball." Hank Aaron and other major leaguers started with the Clowns. The most famous barnstorming team until the 1970s, the House of David, was sponsored by a religious sect. A list of the Clowns' seventy opponents in 1973, recorded in pitcher Bill Heward's memoirs, ranges from the Adams (Massachusetts) All-Stars through Fargo (North Dakota) Glass and Paint to the Holly Springs (Mississippi) Giants. The annals of barnstorming show amateurs, semi-pros, and professional minor leaguers contending at the grass roots.

From such backgrounds came thousands of players who staffed minor league teams of the nineteenth century. In the main this was raw talent, requiring seasons of playing time to develop. Thus, the minors functioned as nurseries of talent, a role that the majors increasingly demanded of them. As for the thousands of hopeful players, few made it to the majors. Records of nineteenth-century teams are scanty at best, but one student of the minor leagues, Robert Obojski, has estimated that 75,000 professional players were active from 1876 to 1911 and that 200,000 more saw pro action from 1911 to 1975. Of this vast number only some 10,000 played in the majors from 1876 to 1975.

Among the deeds wrought by minor leaguers of the 1880s, those of slugger Perry Werden and pitcher Tom Lovett shone like beacons. A versatile player, the popular Werden played twenty-five seasons of pro ball from 1884 to 1908. Werden's long career included seven seasons in the majors, but mostly he toiled in the minor Western League, where

his .341 lifetime batting average and 168 homers rank him among the top fifteen minor league hitters of all time. By contrast, pitcher Tom Lovett's career was shorter, but few hurlers accomplished so much in so short a time. In the years 1886–88 Lovett recorded 103 victories as a minor league pitcher. In 1887 he notched 41 wins, including a 21-3 record with Bridgeport in the Eastern League and a 20-2 record with Oshkosh in the Northwestern League. Lovett's gaudy 41-5 mark of 1887 saw him leading both circuits in winning percentage. Over the years 1888–94 Lovett pitched six seasons in the majors, posting an 88-59 record.

Upping the odds against players making the majors was the shaky nature of many minor league operations. Indeed, the history of minor league baseball is littered with failed teams and leagues. Although actual figures are virtually impossible to obtain, according to one estimate some 850 pro teams were launched in 1869–1900, of which 650 failed soon after they were organized; of the survivors only 50 lasted six years or more. Often entire leagues folded, then regrouped and tried again. For example, the Texas League, organized in 1888, at various times fielded teams from more than a hundred Texas towns and cities. For another example, the Southern League, first organized in 1885, failed and renewed itself at least ten times by 1900.

Although the ups and downs of minor league promotion discouraged many entrepreneurs, John ("Honest John") McCloskey was a bullish exception. In 1888 McCloskey began his promotional career as a key organizer of the Texas League. Over the next forty-four years this "Johnny Appleseed" of minor league promoters helped to organize four more circuits; moreover, McCloskey managed thirty different clubs at all levels of minor league classification. Despite the willingness of this promoter to manage weaker teams, as he often did to help a circuit get

Amateur championship game in Cleveland in September 1914, when an estimated 100,000 fans watched Telling's Strollers play Hanna's Cleaners at Brookside Stadium. (Courtesy Library of Congress and Ronald A. Smith)

started, his lifetime managerial record of .512 attests to his dogged success.

Many factors accounted for the minors' high attrition rate. Mercurial public interest; poorly financed teams; squabbling or crooked promoters, who sometimes absconded with monies; unpaid or ill-paid players (salaries well below $1,000 were normal for the nineteenth century); roster raids by major or higher minor leagues; poor umpiring; religious opposition to Sunday games—all these and more difficulties made minor league baseball promotion a shaky venture.

Nevertheless, the resilience of local fans and promoters was strong enough to lure new leagues; from 1891 to 1899 at least eight new circuits surfaced. Thus, in 1895 a *Sporting Life* cover displayed a montage of pictures of fourteen minor league presidents grouped about a center cut of National League President Nick Young. The fourteen minor leagues recognized under the National Agreement were the Eastern League, Western League, Southern League, Western Association, Interstate League, Western Interstate League, New England League, New England Association, Canadian Association, New York League, Michigan League, Pennsylvania League, Virginia State League, and Schuykill Valley League. In 1895 minor league batters were taking full advantage of the recently extended pitching distance to post some lofty hitting records. Playing for Rockford, Illinois, in the Western Association that year, first baseman Bill Krieg hit .452. Krieg outhit Werden, who batted .428 with forty-five homers for Minneapolis in the Western League.

Among these fourteen circuits, Ban Johnson's Western League (whose ancestry went back to the Northwestern League of 1882) was heading in 1898 towards a rendezvous with destiny. Five years later this thriving circuit successfully warred with the National League for major

Baseball game at a Pennsylvania Railroad athletic meet in Altoona in September 1916. (Courtesy Library of Congress and Ronald A. Smith)

league recognition. In 1903 a new National Agreement conferred major league status upon Johnson's renamed American League; the new agreement also recognized the National Association of Professional Baseball Leagues as the representative association of all accredited minor leagues. The National Association was organized in 1901 by representatives of several minor leagues who resorted to collective action to stop the embattled majors from raiding their player rosters. At their 1901 meetings these representatives formed the National Association, whose ten-year charter empowered the organization to legislate favorable player-draft procedures, to set salary limits and player-reservation policies, and to arbitrate disputes on these and other issues. It was this National Association that the majors, in their 1903 National Agreement, recognized as an integral part of organized baseball. Henceforth, only National Association member leagues were recognized as "organized baseball" leagues. All other professional leagues were "outlaw leagues," with the exception of Negro leagues, which were regarded as existing beyond the pale of organized baseball.

The National Agreement of 1903 also stratified the minor leagues into A, B, C, and D classifications. Class A leagues enjoyed the highest ranking because their teams drew from the more populous cities; their players were paid more and fetched higher prices when drafted by major league teams. In 1908 an even higher ranking, the AA classification, was bestowed upon the elite American Association, Eastern League (later the International League), and the Pacific Coast League. These circuits had threatened to withdraw from the National Association unless they were given drafting rights over the less populous Class A Southern Association and Western League. In 1936 another classification, the A-1 rating, was bestowed upon the Texas League and Southern Association and ranked these fairly populous circuits just a notch below the three elite AA circuits.

In 1946 an AAA rating was conferred upon the three elite circuits, the Pacific Coast League, American Association, and International Association, and the A-1 rating was dropped; minor leagues with smaller population bases were classed as AA, A, B, C, and D. In 1952 another modification took note of the large population base of the Pacific Coast League and bestowed an "open classification" (a super ranking) on that circuit. At that time Pacific Coast League officials had visions of converting their league into a third major league, but these hopes were dashed by the preemption of the populous Los Angeles and San Francisco sites by the major league Dodgers and Giants. Following the 1952 reclassification the number of minor leagues dwindled to the point where the latest reclassification of 1963 abolished all B, C, and D minor league classes; surviving B, C, and D leagues were given the A classification. The majors also staffed and subsidized rookie leagues, which continue to operate.

Behind this brief historical recounting of minor league classification changes lies a tale of rising and flagging minor league fortunes. In the early years of this century, the minor leagues grew rapidly. In 1901 thirteen minor leagues opened play and ten finished their seasons; in 1908 thirty-five opened play and twenty-one finished. By the end of the 1908 season the total value of minor league properties was estimated at $20 million. In 1913 forty-six minor leagues opened play and thirty-six finished, but in the 1918 war year, nine opened seasonal play and only one finished. This mercurial boom-and-bust pattern showed just how vulnerable minor league operators were to social and economic change. In the years 1910–20 two major disruptions resulted from the Federal League war and the nation's participation in World War I. By the 1920s changing leisure fashions, such as automobiling, movies, radio, and rival sports, distracted people from minor league baseball. In the 1930s the Great Depression took its toll of minor leagues; in 1933 only thirteen minor leagues operated. But after bottoming in 1933, the number of minor leagues rose to forty-three by 1940, a year that saw minor league attendance touch a new high with 20 million paid admissions.

For that turnabout credit goes to resourceful minor league promoters for using such successful gimmicks as night ball and sideshow promotions. An outstanding innovator was Frank Shaughnessy, president of

Baseball team of the House of David, popular barnstormers who forswore drinking, smoking, sex, and shaving. (Courtesy Ray Medeiros)

First professional night baseball game at Des Moines, Iowa, in 1929, when that city's team belonged to the Western League. (Courtesy *Des Moines Register and Tribune* and Ronald A. Smith)

the International League, who in 1933 introduced the "Shaughnessy playoff" format. That year the first four finishers in the International League engaged in a playoff to determine the champion who would face their American Association rival in the Little World Series. This "second season" of the International League proved to be popular and profitable. Hard after the Depression recovery came the World War II bust that reduced the number of minor leagues from forty-three to ten by 1944. But peacetime triggered another boom that swelled the number of minor leagues to forty-two in 1946 and to an unprecedented fifty-nine in 1949. In 1949 minor league attendance totaled 41 million, a record never again matched; indeed, in recent years total annual attendance for all minor league parks has been averaging around 11 million. For this sickening decline, the televising of major league games has been blamed, along with the plethora of leisure outlets competing for the public's leisure dollars. The historic bust-and-boom cycle perennially plagued minor league owners and eventually drove most independent operators out of the business. In the years 1900–1920 the National Association tried to shore up its leagues by encouraging member leagues to adopt the policy of making each club annually post a cash guarantee to be forfeited if it dropped out or failed to meet its financial obligations. Unfortunately, the National Association lacked the power to enforce this policy.

On another critical front the National Association waged an unequal struggle with the major leagues over the issues of player drafts and the optioning ("farming out") of major league players to minor league teams. Of these issues, the drafting of minor league players excited the most rancor. Under the player draft system the majors claimed the right to select any minor league player at a fixed price, but minor league operators naturally preferred to sell players at higher negotiated prices. This was a crucial issue to minor league operators because fewer than half of all minor league teams managed to survive on gate receipts alone. From the very beginning this issue was a major bone of contention between major and minor leagues. In 1903 the newly concluded National Agreement fixed draft prices on minor league players; under the ruling, Class A minor league players could be drafted for $750, but no more than two players could be drafted from an A team in any year. In 1905 the price for drafting an A-class player was raised to $1,000. In 1911 the draft price for players from elite AA clubs was raised to $2,500, and only one player could be drafted from an AA team per year. It should be noted that lower-ranked minor leagues received less money for draftees and were also subject to unlimited drafts by the majors and to restricted drafts by higher-ranked minor league teams.

In the years 1919–21 the draft issue exploded anew. In 1919 the National Association abolished the draft. When a settlement was finally reached in 1921, five minor leagues (including the three AA leagues) opted for exemption from major league drafts by agreeing not to draft from the lower minors. This exemption, which lasted until 1931, proved to be a bonanza for independent minor league operators; one of them, Jack Dunn of the Baltimore Orioles in the International League, netted nearly a million dollars in that decade from selling stars to the majors. In one transaction Dunn received $100,000 from Connie Mack of the Athletics for the contract of pitcher Bob ("Lefty") Grove.

Not until 1931 did the majors and minors solve the festering draft issue; then the majors forcibly ended the exemptions. The 1931 agreement saw the draft price for an AA player rise to $7,500, while the majors agreed to draft no more than one player a year from an AA class team. Moreover, the majors agreed to draft only players who had at least four years of minor league experience. Not surprisingly, that latter decision was joylessly regarded by veteran minor league players; it meant that some now faced the grim prospect of toiling seven years in the minors before a major league team would decide on their future. The prospect that an able minor might have to serve a seven-year stretch in the bush leagues resulted from the latest settlement on the option issue. Under the option system, major league teams for years had been optioning out ("farming out") their marginal players to minor league teams. Because such players were owned by major league teams, their employers claimed the right to recall them at short notice. Understandably, minor league operators resented the practice and sought to curb it. Prior to 1923 each major league team might option out no more than eight players during a season, but the 1931 agreement raised the number to fifteen. Moreover, a major league team might option out a player three times; it was these three options that tacked a possible three years atop the four years a player had to spend in the minors. Worse yet from the player's standpoint, when his options were used up, there was only a slim prospect that he would be drafted by another major club.

Yet, many players, including major league discards, accepted their lot as perennial minor leaguers. For such long-term veterans the heyday of the minor leagues from 1900 to 1920 afforded opportunities to continue playing the game they loved before appreciative fans. Thus, at the turn of the century, fans of the Connecticut League could watch Jim O'Rourke, a fabled hero of the nineteenth century, who still caught regularly at age fifty-six in 1908. Likewise, when Joe ("Iron Man")

Dominic ("Dom") DiMaggio was a darling of San Francisco Seal fans in 1938 at the age of twenty-one. Two years later he joined the Boston Red Sox, where he starred in the outfield and had an eleven-year batting average of .298. (Courtesy Michael Mumby Collection)

Pete Gray, who starred as an outfielder for the Memphis Chicks despite the loss of his right arm in an accident at the age of six. In 1944 Gray won the MVP award in the Class A Southern Association with a batting average of .333 and 68 stolen bases along with superb fielding. (Courtesy Michael Mumby Collection)

McGinnity's major league career ended, he pitched regularly in the minors until 1925, when this fifty-five-year-old hurler finally retired. In the years between America's two world wars, Pacific Coast League fans delighted in the hitting exploits of ex-major-league outfielders Smead Jolley (.366 lifetime average compiled 1922–41), Russ ("Buzz") Arlett (.341 lifetime average compiled 1918–37), and Oscar ("Ox") Eckhardt (.367 lifetime average compiled 1925–40). Meanwhile, American Association fans of the 1918–42 era regularly saw Joe ("Unser Choe") Hauser as he batted at a lifetime .299 clip while smacking 399 homers. Equally brilliant were the exploits of a trio of pitchers of this era. Tony Freitas won 342 games over 26 years in the PCL, while Frank Shellenbach racked up 315 wins over 22 years in the same circuit. At the same time, Joe ("Oyster Joe") Martina won 349 games pitching in the Texas League and in the Southern Association.

During the 1920s, when top minor league players fetched high prices from major clubs bidding for their services, some enterprising major league officials found a way to grow their own crop of recruits. To Branch Rickey of the Cardinals goes credit for devising the modern farm system, under which a major club acquires minor league teams by outright purchase or by negotiated working agreements. The limited financial resources of the Cardinals goaded Rickey into reviving and elaborating upon this old baseball stratagem. Unable to outbid richer clubs for minor league stars, Rickey hired and trained scouts, who haunted sandlot, school, and college games in search of promising players. In the years following World War I there were plenty of leagues to scout; high schools, city recreational programs, and American Legion posts sponsored summer leagues that attracted hordes of players. In addition, Rickey sponsored tryout camps to lure any players who might have been overlooked by his scouts. Promising players were signed cheap and assigned to minor league teams owned by or allied with the Cardinals. There the players were subjected to Rickey's astute training and developing regimens. After purchasing his first minor league team in 1919, Rickey added two more by 1927, and on the eve of World War II his Cardinal farm chain numbered thirty-two minor teams at all levels of classification. Thus, the Cardinals could select from 600 minor league players and sell the leftovers; Rickey cannily did such selling at considerable financial advantage to the Cardinals and to himself. His enterprise made the Cardinals not only a feared contender, but also a perennially profitable operation in spite of the club's meager home-attendance record.

By the late 1920s other major clubs imitated Rickey's example and built farm systems of their own. Once established, the farm system trend overrode opposition from critics like Commissioner Landis. As major and top minor league teams acquired farm systems, independent minor league operators became a vanishing species; those who survived found themselves outvoted at league meetings and in National Association councils by major league interests. Throughout the 1930s the farm system was a controversial issue in professional baseball. Defenders argued that the farm systems saved the minors from collapsing during the Depression and that they also made for more efficient player development. But critics retorted that unrestricted drafts of players from farm systems killed local interest in minor league pennant races and contributed to poor attendance. Indeed, few could deny that the minors were hurting from lack of interest, but other forces—such as changing leisure patterns, competition from rival sports, and the inroads of the Depression and World War II—were also factors.

Nevertheless, after suffering grievous setbacks during World War II, the minors rebounded sharply, as has been noted, peaking in 1949 when 59 minor leagues in 464 cities attracted 41 million fans. In the peak year of 1949 there were 9,000 minor league players competing for the 400 playing positions on major teams. Alas, for the minors, this was a pitifully brief renaissance. During the 1950s attendance and leagues declined with sickening speed. Although some blamed the televising of major league games into minor league territories for the decline, other factors were at work. For one, athletes now eyed careers with rival team sports; for another, economic prosperity offered good-paying jobs as alternatives to low-paying minor league careers, while the same prosperity afforded leisure-seeking Americans a wide range of alternative outlets. By 1960 the number of minor leagues shrank to twenty-two, and

Baseball academy and minor league complex of the Kansas City Royals, parent club of teams in Omaha, Jacksonville, San Jose, and Waterloo, Iowa, as well as of two teams in the Gulf Coast Rookie League. (Courtesy Kansas City Royals)

annual attendance at all games fell below 11 million and never reached 17 million thereafter. To shore up the sagging minors, still indispensable for training talent, major league owners in 1956 took to subsidizing minor league operations. A beginning grant of $500,000 was voted that year, and three years later the majors put up $1 million to finance player development and to fund minor league promotional campaigns. Such transfusions came none too soon to relieve the problem. In 1960 the twenty-two minors fielded a total of 3,000 players, or only seven minor league players for every one in the majors. And by 1973 the minors shrank to eighteen leagues and 2,500 players, or only six minor league players for every major leaguer.

To deal with this worsening trend, more drastic salvage measures were undertaken by the majors. In 1962 the majors inaugurated the Player Development Plan, which reclassified the minors into AAA, AA, and A divisions. The A division included all surviving B, C, and D leagues. In addition, an A-1 rookie league was funded by the majors along with annual instructional leagues. Under the Player Development Plan, each major league team agreed to finance at least five minor league teams. This meant subsidizing salaries, travel expenses, and club operations. As a further measure, in 1965 the majors adopted an annual free-agent (rookie) draft, a plan proposed much earlier but damned and rejected as "socialistic" by some major owners. Now it came to pass, and annual drafts of high school and college ball players, with each major league team picking in turn, became the norm. At the same time, each major league team now had to budget at least $1 million annually as the cost of financing its minor league operations.

Given the chronic scarcity of minor league players since the 1950s, it is astonishing that major league executives have done so little to alleviate the spartan conditions endured by minor league players. In the past, minor league players routinely accepted their lot, which included low pay, peremptory dismissal, poor accommodations, hectic travel conditions, and no union protection. Astonishingly, this kind of torture-chamber existence persists and is defended by major league executives as necessary for weeding out the fainthearted from the ranks of starry-eyed young prospects. As always, minor leaguers still endure intense pressures to perform in splendid fashion. But today's minor league player is under increased pressure to make his mark within five years or be dropped. Thus, many minor league players now feel compelled to play extended seasons of winter baseball in Central American leagues to hasten their development. Sometimes this works, but all too often it exacts a physical and mental toll. Although minor league prospects often receive hefty signing bonuses from the rookie draft, once they are assigned to a minor league club, salaries and fringe benefits are low. In 1982 the average salary of an AAA player was $750 a month, and meal money was $15 a day. At spring training, minor league players received $5 a day for expenses, forcing them to augment their expense money from outside funds.

Although Marvin Miller, the former president of the Major League Players Association, tried to organize the minor league players into a protective association, his efforts drew little support from men made cautious by their ambition to make the majors. Aside from typically low pay and benefits, most minor league contracts are easily terminated. Writer Roger Kahn, who in 1983 owned and operated the Class A Utica Blue Sox, summed up the minor leaguers' position: "It seems impossible but in the minor league the owner really does possess something close to absolute power. There is no Players' Association in the minors, so the players have no rights whatsoever."

Minor leaguers also receive little glory for their deeds on the field. According to Miller, minor league fans, whose attendance at games is now pitifully small, tend to lump minor league players with well-paid major leaguers and thus to view all pro ball players as plutocrats. Worse still, the performances of minor league players have been slighted by baseball historians and publicists overawed by the deeds of major leaguers. Although playing conditions in the majors and minors tend to beggar comparisons, minor league partisans can point with pride to some outstanding achievements. Among the offensive records posted by minor leaguers were Smead Jolley's 314 hits in Pacific Coast League play in 1929, Tony Lazzeri's 202 runs scored and 222 RBIs in the Pacific Coast League in 1925, Ike Boone's 553 total bases in the Pacific Coast League in 1929, Joe Houser's 69 homers in the American Association in 1933, and Gabe Hughes's 210 bases on balls in the Sunset League in 1949. And among the pitching records posted were Harry ("Rube") Vickers's 408 strikeouts in the Pacific Coast League in 1906 and Clarence Henly's 48 complete games in the Pacific Coast League in 1910.

The fact that most major league stars learned their trade in the minors poses the most insistent reminder of the continuing importance of minor leagues. Indeed, in every era of baseball history, future stars of the majors arose from minor leagues. Among them were greats like Adrian Anson (from an Iowa independent team in 1870), John Ward, Ed Delehanty, John McGraw, Willie Keeler, Nap Lajoie, Honus Wagner, Ty Cobb, Babe Ruth, Jimmy Foxx, Joe DiMaggio, and Ted Williams. Moreover, leading stars of today—including Don Mattingly, Dwight Gooden, Wade Boggs, Willie McGee, Eddie Murray, and Mike Schmidt—all experienced minor league seasoning. Although annual free-agent auctions allow well-heeled owners the luxury of buying established stars for quick team reinforcement, most major league executives rightly regard subsidized minor league operations as essential player development resources. Indeed, it is the vital function of player development that now carries the minors. Unless some innovator devises a scheme for turning out finished ball players in another fashion, the future of the minor leagues is assured.

BALLS, GLOVES, UNIFORMS, AND SAFETY GEAR

BASEBALL, LIKE ALL GOOD SPORTING GAMES, *changes, but only very slowly. If baseball changed rapidly, it would lose its familiarity and the comparability from generation to generation that is one of its delights. If baseball never changed, it would be stuck in the mud without the benefit of generally accepted improvements.*

Spalding's introduction of the cork-centered ball in 1910 livened up the game permanently. The ball has not changed much otherwise since the days of the earliest clubs in the 1840s. The official ball weighs 5 to 5¼ ounces, measures 9 to 9½ inches in circumference, and is covered with tightly stitched white horsehide (or cowhide made to resemble horsehide). Major league bats are wooden and no more than 42 inches long, though the colleges allow aluminum bats and the Little League limits the length of bats to 33 inches.

The biggest change in baseball attire came in 1868, when the Cincinnati Red Stockings began wearing knickers and comfortable shirts. The New York Knickerbockers, who started the uniform idea around 1849, had worn navy blue trousers and white dress shirts. Uniforms today can be described as streamlined versions of the post–Civil War style. Branch Rickey tried to introduce shorts around 1950, but they never caught on. A major change has been the addition of numbers, and even names, to uniforms for identification of the players. Credit for this seemingly obvious idea is in dispute. The Cincinnati team of the American Association reportedly used numbers as early as 1883. An early bit of photographic evidence shows Cleveland Indians with numbers on their sleeves as early as 1916. By 1929 both the Indians and the Yankees wore numbers on their backs, and this practice was common by the 'Thirties.

Protective gear for catchers began to be developed at the turn of the twentieth century, but protection for the batter was not a concern until the 1930s. Catcher's leg guards are generally credited to Roger Bresnahan of the Giants in 1907, though his claim was disputed by his teammate Matt Fitzgerald and by Red Dooin of the Phillies. Devices for protecting shins and kneecaps have been improved greatly since 1914, but they have changed little in basic design.

The most striking and ongoing changes in the look of baseball have come in gloves and mitts. Gloves of any kind, except for catchers, were considered sissified before 1900, and the attitude toward infield and outfield gloves in the early days was that less is better. The whole picture has changed since the 'Thirties, with the development of webs, traps, and claws. After the first official rules about gloves were set down in 1895, there were no changes until 1931. Since 1931 there have been many rule changes, mostly to make fielding more efficient and comfortable while minimizing George Wright's fear of giving fielders an unfair advantage over batters.

Van Emery, semi-pro catcher in Pennsylvania in the 'Nineties, wearing typical equipment of the time. (Courtesy Charles Burkhardt)

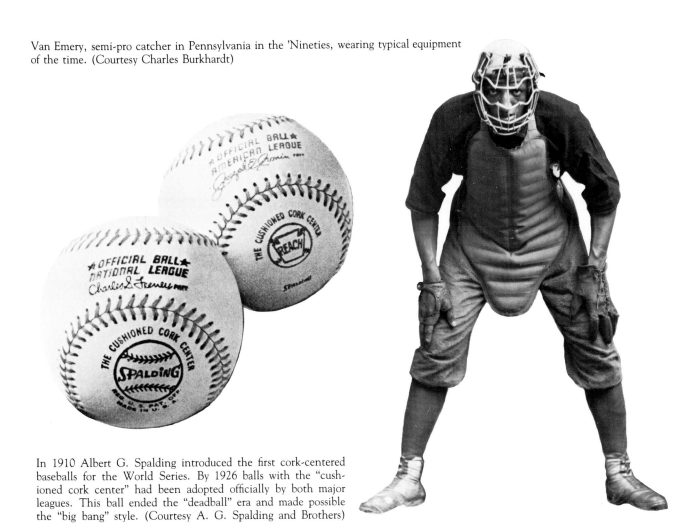

In 1910 Albert G. Spalding introduced the first cork-centered baseballs for the World Series. By 1926 balls with the "cushioned cork center" had been adopted officially by both major leagues. This ball ended the "deadball" era and made possible the "big bang" style. (Courtesy A. G. Spalding and Brothers)

Evolution of the uniform is illustrated with examples from the 1860s to the present—from heavy, baggy flannels to light, fitted double-knits. (Courtesy National Baseball Hall of Fame and Museum, Cooperstown, New York)

Below: Robert ("Braggo") Roth of the Cleveland Indians showing off his numbered uniform in 1916. Many baseball historians credit the Indians with introducing numbered uniforms to the majors. (Courtesy Dennis Goldstein)

Top right: Skeeter Newsome of the Athletics demonstrating a "helmet-liner" type of protective headgear for batters in 1939. (Courtesy Charles Burkhardt)

Bottom right: Jackie Hayes of the White Sox wearing an early helmet during batting practice in the 'Thirties. His teammate wears typical modern catcher's gear. (Courtesy Mike Andersen)

Philadelphia Phillies

*NOTE Pinstripe
color for Home
Jersey and Pants
is PANTONE 200
red. Wide stripings,
logo and numbers
are all PANTONE
209 maroon.

HOME JERSEY

ROAD JERSEY

HOME AND ROAD JACKET
*NOTE: Match attached color swatch or PANTONE 209 to all uniform components and logo
except Home Jersey Pinstripe fabric.

ROAD TROUSERS

HOME TROUSERS

SOCKS

STIRRUP

HOME AND ROAD HELMET

HOME AND ROAD CAP

An example of the modern baseball uniform. (Courtesy National Baseball Library, Cooperstown, New York)

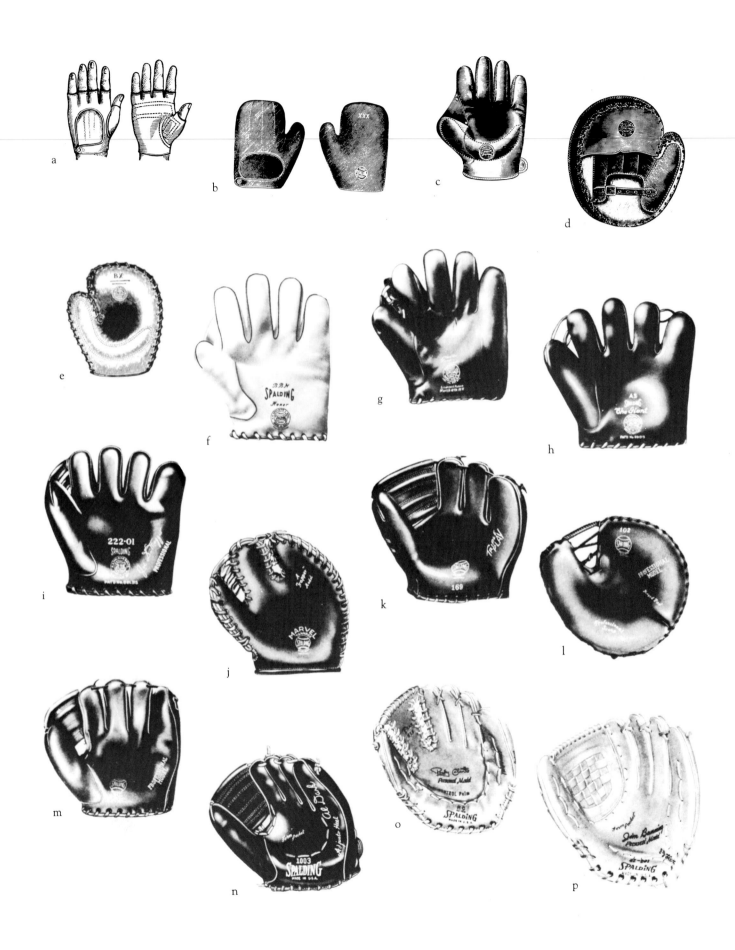

Opposite

Gloved players were usually tagged as sissies for daring to wear the primitive, half-fingered gloves of the 1880s (*a*). Designed for wear on one hand or both, the gloves sold for a dollar apiece.

By 1893, with the advent of overhand pitching from the present distance of sixty feet, six inches, and with catchers stationed behind batters, baseball's rugged style of play demanded protective gloves. Gloves worn by infielders of the 'Nineties closely followed the catcher's mitt in design (*b*). As more players used gloves, purists, including even George Wright, who manufactured them, were afraid that they would give fielders an unfair advantage. To be gloved in the 'Nineties was still socially risky.

By 1900 gloves for infielders and outfielders were an accepted part of the major league scene (*c*) and could be purchased for $2.50.

Because fans more readily conceded a catcher's right to gloved protection, the catcher's mitt evolved rapidly. The "Decker Patent" model (*d*) was equal to the task of catching fastball pitchers like "Cy" Young.

Like catchers' mitts, first basemen's mitts were evolving in a distinctly specialized direction by the early 1900s. A black leather model (*e*) cost $4.00.

In baseball's prosperous era of the 1920s, gloves adapted to cope with sharply batted "lively" balls (*f*) and were commonly used by infielders and outfielders. Although some balls were caught in the primitive "web," most players depended on the "pocket" of the glove. To develop a good pocket required much breaking in, including a trick of binding a ball inside the glove and soaking glove and ball together. By the 'Twenties, such gloves as these cost ten dollars.

A trend toward the efficient traplike gloves of today came in the late 'Twenties and 'Thirties (*g, h*). Figure *g* shows a trend toward a bigger web, and *h* shows a trend toward stringing the fingers together for better snaring of line drives. The latter model took only a timid step in this direction, and, as figure *i* shows, it was briefly reversed in 1938. However, the 1938 model shows a marked improvement of the webbed pocket between thumb and forefinger.

By the end of World War II, the webbed pocket trap was rapidly exploited. In 1944 the first baseman's mitt (*j*) used a double webbed trap to snare thrown balls. Well named "the Trapper," it allowed the first baseman to scoop grounders and snag thrown balls with lessened shock.

Rapid exploitation of the webbed pocket has served infielders and outfielders alike (*k, l, m, n, o, p*). So effective is the webbed pocket trap that most balls are now caught in the webbing. Today, the "pocket" begins at the base of the web, and the rest of the glove is artfully constructed, often with built-in heels, to cause an almost automatic closing of the glove when the ball strikes it. The growing efficiency of gloves seems to verify Wright's earlier fear. Although no restrictive action has been taken yet, the hitting famine of 1968 has prompted suggestions for curbing the size and design of gloves in order to restore hitting to the game. (Courtesy A. G. Spalding and Brothers)

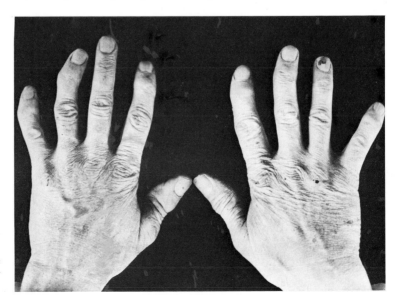

Baseball player's hands in the early 1920s, photographed for the U.S. Surgeon General's Office. Even with improved gloves, the hands of players in the Silver Age took a fierce beating. (Courtesy The New York Public Library)

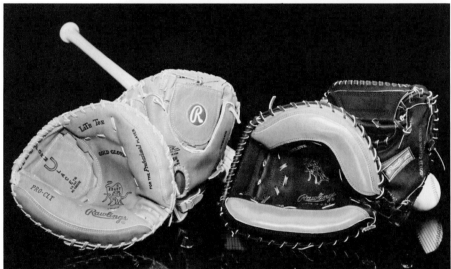

Gloves from 1986 Rawlings catalog: *top:* fielders' gloves with two types of web, basket and "H"; *center:* catcher's mitt with adjustable loops for thumb and little finger; *bottom:* first-base mitt with two-piece pocket. (Courtesy Rawlings Sporting Goods Company)

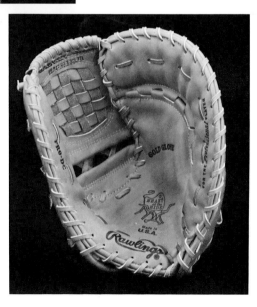

CONSOLIDATION AMIDST CRISES, 1901–1945

IN 1901 "BAN" JOHNSON CHANGED THE NAME OF HIS *Western League to the American League; by 1903 he had forced the National League to recognize the upstart circuit as a second major league. By restoring the dual league system, the 1903 National Agreement placed major league baseball on a stable course that was to last half a century; during that time not a single franchise change occurred in either league. The agreement also revived annual World Series competition, which proved to be immensely popular. Moreover, the appointment of a three-member National Commission to adjudicate inter-league disputes worked well; during its eighteen years of service the commission quelled fears of inter-league wars that so plagued the nineteenth-century game.*

Thus consolidated, major league baseball entered a popular and profitable "Silver Age," which lasted until 1920. Stability was the major characteristic of this age. Stability was a factor in attracting ever-larger crowds to games; by 1909 such gains prompted owners to build the capacious concrete-and-steel parks that served two generations of fans. Stability also characterized the style of play. In this "dead ball" era, pitching predominated; offensively most teams employed a "scientific" style that stressed place-hitting, bunting, stealing, and sacrificing. Manager John McGraw of the Giants was a master of this strategy. Players like Ty Cobb, Honus Wagner, Willie Keeler, and Nap Lajoie were lionized as offensive stars; among the great pitchers, Cy Young, Christy Mathewson, Walter Johnson, and Grover Cleveland Alexander were heroic standouts. At this time player-heroes were acclaimed by fans and glorified in expanding sports pages, books, and theatricals, and by the newly emerging motion pictures.

Baseball's Silver Age reflected the nation's fabulous growth and prosperity. The U.S. population grew from 76 million to 106 million between 1900 and 1920, while the number of city dwellers increased from 30 to 54 million. Big league cities from Boston to St. Louis were linked by railroads, and ballparks were made increasingly accessible by the electrification of streetcars. Prodigious industrial growth gave ever more Americans the money and time for recreational activities, including baseball. The average annual earnings of American workers, adjusted for consumer prices, rose from about $500 in 1900 to $1,489 by 1920. At the same time, the average work week fell from 57.5 hours to 50.4 hours. The big leagues' Silver Age prosperity was set back only by brief business recessions and by the United States' involvement for less than two years in World War I. Ball players' salaries and working conditions improved steadily amid the general prosperity, though their freedom of movement and other contractual rights remained limited.

During the Silver Age, major league baseball extended its mythic hold on Americans. The claim that baseball was the national game was enhanced by the Doubleday "spontaneous-invention myth" and by the popular song "Take Me Out to the Ball Game," which became the game's enduring hymn. Also in these years, President Taft inaugurated the custom of the president throwing out the first ball of a new season. The game's past was covered by Spalding's America's National Game, *a respectable history that appeared in 1911. By then the flood of literary works about baseball included Gilbert Patten's popular "Frank Merriwell" boys' fiction; Zane Grey's novel* The Shortstop; *Owen Johnson's novel* The Hummingbird; *and Ring Lardner's incomparable short stories, among which "You Know Me, Al" became a popular hit when it appeared in 1914. Moreover, major league baseball added its own legendary character to American folklore in the person of "Bonehead" Fred Merkle, the ill-fated butt of the Giants' woeful 1908 season.*

A series of crises—the Federal League war, the impact of World War I, and the Chicago "Black Sox" scandal—combined to end the Silver Age by 1920. Among these crises, the Black Sox scandal outraged myth-bound fans who believed that baseball must always be above suspicion. The Black Sox furor ended the National Commission's reign. In its stead a high commissioner, Judge Kenesaw Mountain Landis, pontificated as the guardian of the game's integrity from 1920 to 1944; such was Landis's style that he too became an American folk hero. Commissioner Landis was a product of what historians call the "Progressive Era" or the "Age of Reform," roughly from the end of the Spanish-American War until the United States' entry into World War I. Landis shared the progressive reformers' paternalistic high-handedness and narrowness of outlook, but he also shared their fury against corruption—a zeal that kept organized baseball "clean" even during the gangster-ridden Roaring 'Twenties.

America always has been a volatile mixture of frontier wildness and Main Street respectability. The New World also possesses an unquenchable impulse for reform. Many American reformers are enlightened, if sometimes overzealous, whereas many are bluenosed imposers of their own brand of respectability. The behavior of certain players, owners, and fans has offended some of their colleagues and the larger public. The extent to which there should be special rules of behavior for persons connected with the national game—regarding such matters as the use of alcohol and drugs, sexual activity, gambling, brawling, swearing, spitting, and even noisemaking—remains an open question in the 1980s.

Sunday baseball and the sale of alcoholic beverages in ballparks provide examples of the uses and abuses of reform. By 1920 prohibitionists succeeded in banning beer not only in ballparks but everywhere. In the half-century since Repeal, a general feeling has evolved that some restrictions on fans' drinking are for the common good. Sabbatarians by 1902 had succeeded in banning Sunday baseball in all big league cities except Chicago, Cincinnati, and St. Louis. In cutting through the thicket of repressive laws, baseball people were supported by "social gospel" clergymen, who believed in the workers' right to recreational leisure. Legalization of Sunday baseball came slowly: in 1918 to Cleveland, Detroit, Washington, and New York; in 1929 to Boston; and in 1933 to Philadelphia and Pittsburgh.

The decline of baseball's Silver Age in the wake of the Black Sox scandal of 1919–20 corresponded with the rise of baseball's greatest folk hero, Babe Ruth, who led the game into its "Second Golden Age." Almost single-handedly, this slugging prodigy replaced the scientific game with his homeric "big bang" style. The popular slugging game attracted bigger crowds and brought more profits and publicity than the game had ever known. During the golden 1920s radio and movies joined with the print media to boost the major league game to record heights of prosperity.

From the earliest days of organized baseball, the national game attracted immigrants and their sons, together with descendants of early settlers. Big league rosters reflected immigration patterns, along with other aspects of American society. The ancestry of early major leaguers was mainly English, Irish, and German—with a dash of French. The flood of immigration after 1900, chiefly from eastern and southern Europe, added many Jewish, Slavic, and Latin names to big league lineups: Greenberg, DiMaggio, Gomez, Musial. Baseball's door of opportunity, however, stayed closed to one group of longtime Americans, those of African ancestry, until after World War II. Denied entry to the white majors, black players were forced to organize their own major leagues, which fielded some outstanding stars.

Major league baseball's Second Golden Age ended with the Great Depression of the 1930s. Falling attendance and income harried owners until 1940. Stylistically, however, the game continued to feature the "big bang." As Ruth faded, new slugging heroes like Jimmy Foxx, Hank Greenberg, Mel Ott, and Joe DiMaggio rose to the fore. In St. Louis, general manager Branch Rickey's farm system produced the talent for his "gas house gang" champions and a new folk hero in pitcher "Dizzy" Dean. Rickey's innovative farm plan helped major and minor league clubs to cope with the ravages of the Depression. So did night baseball, which Cincinnati general manager Larry MacPhail belatedly introduced to the majors in 1935. Radio broadcast fees also helped, after a modest start in 1933. Although financially hard-pressed, major league baseball strengthened its mythic hold on America in 1939 by staging a season-long celebration of the centennial of the game's supposed invention by Abner Doubleday. In that same year the opening of the Baseball Hall of Fame at Cooperstown, New York, began the enshrinement of the game's great heroes. Thenceforth, annual additions to this baseball temple burnished the game's mystique.

Just as major league baseball was recovering from Depression ills, the nation plunged into World War II. By 1943 the burden of total war, with its military drafts and travel restrictions, had seriously crippled the ball clubs. But once victory was achieved, innovators such as Branch Rickey implemented plans that changed the face of the game. As in baseball's past eras, the dynamic growth of the postwar years served as a new reminder to fans that baseball is durable and adaptable.

4

BASEBALL'S SILVER AGE

Byron Bancroft ("Ban") Johnson, who became president of the Western League in 1894, led its transformation into the American League in 1900, and helped force acceptance of his circuit as a major league in the National Agreement of 1903. (Courtesy John Thorn)

THE EARLY 1900s WERE TORNADO TIMES FOR MAJOR league baseball. Like the destructive blasts resulting in a single big league in 1892, new winds carried threats of coming changes in the twentieth century. To be sure, the Western League challenge appeared puny alongside those of the American and Union associations. Indeed, why should a major league magnate of 1899 have worried about an uppity minor league based in peripheral midwestern cities? Yet there was danger in treating the threat lightly. The Western League was brilliantly directed by the burly, convivial, hard-drinking Byron Bancroft ("Ban") Johnson, an ex-Cincinnati sportswriter who knew the game and was determined to make his mark. As a crusading baseball writer, Johnson penned critical gibes so vexing to owner John T. Brush that Brush challenged Johnson to try bettering the game. Accepting the challenge, Johnson assumed the Western League presidency, and by 1899 he and such able lieutenants as Connie Mack and Charles Comiskey had the circuit running as an elite minor league. Further growth was impossible, however, so long as the National League constantly drafted the best Western players. For a start, Johnson demanded and won a time limit on annual drafts, but a surer antidote was major league status, which Johnson set out to get.

When the Nationals reduced their unwieldy circuit to eight teams in 1900, Western teams snapped up surplus National players, emboldening Johnson to rename his league the American League. Then, to test National resolve, Johnson backed Comiskey's plan of invading Chicago. Such poaching on an entrenched National preserve infuriated the Chicago Cubs' owner but incited no massive resistance. With solid financial backing and a new ballpark, Commy's fighting team of major league castoffs and promising youngsters captured the first American League pennant and scored a modest box office success.

Commy's success prompted Johnson to take advantage of the expiring National Agreement and declare major league status for the American League in 1901. Naturally, this meant war, but Johnson prepared by encouraging his promoters to abandon old haunts for new locations in Boston, Baltimore, Washington, Cleveland, Detroit, and Philadelphia. To secure these beachheads, Johnson courted and won new financiers, acquired playing facilities, and stocked teams with major leaguers, including a number of National stars who eagerly jumped for offers of higher pay. Thus, the American League's 1901 campaign saw more than a hundred ex–National Leaguers in the ranks, including such big

Denton True ("Cy") Young, who moved to Boston's new American League club in 1901 from the St. Louis Nationals, thereby helping to speed acceptance of the upstart circuit. (Courtesy John Thorn)

names as Clark Griffith, Jimmy Collins, Cy Young, Buck Freeman, and Napoleon Lajoie.

What the Americans now needed was a rousing pennant race to entice fans and hearten tremulous financiers. Providentially, the 1901 race filled the bill, as Chicago and Boston battled all the way. The victory went to Chicago by four games on good pitching from manager Clark Griffith and Jimmy Callahan, a pair of aces Comiskey had pried loose from his Cub rivals.

For good measure the 1902 season provided another close and lucrative race. Renewed raids on National rosters over the winter strengthened Connie Mack's Philadelphia Athletics. Mack had gained badly needed financial support from Benjamin Shibe, a former Phillies investor, now an Athletic partner. This connection enabled Mack to raid the Phillies, divesting them of star infielder Nap Lajoie and outfielder Ralph ("Socks") Seybold, while a raid on the much-plundered Cubs landed the eccentric pitcher George ("Rube") Waddell. To Mack's dismay, the Phillies won a court injunction barring the A's from playing

George Edward ("Rube") Waddell, stellar left-handed pitcher, whose move from the Cubs to the A's in 1902 helped Connie Mack's team stay at or near the top through 1905. His record of sixteen strikeouts in a single game stood for many years. (Courtesy George Brace)

Lajoie. Forced to dispose of the 1901 batting star, Mack reluctantly sold Lajoie to Cleveland. In the early 1902 season this loss hurt, but after midseason the A's rallied behind pitchers Waddell and Eddie Plank and Seybold's slugging. Rebounding, they overtook Chicago and won the flag by five games over St. Louis. After their rival's sprightly, profitable race, the harried Nationals now sued for peace.

Truthfully, the American victory owed as much to National League disarray as to Johnson's acumen. Left leaderless by Spalding's retirement, National owners were accustomed to doing as they pleased. Often they battled one another in anarchic fashion; while such tiffs grabbed headlines for these owners, they divided and bled the big league. Among the sour results, poor attendance, brawling scenes on diamonds, and public anger over syndicate follies demanded remedies that lack of leadership could not provide.

Ironically, National owners were grappling with this leadership void at the time Johnson challenged them. Thus, in 1901 National owners met to choose a leader but fell to quarreling bitterly. One faction of owners wanted to retain President Young, but that aging figure personified the weak leadership problem, and his candidacy was merely a screen for invoking Freedman's controversial baseball trust scheme. Knowing this, a rival faction countered by proposing Spalding as president. With each side refusing to yield, neither could elect a president. From December 1901 till March 1902 the deadlock persisted, until Spalding's opponents walked out. Then the Spalding faction took advantage of their rivals' absence to declare Spalding elected. Spalding brazenly seized the books and tried to rule, but threatened legal action soon blocked him. Defeated, Spalding yielded to a temporary Control Commission and retired permanently from baseball councils. His departure allowed the Control Commission to restore a semblance of order. In July a major barrier was removed when the controversial Freedman sold his interest in the Giants and quit the game. Freedman exacted more than a pound of flesh, however; not only did he get $125,000 for selling out, but he designated Brush as his presidential successor. Moreover, Freedman forced his colleagues to permit an American League team to enter New York under the ownership of a political crony, Frank Farrell. As the Highlanders, these New Yorkers did little, but as latter-day Yankees, they became an awesome power.

After so much destructive infighting, National owners welcomed a return to a dual major league system. That the American League was preferable to a revived American Association was as plain as a pikestaff to 1902 observers. Hence, once the Control Commission selected Henry Clay Pulliam as the National League's new president, serious peace talks with Johnson began. At a 1903 Cincinnati conference, Johnson and Comiskey met with Pulliam and August ("Garry") Herrmann, and in two days they hammered out a new National Agreement. It was agreed that the National and American leagues would operate as separate but equal major leagues, bound by common playing rules, harmonized playing schedules, and mutually recognized player contracts. That last point ended the player raids, restored the reserve clause, and recognized the existing rosters and territories of each of the sixteen clubs. The agreement also conceded the Americans a foothold in New York, which Johnson immediately secured by moving the profitless Baltimore Orioles to a Manhattan site.

Beyond these points, the 1903 agreement classified the minor leagues anew and redefined rules for drafting players. By creating a board of arbitration to adjudicate trouble cases between major and minor leagues, the agreement stimulated the growth of minor leagues, whose numbers increased by twenty-five over the next decade. The agreement did little for ball players, however; even if it no longer included a salary limitation plank, the document restricted the rights of players by asserting extra-legal baseball law. Not only did the agreement include the reserve clause, but it created a National Commission with the right to control baseball. In lawyer John Stayton's words, the commission ruled "by its own decrees . . . enforcing them without the aid of law, and answerable to no power outside its own." In other words, major league baseball was a closed institution, and those working within its bounds must obey its own peculiar edicts.

The passage of time showed that the Cincinnati conference afforded major league baseball fifty years of structural stability, with not one franchise shift occurring in this half-century. Certainly, this outcome far exceeded the dreams of the delegates, who modestly hoped for ten years of peace at best. That it endured so long can be attributed to the compromising mood of the delegates—a spirit embodied in the newly created National Commission, a high-level executive and judicial group charged with keeping the peace.

The National Commission called for league presidents Pulliam and Johnson to form a three-man ruling body with Garry Herrmann, the Cincinnati magnate, who became chairman. Ostensibly, this gave the National League two voices, but actually Herrmann and Johnson were close friends. While Pulliam contributed to the smooth functioning of the commission, he was manipulated by the Johnson-Herrmann clique, while his limited powers as National League president were outmatched by the absolute powers the Americans invested in their charismatic "czar." Indeed, the sensitive Pulliam was so harried by National owners that in 1909 he suffered a nervous breakdown and a year later took his own life.

By fearing to empower any president, the National League owners forfeited their influence on the commission. Instead of speaking with a single voice, over fifteen years the Nationals matched a quartet of presidents against the entrenched Johnson. There was no such disarray in the American camp. There Johnson led, and his owners empowered him fully. As president, secretary, and treasurer of the American League, he was the most powerful league president in major league history. A combination of personal charisma and proven leadership lent a touch of royalty to this burly, bespectacled leader. In 1901 he was voted a ten-year term at a $7,500 annual salary, raised to $15,000 in 1906; in 1910 his worshipful followers voted him a twenty-year term at $25,000 a year. For his part, Johnson was every inch a potentate. To protect his "great American League" from possible National League

THE NATIONAL COMMISSION

Henry Clay Pulliam, elected president of the National League in time to work on the 1903 National Agreement with the American League, as sketched for the *New York Clipper*. Constantly harried by National League "magnates," he committed suicide in 1910. (Author's Collection)

John Joseph McGraw, player-manager of the New York Giants from 1902 through 1906—a period in which his team won two National League pennants and a world championship. In 1907 the "Little Napoleon" began a brilliant quarter-century as a non-playing manager. Photo from *The Sporting News*. (Author's Collection)

treachery, he personally held all franchise leases, along with an option to buy both the plant and franchise of any member club. Ever the activist leader, Johnson fixed seasonal schedules, ordained a minimum twenty-five-cent admission at all parks, denounced and punished brawlers, and constantly kept an eye on the member teams.

Inevitably, such powers made enemies who eventually clipped Johnson's wings. One of the earliest and bitterest was John McGraw, whom Johnson suspended for umpire-baiting in 1902. Incensed, McGraw quit his post as an American League manager and jumped to the National's Giants, which he soon made into the elite team of the majors, perennially overshadowing their weak American rivals in New York City. While McGraw could be humbled in World Series encounters, not so with Charles Comiskey. From the start Commy was Johnson's ablest lieutenant, but over the years these two friends fell out. Tensions began in 1910 when Johnson fined Commy for umpire-baiting; later the rift widened as Johnson's rulings cost Commy the services of good players. Thus, anti-Johnson sentiment welled and spread, and in 1919 the new owners of the Yankees defied Johnson's dictates and threatened to take him to court. By then Johnson was besieged by hostile owners and haunted by the scandal of the Black Sox. In the aftermath of the Black Sox game-throwing in the 1919 World Series, Judge Kenesaw Mountain Landis was elected high commissioner of baseball, a move Johnson bitterly opposed. Landis's rise marked the end of Johnson's czardom, but while Johnson ruled he restored prosperity to the game.

Over the years 1903–19 Johnson dominated the National Commission, using his close friendship with Herrmann, a pliable man who served as perennial chairman. Moreover, since this pair got on well with the National League presidents, there was little acrimony; indeed, this "Supreme Court of Baseball" was soon credited with saving the game from anarchy.

Foremost among commission achievements was the profitable revival of the World Series. After the two leagues agreed to restage the Series in 1905, the commission took over as its administrators, appointing umps, ruling on eligible players, monitoring the fields, and collecting and disbursing receipts. Since 10 percent of receipts went to finance the commission's office, the popularity of the Series was an important charge; that the commission met the test was evidenced by a tenfold increase in Series profits by 1910. However, the commissioners were vulnerable to any charges of chicanery involving the Series; thus, the "thrown" Series of 1919 brought about the commission's downfall.

Meanwhile, the commission did much to reduce tensions between the major leagues. Many disputes between teams over the rights to player services were resolved by the commission, including seventy-three cases in 1905 alone. Likewise, the commission defended the rights of minor league promoters by effecting the modification of rules for drafting minor league players. Maligned umpires also gained protection from the commission, which judged disputes between players and umps and collected fines. Other commission actions included disciplining players, blunting the threat of a players' union in 1913, fending off Federal League interlopers, and keeping a watchful eye on the growing "farm system" trend in player development.

Handshake between leading players of the American and National leagues symbolizes healthy rivalry of the Silver Age. Nap Lajoie (left) of the American's Cleveland club and Honus Wagner of the National's Pittsburghers exchange greetings before a preseason game in 1904. (Courtesy MacGreevy Collection, Boston Public Library)

"Royal Rooter" for the Boston Pilgrims celebrates their 1903 World Series victory over the Pittsburgh Pirates. (Courtesy MacGreevy Collection, Boston Public Library)

In the main the commissioner system succeeded because it served the interests of the owners. As long as the commissioners acted circumspectly, the owners accepted the illusion of an all-powerful Supreme Court in baseball. Sometimes the commissioners fined owners for misbehavior, but such rulings were wrist-slaps. On those rare occasions when the commissioners harried an owner from baseball, they carried out the wishes of the other owners. Powerful and popular owners could bend rules without drawing commission fire. Hence, the Cardinals began building a thriving farm system, and some teams maintained interlocking ownerships, with no interference from Johnson—perhaps because Johnson himself relied so heavily on joint ownerships to keep his league afloat in the early going. Suffice it to say that, when owner interests counted, the commissioners prudently acquiesced. Thus, continuing requests by players and minor league officials to be represented on the commission were flatly rejected.

Notwithstanding commission biases, or the boozy, easy-going caucuses that marked its deliberations, baseball prospered under this system. By posing as the game's incorruptible Supreme Court, the commission supplied an honest image for the game, a much-needed antidote to the previous robber-baron era. Thanks to this system the game profited, annual paid attendance for both major leagues rose dramatically, and even player salaries improved. Still, if the commissioner era was a profitable and stable time for baseball, it was not a golden age. That lordly label better fits the game of the 1880s or the "big bang" era that followed in the 1920s. Nonetheless, jingling profits and spirited play in some memorable campaigns rightly earned this era the label of the "Silver Age."

DEADBALL DYNASTIES: THE AMERICAN LEAGUE

In this Silver Age it swelled Johnson's pride to behold his "great American League" outdraw and outplay the Nationals. As the detente of 1903 established the dual major leagues, American League stock soared by dint of spirited competition among its Chicago, Philadelphia, Boston, and Detroit teams. Since no other teams scaled the championship heights at this time, these American mini-dynasties reaped most of the cash and glory. In this so-called "deadball era," most teams adopted the "scientific" style of play, with its emphasis on power pitching and low-scoring offenses. Nevertheless, the "manly slugging" style that, in the late 1890s, produced high-scoring games and homer barrages was far from dead; in the 1920s it was gloriously resurrected in the person of Babe Ruth.

By 1902 two American League dynasties, the Chicagos and Philadelphia Athletics, were already on stage with pennants unfurled. In 1903 both were beaten by the rising Boston Pilgrims (or Puritans), a team hastily assembled in 1901 and housed near the playing grounds of the formidable National League Beaneaters. This was stiff competition, but Pilgrim promoters met it by enticing a covey of Beaneaters to jump from that team's $2,400 salary ceiling. For a $4,000 salary, the Pilgrims signed third baseman Jimmy Collins as playing manager, and for lesser sums they lured star outfielder Chick Stahl, slugging first baseman Buck Freeman, and able pitchers Bill Dinneen and Ed Lewis. Then a raid on the St. Louis Nationals landed the fabulous pitcher Cy Young and his catcher Lou Criger. With Young winning thirty-two games in 1902, the upstart Pilgrims attracted 527,000 fans, double that of the enfeebled Beaneaters.

Rebounding from a 1902 third-place finish, the 1903 Pilgrims won big, beating the second-place Athletics by 14½ games. Brilliant pitching told the tale, as Young won 28 and Tom Hughes and Dinneen each notched 21. Dazzled by this victory, Pilgrim fans clamored for a World Series test against the National League champion Pittsburgh Pirates. With misgivings, Johnson assented to a best-of-nine-games test. The Pirates took an early lead, but the Pilgrims closed fast, Young and Dinneen winning five games to complete a 5-3 Series victory. For Johnson this was a public relations coup, while the Pilgrims gained a well-heeled financier, John Taylor, along with hard-won bragging rights.

Unwise player trades by new owner Taylor nearly derailed the 1904 Pilgrims. Still, the Pilgrims fought off the stubborn New York Highlanders and their 41-game-winning pitcher, Jack Chesbro. On the last day, the Pilgrims beat the Highlanders to take the league championship; defeat dealt a hard blow at the hard-luck Highlanders, whose bid for support from Gotham fans lost to the rising National League Giants. The league champion Giants lost face, however, by refusing to engage the Pilgrims in a Series test; such was the outcry over that refusal that the two leagues speedily adopted a permanent World Series format.

This promise of added cash and glory at the end of the season fired up competitors in the 1905 race. Boston, however, suffered the loss of key players; Highlander pitching slumped; and Chicago strained for offensive strength. Given a clear road, the Athletics got eighty-eight victories from pitchers Eddie Plank, Rube Waddell, Andy Coakley, and Albert ("Chief") Bender. It was barely enough, as the weak-hitting Chicagos, now flaunting their new "White Sox" identity, hung close and lost by only two games. The victory sent the A's against McGraw's Giants in the World Series, but a suspicious injury sidelined Waddell and crippled the A's, who fell ignominiously, losing four games to one. Since Waddell was often drunk and disorderly, no one knew whether he hurt himself by accident or for a bribe.

Demoralized by the defeat, Mack's great pitching staff floundered in 1906; not so the White Sox staff, whose quartet of Frank Owen, Nick Altrock, Doc White, and spitballer Ed Walsh won 77 games. By winning 19 games in August this staff carried one of baseball's weakest batting teams to a narrow victory over the Highlanders. Dubbed the "hitless wonders," the White Sox batted a mere .228, scored only 570 runs, and were shut out in 16 games. Moving into the World Series against the National's Cubs, winners of 116 games, the Sox seemed ludicrously overmatched. Still, they hung tough, and by dint of good pitching and timely hitting by substitute George Rohe, the Sox deadlocked the Cubs after four games. Then, Frank Isbell smote four doubles to pace an 8-6 White Sox win, and Doc White's pitching and another

Samuel Earl ("Wahoo Sam") Crawford, whose steady hitting and fielding helped the Detroit Tigers to three American League pennants from 1907 to 1909. (Courtesy National Baseball Library, Cooperstown, New York)

eight-run outburst won the deciding game. Overjoyed by this unexpected victory, Johnson kissed owner Comiskey, while the celebrated "hitless wonders" became an enduring baseball legend.

Poor Johnson! His joy was soon damped by three seasons of humiliation at the hands of Nationals. As the White Sox faded, a fourth dynasty, the Detroit Tigers, carried the American banner. Managed by Hugh Jennings, one of the "old Orioles" whom Johnson ever mistrusted, the Tigers mounted a powerful hitting attack behind outfielders Sam Crawford and young Ty Cobb. For the nonce, Crawford was the Tiger hero; fast and powerful, "Wahoo Sam" reaped honors, eventually producing a lifetime .312 average and a record number of triples, enough to land him a niche in the Hall of Fame.

In 1907, however, Cobb rivaled Crawford and soon reigned as the superstar of the Silver Age. Born Tyrus Raymond Cobb, this scion of an aristocratic Georgia family bore a burden of psychological problems that both marred and inspired his diamond achievements. For one, his father disapproved of his baseball career, and when the father died tragically in 1906, the guilt-ridden son reacted with terrible resolve to justify his course. For another, this proud, humorless twenty-year-old responded to anti-southern gibes with furious fisticuffs that left him friendless and alienated. Yet, the driven rookie fought his way into the 1906 Tiger lineup, and by 1907, using his spread-handed batting grip and smooth left-sided swing, he mastered all forms of scientific batting. A dazzling speedster, he beat out bunts and stole bases in unprecedented numbers, while his mastery of place-hitting, combined with slugging ability, defied defense. In 1907 he notched the first of a string of nine consecutive batting titles.

That year manager Jennings infused old Oriole spirit into the Tigers, who climbed to the top of the league. Tiger pitching was good, but other staffs were better, including the A's, who finished 2½ games behind. The tense race boosted American League attendance even in the teeth of a national business depression. In the World Series, however, the Tigers came off depressed, losing to the National champion Cubs in four straight games.

The next two seasons had the same grim finish. Each time, Detroit won a close American race only to lose the World Series. In 1908 they edged the Cleveland "Naps," a team honorific for manager Nap Lajoie's prowess, by a mere half-game. Naturally, this close race spurred attendance again, but the even closer National race attracted a record 910,000 fans to Giant games. After beating the Giants in an unprecedented postseason playoff, the Cubs again humbled the Tigers in the World Series.

Stunned by this second humiliation, the Tigers regrouped in 1909 and downed Mack's rising young A's to land a third straight pennant. Again the race was close, and in an ugly late-season incident, the hard-sliding Cobb spiked shortstop Jack Barry of the A's, sidelining him and derailing the A's pennant hopes. The spiking triggered a wave of anti-Cobb hostility, but the redoubtable Cobb won batting and stealing honors for a third straight year. However, Cobb hit a mere .231 in the World Series as the Pittsburgh Pirates bested the Tigers.

Tyrus Raymond ("Ty") Cobb, the Georgia aristocrat as Tiger. (Courtesy Gordon Miller)

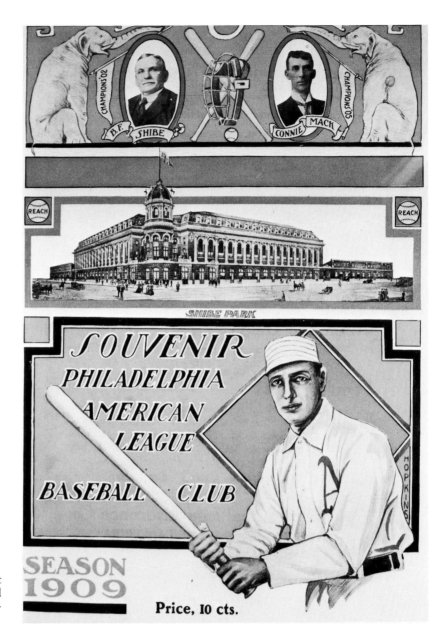

Athletics souvenir program, sold at their new park on opening day, April 12, 1909. (Courtesy Dennis Goldstein)

Now thoroughly disgusted with the Tigers, Johnson yearned for a new champion who might burnish the American escutcheon. Happily, rescue was at hand in the persons of Mack's Philadelphia A's. Although only forty-eight in 1910, manager Mack was already the "dean of American League managers." Though he was respected, his habit of wearing his business suit on the field and his faith in college-bred players drew ridicule. But Mack was a sound tactician and player developer, and as part-owner of the A's he was bold enough to invest in a capacious new park; named Shibe Park after his partner, it was a harbinger of more concrete-and-steel parks that soon dotted the major league landscape. In 1910, however, scolding critics dubbed the park the "white elephant," a name Mack blithely appropriated for his young team.

Once unleashed, Mack's pachyderms stomped all comers, winning 102 games and finishing 14½ games up on their closest pursuers, the Yankees (as the former Highlanders now were known). A well-balanced team, the A's got first-rate pitching from Jack Coombs, Cy Morgan, Bender, and Plank, and sturdy catching from Ira Thomas and John Lapp. While the outfield was adequate, the sparkling inner defense won for John McInnis, Eddie Collins, Jack Barry, and Frank Baker the awesome appellation of the "$100,000 infield." Paced by Collins, whose all-round play compared with that of the great Lajoie, the A's crushed the Cubs four games to one in World Series play.

Besides restoring smiles to the broad face of the three-hundred-pound President Johnson, this victory triggered a new wave of baseball enthusiasm. This year brought the new cork-centered ball, which soon made for heavier hitting and a departure from the stylized deadball game. More immediately, in 1911 more than 10 million fans jammed big league parks, vindicating the big-park innovators. As imitators rushed to catch the innovators, Mack drove his A's to another victory in 1911, this time a 13½-game romp over the Tigers. In winning, the A's batted a league-leading .297 and led in pitching and fielding, prowess much needed in their Series duel with the Giants. What followed was Mack's revenge for his 1905 loss to the Giants; strong pitching and two homers from Baker, whose long blows soon nicknamed him "Home Run" Baker, carried the A's.

The following year Mack's bid for a third straight conquest ran afoul of faltering pitching, as injuries and aging took their toll. Although Mack's scouts signed future pitching stars Herb Pennock, Joe Bush, and Bob Shawkey with catcher Wally Schang, these rookies were too green to help the 1912 team, which won 90 and yet finished a distant third to the winning Red Sox.

Boston's 1912 resurgence defied critics and reminded fans of the uncertainties of baseball forecasting. After winning consecutive flags in 1903–4, Boston's chief distinction was changing its totem from Pilgrims to Red Sox. Playing under that proud old name, the 1911 Red Sox finished a sorry fifth, a failure that persuaded owner Taylor that his recruiting attempts and his costly new Fenway Park were liabilities. In selling out, Taylor rued his lost confidence, as protégés like pitcher "Smokey Joe" Wood and outfielders Tris Speaker, Duffy Lewis, and Harry Hooper burst into stardom. Brightest was Wood, whose 34-5 pitching outshone Washington's great Walter Johnson, whom Wood defeated 1-0 before a huge Boston crowd. That victory keyed a 16-game winning streak by Wood that tied Johnson's earlier 16-game streak. The Red Sox won 105 games overall to outpace the Senators by 14 games. In the World Series, McGraw's Giants fell to Wood's pitching, and the victory put the Americans ahead to stay in this annual inter-league test of strength.

Tragically for Wood, arm trouble starting in 1913 ended his great pitching career and, with it, Boston's chances. As the Sox faded, Mack's revitalized A's took the measure of Clark Griffith's Washington Senators. Backed by good hitting, Mack's rejuvenated pitchers won by 6½ games, and the A's easily trampled the Giants in the World Series.

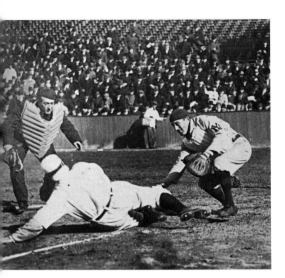

A rare early action photograph caught a play at home plate in a game between the New York Highlanders and the Boston Red Sox. The game was at Boston's Huntington Avenue Grounds around 1910. (Courtesy Dennis Goldstein)

Now, however, storm clouds threatened the profitable major league scene. Smelling profits, prosperous industrial investors launched a rival major league, which in classic fashion enticed major league stars by higher salaries. This menacing Federal League lasted two seasons, during which a business depression and war fears also contributed to hard times in baseball. Against this gloomy backdrop Mack led his 1914 A's to an easy 8½-game win over the Red Sox, but losses totaling $60,000 soured him. Having stretched himself thin by buying half-ownership in the club, Mack was dismayed by the team's four-straight-game loss to the "Miracle" Boston Braves in the Series. To recoup his finances, Mack retrenched, ruthlessly cutting his payroll by releasing veterans and selling stars for cash. To his lasting regret, Mack even refused to invest $10,000 for promising youngsters Babe Ruth and Ernie Shore, a piece of penury that helped consign the A's to the league's cellar for seven years.

For the short run this kind of conservatism made sense, as only seven major league clubs made money in 1915; however, optimistic owners Comiskey of Chicago and Joe Lannin of Boston, who snapped up Mack's stars, profited by capturing the next five pennants. First blood went to Boston by dint of acquiring shortstop Jack Barry, as well as Ruth and Shore. Managed by catcher Bill ("Rough") Carrigan, the 1915 Red Sox fought a furious battle with the Tigers. In this test, pitchers Ruth and Shore responded by winning 37 games as Boston won by 2½ games. In the World Series, the battle-hardened Red Sox won four close games in beating the Phillies four games to one. Because Boston lost the services of outfielder Speaker, they suffered another close call in 1916. For demanding more pay, Speaker was dealt to Cleveland, where his batting ended Cobb's nine-year skein of titles. Nevertheless, Boston's pitching quintet of Ruth, Shore, Dutch Leon-

American League all-star team of 1911, assembled at Cleveland to play a benefit game for the family of Indians pitcher Addie Joss, whose death from a lung ailment ended a brilliant career. Seated, left to right: Herman Schaefer (Washington), Tris Speaker (Boston), Sam Crawford (Detroit), president McAleer (New York), Ty Cobb (Detroit, in Cleveland uniform), Gabby Street (Washington), Paddy Livingston (Philadelphia). Standing: Bobby Wallace (St. Louis), Frank Baker (Philadelphia), Joe Wood (Boston), Walter Johnson (Washington), Hal Chase (New York), Clyde Milan (Washington), Russ Ford (New York), Eddie Collins (Philadelphia). Photo by L. Vandeven. (Courtesy John Thorn)

Tristram E. ("Tris") Speaker, slugging outfielder for the Boston Red Sox, 1907–15, then player and player-manager for the Cleveland Indians, 1916–26. A Silver Age marvel, he had a .344 career batting average for twenty-two seasons. (Courtesy John Thorn)

Napoleon ("Nap") Lajoie, player-manager of the Cleveland Indians, 1905–9. Both graceful and durable, he played twenty-one seasons, with a career batting average of .339. (Author's Collection)

Right: Walter P. ("Big Train") Johnson, whose entire brilliant career, 1907–27, was with the Washington Senators. In 1912 his record was 32 and 12; in 1913 it was 36 and 7. (Courtesy National Baseball Library, Cooperstown, New York)

Below: Cleveland "Naps" pitchers of 1914: from left, Willie Mitchell, lefty Bill James, Norman ("Nick") Cullop. (Courtesy Dennis Goldstein)

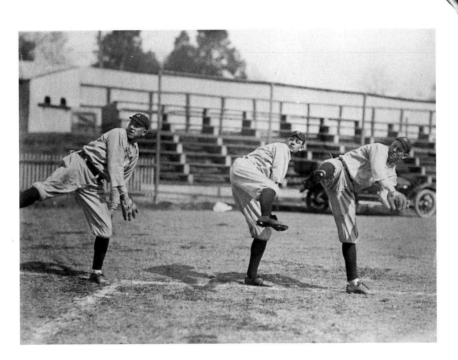

ard, Rube Foster, and Carl Mays carried the Sox to a two-game victory over Chicago, then to an easy 4-1 sweep of the Dodgers in the World Series.

Although few saw it coming, Boston's decline was nigh. In 1917 manager Carrigan resigned, and theatre producer Harry Frazee appeared as a new Boston owner. If Carrigan's departure had a temporary ill-effect, Frazee's accession was a long-term disaster; within a few years his sales of star players prostrated the Sox. Meanwhile, Jack Barry managed the 1917 Red Sox to a second-place finish, only nine games back of the White Sox.

To relieve an eleven-year pennant drought, Comiskey spent big, including $130,000 in 1915 to get Eddie Collins and outfielder Joe Jackson. Installing Collins as the team's well-paid captain and Clarence ("Pants") Rowland as manager, Commy chose well, but the rest of the team was poorly paid and, given their talent, rightly envious. Still, they stormed the league, then handed McGraw's Giants a fourth Series defeat. After the 1917 Series, baseball felt the squeeze of total war, which forced clubs to cut the 1918 playing schedule to 128 games. Although Boston won the inglorious 1918 race by 4½ games over Cleveland, little cash or glory was realized thereby or in their Series victory over the Cubs. That year World War I involvement claimed many players for military service and embarrassed those who kept playing; as war fever rose, baseball seemed irrelevant, attendance flagged, and it took a special War Department dispensation to schedule the World Series. No wonder some owners despaired and retrenched or sold out. Yet it was no time for faintheartedness; despite baseball's wartime decline, the post-Armistice period triggered a mighty baseball boom in the land. But if sentimentalists expected baseball as usual, they were hit by sweeping changes. In the hands of bold innovators the game, like the nation, was being transformed. For baseball, changes brought both woe in the form of scandal and good fortune via the marvelously popular "big bang" style of play. Symbolized by that homeric star Babe Ruth, the dawning new era would emerge a new Golden Age.

DEADBALL DYNASTIES: THE NATIONAL LEAGUE

Joe Wood of the Boston Red Sox (left) and Christy Mathewson of the New York Giants pose together before a 1912 World Series game. (Courtesy National Baseball Library, Cooperstown, New York)

As the new American League freed fans from monopolistic baseball organization, so the former also-rans of the National League overthrew the pennant monopolists of the 1890s. Or so fans thought, as they really exchanged one oligopoly for another; beginning with the 1901 season, the next thirteen pennants went to the mini-dynasties of Pittsburgh, Chicago, and New York.

Pittsburgh was the first newcomer to scale the heights. A chronic loser until 1900, the Pirates flexed their muscles as owner Barney Dreyfuss abandoned Louisville for Pittsburgh. Convinced the Pittsburgh fans would support a contender, Dreyfuss demanded that his manager finish every season in the first division. Presumptuous as this was, Dreyfuss had his way for fourteen seasons, during which his teams also won four pennants. At the start, Dreyfuss's pronouncement seemed reasonable, since he was able to pick his 1900 team from two major league clubs. From the defunct Louisvilles he named outfielder Fred Clarke as Pirate playing manager, and Clarke selected pitchers Charles ("Deacon") Phillippe and Rube Waddell, catchers Charles Zimmer and Cliff Latimer, and the bowlegged shortstop John ("Honus") Wagner. These Louisvillians went with Clarke to Pittsburgh; Wagner was the gem of the lot, for his fielding and batting (eight titles and a record total of hits) ranked the "Flying Dutchman" second only to Cobb in this era. Clarke retained such Pirates as pitchers Jack Chesbro and Jess Tannehill, infielders John Williams and Fred Ely, and outfielders Clarence ("Ginger") Beaumont and Tom McCreery, and elected to promote rookie first baseman Bill ("Kitty") Bransfield.

In 1901 Clarke led this team to the first of three consecutive flags. With Wagner hitting and stealing, and pitchers Chesbro, Phillippe, and Tannehill winning 61 times, the Pirates beat the Phils by 8½ games. Then, having avoided devastating roster raids by American Leaguers, the 1902 Pirates repeated, winning 103 games and leaving

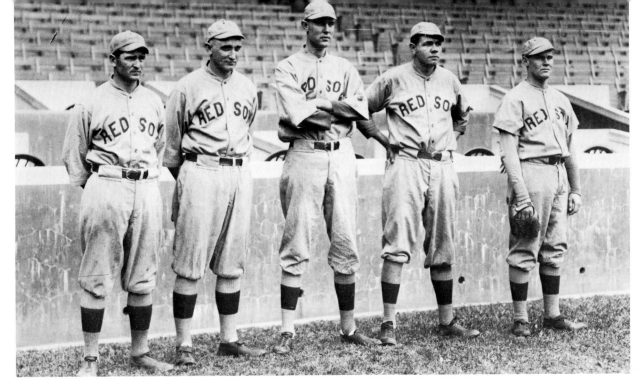

Boston Red Sox pitching quintet of 1915: from left, Rube Foster, Carl Mays, Ernie Shore, Babe Ruth, Dutch Leonard. (Courtesy Library of Congress)

the pursuing Dodgers 27 games behind. In 1903, however, the raiders stripped the Pirates of pitchers Chesbro and Tannehill; even so, Clarke added a third flag. With Wagner leading league batters and Sam Leever pitching 25 victories, the 1903 Pirates beat the Giants by seven. But then came the test of the first modern World Series, which the Pirates failed, losing to the Boston Americans.

Pirate domination faded after that, and in 1904 owner John Brush goaded his Giants to the top. Not even a crippling stroke stayed Brush's determination to make New York a National League bastion. From a wheelchair Brush watched approvingly as his hard-bitten manager John McGraw, who nursed his own grudge against Ban Johnson, turned the lowly Giants into the era's winningest team. Schooling his charges in scientific baseball fundamentals of sound defense and hit-and-run offense, taskmaster McGraw controlled strategy and tactics, sometimes even signaling each pitch of a game. If at times players chafed under this Napoleonic regimen, most Giants respected the man whose thirty-one seasons as team manager produced ten pennants. No other major league team matched this performance, and for dominating the lucrative Gotham area, McGraw was a major irritant to Johnson.

In 1903 McGraw's masterly touch rallied the former cellar-dwellers to second place. A major factor was the pitching of Joe McGinnity and Christy Mathewson. Inspired by McGraw's friendship, the husky collegian Mathewson became one of the greatest pitchers in this age of pitching greats. Likewise, utility player Roger Bresnahan developed into an innovative catcher. In girding for 1904, McGraw added pitcher George ("Hooks") Wiltse and revamped the infield, installing Art Devlin at third and Bill Dahlen at short; at the same time, "Moose" McCormick and "Turkey Mike" Donlin strengthened the outfield.

With McGraw directing action from the bench, the 1904 Giants won 106 games, 13 more than the runner-up Cubs. Strong pitching told the

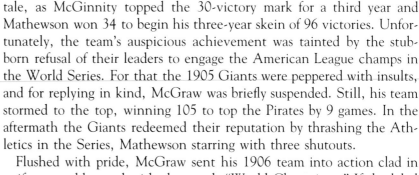

tale, as McGinnity topped the 30-victory mark for a third year and Mathewson won 34 to begin his three-year skein of 96 victories. Unfortunately, the team's auspicious achievement was tainted by the stubborn refusal of their leaders to engage the American League champs in the World Series. For that the 1905 Giants were peppered with insults, and for replying in kind, McGraw was briefly suspended. Still, his team stormed to the top, winning 105 to top the Pirates by 9 games. In the aftermath the Giants redeemed their reputation by thrashing the Athletics in the Series, Mathewson starring with three shutouts.

Flushed with pride, McGraw sent his 1906 team into action clad in uniforms emblazoned with the words "World Champions." If the label was intended to cow rivals, it had the opposite effect on the Chicago Cubs. Pennantless for twenty years, the Cubs now belonged to Charles Murphy and Charles P. Taft, the latter a brother to the future president. Murphy's shrewd move was to appoint first baseman Frank Chance, a devotee of scientific baseball, to manage the team. Planting wispy Johnny Evers at second base, Joe Tinker at short, and Harry Steinfeldt at third, Chance assembled a legendary infield, whose exploits, however, produced far fewer double plays than their myth proclaimed. With scout George Huff discovering pitchers Jack Pfeister, Carl Lundgren, and Ed Ruelbach, and outfielder Frank ("Wildfire") Schulte, the Cubs became contenders. Led by Mordecai ("Three-Finger") Brown's 26 pitching wins, the lightly regarded Cub pitching staff turned tigers. In June the Cubs beat the Giants thrice, then outdistanced the fading champs by winning 14 straight in August. Chance's men finished with a record 116 wins, a most auspicious debut for this third dynastic power. Alas, their glory evaporated in one nightmarish week when the White Sox, despised urban rivals to these mighties, unexpectedly scored a 4-2 Series victory.

Over a winter of recriminations, Chance regrouped and drove his men to another pennant, his 1907 team winning 107 to outlast the Pirates by 17. Better still, the Cubs swept the Detroit Tigers in the Series. It was glory aplenty, but the 1908 Cubs added a baseball miracle. Worsted by the Giants most of that season, the Cubs were nearly eliminated by September. At the Polo Grounds on September 23, the Giants seemingly dealt the final blow by scoring what appeared to be the winning run in the last of the ninth. But Johnny Evers noted that Giant base runner Fred Merkle failed to touch second base on the winning hit. Evers yelled for the ball, got one, tagged second, and

Top: Knuckleball of right-hander Eddie Cicotte, who pitched for the White Sox from 1913 to 1920. Photo by Conlon in 1913. (Courtesy Gordon Miller)

Bottom: Joseph Jefferson ("Shoeless Joe") Jackson, consistent hitter acquired from Cleveland by the White Sox in 1915. Implicated in the "Black Sox" scandal, he was banned from organized baseball in 1920. (Courtesy George Brace)

appealed to umpire Hank O'Day for a force-out decision. Amidst the confusion of milling Giant fans, O'Day called Merkle out; when sustained, that verdict declared the game a tie. At the time it meant little, as the Cubs needed to win 11 of their last 12 games to tie the Giants. By doing just that, they forced a "sudden death" playoff game; playing at the Polo Grounds, the Cubs won it 4-2 and landed a third straight pennant. A legendary victory, it forever stigmatized Merkle as "Bonehead Fred," while the heroic Cubs added more glory by again beating the Tigers in the Series.

In a far calmer 1909 race the Cubs easily outran the Giants but finished second to the Pirates, who won 110 games. The Pirates were rejuvenated by such newcomers as rookie pitcher Charles ("Babe") Adams, catcher George Gibson, a trio of new infielders, an outfielder, and even a new playing field—capacious, triple-decked Forbes Field. The park investment was a gamble, but the Pirate victory justified Dreyfuss's faith, as did the team's thumping win over the Tigers in the Series.

This latest humiliation of the Americans had National leaders gloating, but their euphoria soured in the fall of 1910. That season Chance's Cubs reclaimed the pennant, winning 104 games to lap the Giants and become the first major league team to average 100 or more victories over five seasons. It was the high tide of National League predominance; beginning with the Cubs' fall defeat at the hands of the Athletics, the tide turned. The following year the Cubs faltered, and when the Pirates failed to move up, McGraw's revamped Giants took command.

Fielding young, educable newcomers like outfielders Fred Snodgrass and Josh Devore, infielders Art Fletcher, Larry Doyle, and Charles Herzog, pitcher "Rube" Marquard, and catcher John ("Chief") Meyers, McGraw established a monopoly. Over the years 1911–13, backed by league-leading batting, pitchers Mathewson and Marquard each won 73 games to lead the Giants to three flags. Ironically, though winning 303 games in those three years, the Giants never won a World Series; twice they fell to the Athletics, and in 1913 the Red Sox supplied the crusher.

Such failures suggested that the Nationals might be better served by a new champion. In 1914 this was a most unlikely prospect; not only had the three mini-dynasties captured all pennants since 1901, but only thrice in that span did an outsider rise as high as third place. But now change was in the air; in world politics a colossal European war loomed, threatening to topple old ruling dynasties, and in baseball the rival Federal League threatened to force a new order. At the same time, slumps took their toll on the National mini-dynasts. Still, at the outset of the 1914 race, the Giants took a big lead. Then, midseason arm miseries hampered Marquard, who lost 12 straight games. As a result, the race by mid-July was so tight that even the last-place Boston Braves were only 10 games off the pace. Once the terrors of the league, the Braves since 1903 had seemed beyond help; not even a succession of name changes and ownership shifts roused the team. Now managed by hard-driving George Stallings, the Braves were captained by ex-Cub Johnny Evers, who teamed with shortstop Walter ("Rabbit") Maranville in the infield. In addition, Stallings had three good pitchers, Dick

Chick Shorten of the Red Sox is caught trying to steal second by Ivy Olson, Dodger shortstop, in the 1916 World Series. George Cutshaw, Brooklyn second baseman, backs up the play, while third baseman Mike Mowrey looks on. (Courtesy Michael Mumby Collection)

Left: Fred Clifford Clarke, player-manager of the Pittsburgh Pirates from 1900 to 1915; he was elected to the Hall of Fame for his .315 career hitting and his leadership. (Author's Collection)

Right: John Peter ("Honus") Wagner, a mainstay of the Pirates from 1900 to 1917 and one of the superstars of baseball's Silver Age. (Courtesy National Baseball Library, Cooperstown, New York)

Rudolph, Bill James, and George Tyler, and able catcher Hank Gowdy. Otherwise the team was a nondescript tribe, but in the second half of the '14 season the Braves staged a massacre, winning 60 of 76 outings to beat out the Giants by 10½ games. Now dubbed the "Miracle Braves," the team swept the A's four straight in the World Series.

Hoping to retain their good fortune, the Braves opened the 1915 season in a new park. Yet, ironically, the luck force shifted to the major leagues' oldest park, the Phillies' ramshackle Baker Bowl. Never having known a pennant, the Phillies were now managed by tough Pat ("Whiskey Face") Moran, whose effectives included star pitcher Grover Cleveland Alexander and slugger George ("Gavvy") Cravath. Snatching an early season lead, the Phillies got 31 victories from Alexander and an amazing 24 homers from Cravath, ending ahead of the Braves by 7 games. Then the miracle ended, as the Red Sox methodically swept the World Series.

After this debacle another inspired outside force, the Brooklyn Robins, surged to the top in 1916. Like Boston, Brooklyn had been a league power, but owner Charles Ebbets had despaired of attracting fans to his new Ebbets Field park. An upturn came in 1913 when he hired old Oriole Wilbert Robinson to manage the team. By his humorous antics, Robinson charmed fans, who took to calling the team the "Robins." Yet Robinson the buffoon was also a sound judge of pitchers; in 1916 he got 25 wins from Ed Pfeffer and stout support from castoffs Jack Coombs and Rube Marquard. With solid hitting from Casey Stengel, Zack Wheat, and Jake Daubert, the Robins edged the Phillies by 2½ games. Unfortunately, the victory was tainted by charges that the Giants had thrown games to help the Robins win. Be that as it may, the Red Sox easily dispatched the Robins in the World Series.

After this incursion the waning Silver Age saw no more miracle pennant dashes by outsiders. America's all-out effort in the Great War saw to that. As the war claimed players and caused falling attendance, some owners retrenched or sold out. In 1918 Giant owner Harry Hempstead sold out to Charles Stoneham, but not before McGraw had landed another pennant. With help from newcomers like pitcher Ferdie Schupp and outfielders Benny Kauff and George Burns, the 1917 Giants won 98 games for an easy 10-game win over the Phillies. McGraw's reputation suffered, however, when for the fourth straight time his men lost the Series, this time to the Chicago White Sox.

In 1918 the full impact of war austerity took its toll on baseball. After a debate over whether to play the season, an attenuated schedule was set and a World Series grudgingly approved. In a forlorn race the Cubs beat the Giants by 10½ games; in the gloomy aftermath, a National League entry lost the World Series for a fourth straight time, as the Red Sox again triumphed. That fall the Armistice ended the war, but fearful major league owners voted to play another shortened season in 1919. Such was the depth of their pessimism, but how were they to know that a great surge of public interest was nigh? Or that winds of change unleashed by war were blowing away the Silver Age and ushering in a new free-swinging style of play?

Charles Louis ("Deacon") Philippe, who had eight outstanding seasons as a pitcher for the Pirates in the Silver Age. (Courtesy George Brace)

TIME OF TROUBLES, 1914–1919

When the Silver Age sparked interest in baseball, bullish promoters responded by building more capacious parks, inspiring the timorous to follow suit. Owners were well advised to conceal their prosperity, however, as past experiences warned of interlopers attracted by conspicuous display. Indeed, an abortive attempt by poorly organized poachers to launch a rival "United States League" failed miserably in 1912, the same year that another group failed to plant a western-based "Columbian League."

Shaken by such feints, major league owners took the drastic step of censoring figures on attendance and profits from official publications. It was too late, because two perceptive Chicagoans, John T. Powers and James A. Gilmore, already eyed a piece of the profitable action. Boldly defying the major league establishment, Powers in 1913 floated the "outlaw" Federal League, which finished the season inauspiciously as a western-based circuit. While this attempt appeared feeble, Gilmore's advent soon had major league owners quaking. Meeting with disheart-

John J. McGraw, "Napoleonic" manager of the Giants, surveys his forces at Manhattan's Polo Grounds. During McGraw's thirty-three years as Giants manager, his teams captured ten National League pennants but won only three world championships. (Courtesy George Brace)

ened Federal owners in the fall of 1913, the glib Gilmore dazzled them with visions of profits to come from expanded operations. Seduced by such talk, the Federal owners ousted Powers and named Gilmore president. Thereupon Gilmore lined up a bevy of wealthy backers, including some who had been turned down in efforts to buy into the established majors. Hence, with dramatic suddenness, the Federal League rose in 1914 with teams planted in Chicago, Baltimore, Buffalo, Pittsburgh, Indianapolis, Brooklyn, St. Louis, and Kansas City. A brilliant coup, the Federal incursion struck terror by building parks and seducing major league players with high salary offers. It was a classic invasion; because the stakes were higher, the threat was more menacing than those of the old Union or American associations.

To fend off the threat, the majors threatened jumping players with blacklists and expulsions, but they were obliged to raise salaries. These moves failed to stay the Federals, but too much baseball resulted in losses all around. Although the Federals lost more money than the big two, they survived, and Indianapolis won the league's 1914 championship. Undaunted, the Federals fought on in 1915, transferring the Indianapolis club to Newark, where new money from oil king Harry Sinclair was pumped in. That year manager Joe Tinker's Chicago Whales edged St. Louis and Pittsburgh in a close race. But this was the Federal League's last shot; continuing losses, plus the untimely death of the league's outstanding financier, Robert Ward, staggered the Federal promoters.

In suing for peace, the three leading Federal owners accepted offers to become major league owners: one buying the Browns and a duo acquiring the Cubs. This classic settlement to a classic baseball war ignored the plight of more modest Federal financiers. All were losers, even though the established majors shelled out $5 million as partial compensation. While that payoff ended most of the antitrust suits filed by Federal investors against organized baseball, one suit by Baltimore investors eventually reached the United States Supreme Court. Speaking for the unanimous court in 1922, Justice Oliver Wendell Holmes, Jr., disallowed Baltimore's suit and held major league baseball to be mainly a sport, at least not a commonly accepted form of commerce. While this decision relieved baseball from antitrust suits, it was not considered irreversible; consequently, later generations of major league owners still trembled over possible Federal suits or prospective congressional investigations of their enterprise.

A year's respite followed the Federal League settlement, after which owners faced the formidable threat of America's entry into World War I. Except for the Spanish-American War, which caused falling attendance in 1898, baseball owners knew nothing of wartime austerities. Hence, after the profitable 1916 season, owners were stunned by the impact of wartime demands. Although the 1917 season was little affected, owners were hard-pressed to justify their enterprise, which they did by staging patriotic displays and admitting soldiers free of charge. In 1918, with the AEF in the trenches, much more was demanded, summed up in the slogan "Work or Fight." Far from being seen as heroes, players were branded as slackers, and teams faced severe restrictions on travel and accommodations. It mattered little that some 550

Chicago Cubs' acclaimed infield of the 1900s: from left, Harry Steinfeldt, third base; Joe Tinker, shortstop; John Evers, second base; Frank Chance, first base and manager. Celebrating the artistry of the Tinker-to-Evers-to-Chance fielding combination, newsman Franklin P. Adams described them as "a trio of bear cubs, fleeter than birds." (Courtesy George Brace)

Mordecai Peter Centennial ("Three Finger") Brown, a great starter and reliever despite the absence of an index finger on his pitching hand. His eighteen relief points in 1911 remained the National League record for two decades. (Courtesy George Brace)

pro players entered military ranks, as those who stayed out were scorned. In May 1918 the provost marshal held baseball to be nonessential to the war effort. This stunning blow threatened to halt the season, and pleas for an extension evoked only grudging permission to complete the World Series by mid-September. Thus, the combination of bad publicity and attenuated play made the 1918 season the worst financial flop of the era. Fearing worse to come, the owners voted to shorten the 1919 season even as news of the Armistice rang through the land.

While reeling from wartime buffets, baseball suffered another crusher in 1919. Welling up from inside the game, the Black Sox scandal, telling of gamblers fixing World Series games, struck at the integrity of organized baseball. To be sure, baseball's past showed periodic corruption involving conniving owners and gamblers bribing players to throw games. As recently as 1918 infielder Hal Chase of the Reds was accused of tampering with games, and that same year the A's defiantly signed a pitcher who belonged to the Braves. Although baseball law called for the National Commission to settle such troubles, in another instance the plaintiffs skirted baseball law by appealing to civil courts. Such defiance undercut the National Commission and invited more of the same; thus, the Yankees circumvented league president Johnson's refusal to approve a 1919 player purchase by appealing to the courts.

While baseball's authority structure was being undermined, opportunity and greed combined to create an explosive scandal in 1919. As unanticipated high attendance brought unprecedented profits, a group of underpaid Chicago White Sox players engaged in a profitable game-fixing scheme. Playing before huge crowds, the White Sox won a hard-fought American race by beating Cleveland by 3½ games. The victory sent the White Sox against the Cincinnati Reds in the World Series, with the Sox heavily favored to win. The Reds had won their first pennant in this century over the Giants by 9 games. With public interest in the Series outcome at high pitch, the owners voted to extend the number of games to best of nine. (The big leagues kept the best-of-nine format for three seasons, but then returned to the best-of-

Jiggs Donahue of Chicago's American League team tries to tag out Frank Chance of Chicago's National League team during the 1906 World Series. (Courtesy MacGreevy Collection, Boston Public Library)

seven format that had been traditional *since* the first modern World Series in 1903, itself a best-of-nine event.)

Given the superbly balanced White Sox, few expected the over-matched Reds to survive. Nevertheless, the Reds won four of the first five; then, after losing a pair, they hammered Chicago pitching for ten runs to win the Series 5 games to 3. On the face of it, the Red victory looked like an inspired underdog triumph, but there were rumors of collusion that could not be stilled.

Not long afterwards, a detailed exposé of some questionable plays, compiled by sportswriter Hugh Fullerton with help from Christy Mathewson, stirred an investigation. This led in mid-1920 to charges that eight White Sox players had taken bribe money from gamblers to throw the 1919 Series. When these allegations were blended with charges that more game-fixing was going on in 1920, baseball's credibility took a terrible beating. By September, published particulars of the 1919 "Black Sox Scandal" forced the suspension of the eight accused players. Haled before a Chicago grand jury, some of them admitted to taking bribes of as much as $10,000 and implicated others. The confessions prompted a 1921 conspiracy trial. Astonishingly, all the grand jury records were missing, prompting the defendants to repudiate earlier confessions, whereupon a friendly jury held all eight to be innocent. Baseball law had the final say, however, when newly appointed High Commissioner Kenesaw Mountain Landis summarily banned the eight "Black Sox" from the game.

Such was the mood of the times that Landis's draconian ruling, with its blatant disregard for the civil rights of the accused, held firm. None of the accused ever again played in the majors. A realist (or cynic) might say that the restoration of baseball's integrity demanded scapegoats and that the eight Black Sox filled the bill. Furthermore, by blaming the players, Chicago owner Comiskey escaped punishment, even though he had withheld evidence of his men's wrongdoing in the vain hope that the storm might blow over.

Nevertheless, the course of major league baseball was altered by this shabby incident. While panicking under the adverse publicity and putting on guilty faces, the owners hastily drew up a new National Agreement that replaced the old commission with a single high commissioner, Judge Landis. Over the next twenty-three years Landis's presence reshaped baseball's authority structure, causing some owners to rue the day they empowered him. Thus, the purging of the Black Sox Scandal propelled baseball into a new era, leaving the Silver Age as a fading memory.

The hallmark of the Silver Age was the restoration of the dual major league system, which blessed the game with fifteen seasons of comparative prosperity. Under a competitive format and a consistent style of play, baseball became an established, mature spectacle. Over the years 1903–17 most teams embraced the "scientific style" of play, relying on strong pitching and tight defenses to guard the skimpy run productions that offenses managed by dint of short hits, bunts, and stolen bases. To some critics, this was the "deadball era," a time when batters pushed, poked, shoved, and chopped at pitched balls to score scarce runs. In its time this was popular enough, but compared with the dynamic, high-scoring "big bang" style of the 1920s, it seemed like a dull show.

In the Silver Age it was astonishing to find pitchers rebounding from the batterings they took in the 1890s to once again dominate the game. They did so by adapting to the extended distance: Some used natural talents to deliver overpowering fastballs, deceptive curves, and off-speed pitches, all with pinpoint control; others used artifices like spitballs, paraffin balls, and other trick pitches to bewilder batters. Altogether it was pitching that accounted for drastically lowered batting averages. In an age of pitching tyranny, naturally endowed aces like Cy Young, Walter Johnson, Kid Nichols, Eddie Plank, Grover Alexander, and Christy Mathewson each recorded well over 300 victories, with Young's 511 and Johnson's 414 totals setting Olympian standards. At the same time, tricksters like spitballers Ed Walsh, Burleigh Grimes, and Urban ("Red") Faber won enough games to join the others in the Hall of Fame.

What made spitballs so controversial, aside from their gross dependence on saliva-facilitating substances like slippery elm and tobacco juice, was that they spawned other artifices. By 1909 so many hurlers doctored balls with sandpaper, paraffin, hair oil, and cutting devices that the banning of all trick deliveries was urged. At last, in 1920, the ban was invoked, although veteran practitioners were permitted to use the spitter until they retired—this was a loophole enabling young pitchers to learn the forbidden lore and to continue its clandestine use down to the present day.

Meanwhile, pitching dominance showed vividly in earned run averages, which rule makers now added to baseball's growing statistical lists. In fourteen of the years between 1901 and 1919, American League pitchers yielded fewer than three earned runs per game, while in thirteen seasons National pitchers did the same. Under such pressure, annual batting averages in both leagues barely reached .250 and ac-

THE SILVER AGE STYLE

Frederick Charles Merkle, who became a solid first baseman with a .273 batting average for sixteen seasons, in spite of one costly slip in his second season. His likeness is on a Sweet Caporal cigarette baseball card, which preceded the bubble gum card. (Courtesy Goulston Collection, New York Public Library)

Bevy of Giant pitchers of the Silver Age: from the left, Rube Marquard, Jeff Tesreau, Christy Mathewson, Red Ames, George Wiltse, Doc Crandall. Supplementing the stellar work of Marquard and Mathewson, newcomer Tesreau won 38 games in 1912–13; Wiltse won 23 in 1908 but slipped to zero by 1913; veteran Ames won 22 in 1905, then leveled off at about a dozen wins per season; Crandall won 32 in 1911–13. (Courtesy National Baseball Library, Cooperstown, New York)

counted for limited run production. Also, few long hits were struck, home run output averaging fewer than 20 per team.

Almost as much as intimidating pitching, improved fielding and the quality of the balls used stamped this age as the deadball era. Compared with balls used in the 1920s, those of this era were less resilient and less often replaced. In 1910 a livelier cork-centered ball appeared, but it was not widely used in this era. Meanwhile, improved gloves sent fielding averages up by 15 points over the 1890s. As these factors curbed hitting, managers more often loosed base runners on stealing ventures; thus, teams averaged 100 steals a year, with American teams five times averaging more than 200.

Still, it must not be supposed that batting became a lost art. On the contrary, demigods Ty Cobb and Honus Wagner yielded to no rivals of any era. In a class by himself, Cobb zealously compiled the highest lifetime average (.367), the most hits (4,191) until 1985, and the most batting titles (13) of any batter in history. In addition, Cobb's seasonal and lifetime stolen-base records endured to the 1970s. Meanwhile, Wagner set long-lasting National League marks for total hits (3,415) and stolen bases, while his record of eight batting titles still endures.

Although outshone by this pair, other hitters of the era claimed shares of glory. Before Cobb burst on the scene, American League fans doted on Nap Lajoie, the handsome, slick-fielding second baseman who captured three of the first four American batting crowns and dogged Cobb each year until 1912. Another challenger was Cobb's teammate Sam Crawford, who never won a batting title but twice led the American League in homers and smote a record 309 triples. At this time the deadball and capacious new parks penalized sluggers like Crawford, Buck Freeman, and Ed Delehanty. As a result, they and other sluggers spent their strength in compiling modest seasonal totals. Because one might become a homer king with as few as eight home runs in a season, scant recognition fell to Harry Davis of the A's for his four titles. The turnabout in recognition began in 1911 when Frank ("Wildfire") Schulte of the Cubs pounded 21. After that, Clifford ("Gavvy") Cravath of the Phillies won six titles, including one in 1915 when he hit 24. In the American League meanwhile, Frank ("Homerun") Baker of the A's won his nickname for capturing consecutive homer titles in 1911–14. Such feats glamorized sluggers, so, when Babe Ruth of the Red Sox smashed a record 29 in 1919, his blows tolled the death knell of the deadball era.

Nevertheless, while that era lasted, fans doted on deadball batters like Cobb, Wagner, Lajoie, Eddie Collins, Tris Speaker, and the versatile "Shoeless Joe" Jackson, whose career ended in disgrace as one of the Black Sox. Indeed, the era offered enough varied heroes to meet any fan's tastes. For those craving respectability, college-bred stars like Collins, Christy Mathewson, and Eddie Plank served; for those doting on power pitching, there was Joe Wood or the matchless Walter Johnson; for lovers of raw power, there was Joe Jackson or Jim Thorpe, the famous native American track star who never fully blossomed as a player; for regional-minded fans, there were players from every section, although more than 500 hailed from New York and Pennsylvania; for identity-seeking hyphenated Americans, there were compatriots like Stan Coveleskie and Francesco Pezzolo (who changed his name to Frank Bodie). If fans wanted villains to hiss, they had the imperious Cobb or the corrupt Black Sox; for those seeking victims for ridicule, there was "Bonehead" Fred Merkle, zany Rube Waddell, or the notorious lush "Bugs" Raymond.

That fans liked the game of this era was attested by the growing numbers of paid admissions. From 4.7 million in 1903, major league attendance reached 7 million in 1908 and peaked at 10 million in 1911. It was such jingling support that inspired the ballpark building

Yankees in military drill in 1918. (Courtesy Dennis Goldstein)

Ty Cobb of the Tigers sliding into
third base, manned by Jimmy Austin
of the Browns. "The Georgia Peach"
epitomized the "scientific" yet heroic
style of the Silver Age. (Courtesy
Ronald A. Smith)

chronicling of black baseball feats kept alive its heroes. Even so, black
baseball, like other forcibly segregated black institutions, remained a
largely invisible and unsung chapter of American life.

Meanwhile, major league umpires lived a despised existence, somewhat above that of the black pariahs. As manufactured villains, they
suffered insults and abuses from fans and players. To his credit, President Ban Johnson successfully defended American umpires, but not
until 1911 did both leagues adopt the dual umpire system. Then umps
also received travel expenses, but they still footed the costs of uniforms
and equipment. Welcome as such reforms were, umps still lacked job
security and drew niggardly pay. In 1910 $3,000 was the top salary of
any ump, and as late as 1920 a budget of $41,000 took care of thirty-
two umpires. Nevertheless, standouts like Bill Klem, Tim Hurst, "Silk"
O'Loughlin, Tom Connolly, and Billy Evans starred; by their personal
charismatic styles they set standards that enhanced the profession.

At least baseball owners of this age no longer lorded it in the fashion
of the magnates of the 1890s. By 1912 most of that old breed had gone,
replaced by newcomers who styled themselves as gentlemen-sportsmen
but who mixed altruism with avarice. Although considerable profit
could be made from baseball, the usual gaps between have and have-not
clubs persisted. Overall American League profits exceeded the National's, but such profits were unevenly distributed. Thus, in 1911–20
six American clubs collected 79 percent of the wealth, and in the

National the greater "attendance strength" of New York, Pittsburgh, Chicago, and Philadelphia gave these the lion's share. Such disparities incurred jealousy, and the National Commission was hard put to get owners to cooperate with each other. To screen out troublemakers, both leagues by 1910 had devised elaborate and secret policies for weighing new applicants and for ousting unwanteds. Although the utility of this fraternal policy can be defended, its legal status was shaky. Moreover, since a nearly unanimous vote of league owners was needed to oust an unwanted one, a small clique often would resort to stirring up a hornet's nest of dissent. In the wake of the Black Sox scandal, organized dissenters won a majority and voted to abolish the National Commission. Thus, by installing a high commissioner, they put the quietus on the Silver Age and helped to inaugurate a new era.

Jim Thorpe, who came from the Carlisle Indian School to gain fame as the greatest all-around athlete. In his six-year big league baseball career with the Giants, Reds, and Braves, he never made the regular lineup and posted a .252 batting average. (Courtesy George Brace)

A cartoonist for *Puck* lampooned the idea that baseball players were underpaid victims of a "baseball trust," in the humor magazine's issue of May 14, 1913. (Courtesy John Thorn)

5

THE BIG
BANG ERA

LTHOUGH FEW SAW IT COMING, A SECOND GOLDEN
Age dawned for major league baseball in the 1920s. A time of
unprecedented profits and popularity, this new era owed its success to the popular "big bang" style of high-scoring games, often
decided by home runs. With electrifying impact this new style burst
over the baseball world of 1920. That year Babe Ruth, the high-priced
Yankee outfielder, smote 54 homers, a prodigious total that not only
exceeded any individual's seasonal output before then but dwarfed the
annual seasonal totals of most teams since the dawn of the major
leagues. No wonder fans sainted this young Goliath. For a rough perspective on his achievement, consider the fact that as recently as 1918
the entire Senators team hit five homers in a season, or the fact that
never during the Silver Age did any American League team's seasonal
total approach Ruth's 1920 mark. True, the National League's Phillies
had topped it, but they were assisted by shortened fences in their
obsolete park. Also, older fans recalled the 1884 season, when shortened fences allowed Anson's Colts to exceed 100 homers. Since then,
however, no team's annual homer output had matched the 115 blows
unleashed by the 1920 Yankees.

Enthralled by this explosive style, the powerful New York press
touted the big bang over the fading scientific style of the deadball era.
Responding to this appreciative chorus, Ruth and his Yankee mates
lived up to their role of pace-setting sluggers. Over the years 1921–31
Ruth notched nine homer titles, and on nine occasions his Yankee
team belted over 100 homers a year. Such consistent slugging stamped
the Yankee brand on the big bang style, and except for occasional

Babe Ruth following a ball he has sent
on its way. The "Sultan of Swat" set
the style of the Big Bang Era. (Courtesy National Baseball Library, Cooperstown, New York)

flurries by the A's, Tigers, and Browns, no American team challenged the Yankee Bombers.

This was not the case in the National League, where since 1904 sluggers consistently had overpowered the Americans. In this era they still did; nine times in the years 1920–31 National sluggers led Americans, usually by wide margins. Indeed, in their awesomely explosive 1930 season, the Nationals struck 892 to 673 for the Americans. While this was proof aplenty that National sluggers were the big bang masters, the added fact that half a dozen National teams posted 100-plus homer seasons clinches the point. Be that as it may, baseball mythology still credits the Yankees with authoring the big bang style, and no one can gainsay their achievements. Although four National clubs repeatedly notched 100-plus homer seasons, no National team matched the Yankee team's consistency, and no National slugger rivaled the great Ruth.

A TRIO OF DEMIGODS

Ironically, at the very time the new style was captivating fans, major league owners despaired of baseball's future. Despondent over the Black Sox scandal, the owners scuttled both the National Commission and its leader, Ban Johnson, who symbolized the Silver Age. Fearful that baseball's credibility had been undermined by the Black Sox, the owners frantically sought a leader who might wash away the guilty season. In their searchings they settled on Judge Kenesaw Mountain Landis as the purging force. Although time would show that Landis would indeed furnish an honest image for baseball, already on hand was a pair of leaders whose impact on baseball's growth and prosperity would be greater. One was Babe Ruth, the superstar slugger who outmatched all players in popular favor; the other was Wesley Branch Rickey, a genius at recruiting players and building teams of championship caliber. Together, this great trio of Landis, Ruth, and Rickey led the major leagues into a new Golden Age.

The 1920s seem made to order for baseball's Second Golden Age. The people of the United States were ready to forget World War I and the "European entanglements" that got them into it—as well as the flu epidemic of 1918–20 and the brief recession of 1920—and to have some fun. They elected glad-handing Warren G. Harding to the presidency on his promise of a "Return to Normalcy." National pride was at a high level, as was the habit of hero worship. What better opportunity for the "national game" with its propensity for making heroes? "Black Jack" Pershing and Sergeant York opened the way for heroes of the diamond. Even the widespread corruption of the Roaring 'Twenties, reaching as high as Harding's White House, served baseball's interests. Baseball represented the true, incorruptible America—with the crusty father figure of Judge Landis taking charge. American prosperity gave fans the means to go to ball games. While there were large pockets of poverty in city slums, and while many farmers suffered hardships, millions of workers—both white-collar and blue-collar—had time and money to spend at ballparks. Prosperous fans were especially numerous in the growing metropolises with major league franchises.

Of the three Golden Age demigods, only Landis's appearance was

Kenesaw Mountain Landis throwing out the first ball in the 1926 World Series. The Cardinals beat the Yankees 4-3 that year, while the commissioner was in his feisty prime. (Courtesy Library of Congress)

formally noted. At a Chicago meeting in November of 1920, the baseball owners overthrew the National Commission and immediately dispatched a delegation to persuade District Judge Landis to accept a call to become the game's high commissioner. Given advance warning of the mission, Landis used his judicial trappings and raspy voice to intimidate the delegation, but after a ceremonial refusal he pounced on the $50,000-a-year offer. To relieved owners, Landis's acceptance was a form of redemption; surely he would be the cleansing savior who would wipe away the Black Sox scandal. Two months later the owners signed a new National Agreement, which not only established the exalted post of high commissioner but also stated that in the event of Landis's death the president of the United States would be asked to name a replacement. If this sounded fanciful, so was the depth of the owners' guilt feelings. In waiving their rights to take their baseball troubles to the civil courts, the owners empowered Landis as a baseball Solon, a lawgiver who might rule on matters "detrimental to the game" and who could fire, suspend, dismiss, and rebuke any wrongdoers. In retrospect, it seems incredible that the owners should have enthroned such an erratic, headline-grabbing character.

A semi-educated lawyer, Landis owed his 1905 appointment to a Federal District Court bench in Illinois to political pull provided by his father and his two Congressmen brothers. Landis was a courtroom showman whose histrionics extended to badgering principals and reporters. A sometime big-business baiter, he titillated the nation in 1907 by slapping a $29 million fine on Standard Oil of Indiana for antitrust violations. Although the decision was speedily overturned, the publicity made him famous. So did public approval of his bellicose wartime decisions against Bill Haywood of the Industrial Workers of the World, Socialist Congressman Victor Berger, and Kaiser Wilhelm II, whom Landis tried to subpoena to answer for the *Lusitania* sinking.

While such theatrics made Landis's national reputation, he also won the respect of baseball owners for delaying his decision on an antitrust suit filed by Federal League promoters against the major leagues. By delaying, Landis gave the big league moguls time to settle the case out of court. More than anything else, that gesture by Landis persuaded owners that he was the man who could now burnish baseball's tarnished image. Measured by the warm public response to the appointment, their judgment was right. Shortly after accepting the commissionership, Landis occupied spartan headquarters in Chicago, where the black-lettered "BASEBALL" caption on his office door symbolized the official residence of the game's "Integrity Mountain."

As defender of baseball's integrity, Landis held his post from 1921 to 1944, during which time he administered the millions of dollars that flowed from World Series and other special game receipts, from fines, and from radio contracts that he negotiated. Still, if Landis was the responsible "czar," most of the details were handled by his handpicked lieutenant, lawyer Leslie O'Connor, who advised and assisted Landis throughout his tenure.

Among the varied troublesome cases handled by Landis during his twenty-three years as commissioner, one traces the pattern of baseball's adaptation to a fast-changing society. Above all, Landis strove to keep

Branch Rickey, baseball's top innovator from 1912 until his death in 1965. (Courtesy National Baseball Library, Cooperstown, New York)

Opposite:
George Herman ("Babe") Ruth, photographed by Nickolas Muray for the National Portrait Gallery. (Courtesy Smithsonian Institution)

Babe Ruth in friendly consultation with Colonel Jake Ruppert, Yankee owner, while general manager Ed Barrow looks on. (Courtesy National Baseball Library, Cooperstown, New York)

the game honest. Beginning with his expulsion of the eight Black Sox players, Landis ousted and disciplined other players suspected of wrongdoing, and he issued a stream of edicts banning players from fraternizing with fans, betting on horses, engaging in prizefights and in forbidden postseason games, and committing other tabooed acts. Such rulings cast him as a tough overseer; certainly, players feared him, and black players, hoping forlornly to play in the white majors, found him stubbornly opposed to baseball's integration. While Landis's moral dictates often flouted the civil rights of players, in his time they struck a popular chord. All in all, Landis used baseball law of his own fashioning to cow players into submission.

Charged with protecting the integrity of the World Series, Landis made many rulings and gained most of the operating expenses of his office while supervising the fall classic. Determined to keep the Series above suspicion, Landis attended games, supervising the collection and disbursement of money, ruling on player decorum, and sometimes second-guessing umpires.

Another set of troublesome cases confronting Landis involved the tottering independent minor leagues. From the 1920s onward, economic pressures hurt independent minor league promoters, threatening to block the flow of youthful talent to the majors. To cope with this threat, farsighted officials like Rickey of the Cardinals purchased minor league teams and built vast "farm system" empires. Landis strongly opposed such ventures, but he could not stem the trend towards major league control over minor league operations. Sometimes Landis made headlines by freeing minor league players from major farm systems, but by 1941 every important minor league was controlled by the majors. For his stubborn opposition in this matter, Landis faced mounting opposition among owners.

In this era owners also accused Landis of wrongheaded nostalgia when he opposed radio broadcasts of Series games. Belatedly recogniz-

Miller Huggins, Yankee field manager, flanked on his right by Babe Ruth and Waite Hoyt, on his left by Bob Meusel and Bob Shawkey. Huggins, after thirteen quite respectable years as a National League second baseman and player-manager, led the Yankees from 1918 to 1929, a period when they won six pennants and three world championships. (Courtesy National Baseball Library, Cooperstown, New York)

ing radio's profit potential, Landis in 1934 negotiated the first contract for exclusive rights to such broadcasts. Thereafter, such contracts provided owners with welcome windfalls, but some criticized Landis for selling rights too cheaply, while announcers chafed at his meddlesome, style-cramping injunctions.

Under increasing fire from owners, Landis's public image alone kept him in his post. Among his last acts was his effort to sustain baseball during the crisis of World War II, but Landis's injudicious criticisms of President Roosevelt hampered his efforts. Fortunately, owner Clark Griffith of the Senators, a friend of the President, managed to get a "green light" for baseball's continuance. Working within restricted guidelines, Landis managed to keep baseball going, albeit with many curtailments.

In retrospect, Landis's death in 1944 relieved owners of a burdensome liability. Ever since his accession, owners had chafed under his self-righteous criticisms; moreover, during the Depression some charged Landis with imprudent investments of baseball funds. In 1932 a cabal of owners tried to block his reelection; failing, they cut his salary and forced him to conform more to their wishes. Landis's public support never faltered, however. Acclaimed as the man who cleaned up baseball, he inspired imitators like "Czar" Will Hays, the Hollywood film censor. Saddled with such an Olympian figure, owners were reminded, so long as Landis served, that having empowered a saint they cast themselves as sinners. No wonder they sought to bury the autocratic commissionership with Landis. But if Landis's death disenthralled baseball owners, he left an enduring legacy of incorruptibility that forced owners to maintain the commissioner's post, even if all subsequent incumbents were hog-tied.

In strange counterpoint to the stern, patriarchal Landis, the Second Golden Age also hosted the greatest of player-heroes in George Herman ("Babe") Ruth. Comparing these two demigods is like weighing Zeus the cloud-gatherer against the powerful but all-too-human Hercules. On and off the field the colorful Ruth lived life to the hilt. His prodigious slugging was matched by a gargantuan appetite for worldly pleasures. Not seldom, his excessive boozing and wenching marred his performance on the diamond, but when upbraided, this man-child remorsefully picked himself up and rose to greater heights. No wonder fans took the big guy to their hearts, or that America's "Ruthomania" endured for so long.

Big, powerful, immensely talented, Ruth single-handedly carried the big bang style into baseball. Year after year he won homer titles; in 1927 he set a seasonal record of 60, and he retired in 1935 having blasted 714. Like Cy Young's 511 wins or Cobb's .367 lifetime batting average, Ruth's production was Olympian. No mere powermonger, his lifetime .342 batting average bespoke hitting virtuosity, and his incredible versatility showed in defensive ability, speed afoot, and a remarkable pitching record compiled early in his career.

Yet, to attempt to plumb the Ruth mystique or to explain his charismatic appeal one must dwell on his rags-to-riches rise. A deprived child, he ran wild in the streets of Baltimore, cursing, drinking, fighting, and stealing. His parents judged him incorrigible at age seven and

Top: Babe Ruth and Bob Meusel are reinstated in 1922 after a two-month suspension for postseason barnstorming. (Courtesy Dennis Goldstein)

Bottom: Henry Louis Gehrig (left), who joined the Yankees from Columbia University in 1923, discoursing with "The Bambino." (Courtesy Herman Seid)

Harry Edwin Heilmann, hard-hitting outfielder for the Tigers, 1914–29. He was the American League's top hitter four times during baseball's Second Silver Age, with averages between .393 and .403. (Courtesy *Detroit News*)

Opposite:
Top: Athletics posed in front of their home field in 1926, when the automobile began to take over from street railways. (Courtesy Charles Burkhardt)

Bottom: Rooftop bleachers and second-story boxes enable fans to watch 1929 World Series action inside Shibe Park. A *Philadelphia Bulletin* photograph. (Courtesy Photojournalism Collection, Temple University Libraries)

committed him to the St. Mary's Industrial Home for Boys. There, under the tutelage of Xaverian fathers, he grew to young manhood, fleshing out to six feet, two inches of muscular brawn, with "a flat nose and little piggy eyes and a big grin" that Ruth worshippers came to recognize on sight. A baseball-playing genius, he became a star Red Sox pitcher after the briefest minor league seasoning. Such was his hitting ability, however, that he was converted to full-time outfield play, and in 1919 he slugged 29 homers. Sold to the Yankees in 1920 for an unheard of $125,000, and paid $20,000, the twenty-five-year-old star responded by poling 54 homers. From then on, the powerful Gotham publicity mills dinned his exploits into every corner of the land.

As baseball's reigning demigod, Ruth attained international fame. By 1930 he was said to be the most photographed American. Nearly everything he did made news, the press straining to whitewash his tabooed, hedonistic antics. His binges and excesses were followed by reformations that always redeemed him, as did public appearances and kindly acts toward children. Such an idol was he that by 1930 he was paid $80,000 a season; in vain moralizers tried to drag him down by questioning the morality that elevated "a subnormal giant" above the president. To such a charge in 1930 Ruth delighted fans by quipping, "Why not, I had a better year!"

His exuberant, upstaging presence so threatened baseball officials that, following his retirement, Ruth found no permanent place in baseball. At least his adoring public never forgot; until his death in 1948 his public appearances attracted worshipping crowds. When he died, 100,000 fans passed by his bier in the rotunda of Yankee Stadium, "the house that Ruth built." Since Babe Ruth's passing, American baseball has yet to produce an equivalent hero. His legend haunted Roger Maris and Henry Aaron, players who broke Ruth's greatest homer records. Indeed, after Aaron passed Ruth's lifetime homer mark in 1973, four new books on Ruth's life appeared. It was as if a message hurled from Olympus had served notice that the Golden Age gods were angered.

Wesley Branch Rickey was the other member of the Second Golden Age trio of demigods. At first glance the bespectacled, owlish-looking Rickey seemed misplaced in company with the rambunctious Ruth and the lawgiver Landis. So it was with the Olympian Vulcan, whose skillful fashioning of weapons used by the gods transcended his unimpressive appearance. Indeed, Rickey had a penchant for wearing rumpled clothes and for chain-smoking cigars, affectations that oddly enhanced the image of this great baseball innovator.

Howard Ehmke, a surprise starter at the age of thirty-five, won the 1929 Series opener for the Athletics. The A's took the Series 4-1 against the Cubs. (Courtesy Michael Mumby Collection)

Born of pious Methodist parents in 1881, Rickey grew up on an Ohio farm, where he was imbued with an appetite for hard work and pledged never to drink, to swear, or to profane the Sabbath. Happily, a tolerance for sports on the part of his parents gentled his austere upbringing, enabling this gifted student-athlete to pay his way through college and law school by coaching baseball. An average catcher, he reached the majors in 1904, but poor health and limited ability ended his playing career in 1907. Still, that was time enough for his knowledge of the game and his coaching talent to excite official interest.

In 1912 the Browns handed him a $7,500 annual contract to scout and develop young players. By discovering and cataloging hundreds of young players, Rickey devised his lifelong philosophy that in quantity there is quality. Determined to keep the most promising players, Rickey conceived the idea of stocking them on minor league teams that were wholly or partly owned by the major league team. While this scheme revived the discredited "farming systems" of the 1890s, Rickey gave it a new twist, building an efficient network that supplied a steady source of championship-caliber talent for his St. Louis Cardinals.

Following a dispute with the Browns' owner and time out for World War I service, Rickey joined the moribund Cardinals in 1919 as president and team manager. With a three-year contract that also guaranteed him a percentage from any player sales, Rickey perfected his farm system scheme and soon waxed moderately wealthy from shares of player sales. Nor did his Cardinals ever want for good, cheap talent; indeed, after Rickey purchased an established pitcher in 1919, never again during his twenty-five years as a Cardinal executive did he purchase an established big league player. Instead, by dint of advanced scouting and developing methods and at small cost for salaries, Rickey's scouts signed and assigned scores of young players to the Cardinal farm network. There, under a graded system, the young players vied for promotion to the higher leagues; the best moved upward to the Cardinals or were sold at a profit to needy major league teams. For a cash-poor team like the Cards, this system meant freedom from the costly bidding wars of the old system, which had independent minor league operators auctioning stars at steep prices, affordable mainly by well-heeled clubs. Indeed, such was the efficiency of the Cardinal feeder system that critics accused Rickey of cornering the talent market. Partisans of other clubs also envied Rickey's lucrative sales of surplus playing

Jimmy Foxx approaching home plate in the Athletics' 1931 opening game against the Senators in Washington. "Double X" became the regular first baseman for the A's in 1929, when he batted .354. (Courtesy Charles Burkhardt)

talent, which made the Cards a perennially profitable franchise despite the club's poor attendance records.

Among his severest critics, McGraw and Landis denounced Rickey's system as a threat to the independent minors. That it was, but these nostalgists ignored the fact that under independent operations the minors never had been stable, nor was such a prospect likely in the 1920s. By then, impersonal forces like autos, mass newspapers and magazines, movies, and radio had turned Americans' attentions outward, away from local themes. Thus, interest in major league baseball greatly over-shadowed the minors. Mindful of this effect, Rickey argued that, for minor leagues to survive, subvention in the form of major league ownership was crucial. Dissenting, Landis spoke for a minority of owners in branding the farm system scheme as "communistic." Of course, the same epithet might have fit Landis's vague counter-proposal calling for a universal player draft to equalize the talent. Ironically, when faced with acute talent shortages in the 1960s, the majors adopted a draft program that went far beyond Landis's fuzzy proposal. But in the 1920s it was helpful for both the majors and the minors that Rickey's farm system won out. Indeed, other clubs rushed to imitate Rickey, so that by 1939 nearly all minor league teams were controlled by major clubs.

Yet, no imitator ever caught up with the zealous Rickey. Always a step ahead, he first conducted mass tryout camps for young hopefuls; he recognized after World War II that young players, and not returning vets, would carry the game; and he first exploited the vast reservoir of black players. Had Rickey been only an imaginative player recruiter his fame would have been assured, but his extraordinary teaching ability raised him above others. Never a championship manager, Rickey stepped down from his field post in 1925, whereupon with players developed by him the Cardinals won two flags in three years; then, under Rickey as general manager, they reigned as a league power in the 1930s and 1940s. As a player developer, Rickey devised a variety of teaching aids, including sliding pits, batting cages, strike-zone outlines for teaching pitching control, and, later, pitching machines for batting practice. Moreover, Rickey's legendary chalk-talks on tactics and strategy inspired a cadre of disciples, including some who now carry on the Rickey gospel.

In retrospect, baseball's adaptive success owed more to the insightful Rickey than to Landis or Ruth. Like comets, that pair illuminated the Second Golden Age and soon burned out, but Rickey's guiding hand shaped the course of baseball far beyond that era. Although much criticized for pinch-penny practices and for exploiting hungry young players, Rickey planted his ideas of efficient recruitment and player development, which after World War II made him the pioneer in racial integration of the majors. Nor did advancing age dim his genius. He was seventy-eight in 1959 when his Continental League movement threatened to carry major league baseball into the newer urban regions of the land. That abortive threat forced major league owners to expand operations to these sites lest old Rickey do it for them. Like most of his ideas, this one drew critical fire; indeed, fame was granted grudgingly to this creative gadfly. Only after his death in 1965 did baseball men

Manager John McGraw coaching a rookie pitcher during spring training on how to avoid foot-faulting. (Courtesy Dennis Goldstein)

appreciate his ingenious tinkering, and they have yet to exploit enough of his saving ideas.

YANKEE TYRANNY: THE AMERICAN LEAGUE, 1920–1931

Emil ("Irish") Meusel of the Giants, Bob Meusel's brother, scoring the winning run in the final game of the 1922 World Series. Frank Frisch, who scored on the same hit by George Kelly, is behind the umpire. The Yankee catcher is Wally Schang. (Courtesy Michael Mumby Collection)

In the 1920s the star of empire hung over Ruth and the New York Yankees. Led by their big-banging Babe, the Yankees took six American League pennants and three world titles over the years 1920–30. In the entire span of major league history, only Wright's Boston Reds of the 1870s matched this feat of domination. Yet, this was but the beginning of the awesome Yankee hegemony. Thenceforth, each passing decade saw Yankee teams grind rivals beneath their spikes. The 1930s saw the "Bronx Bombers" win five world titles in as many tries; in the 1940s they won four of five attempts; in the 1950s they won six of a possible eight! (Mercifully for American contenders, that was the apogee of the Yankee star of empire. Thereafter, the New Yorkers slipped from being overlords to being mere terrors, winning two world titles in five attempts during the '60s, two of three in the '70s, and one league championship in the first half of the '80s.) Such devastating dominance ruthlessly erased memories of lesser dynasts, such as Wright's Reds, Anson's Colts, Comiskey's Browns, Hanlon's Orioles and Superbas, Selee's Beaneaters, Mack's A's, or McGraw's Giants. Naturally enough, the Yankee teams paid an emotional price for their massacres. By the 1930s Yankee hatred was endemic in the land, with locals turning out in every league city hoping to see the pin-stripers get their comeuppance. Yet, more often than not, the Yankees sent them home in despair.

As early as 1920 some observers predicted a Yankee breakthrough, but nothing of the sort happened. Moreover, since joining the American League in 1903 as the Highlanders, only thrice had the renamed Yankees finished as high as second; usually, they had languished in the second division. As chronic losers, the Yankees looked like ugly ducklings alongside their elite hometown rivals, McGraw's National League Giants. Proud of their status as the winningest team in the majors, the Giants were so smug about their superior drawing power that they had condescendingly allowed the Yanks to become their Polo Grounds tenants.

This embarrassing situation grated on President Ban Johnson. Hoping to turn the tide with a change in ownership, he had encouraged brewer Jacob Ruppert and engineer Tillinghast Huston in 1913 to buy the Yanks from Frank Farrell. Although Johnson rejoiced in landing two wealthy, resolute men, they were ill-matched as partners. For a time they cooperated, but five years of fruitless spending on failed players strained their relationship. Their frequent bickering ended briefly when war service sent Huston to France, although Huston found time to dispatch cabled objections to Ruppert's 1918 choice of Miller Huggins as team manager. Returning home after the Armistice, Huston widened the rift by undercutting Huggins and protesting the hiring of Edward G. Barrow as general manager. Nor did Huston like Ruppert's choice of a site for a proposed new stadium.

The Giants precipitated the owners' stadium quarrel by refusing to extend the Yankees' tenancy lease. But if the Giants hoped to cripple the Yankees by exploiting the ownership rift, they were misguided. Relenting, Huston gave expert engineering advice on constructing the new stadium, which rose in full view of the Polo Grounds with the Harlem River between the two edifices. Thus, in 1923 the Yankees occupied Yankee Stadium, a $2 million citadel that came to be known far and wide as "the house that Ruth built." By then the Yankee ownership crisis had ended; Ruppert solved it by buying out Huston for $1.5 million. The settlement freed Ruppert's lieutenants, Huggins and Barrow, to do their best, and the aristocratic Ruppert, who never called an employee by his first name, let it be known that he expected championship results.

Ruppert could be forgiven his impatience. Prior to 1920 his eight years as a Yankee owner had produced only two winning seasons. In 1919 the purchase of pitcher Carl Mays from Boston produced one of these, and attendance rose to 619,000. Then in 1920 Ruppert stunned the baseball world by paying Boston $125,000 for Ruth. Though it was a much-criticized move, detractors shut up when Ruth smashed 54 homers, and an unprecedented 1,289,000 fans jammed the Polo Grounds for Yankee home games.

Indeed, few American League campaigns provided more drama than the 1920 race. All season long the Indians, White Sox, and Yankees flailed away, and the struggle ended with but three games separating the third-place Yanks from the winning Indians. While glittering performances marked the struggle, it was marred by woeful tragedy. On the bright side, Cleveland playing manager Tris Speaker's .388 batting inspired his team to a .303 team batting average. This attack neutralized the 115 homers slugged by the Yanks and .294 hitting by the White Sox; still, it took superb pitching from Jim Bagby (31-12) and Stan Coveleskie (24-14) to carry the Indians to the top.

On the darker side, such performances were upstaged by a pair of tragedies. In mid-August one of Yankee pitcher Carl Mays's "submarine" fastballs struck Ray Chapman of the Indians on the head; the next morning the young shortstop died. A shocking tragedy, Chapman's death established the Indians as sentimental favorites. Respond-

Melvin T. ("Mel") Ott, who joined the Giants in 1926 to spend twenty-two years with them as outfielder and manager. His career batting average of .304, with 511 homers, won this left-handed slugger early election to the Hall of Fame. (Courtesy Michael Mumby Collection)

Giants' star infield of 1924: from left, Heinie Groh, third base; Travis Jackson, shortstop; Frankie Frisch, second base; George Kelly, first base. (Courtesy Dennis Goldstein)

Harold Joseph ("Pie") Traynor, a main-stay of the Pirates as third baseman, player-manager, and manager from 1920 to 1939. A brilliant fielder, he had a lifetime batting average of .320. (Courtesy John Thorn)

ing courageously, they struggled on, leading the second-place White Sox by half a game with three games left to play. Then, like a fast-breaking summer storm, a second tragedy opened the way to Cleveland's victory. After a month of thundering newspaper revelations telling of the crooked World Series of 1919, Comiskey abruptly suspended his eight accused players. Thus decimated, the Sox lost their final series to the Browns and finished two games behind the Indians. It was a tainted victory, but the Indians made the most of it by downing the Dodgers five games to two in the World Series. After losing two of the first three games, the Indians won the next four; a sparkling unassisted triple play by Indian second baseman Bill Wambsganss in game five provided a memorable highlight to a much-darkened season.

The shocking news of the Black Sox sellout had some alarmists forecasting an attendance recession for 1921. They were wrong; Commissioner Landis's pitiless banishment of the accused players appeased public blood lust, and Ruth's homer barrages dispersed much of the remaining stench. With Ruth poling 59 homers in 1921, American League attendance held firm, demonstrating how easily Ruthomania displaced Black Sox–phobia. Of course, New York fans were the most rabid Ruth worshippers, lacking only a Yankee pennant to complete their joy. To insure that outcome, general manager Barrow turned once again to Boston and to his financially strapped ex-boss, owner Harry Frazee. Mostly for cash, Frazee sold catcher Wally Schang, pitcher Waite Hoyt, and utility infielder Mike McNally to the Yanks. Barrow then lured veteran Frank Baker from retirement to fill a gap at third base. Thus, with Wally Pipp at first, Aaron Ward at second, and Roger Peckinpaugh at short, the infield was set. With sophomore Bob Meusel coming on strong with a .318 batting average and 24 homers, the outfield was even better. As for pitching, Hoyt buttressed the veteran staff, which included Mays, Bob Shawkey, Harry Collins, and Jack Quinn.

Unleashed, this augmented team met its expectations. To his homerics, Ruth added a .378 average and 170 RBIs, and the team averaged .300. Mays led the league with 27 wins and Hoyt won 19 as the Yankees defeated the Indians by 4½ games. That left one remaining hurdle—the tough task of beating their local rivals, the Giants, in the World Series. Indeed, the Yanks won the first two games, but a leg injury sidelined Ruth, and McGraw's men rallied to win the match by five games to three.

Yankee hopes for settling the score in 1922 took flight when Ruth and Meusel drew two-month suspensions for defying Landis's ban on postseason barnstorming. To plug the outfield gap till the pair returned, Barrow purchased Whitey Witt from the A's; for added pitching strength Barrow again tapped Frazee, getting Sam Jones and Joe Bush. Later, Frazee also sold shortstop Everett Scott and third baseman Joe Dugan to the Yanks. In the grim struggle with the hard-hitting Browns that marked the 1922 campaign, these newcomers made the difference. By combining for 39 wins, Bush and Jones overcame Mays's slump; Dugan and Scott shored up the infield; and Witt batted .297 as the regular center fielder. After serving their punishment stints, Ruth and Meusel returned to key the offensive, but the lost time cost Ruth the homer title. Moreover, Ruth's unrepentant attitude and his defiance of Huggins's authority undermined team morale. Although the Yanks won the pennant by one game over the Browns, they were manhandled by the Giants in the Series. Except for a tie game, the Giants won all four games; moreover, McGraw humiliated Ruth by calling pitches when he batted and holding the slugger to a meager .118 average.

Ruth was crushed, but such was his charismatic genius that he took his lumps manfully, came back strongly, and regained his lofty stature. Clearly, 1923 was the time for his redemption; the new Yankee Stadium was ready, and Ruppert wanted his full measure of glory. Wasting no time, Ruth baptized the citadel on opening day with a game-winning homer before 60,000 fans. After that he batted .393, leading the league in homers and RBIs. That year, only Harry Heilmann's .403 hitting barred Ruth from the Triple Crown, but Heilmann's Tigers, while outhitting the Yanks, finished a distant second to the New Yorkers. Yankee pitching told the tale; led by lefty Herb Pennock, yet another Boston acquisition, the Yankee staff was the league's best, as was the team's defense. Clinching early, the well-rested Yankees awaited a third Series test against their Giant tormentors. It looked bad for the Yankees as they lost the first two; however, Ruth blasted three homers to pace a four-game sweep that carried the team to its first world title.

This timely victory, followed by another Giant loss in the next World Series, completed the Yankee conquest of New York City. That the Yanks failed to win the 1924 American race was Washington's doing. Since owner Clark Griffith's perennially shaky franchise depended mostly on ace pitcher Walter Johnson's drawing power, few experts expected much more from these Senators, who were led by their "boy manager," second baseman Stanley ("Bucky") Harris. However, outfielders Sam Rice and Leon ("Goose") Goslin keyed a .294 offensive; veterans Harris, Joe Judge, and Roger Peckinpaugh provided a stout infield defense; and Johnson, Tom Zachary, and reliefer Firpo Marberry accounted for the league's stingiest pitching. When a rash of sore arms crippled Yankee hurlers, the Senators moved up; from seventh in May they climbed to the top in the September stretch and edged the Yankees by two games. The popular victory heaped glory on Walter Johnson (the league's Most Valuable Player) and "boy wonder" Harris. Still, the Senators entered the Series as underdogs to the Giants. The Senators thrice rallied to square the Series, however, and in the final game the indomitable Johnson came on in relief to record his first Series pitching victory. A missed pop foul and an erratically bouncing grounder that went for a hit gave the Senators the twelfth-inning run they needed to win the decisive game. Although nobody then knew it, this fourth straight Series appearance by the star-crossed Giants would be their last under McGraw's leadership.

The stars favored the Senators, who won again in 1925. Over the winter, veterans "Dutch" Reuther and Stan Coveleskie were obtained to shore up the pitching; along with Johnson and Marberry they accounted for another league-leading effort. In support, Rice, Goslin, and Judge again keyed a formidable (.303) batting attack. Even so, most experts predicted a Yankee victory; however, Ruth was felled by serious

James LeRoy ("Sunny Jim") Bottomley, regular Cardinal first baseman, 1923–32. He led the National League in RBIs and doubles in 1926; in triples, homers, and RBIs in 1928. (Courtesy Charles Burkhardt)

illness. Returning, he slumped badly and behaved worse; by season's end he was chastised by the club, which fined him $5,000 and suspended him. On top of this, attrition struck down other men, forcing Huggins to rebuild the infield with rookies Lou Gehrig, Mark Koenig, and Tony Lazzeri. Out of contention early, the Yanks dropped to seventh, leaving only Mack's rising Athletics to challenge the Senators. The Mackmen finished 8½ games behind the Senators, who proceeded to squander a 3-1 lead in World Series games and go on to suffer a humiliating loss to the Pirates.

Although the 1926 Senators seemed ripe for the plucking, only one expert, Fred Lieb, picked the Yankees to win. Eyeing such rising A's stars as pitcher Lefty Grove and slugger Al Simmons, most others picked this team. Ruth, they said, was washed up, but they misjudged his resilience. Contrite, he worked to atone for his latest failing and succeeded brilliantly; if afterwards he still followed his fun-loving paths, at least he never again plumbed such depths as in 1925. Bouncing back, Ruth batted .372 and regained his homer and RBI crowns. Joining him, Gehrig, Lazzeri, Meusel, and young Earl Combs headed a .289 batting attack that more than compensated for average pitching. In beating Cleveland by three games and the A's by six, the Yanks won the pennant, but lost a hard-fought seven-game Series struggle to the Cardinals.

Battle-hardened, the Yanks returned to action in 1927 and mounted the most murderous assault of this century. In crushing their closest rivals, the A's, by 19 games, they won 110 games. Dominating all major categories, they led in batting (.307), homers (158), triples (105), and pitching (ERA, 3.20). Leading the offensive, Ruth crashed 60 homers, a record that stood until 1961; Gehrig batted .373 and drove in 175 runs; pitcher Pennock led in victories (22) and ERA (2.63). Arrayed against the Pirates in the World Series, the Yankee juggernaut swept all four games.

They made it three pennants in a row in 1928, although this time the A's pressed them hard, finishing 2½ behind. Outpitched and nearly outbatted by the Mackmen, Yankee hitting was decisive: Ruth led the 133-homer barrage, and his 142 RBIs tied Gehrig; overall the team batted .296. Then, proving that their victory was no fluke, they avenged their 1926 Series defeat by sweeping the Cardinals in the fall classic.

On the face of it, the awesome Yankees left little hope for outsiders, but the balance of power was shifting. At Philadelphia a new dynasty was aborning as Mack gathered his forces for 1929. Paced by slugger Al Simmons, teamed with Bing Miller and Mule Haas, the Athletic outfield matched any rival's; at first base, slugger Jimmy Foxx, Simmons's equal at bat, anchored an infield completed by Max Bishop, Joe Boley, and Sam Hale. Catcher Mickey Cochrane was the league's best; a .331 hitter and shrewd handler of pitchers, he backed a great pitching quartet of Lefty Grove, George Earnshaw, Rube Walberg, and Ed Rommel. Paced by Grove, the Athletics' pitching ERA of 3.44 was the league's best. Although outhit and outhomered by others, the A's won 104 games to lap the Yanks by 18. In the World Series the A's dueled manager Joe McCarthy's hard-hitting Cubs, downing the Chicagoans in

Player-manager Rogers Hornsby of the Cardinals visits with player-manager George Sisler of the Browns before a 1926 World Series game in St. Louis. Between the future Hall of Famers is Dick Sisler, destined to become a major leaguer twenty years later. (Courtesy Dennis Goldstein)

five games, including one momentous victory that saw the A's overcome an 8-0 deficit with a 10-run inning.

The Athletics' dazzling 1929 victory was the first of three consecutive conquests, which unfortunately coincided with the onset of the Great Depression. By 1932 baseball felt the crushing impact of the widespread income decline that was precipitated; meanwhile, Mack suffered attendance reverses in 1930–31 that blighted his victories. In 1930 Simmons batted a league-leading .381 to pace the A's to an easy eight-game pennant victory over Washington; they followed with a 4-2 conquest of the Cardinals in the World Series. In 1931 the A's exceeded their 1929 effort, winning 107 to land a third straight pennant. However, this time the Cardinals, dubbed the "gas house gang" for their Depression austerities, beat Mack's team in a seven-game World Series. For Mack this loss was doubly depressing, for it was accompanied by serious attendance losses. After another year the desperate Mack would again sell off star players for cash. In the past this measure had worked by allowing Mack to ride out the economic storm and then rebuild. This time, however, the enduring Depression, followed by four years of world war, was too much of an obstacle for the aging leader to overcome. Meanwhile, as baseball battled to survive the Depression's onslaught, the immediate glory belonged to the more prosperous owners of the Yankees and Tigers.

IN RUTH'S SHADOW: NATIONAL LEAGUE CHAMPIONS, 1920–1931

It must not be supposed that all power and glory belonged to the American League in this era. On the contrary, National Leaguers gave their rivals as good as they got. Although American teams won seven of twelve Series duels and American batters outhit the Nationals in six of ten seasons, in other important performance areas the Nationals outdid their rivals. Astonishingly, one of these areas was annual homer production. Despite the apparent Yankee patent on the big bang style, National sluggers consistently outslugged their American rivals. For nine consecutive seasons (1922–30) they did so, and most often decisively, notably in 1930 when their 892 blasts topped the Americans' total by more than 300. Moreover, the Nationals mounted a better-balanced homer attack, as more teams weighed in on the slugging. Thus, on nineteen occasions National teams each struck more than 100 a season, including a record 171 blasts by the Cubs in 1930. True, no National team matched the Yankee consistency in topping the 100 mark each season, but neither did other American teams; during the 'Twenties only six others ever posted seasonal marks of a hundred or more. Nor did American batters equal the seasonal batting averages of .294 and .303 racked up by National hitters in 1929–30; nor did American League pitchers match the ERAs of National hurlers. Nevertheless, such figures testifying to National strength pale before the mythical aura that surrounded Ruth, his Yankees, and Connie Mack's Athletics of the Second Golden Age.

Ironically, McGraw, the canny Giant manager, saw Ruth's potential early; failing to pry him loose from Boston, McGraw set his sights on getting second baseman Rogers Hornsby from the Cardinals. In 1919 he

Paul and Lloyd Waner, who starred in the Pirates' outfield from the mid-1920s until 1940. Paul led the National League in hitting during three seasons, and Lloyd was never far behind. Both were elected to the Hall of Fame. (Courtesy Dennis Goldstein)

offered Rickey $250,000 for Hornsby, a sum greater than what the Yanks paid for Ruth the following year. Still, he would have been well worth the price; in 1920–25 the versatile right-handed hitter won six National batting titles, including two Triple Crowns, while *averaging* close to .400! Indeed, Hornsby in a Giant uniform might have prevented Ruth from monopolizing the headlines in New York. The proposal fell through, however; Rickey was tempted, but McGraw refused to yield to the demand that he throw in Frank Frisch as part of the deal.

After this failure, McGraw turned to the Braves, Phillies, and Reds for deals that landed pitcher Art Nehf, shortstop Dave Bancroft, third baseman Henry ("Heinie") Groh, and outfielders Emil ("Irish") Meusel and Casey Stengel. Blending these newcomers with a homebound nucleus of outfielder Ross ("Pep") Youngs, first baseman George Kelly, second baseman Frank Frisch, catcher Frank Smith, and a veteran pitching staff, McGraw forged a winning dynasty that snared four consecutive pennants. But if McGraw equaled a mark of the 1880s with his four straight flags, Rickey's decision to keep Hornsby paid the Cardinals a pair of championships.

In 1920 neither of these rivals scaled the heights. That year the rising Giants finished behind manager Wilbert Robinson's Brooklyn team. The Robins' easy seven-game victory resulted from league-leading pitching and .277 batting. They fell to the Indians in the World Series, however, and it would be twenty-one years before Dodger fans saw another pennant hoisted at Ebbets Field.

As mediocrity settled over Brooklyn, McGraw's star of empire rose over Manhattan. The next four National pennants went to the Giants, who edged the Pirates by 4 games in 1921, lapped the Reds by 7 in 1922 and by 4½ in 1923, then eked a 1½-game victory over the Dodgers in 1924. In the World Series, the Giants beat the Yanks in 1921 and 1922 but fell to them in 1923 and to the Senators in 1924. The Giants' relentlessly efficient team effort earned McGraw the nickname of the "Napoleonic genius." Over these years his team batted .300, smacked 335 homers, excelled in fielding, and benefited from the effective pitching of Nehf, Phil Douglas, Jack Bentley, and relievers Wilfred ("Rosy") Ryan and Claude Jonnard.

Under ordinary circumstances, such teamwork would have endeared the Giants in the hearts of New Yorkers, but not now. To McGraw's utter frustration, his team was upstaged by his Polo Grounds tenants. Nor did it matter that the Yanks twice lost to the Giants in Series play, as fans clearly preferred their Ruthian delights. Stung by this rebuff, McGraw ended the Yankee lease; however, this proved a blunder when the Yankees opened Yankee Stadium across the river. In that palace's first year, the Yanks won a pennant, outdrew their cross-river rivals, and crushed the Giants in the World Series. From then on the Yankees were the number one team in New York City; for McGraw, who resisted stoutly, his luck was running out. Even the presence of a new slugger, first baseman Bill Terry, and a chance to upstage the Yankees in 1924 backfired. After the Giants won a fourth straight pennant by the narrowest of margins, McGraw's joy turned to ashes; the victory was tainted by rumors of game-fixing by Giant personnel. So pervasive was the stench that Landis nearly canceled the World Series. In retrospect, McGraw would have been better off if it had been canceled. Forced to battle the popular Senators, the maligned Giants squandered a 3-2 lead in games, losing the seventh game when a missed foul fly and a crazily bouncing ball handed the Senators the run they needed to win the title. On this sour, fateful note, McGraw's fortunes sank; he never again managed a championship team.

The following year failing health took its toll on the Giants, sapping McGraw's strength and felling coach Hugh Jennings and outfielder Ross Youngs. Seizing an opportunity, the Pirates took the lead, and on the strength of .307 team batting and 159 stolen bases, they lapped the Giants by 8½ games. Three future Hall of Famers, third baseman Hal ("Pie") Traynor, Max Carey, and Hazen ("Ki-Ki") Cuyler, starred with the 1925 Pirates, but this was a clique-ridden team. Although they rose dramatically from a 3-1 deficit to beat the Senators in the World Series, they looked like one-shot champions.

Indeed, the 1926 Pirates fell to the Cardinals, Rickey's handcrafted club that would win nine pennants over the next twenty years. By 1926 Rickey's farm system sent stars like first baseman Jim Bottomley, short-stop Tom Thevenow, and outfielders Chick Hafey and Taylor Douthit to the Cards. Veteran pitchers Flint Rhem, Jess Haines, Bill Sherdel, and Grover Cleveland Alexander steadied a team now managed by superstar second baseman Rogers Hornsby. Over the past six seasons Hornsby's six batting crowns cast him as the best right-handed batter in baseball history. Now the newly installed playing manager of the Cardinals, he led them to a memorable victory over the Yankees in the 1926 World Series, a tussle that lasted seven games. For all that, Hornsby was a marked man; the dictatorial style of this blunt, outspoken perfectionist had alienated his players and his bosses. Fed up with his prima donna antics, Rickey noted the Rajah's "slumping" batting effort of .317 and swapped him to the Giants for Frank Frisch. The move infuriated Cardinal fans, who roasted Rickey throughout the 1927 season as the Cards lost a close race to the Pirates.

In his Giant flannels Hornsby had little reason to gloat. Although he won the batting title, the Giants finished third; afterwards, for defying McGraw, the testy star was packed off to the Braves. Meanwhile, the reformed Pirates edged the Cardinals by a game and a half. Revamped by manager Donie Bush, who added the hard-hitting Waner brothers, Paul and Lloyd, to his outfield, the 1927 Pirates batted .305. Up against the Yankee colossus, however, they were crushed in four straight games in the Series; following that defeat, the Pirates waited more than thirty years before unfurling another championship flag.

Not so with the Cardinals, who rose up again in 1928 but who then received the same treatment from the Yankees in the Series. This was a more resilient Cardinal team. Managed by Bill McKechnie, the 1928 Cards held off the Giants to win by two games. "Sunny Jim" Bottomley's .325 batting, which included 31 homers and 136 RBIs, led the team's .281 offensive. For losing the Series, however, McKechnie was sacked.

Scapegoating the manager failed to fire up the Cardinal team in 1929. That year three managers, including the recalled McKechnie,

Rogers Hornsby showing his perfectionist style at bat. Ranked as the greatest right-handed batter in baseball history, Hornsby thrice topped the .400 batting mark, and in 1924 he set the modern record of .424 while playing with the Cardinals. (Courtesy George Brace)

managed only a fourth-place finish. In Chicago, however, the Cubs were touting their manager as a genius. Never a major league player, Joe McCarthy earned his spurs in the minors. Tapped to manage the Cubs, he speedily transformed a loser into a contender. In 1929 his power-packed team, which blended peripatetics Hornsby and Ki-Ki Cuyler with the likes of Riggs Stephenson and Hack Wilson, stormed to victory by 10½ games. But like the stock market that fall, they fell resoundingly, losing the Series to Mack's Athletics in five games.

For that McCarthy was scapegoated, but he soon surfaced as the manager of a reviving Yankee powerhouse. Meanwhile, his departure failed to redeem the 1930 Cubs, who lost a close race to the Cardinals. Managed now by ex-catcher Charles ("Gabby") Street, the Cards won two in a row. Newcomers included infielders Frisch, Charley Gelbert, and Earl ("Sparky") Adams, outfielder Johnny ("Pepper") Martin, and pitchers Bill Hallahan, Burleigh Grimes, and Paul Derringer. Otherwise, the team fielded the stars who had scaled the heights in 1928. After edging the Cubs by two games in 1930, a year that saw National League hitters *average* .303, the heavy-hitting Cards lost the World Series in six games to Mack's A's.

It was a different story in 1931. With Street still at the helm, the vengeance-minded Cards repeated; winning 101 games, they lapped the Giants by 13. Then they turned on the A's; with Pepper Martin slashing 12 hits and stealing 5 bases, they won the Series in 7 games. The unexpected Cardinal victory sank the Athletic dynasty. Although Mack never won again, the Cardinals did time and again, thus becoming the winningest National dynasty during the troubled years that followed this passing Golden Age.

THE GOLDEN AGE STYLE

In assaying the human achievements of various times, historians only rarely agree that an era's splendid performances rate the appellation of a "golden age." Among essential qualifications for such an accolade would be brilliant achievements by heroic individuals, realized in unique style, accompanied by intense public acclaim, and showered with rewards. In everyday language these spell cash and glory, which major league baseball obtained in full measure during the 1920s. Thus, like the golden 1880s, the 'Twenties in baseball history deserve a similar accolade.

That cash came from baseball promotion at this time was revealed by attendance figures that surpassed the previous era's by as much as 40 percent. Such gains came early and whetted owner appetites. Indeed, an astonishing attendance breakthrough occurred in 1920, when, for the first season ever, a major league (the American) attracted more than 5 million paying fans. Thenceforth, matching that mark became a goading dream, even as each league usually settled for some 4 million fans a year. Even these shortfalls were profitable, however; in 1929 club receipts peaked at $17 million for the two leagues, only to turn sharply downward under the Depression's impact.

However, since attendance strength was highest among contending clubs located at the more populous sites, the profits were maldistributed. At this time an annual team profit of $100,000 was considered good, with some favored clubs netting as much as $500,000. In the National League fortune favored the Giants, Dodgers, Pirates, and Cardinals, with the Braves and Phillies on the least profitable end of the scale. In the American League the Yanks and Tigers were the plutocrats; the 1927 Yanks accounted for 25 percent of the league's attendance. Not surprisingly, the Yankee presence made for greater imbalance, with the chronically depressed Red Sox leading the losers.

Such disparities arose from the ruthless, dog-in-the-manger attitude of owners who insisted that each home team keep the lion's share of gate receipts. Moreover, imbalance resulted from the continuing existence of ramshackle parks like the Phillies' Baker Bowl, which housed only 18,000; the limited number of charismatic stars like Ruth, Cobb, and Hornsby; and such perennial pennant monopolists as the Yankees, Giants, Cardinals, and A's. One might think that prosperity would have driven owners to build new parks, with parking lots to accommodate the suddenly ubiquitous automobiles; however, if such a building boom had occurred, the ensuing Depression would have made white elephants of new parks. As it was, only the Yankees built a grandiose park; capable of seating 70,000, Yankee Stadium stood alone as the symbol of Golden Age munificence.

Dubbed "the house that Ruth built," Yankee Stadium housed the supreme folk hero of the era. With Ruth authoring the big bang style, high-scoring games erased memories of the low-scoring Silver Age. Having found a successful phenomenon, clubs have clung to the big bang style ever since, except for the ersatz years of World War II. Certainly, the slugging style made for higher-scoring games. In the deadball era, runs scored per game averaged fewer than four; with pitching dominant, clubs relied more on base stealing, as evidenced by seasonal averages of more than a thousand thefts a year. But the big bang changed all that. Over the years 1920–31 runs scored per game averaged nearly five, and annual base-stealing totals shrank to 750. Homer production, averaging over 500 a year, made the difference.

In accounting for the sudden appearance of slugging players, one must not suppose that players suddenly waxed bigger and stronger. True, the new emphasis had scouts searching for muscular giants, but guile and technology did just as much to foster the slugging style. Sensing that fans preferred the big bang, canny owners moved outfield fences closer to home plate to accommodate slugging. As for technology, livelier balls and tapered "whippy" bats abetted the new style. Moreover, new balls were now more frequently inserted to replace scuffed ones, and the ban on spitters and doctored balls robbed pitchers of an effective countermeasure. Not surprisingly, pitchers were more frequently battered, so much so that an ERA of 4.00 was now considered adequate for a pitcher. To cope with the homerics, managers now used more pitchers, employing seven-man staffs and using relievers to bail out starters. The trend was more noticeable in the American League, where ERAs were higher; there, teams like the Senators and Yanks employed specialized relievers. Thus, Firpo Marberry and Wilcy Moore heralded a coming bullpen revolution, but most clubs continued to use starters or marginal pitchers for relief chores. All in all, pitchers

Lewis ("Hack") Wilson, Cub outfielder, and Fred ("Cy") Williams, Phillie outfielder, when they tied for the National League home run championship in 1927, with 30 each. Williams had been number one in 1923, with 41 homers; Wilson far surpassed this in 1930, with 56. (Courtesy Dennis Goldstein)

had a right to complain, as shutouts became rarer and 40- and even 30-game winners virtually disappeared. Yet by dint of learning deceptive deliveries like sliders, knucklers, sinkers, and screwballs, and occasionally smuggling in forbidden deliveries, good pitchers adapted.

On balance, it was the big bang that propelled baseball into this new Golden Age. Certainly, the power game appealed to fans, creating a second honeymoon for baseball just about the time that rival spectacles like boxing, football, basketball, and tournament golf and tennis became distractions. Of course, there was no wooing fans from movies, autos, and radios, the three greatest leisure innovations of this era. Yet even these proved to be more blessing than curse for the game. While America's love affair with autos contributed to the accelerating decline of minor and sandlot leagues, the majors benefited, as autos carried fans from suburbs and exurbs to urban parks, where they often created fearsome parking problems.

Despite Luddite owner fears, radio proved just as promising. Like their tremulous nineteenth century forebears who at first saw threats in newspaper coverage and telegraph-board descriptions of games, this generation trembled at the prospect of radio making a free show of games. In time the airing of games proved to be a stimulant for live attendance, but radio baseball did create serious competition for newspaper reporters. Still, regardless of the weal and woe resulting from radio baseball, it was too powerful a force to restrain; by 1925 most American households owned sets, and public demand for radio sports soon led to the airing of World Series games. As watchdog over the fall classic, Commissioner Landis brooded over how much to charge for the concession and how to force sportscasters to meet his fussy standards. Owing to radio's newness at this time, no individual clubs let contracts for broadcasts of their seasonal games; what radio income the owners got came only from shared Series revenue, and this was a pittance. Hence, the tapping of radio's wealth awaited the Depression era, when owners relaxed their fears and snapped up offers from local stations.

By then owners also had learned to regard movies as an asset. Newsreels, special features, and baseball themes in regular-length films boosted the game; moreover, films served as useful training aids and public relations devices. Yet if owners now shed some of their fears of

President Herbert Hoover preparing to toss out the first ball in the 1930 season opener between the Red Sox and Senators at Washington. (Courtesy Dennis Goldstein)

radio and movies, they remained cautious; more profitable exploitation of these media—as well as their successor, television—awaited the post–World War II era.

While owners of this era eyed the live gate crowds as their biggest profit source, the ever-larger throngs excited both joy and fear. This dual attitude was understandable, as little was known of crowd psychology. Although less prone to riots and mobbings than baseball crowds of the 1890s, fans occasionally got carried away. Moreover, abusive and unruly types and zany characters existed in any crowd. To keep peace, owners hired police, but players learned to expect some abuse along with cheers.

If students of the 'Twenties believe ballpark fans came solely to see games, they are deluded; indeed, catering to a fan's food-and-drink and souvenir wants could net an owner a tidy profit. That more money might be made via night baseball was a possibility unexploited by any major league owner of this time, although some minor league and Negro league teams played night games. Nor did owners much grasp the fans' wishes for extra entertainment. Back in the 1880s Von der Ahe had done so profitably, and some owners now supplied musical acts, clowns, occasional free lunches, lotteries, fireworks, and the like. At this time the Yankees struck a responsive chord by assigning uniform numbers to players, a sound psychological ploy that had been tried earlier but failed to catch on. By the 1930s all clubs followed the example. However, few owners went far with gimmicks. The mass sale of uniform replicas was unknown, and some owners even resented fans' scrambling to grab and keep foul balls hit into the stands. The tendency for teams to use more balls during games stemmed from the fatal beaning of Roy Chapman in 1920. Following that tragedy officials decided that the traditional practice of retaining scuffed and darkened balls was hazardous to batters; hence, they ordered the frequent replacement of balls, including those hit into the stands. By 1930 fans won the right to keep balls hit into their territory, although some owners mourned the loss of as many as 150 balls by this route during the course of double-headers.

Meanwhile, attending baseball games continued to become more respectable. Following a trend begun by President Taft, American presidents found it politically expedient to attend key games, such as opening day at Washington's Griffith Stadium or one of the World Series games. Sometimes fans turned on them, however; while attending one of the 1929 Series games, Hoover was blasted by angry shouts of "We Want Beer," and at the 1932 Series fans jeered him as the Depression's blamesake. Such outbursts bespoke the troubled marriage between baseball and politics, a bond that might bring weal or woe to either partner.

When not booing presidents, players, or owners, fans reveled in the exploits of player-heroes who glorified these times. Babe Ruth, of course, predominated, extending his charismatic presence by means of barnstorming games, movies, vaudeville appearances, endorsements, and ghosted books and articles. Such was his stature that he was said to be the most recognized American of the times. Of lesser magnitude were stars like Ty Cobb, who finished his brilliant career owning the highest batting average, the most hits and stolen bases, and other mosts of any player; not far behind him was Hornsby, winner of two Triple Crowns in this era, who owned the second highest batting average when he retired in the 1930s. These were titans, but sluggers Jimmy Foxx, Al Simmons, Hack Wilson, and Chuck Klein, and dependable hitters like Harry Heilmann, Edd Roush, or the Waner brothers, also were to be counted among the immortals. Likewise, stalwart pitchers like Johnson, Alexander, Grimes, Pennock, Grove and Dazzy Vance were popular heroes.

For consistently performing in splendid fashion, these men became consensus heroes, but the varying tastes of fans allowed for a bewildering variety of lesser heroes, villains, and fools. Reflecting the immigration waves that lent a rich diversity to the American population, fans naturally sought heroes of similar backgrounds. Indeed, this age spawned the myth that immigrant sons were taking over baseball; as one fearful writer, noting the numbers of Italian-American players in the ranks, warned, "These Tonies . . . take to baseball quicker than they take to spaghetti." Like this crude gibe the myth was also absurd; obviously the plenitude of ethnic groups made it unlikely that any one would take over. Besides, the pressures of Anglo-conformity persuaded some ethnic stars to anglicize their surnames. Understandably, such changes were made in hopes of escaping ethnic insults from fans, bench jockeys, and reporters. Aside from shared ethnicity, fans identified with players in other ways. Rural fans doted on such stars as Pepper Martin or Walter Johnson; sophisticated urbanites followed preppy-collegiate types like George Earnshaw; and sectionalists, especially those with southern or western backgrounds, had no trouble finding kindred spirits amongst the players.

At the same time, misanthropic fans seeking hate objects made a villain of Carl Mays, who had beaned Ray Chapman; stars like Cobb, Ruth, and Hornsby also served abusive fans, as did any star who had an off-day. Likewise, those fans who enjoyed mocking and ridiculing players found targets in poor fielders like Hack Wilson, braggarts like Art Shires, or boozers like "Shuffling Phil" Douglas.

As ever, umps were targeted for ritualized abuse. Although they caught flak from all sides, at least the new double-umpire system afforded bluecoats some safety in numbers. Moreover, umps now benefited from better support from league officials, who backed the fines and disciplinary measures meted out by umps. More encouragingly, the standards set by heroic umps like Bill Klem, a doughty martinet who worked thirteen full seasons behind the plate, or reliable Tom Connally boosted the status of umpires.

Of course, no umpire of this age enjoyed such plaudits as players received. In this era fans opened their hearts to players and placed them onstage as never before. Extended newspaper coverage, replete with action photos and feature articles, exalted players, as did books, magazines, radio, and films. Worshipping reporters contributed by coining heroic nicknames for stars. Such deification was a heady experience for players; if some found it hard to match their folk-hero images, at least they enjoyed the acclaim. Better still, salaries rose to unprecedented levels. Ruth was the propelling force moving salaries upward. When he signed for $80,000 for the 1930 season, he set a salary record that was

Robert (Bob) Hart

(Barry) McCormick

Ernest C. (Ernie) Quigley

Frank Wilson

J. Monroe Sweeney

Robert D. (Bob) Emslie

Charles (Cy) Pfirman

William J. (Bill) Klem

Jack Powell

Henry (Hank) O'Day

Charles B. (Uncle Charlie) Moran

Umpires of the Second Golden Age in a 1924 International News Service photographic collage, published in the *Philadelphia Bulletin*. (Courtesy Photojournalism Collection, Temple University Libraries)

unmatched until the post–World War II era. What's more, Ruth's endorsement income surpassed his baseball earnings. Buoyed by Ruth's example, stars like Cobb and Hornsby each collected as much as $40,000 a year; lesser stars like Dazzy Vance got $25,000; the average salary of the 1924 Yankee team was $12,000. No wonder one Yankee exulted, "It's great to be young and a Yankee." The bottom line showed ordinary players of this era collecting salaries equal to those of superstars of the 1880s. In 1923 the average salary was $5,000; in 1924, $6,000; in 1930, $7,000. With little exaggeration, *The Sporting News* in 1925 proclaimed player salaries to be the equal of most professions, and if a player happened to play for a winning World Series team in this era, he could count on getting at least $5,000 more.

Like mythical Sirens, such baseball dollars lured hordes of young hopefuls who aspired to beat the brutal odds against making it to the majors. Most never even got to the minor leagues, where teams increasingly became part of a major club's farm system. This was Rickey's doing, and other baseball executives followed suit, hiring specialists to oversee player recruitment. Ever the innovator, Rickey hired and trained more scouts, using them to run tryout camps where hopefuls were invited to show their stuff. It was Rickey's belief that quality was to be found amidst quantity, but even many of the chosen saw their dreams dashed by poor pay and inability to rise to the majors.

While Rickey's pinch-penny salary schedule took advantage of young players' ambition to reach the majors, Landis's racist stance brutally robbed black players of any hopes of playing in the majors. Convinced that blacks had no place in the white majors, Landis even frowned on exhibition games played between white major leaguers and black major leaguers, especially since black teams frequently bested the whites. Convinced that the walls of discrimination would not fall down, in 1920 Andrew ("Rube") Foster founded the Negro National League, which lasted until 1948. When the games attracted sizable crowds, some players in the white majors booked exhibition games against their black counterparts, despite Landis's disapproval, and some white owners profited by renting their grounds to black teams. In 1923 another black major league, the Eastern Colored League, appeared, enabling the champs of these two black majors to meet in the annual Negro World Series. When the Eastern Colored League folded in 1928, a Negro American League took the field in 1929. Although this venture also folded, it was revived in 1937 and lasted until 1950. Overall, these were shaky ventures; black major leagues suffered heavily from segregation and from the impact of the Depression. As a result, black players saw little of the cash and glory that blessed the white majors. Nevertheless, stars like shortstop John Henry Lloyd, pitcher Leroy ("Satchel") Paige, and young catcher Josh Gibson delighted black fans. Unquestionably, if their skins had been white, these and others would have held their own in the white majors. Forced to play in segregated major leagues, such unsung heroes at least inspired black hopefuls to pursue baseball careers. More than any other single individual, Rube Foster was the administrative genius who kept such hopes alive. His untimely death in 1930 was a cruel blow to this cause.

That same year the gathering storm of the Great Depression dealt harsher blows to all baseball operations. As hard times descended, the Second Golden Age ended. As chronic depression blighted the land, major league baseball faced economic austerities followed by equally trying wartime austerities.

6

SURMOUNTING DEPRESSION AND GLOBAL WAR

ORGANIZED BASEBALL, ALONG WITH OTHER AMERI-can institutions, reeled under the staggering blows of the Great Depression and World War II during the decade and a half from 1930 to 1945. Baseball, like the nation, came through this challenging era with remarkable strength—thanks to American ingenuity, resilience, and luck.

The stock market crash of October 29, 1929, was the most dramatic in a series of blows to the economy of the United States and the world. For organized baseball, a gradual but substantial decline in attendance was the most serious Depression problem. Retrenchment in business spending, on such items as entertainment and radio broadcasts, was another problem. Declining income among individuals—whether from layoffs, wage cuts, or investment losses and business failures—led to cuts in recreational spending. Such cuts became more likely as prospects for restored income dimmed. Spending on ball games and other recreation depends on confidence that the money spent will soon be

Bucky Harris and Joe Cronin were unaware, in this 1934 photograph, of the roles they were slated to play in a Depression drama. Cronin (right), "boy manager" of the pennant-winning Senators in 1933, was about to be sold to the Red Sox by his financially pinched father-in-law, Clark Griffith. Harris, "boy manager" of the Senators in the 1920s, was about to return to Griffith's declining empire after five seasons with the Tigers and one with the Red Sox. (Courtesy Mike Andersen)

Jimmy Foxx looks happy in his Red Sox uniform, though Athletics fans were shocked in 1935 when Connie Mack took needed cash for his slugging first baseman. "Double X" played six and a half seasons with the Red Sox after his decade with the A's. (Courtesy Herman Seid)

replenished. Optimism, the prevailing mood of the Golden 'Twenties, was a boon to professional baseball.

Optimism declined in the early 1930s as the economy slid downhill, revived in 1933–35 during the early New Deal, faltered when the New Deal proved less than a cure-all, and rose steadily after the United States became the "arsenal of democracy" in 1939. Although World War II brought tragedy for many Americans (even before Pearl Harbor for those with relatives in Europe or Asia), it brought prosperity for most Americans and hope for virtually all. A hopeful climate is healthy for organized baseball.

The fortunes of professional baseball fell and rose with the national economy during the Great Depression and the slow recovery that followed. National income fell from more than $80 billion in 1929 to $50 billion in 1932, while big league baseball attendance dropped from 9.6 million fans to 8.1 million. By 1933 a quarter of the nation's work force had been idled, and major league ballpark turnout had sagged to its low point of 6.3 million. American business as a whole endured a net loss of $5 billion in 1932, while the National and American leagues suffered overall losses of $1 million apiece. New investments in all businesses declined from a grand total of $10 billion in 1929 to $1 billion in 1932, while ballpark improvements ground to a halt.

National recovery came slowly and not always steadily, as was the case with baseball recovery. National income did not reach the 1929 level until 1941. Big league attendance recovered a little faster, surpassing the pre-Depression level in 1940. Business conditions improved after Franklin Delano Roosevelt's inauguration in March 1933 but slumped during the 1937 "Roosevelt recession," not fully recovering until the first war orders arrived from Europe. The National League suffered heavy losses from 1932 through 1934 and did not reach pre-Depression profit levels until after 1941. American League losses started a year earlier than those of the senior circuit, but they were turned around a little sooner. By 1940–41 American League earnings surpassed those of the National clubs.

Although professional baseball was not rescued from the maelstrom of the Great Depression until defense plants started humming, most historians view the New Deal as a life preserver that helped keep American

Commissioner Landis removes Joe Medwick of the Cardinals from the final game of the 1934 World Series at Detroit, over the objections of manager Frank Frisch. Tiger fans, angered by Medwick's aggressive sliding, were pelting him with missiles. The Cards, with Dizzy Dean pitching, won the game and the Series. (Courtesy Michael Mumby Collection)

society afloat, sports and all. It may be that only a little income from "work-relief" programs—Works Progress, Farm Security, Social Security, and Civilian Conservation—went to ballparks, but it is likely that ball games were patronized by some businessmen and skilled workers who benefited from "pump-priming" and public works. The Public Works Administration began the tradition of federal aid to municipally financed ballparks when it helped build Cleveland's Municipal Stadium. Above all, FDR's personal popularity—despite constant and vocal detractors—helped to restore the optimistic climate required by the national pastime. "The Chief's" Fireside Chats could be regarded as keeping the airwaves open for World Series broadcasts by Graham McNamee and Red Barber.

A young baritone singer, McNamee had come to New York in 1923 and landed an announcing job with station WEAF. McNamee's rich voice and varied experience as a high school athlete served him well when he was assigned to broadcast a championship fight and the World Series that same year. With no guidelines to follow, McNamee drew upon his school days as a boxer and baseball player (he also had played hockey, basketball, and football). An honest announcer, McNamee acknowledged his mistakes; his candor and his enthusiastic descriptions made him a colossal favorite with radio listeners. The NBC network assigned him to broadcast every World Series from 1923 through 1934. But McNamee was handed so many diverse assignments, including covering ten different sports as well as operas and political conventions, that he was burned out by the mid-1930s. Red Barber, who succeeded him as a World Series commentator in 1935, readily acknowledged his debt to this pioneer. Barber even remembered McNamee's generous appraisal of the newcomer's microphone work during the 1935 Series. "Kid," said McNamee to Barber, "kid, you've got it."

Dick Sisler signs on with the Cardinal farm system in 1939, while Branch Rickey points to the dotted line and father George smiles approval. George Sisler's former club, the Browns, became more impoverished than ever during the 'Thirties. (Courtesy Dennis Goldstein)

BASEBALL'S SURVIVAL MEASURES IN THE DEPRESSION DECADE

Retrenchment was the initial response of most ball clubs to Depression losses in income and profit. Budget cuts were made in payroll, player development, scouting, and park improvement. Some clubs sold major assets—namely, proven or promising players. A few clubs, whose owners had outside wealth, bought stars sold by their distressed competitors. Finally, in the mid-1930s, halfway through the Great Depression, organized baseball's emphasis shifted from retrenchment to market expansion. Night baseball catered to fans with daytime working hours, while radio broadcasting contracts not only generated fees but also stimulated ballpark attendance.

Owners in both leagues employed a variety of austerity measures. Some, whose livelihood depended on baseball earnings, slashed budgets ruthlessly. Thus, Connie Mack sold his stars for cash and replaced them with lower-paid ordinaries; for this he took his lumps on the field and at the turnstiles. So did Clark Griffith of the Senators; after winning the 1933 American League pennant and luring only 437,533 home fans, Griffith soon sold three stars for cash. In his major cash coup, Griffith sold Joe Cronin, his son-in-law and star shortstop, to the Red Sox for $250,000.

Other clubs suffered as much, if not more. In 1934 the World Champion Cardinals drew only 325,056 paying customers, while the Tigers, who had lost to them in the Series, drew 910,000. In three other seasons the Cards drew fewer than 300,000 annually. Yet even they fared better than the Braves, Phillies, and Pirates. Of this trio, the Pirates rebounded after five losing seasons, but the Braves and Phillies never recovered until the 'Forties. After 1933 the Braves' best attendance year was 385,339 fans; as for the Phillies, at no time in the decade did they lure as many as 300,000 a season. To cope, the penurious owners of these two clubs took to playing untried players and selling those who blossomed for much-needed cash. Incredibly, even these flesh merchants did better than the St. Louis Browns. Overshadowed by the Cards at home, the Browns' best seasonal attendance in this decade was 239,591 in 1940. In no other year did they draw as many as 200,000, and thrice they failed to lure even 100,000 in a season. Small wonder then that the Browns were reduced to accepting subsidies from the American League.

In employing such tactics as selling off stars for cash, cutting budgets for scouting and player development, and cutting promotional and maintenance costs, owners acted out of desperation, hoping to ride out the hard times and rebuild; however, they underestimated the length of the Depression or the lingering impact of their pinch-penny practices. Thus, clubs like the Braves, Browns, and Athletics gained reputations of being chronic losers that were virtually impossible to surmount.

Left:
Joseph Paul ("Joltin' Joe") DiMaggio (right), who began a brilliant career as a Yankee in 1936, with Lou Gehrig. Three years later a fatal illness was to force DiMaggio's revered teammate to hang up his shoes. (Courtesy Herman Seid)

Right:
Robert William Andrew ("Bob") Feller, who signed on with the Indians in 1935 while only seventeen. In the generation from 1936 to 1956, Feller won 266 games and lost only 162. (Courtesy Herman Seid)

Smug hindsight prompts one to say that boldness was the course to pursue. But boldness, defined as willingness to spend money to promote one's team, was a luxury mostly enjoyed by well-heeled owners. Among the boldest of Depression-era spenders was new owner Tom Yawkey of the Boston Red Sox. Yawkey spent over $1 million buying up stars from Mack and Griffith; if his spending failed to buy a championship, at least it undermined the rival Braves by enticing giddy fans to come to Fenway Park. Other owners whose spending paid off in pennants and fan support included Philip K. Wrigley of the Cubs, whose chewing-gum enterprise seemed to be depression-proof; Powel Crosley of the Reds, whose radio industry thrived; and Walter Briggs of the Tigers, an auto executive whose spending not only produced three pennants but also won for him the best seasonal attendance marks at this time. Likewise, the Giants and Yankees, blessed by their location in baseball's most populous area, thrived, as did the Dodgers, who came under new ownership and general management late in the Depression decade. As ever, such clubs demonstrated that contenders and pennant winners were essential to baseball promotion.

Yawkey's lavish spending on established stars was a bold course to follow, but it was by no means the most successful. At St. Louis, Rickey's farm system, which grew to thirty-two clubs by 1939, proved to be an efficient, cost-effective approach to cushioning poor attendance at Cardinal home games. By expanding the number of Cardinal-controlled minor league teams, and by hiring more scouts to sign more youths at low salaries, Rickey could develop and promote the best young players to his Cardinal team and sell his surplus talent at a profit to needy rivals. However, Rickey's farm system faced competition from imitators, notably the Yankees, who employed George Weiss to build a rival system. By hiring canny scouts and effective minor league managers and zealously supervising their activities, Weiss built a farm network that furnished the raw material for a renewed Yankee tyranny. Although other clubs built farm systems, these two were the best of this era; however, when Rickey quit the Cardinals for the Dodgers in 1942, it was only a matter of time before the Dodger farm system would rank among the best.

At a time when player surplus was the rule, some teams benefited by the successful "ivory hunts" of bold talent scouts. Although clubs of this era employed only a handful of paid scouts, some scored memorable coups. In 1935 Cy Slapnicka of the Indians saw and signed Iowa pitcher Bob Feller, a fireballing right-handed pitcher destined for the Hall of Fame. Unfortunately for the Indians' pennant chances, Yankee scouts were equally successful; that same year Bill Essick persuaded the Yankees to spend $25,000 for the contract of a gifted outfielder with a gimpy knee. Thus, Joe DiMaggio joined the Yankees in 1936. Meanwhile, scout Joe Cambria, working for Griffith of Washington, found promising players available for cheap prices in Cuba. In time, Latin America would prove to be a rich lode of player talent.

With little competition as yet from rival professional team sports, baseball enjoyed a talent surplus. With amateur baseball programs thriving, scouts could eye plenty of players, while Rickey, by dint of tryout camps, could ply his thesis that in quantity there is quality. Not

Top:
Night game at Sportsman's Park, St. Louis, in the early 'Forties. Cincinnati's Crosley Field was the scene of the first major league game played under lights, on May 24, 1935. (Courtesy Dennis Goldstein)

Bottom:
New York Giants' Polo Grounds being prepared for night games, as lighting engineers set out "measuring targets" for the proper installation of 836 lights. (Courtesy Dennis Goldstein)

Henry Benjamin ("Hank") Greenberg of the Tigers getting a hit against the Indians. "Hammerin' Hank" led the American League thrice in both homers and RBIs between his first season as a regular in 1933 and his military service in 1941–45. (Courtesy Herman Seid)

surprisingly, qualified ball players who made the majors in this period of austerity were paid less than their forebears of the 1920s. During the Depression decade clubs slashed salaries, and during the war years salaries were frozen. Indeed, total player salaries, budgeted at nearly $4 million in 1929, sagged to $3 million in 1933, and as late as 1939 still fell below the 1929 figure.

In individual terms, the average player salary of $7,500 in 1929 skidded to $6,009 in 1933, and climbed back to $7,306 in 1939. Compared to the wages of American industrial workers, however, this was princely pay for the times; such workers averaged $1,421 in 1929, $1,064 in 1933, and $1,269 in 1939. At this time an estimated 35 percent of a club's income went to salaries. During World War II, however, this figure fell below 30 percent and thenceforth remained below that figure.

On the revenue side, income was coming from sources other than attendance. In this era owners wrung more money from concessions; by 1939 such income amounted to 7 percent of a club's total income. Also, income from the sale of radio broadcast rights was rising; from a negligible 0.3 percent in 1930, radio fees rose to 7.3 percent of a club's total income by 1939. At the same time, owners were finding night baseball to be an attendance stimulator—so much so, indeed, that in the years after the war baseball became for the most part a nighttime spectacle. Cincinnati general manager Larry MacPhail is credited with staging the first major league night games in 1935, but he imitated a practice already successfully tested in the minor leagues and in the Negro majors. Minor league promoters also taught major league promoters the wisdom of using sideshows and giveaways to entice paying fans.

If by 1940 most clubs were installing lights for night baseball, at no time in this decade did any club build a new park. Only one new park, Cleveland's Municipal Stadium, with the largest seating capacity in the majors, was constructed at this time. Available in 1932, this publicly financed park was a harbinger of the postwar trend wherein new parks were either wholly or partially financed by public monies. The Cleveland Indians used this new park sparingly, preferring the cheaper course of using their own League Park. During the Depression decade, all major league parks waxed older and shabbier. One dilapidated structure, the Phillies' Baker Bowl, was abandoned when the Phillies became tenants of the A's at Shibe Park. Two other major league parks were modified. At Chicago, owner Wrigley added a new scoreboard and new bleachers in 1937, increasing the seating capacity to over 40,000. At Detroit, some modifications were undertaken in 1938 when the park's name was changed from Navin Field to Briggs Stadium in honor of the latest owner.

Although owners were challenged to find ways of coping with austerities imposed by depression and war, at least they faced no opposition from organized players. At this time players bargained individually for pay and in most cases took what was offered. Salary cuts were a fact of life, and even the mightiest were affected. Babe Ruth, admittedly aging, but still popular, remained the highest-paid player until he retired. His annual salary fell steadily; from a peak of $80,000 in 1931, it dropped to $70,000 in 1932, to $52,000 in 1933, to $35,000 in 1934, and in his last year of 1935, which he did not complete, he had signed for $25,000. That the aging warhorse could be paid so well when his skills were fading was a tribute to his continuing hold on the public. By

Joe DiMaggio showing his form against the Indians. (Courtesy Herman Seid)

comparison, in 1934 the more productive Lou Gehrig signed a $23,000 Yankee pact with the understanding that he'd not be paid less the following year!

As baseball income was always unevenly distributed between have and have-not clubs, so player salaries varied. During the Depression, fortune still favored players who wore Yankee or Cub uniforms. In the boom year of 1929, no club topped the average Yankee salary of $14,000; even if it dipped to $11,000 in 1933 and did not return to $14,000 until 1939, this average led all others. In the National League, the Cub players led all the rest; in 1929 the average Cub salary was $12,000, in 1933 it was $11,000, and in 1939 it was $12,000. By comparison, the Browns' average salary was $8,000 in 1929; it fell to $6,000 in 1933 and stayed there. Reportedly, the Pirates had the lowest salary average in the Depression era; Pirate pay averaged less than $6,000 in 1929 and was less than $6,000 in 1939. Between these extremes ranged the average salaries of all other teams, with American League players generally drawing somewhat lower average salaries than National Leaguers.

AMERICANS TO THE FORE

If American Leaguers played before smaller crowds and drew smaller paychecks than their National League brothers, at least they enjoyed the satisfaction of besting the Nationals on the playing field and in record books. By most standards the Americans overwhelmed the Nationals. Of the ten World Series battles fought in 1932–41, American teams won seven—a feat of mastery that stood second only to the eight Series victories notched by American teams in the 1911–20 decade.

What's more, in such basic offensive areas as batting averages, homers, RBIs, and stolen bases, the Americans outshone the Nationals in every season from 1932 through 1941. American superiority showed most tellingly in homer hitting. As if to atone for being outslugged by the Nationals during the 1920s, American clubbers exploded with a vengeance in the next decade, outsmiting their rivals each year. Since American League hitting naturally hurt its pitching, Nationals could at least tout their superior pitching. In this decade National hurlers allowed an average of 3.6 runs a game, while buffeted American pitchers yielded four-plus ERAs on the average, and in one season averaged over five per game.

The Americans also had the edge in individual heroics. In this decade nothing lower than a .349 batting average won the annual American League batting title, whereas .342 might do it in the National. In homer hitting no American slugger won with fewer than 35 blows, whereas 28 once sufficed in the National. Also, American RBI leaders annually topped their counterparts. Hence, it was hardly surprising that no National batting star matched Ted Williams's .406 average of 1941; or Joe DiMaggio's sensational 56-consecutive-game hitting streak of that year; or Jimmy Foxx's 58 homers in 1932, which Hank Greenberg matched in 1938; or Greenberg's awesome 183 RBIs of 1937. Put down by such titans, National partisans were better off boasting Dizzy Dean's pitching, citing the Cardinal ace's 30 wins in 1934 and his 28 the following year. Indeed, Dean's 30-victory season stood as a record for thirty-three years.

To be sure, there were vulnerable chinks in the American League superiority armor. As it was in the 1920s, but even more so later, the power-bloated Yankees made for a woefully unbalanced league. Indeed, were one to subtract Yankee Series victories from the American total of seven, only the Tigers' 1935 triumph would remain. By winning six pennants and as many world titles in this decade, the Yankees seemingly made the American League their fief. Nor would Yankee owner Ruppert have it otherwise; in nixing a proposed profit-sharing scheme aimed at helping lowly clubs cope with Depression vicissitudes, this conservative clung to his dog-in-the-manger philosophy, saying: "I found out a long time ago that there is no charity in baseball, and that every owner must make his own fight for existence." A pitiless philosophy it was; yet with rare exceptions, such as bailing out the moribund Browns, it prevailed then and still does.

In 1932, following three consecutive losses to the Athletics, Ruppert's pennant hunger was voracious. With Joe McCarthy, a former Cub manager, at the helm, the Yankees helped to divert some of the Gothamites' miseries over the spreading Depression and still lingering Prohibition by winning 107 games, good enough to crush the A's by 13. Ruth and Gehrig accounted for 75 of the team's 160 homers; overall, the team batted .286. Although the A's, led by Foxx's 58 homers and 169 RBIs, outslugged and outhit the Yanks, they could not match Yankee pitching. Only Lefty Grove did so, but the Yankee staff, including starters Lefty Gomez, Red Ruffing, Johnny Allen, and George Pipgras, owned the league's best ERA. Thenceforth, pitching dominance became a hallmark of McCarthy's teams; in an era when most other American staffs yielded more than four earned runs a game, Yankee flingers consistently yielded fewer than four, approaching the National average of 3.6.

Left:
Babe Ruth, who remained a powerful Yankee until 1934, showing nine-year-old John Dell how to use a bat. (Courtesy Dennis Goldstein)

Right:
Jay Hanna ("Dizzy") Dean arguing with umpire George Barr during the 1935 season, in front of nearly empty bleachers. Dizzy was 28 and 12 that year, when his Cardinals finished second. (Courtesy Dennis Goldstein)

That summer more than 900,000 fans attended Yankee home games, while an equal number watched the National League's champion Cubs. With McCarthy seeking revenge for his 1930 sacking as manager of the Cubs, the 1932 Series shaped up as a grudge-match between two power-packed teams. At the opener in New York the fans joined in with raucous jeers aimed at the Cubs and also at President Hoover, targeted as the Depression blamesake. Once the games began the clubs heaped insults upon each other, but the Yanks backed theirs with a fusillade of hits that dropped the Cubs in four straight games. For the aging Ruth, playing in his last Series, new luster was added to his legend. His glory moment came in Chicago, in the fifth inning of the third game, when he silenced Cub tormentors with a "called shot" homer. Whether or not he signaled his intent to homer is still hotly debated, but that Ruthian shot was the Series highlight.

No such dramatics illuminated the austere year of 1933. That year the Depression's impact resulted in sickening attendance declines and widespread financial losses. The hard-pressed Connie Mack sold star players Dykes, Simmons, and Haas to the White Sox, who benefited by moving up one notch to sixth place. Ruppert's bullishness was more successful, at least over the long haul; he hired George Weiss and charged him with building a farm system to rival Rickey's. To provide a staging ground for future Yankee stars, the Yanks purchased the Newark club of the International League. Although such moves augured well for the future, the 1933 Yankees needed immediate help to spell aging veterans and faltering pitchers. When such aid was unobtainable, the Yankees fell to second place.

While the Yankees were winning only 91 games, the long-dormant Senators rose and passed them with 99 victories. Once again a boy-manager led, this time shortstop Joe Cronin. Though lacking power, the Senators got steady hitting from Joe Kuhel, Buddy Myer, Heine Manush, and Goose Goslin, as well as able pitching from "General" Al Crowder (24-15), Earl Whitehill (22-8), and "Lefty" Walt Stewart (15-6). Yet, sad to say, only 437,000 fans paid to see this darkhorse team oust the Yankees. It was the same grim story elsewhere; 250,000 fewer fans attended Yankee games, and the A's, though boasting Triple Crown winner Jimmy Foxx, drew only 297,000. Not surprisingly, World Series attendance fell off, as the mismatched Senators succumbed to the Giants in five games.

As predicted, the Senators slipped back to the depths in 1934. Goslin's sale to Detroit was a factor in their seventh-place finish; in the wake of his Cinderella team's collapse, Griffith sold Cronin to Boston for $250,000. Now under wealthy and bullish new ownership, the Red Sox were buying instead of selling. Ever willing to fish in troubled waters, owner Tom Yawkey purchased Lefty Grove and two other stars from Mack, who also sold pitcher George Earnshaw to the White Sox and Mickey Cochrane to the Tigers. As expected, these acquisitions altered the power balance, though not to Chicago's advantage, nor Boston's when Grove won only eight games.

While these bullish teams faltered, Detroit struck a bonanza by purchasing catcher Cochrane. Installed as playing manager, "Black Mike" immediately turned a fifth-place team into a two-time champion.

While personally batting .320, Cochrane also shaped pitchers Tommy Bridges (22-11), "Schoolboy" Rowe (24-8), Eldon Auker (15-7), and old Firpo Marberry (15-5) into a formidable staff. The veteran Goslin stabilized the young outfield; at first base young Hank Greenberg ranged alongside infielders Charley Gehringer, Bill Rogell, and Marv Owen. Hitters all, they paced a .300 team batting average and led the team to 101 wins, enough to lap the Yanks by seven games. The 1934 Tigers drew 919,000 fans at home, 600,000 more than in bleak 1933. Local dreams of a first Tiger world title since 1887 collapsed, however, when the Cardinals won the Series four games to three.

Bolstered by the acquisition of pitcher Crowder from the Senators, the Tigers repeated in 1935. This time over a million fans turned out as

Yankee dugout scene in 1936, the first of four straight world-championship seasons: from left, Joe McCarthy, manager; Lou Gehrig, first base; Joe Glenn, catcher; Joe DiMaggio, outfield. (Courtesy Dennis Goldstein)

Lou Gehrig connecting for a homer in 1938, his last full season. "The Iron Horse" was wearing the logo of the upcoming 1939 New York World's Fair on his left sleeve. (Courtesy Herman Seid)

the Tigers edged the Yankees by three games. Batting .290 with power, Greenberg led the attack; his 36 homers tied for the league lead, and his prodigious 170 RBIs left all others far behind. Pitted in the World Series against the rampaging Cubs, who had won 21 straight games in September, the Tigers lost heart when an injury sidelined Greenberg. Nevertheless, the Tigers went on to win in six games, handing delighted Detroiters a long-sought world title.

Alas, the view from the top was brief. In 1936 sickness felled Cochrane, while a broken wrist sidelined Greenberg for much of the season; hard luck dogged Cochrane when in 1937 a pitched ball fractured his skull, virtually ending his career. In 1936 not even the acquisition of Al Simmons from the White Sox could overcome such losses. Besides, rival scouts had turned up priceless gems for Cleveland and New York. Cleveland signed seventeen-year-old Bob Feller, a pitching phenomenon two years away from stardom. Not so with the Yankees' find; in signing Joe DiMaggio, a coast league batting prodigy, they picked up a fully ripened outfielder.

Left Ruth-less in 1935, Gotham fans in 1936 adopted DiMaggio as the hero who came closest to replacing the Babe in their hearts. Installed in center field alongside George Selkirk and Jake Powell, the taciturn youngster's regal dignity and matchless fielding captivated fans and teammates; his batting debut of .323, 29 homers, and 125 RBIs stood second only to Gehrig's .354, 49, and 152 production. With such pacesetters as this pair, the team batted .300, smote 182 homers, and boasted the league's most effective pitching. The results were awesome; winning 102 games, the Yankees left the runner-up Tigers 19½ games behind. In the "Subway Series" that followed, they thrashed the Giants in six games.

This conquest was the first of an unprecedented four straight World Series titles racked up by McCarthy's men. Helping to keep the team strong was Weiss's farm system, which provided able replacements. Pitcher Spud Chandler and outfielder Tom Henrich came up in 1937; pitcher Steve Sundra and second baseman Joe Gordon joined in 1938; and pitchers Atley Donald and Marius Russo and slugging outfielder Charley Keller debuted in 1939. Thanks to the steady mastery of veteran pitchers Gomez, Ruffing, and reliefer Johnny Murphy, the pitching was the league's best. In slugging, the Yanks yielded to none, poling at least 166 homers in each of these years. So balanced was the hitting and slugging that not even Gehrig's tragic collapse from multiple sclerosis in 1939 halted the juggernaut. Although Weiss never found a first baseman to equal the "Iron Horse," DiMaggio, Gordon, Henrich, Keller, and Dickey took up the hitting slack.

With this personnel advantage, McCarthy led his team to a 13-game victory over the Tigers in 1937, a 9½-game win over the Red Sox in 1938, and a 17-game conquest of the Red Sox in 1939. On top of these victories, each fall saw another Series banner go up, raising the team's total to eight by 1939. Astonishingly, each Series victory was more decisive than its predecessor: In 1937 the Giants fell in five games; in 1938–39 the Cubs and the Reds were each swept in four games. Handed such brutal treatment, rivals again raised the cry of "Break up the Yankees!"

Rivals gained momentary succor at the dawn of a new decade. As the 1940 campaign opened, nagging misfortunes plagued the Yankees. Failure to find a hitting first baseman, plus weak batting by Crosetti and Dickey, accounted for the anemic .259 team hitting, while arm trouble sidelined pitcher Gomez. Still, 155 homers carried the team to 88 wins;

Lou Gehrig being honored by teammates and dignitaries at a game in Yankee Stadium in 1939, two years before his death. In accepting the tribute before 60,000 fans, Gehrig said, "Today I consider myself the luckiest man on the face of this earth. . . ." (Courtesy John Thorn)

Tigers celebrating the pennant-clinching victory of Floyd Giebell, second from left, over Bob Feller and the Indians in their last game of the 1940 season. Giebell is on the shoulders of Bill Sullivan and Johnny Gorsica. Also lifted is Del Baker, leaning on Rudy York, while Hal Newhouser stands behind. (Courtesy Michael Mumby Collection)

Ted Williams scoring the winning homer for the American League in the 1941 All-Star game. (Author's Collection)

but this was two short of what was needed in the torrid 1940 race. That year Detroit and Cleveland finished ahead of the Yankees. With young Feller firing his fastball for a league-leading 27 wins, the Indians contended till the final day. Were it not for a serious dispute between Indian players and their manager, they might have won. Such tensions hampered them in their duel with the Tigers. League-leading batting boosted the Tigers from fifth in 1939 to the top in 1940. Manager Del Baker's decision to move Greenberg to the outfield, in order to fit good-hitting but poor-fielding Rudy York into the lineup, greatly enhanced the offense. Moreover, pitcher Louis ("Bobo") Newsom (21-5) and reliever Al Benton shored up the mound staff. Not till the last day was the issue decided; in a must-win final game between these contenders, Tiger rookie Floyd Giebell outpitched the great Feller; ironically, Giebell's 2-0 shutout that day was his last major league victory.

As champs, the Tigers faced the Reds in a final struggle. Not till the last out of the seventh game was the World Series decided; then, by dint of a 2-1 victory, the Reds won. For over a million Tiger fans who had thronged Briggs Stadium that year, the loss was a bitter pill.

Hard after this loss, ominous preparations for impending war sank Tiger hopes for a comeback. After playing only 19 games in 1941, Greenberg was drafted into the army; his loss was a major factor in a Tiger slump. In what was to be baseball's last peacetime campaign until 1946, the Yanks took charge, winning 101 games to finish 17 ahead of the Red Sox. Not even the .406 batting of outfielder Ted Williams atoned for weak Sox pitching. Even Williams was upstaged by the great DiMaggio's record-shattering 56-consecutive-game hitting streak. And rightly so; for when DiMaggio began his skein, the Yanks stood 5½ games behind Cleveland with a 14-14 record. But when the long streak was ended, the Yankee record was 55-27 (two ties) and the team led the Indians by seven games. That year DiMaggio's .357, 30 homers, and 125 RBIs led a Yankee resurgence, including a 4-1 victory over the Dodgers in the World Series. A Merkleian blunder by Dodger catcher

Mickey Owen, whose muffed third strike allowed the Yanks to rally for four runs in the last inning of the fourth game, cast a legendary aura over this last peacetime Series.

By 1941 the National League had grown accustomed to losing World Series matches; such annual humiliations, along with similar setbacks in annual All-Star games (instituted in 1933, mostly for the benefit of indigent ex-players), seemed to verify American superiority. Yet, it could be argued that the National League was better balanced and that its annual campaigns were more exciting. In the 'Thirties, five National teams scaled championship heights; moreover, every race but one was hotly contested, and in all but two races the team with the best pitching ERA won. Not surprisingly, the longest reign of any would-be dynasty during this decade was two years.

As the Depression gripped the game, the 1932 Cubs won a hotly contested race over the Pirates by four games. An oddly resilient team, the Cubs at this time seemed to surface as champs every three years; thereupon they would lose the World Series and go into a two-year swoon. This pattern began in 1929 and resurfaced in 1932, 1935, and 1938. In 1932 the Cubs held first place in early August, at which time the ever-testy manager, Rogers Hornsby, was sacked for insubordination. His successor was first baseman Charlie Grimm, who drove the team to victory. Himself a .300 hitter, Grimm was joined by young Billy Herman, Riggs Stephenson, and Johnny Moore as offensive standouts. Young Lon Warneke (22-6) and a corps of veterans served up the league's best pitching. The Cub victory attracted 974,000 home fans, but the team ran afoul of Yankee manager Joe McCarthy; still seething over his 1929 sacking by the Cubs, McCarthy led his Yanks to a crushing sweep in the World Series.

As the Cubs slipped to third in 1933, the Giants won for the first time since 1924. Gone was their great helmsman McGraw, now replaced by first baseman Bill Terry. In his first full year as manager, Terry batted .322 and, with outfielder Mel Ott (23 homers and 103 RBIs), led the attack. Most of the credit for the five-game pennant victory over the Pirates belonged to the pitching staff; headed by lefty Carl Hubbell (23-12), the pitchers yielded fewer than three runs a game. Thus armed, the Giants climaxed their 1933 season with an easy 4-1 win over the Senators in the World Series.

Giant pitching again topped the league in 1934, but in the very last week of the race the onrushing Cardinals overtook Terry's men and won by two games. The Card victory captured some of the spirit of the times. Led by playing manager Frank Frisch, the scrappy, ill-paid Cards attracted only 325,000 home fans. Undaunted, they batted a league-leading .288, finished second in homers, and trumped Giant pitching aces with the Dean brothers. Arkansas-born and folksy-funny, Jerome ("Dizzy") Dean won 30 games, while his more reticent brother, Paul, added 19. Five regulars batted above .300, including Frisch, Jim ("Ripper") Collins, Ernie Orsatti, Spud Davis, and young Joe ("Ducky") Medwick; two others, Pepper Martin and Leo Durocher, fired the club

NATIONAL LEAGUE CAMPAIGNS

Tiger manager Steve O'Neill (center) and Tigers Rudy York (left) and Jim Bloodworth brawl with umpire Larry Grieve in a 1943 game against the Athletics at Philadelphia's Shibe Park. Photographed for the *Philadelphia Bulletin*. (Courtesy Photojournalism Collection, Temple University Libraries)

Pete Gray was called up from the Memphis Chicks by the St. Louis Browns in the wartime year of 1945. The one-armed lefty batted .218 for the Browns. (Courtesy George Brace)

baseman Frank McCormick, outfielder Ival Goodman, and slugging catcher Ernie Lombardi mounted enough of an offensive to send the Reds against the Yankees in the World Series. Yankee pitching and hitting ousted the Reds in four games, however.

Regrouping, the Reds drove to a 12-game victory over the rising Dodgers in 1940. Once again the pitching was superb; Walters (22-10) led the league, Derringer won 20, Thompson won 16, ex-Brave Jim Turner won 13, and ex-Yankee Joe Beggs won 12. Combined with the league's best fielding, such performances atoned for mediocre hitting. The same prowess enabled the Reds to recover from a 3-2 games deficit in World Series play to defeat the hard-hitting Tigers.

This was as far as the Reds could go. A sorry .247 batting performance dropped them to third in 1941, far behind the Cardinals and Dodgers, who battled into the last week of play. In eking a 2½-game victory, the Dodgers led the league in runs, homers, and pitching ERA, and tied the Cards in team batting. Managed by ex-Cardinal Leo Durocher and knit together by ex-Red general manager Larry MacPhail, the Dodger team was an assemblage of bartered stars. Some were ex-Cardinals acquired from Rickey. Among them were pitcher Curt Davis, catcher Mickey Owen, and outfielder Joe Medwick; they performed stoutly but were excelled by rookie outfielder Pete Reiser, an ex-Cardinal farmhand, who won the batting title. Meanwhile, other deals with other teams had made Dodgers of first baseman Dolph Camilli, whose 34 homers and 120 RBIs led the league; second baseman Billy Herman; shortstop Harold ("Pee Wee") Reese; third baseman Harry ("Cookie") Lavagetto; infielder Lew Riggs; outfielder Dixie Walker; and pitching aces Kirby Higbe, Whit Wyatt, and Fred Fitzsimmons. Indeed, no Dodger regular of 1941 was a homegrown product; still, goaded by Durocher, the team jelled into a formidable array. Over a million Brooklyn fans, the league's largest home attendance of the Depression era, took them to heart, cheered them to the pennant, and mourned their loss to the Yankees in the subway World Series. Catcher Owen's missed strike virtually handed the Yanks one victory. In the aftermath of defeat, defiant Dodger fans groused, "Wait till next year."

WARTIME BASEBALL

Unfortunately, before the old year was over the nation plunged into total war against the Axis powers. By the time the war ended in 1945, some 12 million Americans were mobilized, including at least 500 major league players and 3,500 minor leaguers. Bled by the manpower drain, the minors shrank to nine leagues in 1943. Although the hardhit majors were given a "green light" from President Roosevelt to continue play, they were obliged by the military draft to play underage youngsters, overage veterans, draft rejects, and aliens—such as some 50 Cubans recruited by scouts. Under the circumstances, the quality of play deteriorated, but even ersatz major league ball seemed likely to end in 1945. Just before that season was due to start, draft boards, responding to protests about allegedly unfit men playing a strenuous game, reexamined and conscripted many of the 200 draft rejects in major league uniforms. At the same time, a "work or fight" proposal, aimed at putting all draft-age men into war work or military service, threatened, if adopted, to denude player ranks. However, Germany's imminent collapse, and persuasive politicking on behalf of baseball by prominent figures like J. Edgar Hoover and Senator A. B. ("Happy") Chandler, saved the 1945 season. In April the Senate killed the "work or fight" proposition.

If finding able players to fill vacant ranks vexed owners the most, other problems were sorely trying. For one, overall attendance, which averaged 10 million over 1940–41, fell to 8.8 million in 1942 and to 7.7 million in 1943. Then, however, it rebounded to 9 million in 1944 and soared to a record 11.1 million in 1945. The turnabout boosted reported overall earnings figures from a $240,000 loss in 1943 to a $1.2 million gain in 1945. Indeed, twelve clubs reported modest profits during the war years; the profit leaders were the Tigers, whose $532,000 headed the Americans, and the Cards, whose $410,000 led the Nationals.

Player salaries, however, received no boost; indeed, the average fell from $7,300 in 1939 to $6,400 in 1943. A federal wage-limiting edict, intended to combat inflation, was the chief reason. Invoked in 1943, the rule as applied to baseball salaries barred a player from earning more than the top salary his team paid to any man in 1942. For Cardinal players this meant that nobody earned more than $13,500 in 1943–45; for Braves it was $12,500; and for Giants it was $17,500. Such dammed-up salaries inspired union sentiment among players, and once the wage restriction was lifted this erupted. Thus, from the postwar era onward, salary disputes plagued owner-player relations.

Wartime austerities also handed major league promoters major problems involving team transport, hotel accommodations, and food and equipment procurement. By 1945 travel limitations eliminated spring-training programs in the South, forced the cancellation of that season's All-Star game, and for a time threatened to bring about a realignment of the leagues. Earlier on, a serious rubber shortage had the Spalding Company introducing an ersatz ball with a center core made of balata; hitters in 1943 complained of its deadness, but pitchers rejoiced. Happily for hitters, a timely supply of synthetic rubber improved the resiliency of balls in 1944. But obtaining good wood for bats awaited the war's end. Night baseball in the New York City area was also curtailed for a time; dimout orders forced the cancellation of such games at the Polo Grounds and Ebbets Field. In 1944, however, this restriction was lifted, and clubs scheduled more of these increasingly popular games.

All in all, baseball men were fortunate to be able to continue their game through the war. Moreover, promoters won plaudits for contributing their bit to the war effort by such patriotic gestures as admitting servicemen free to games, staging war bond benefits, and supplying used equipment and transmitting game broadcasts to military units.

If wartime diamond campaigns pale by comparison with others, at least the struggles afforded excitement enough to sustain public interest in the game. In the American League, the Yankees, benefiting from the temporary retention of able veteran players in 1942 and by their productive farm system, won back-to-back pennants in these years. Despite Ted Williams's Triple Crown batting performance of 1942, Yankee pitching and slugging consigned the Red Sox to second place, nine

William Harold ("Bill") Terry, Giant player-manager, being interviewed by Orene Muse of the Baton Rouge *Star Times*. (Courtesy Dennis Goldstein)

Left:
Stan Musial, playing for Bainbridge Naval Training Station in 1945, runs home, while Ernie Lombardi of the New York Giants waits for the ball. (Courtesy Michael Mumby Collection)

Right:
Johnny Vander Meer, who pitched strongly for the Cincinnati Reds from 1938 to 1948. On June 11 and 15, 1938, Vander Meer pitched consecutive no-hit games, an unparalleled pitching feat. (Author's Collection)

games off the pace. With Williams gone by 1943, Washington challenged the Yanks, but superb pitching and good hitting by newcomers Nick Etten, Bill Johnson, and Johnny Lindell, acquired as replacements for departed stars like Buddy Hassett, Tommy Henrich, and Joe DiMaggio, enabled the Yankees to win by 13½ games. In World Series play, the Yanks fell to the Cards in 1942 but scored an avenging victory over the same team in 1943.

By 1944 the leveling impact of the military draft depleted all teams; still, if the quality of play was low, attendance now rose under the stimulus of the lively three-way race among the Yankees, Tigers, and Browns. It ended with the Browns atop by a game over the Tigers and six over the Yanks. For the Browns it was their first and last American League pennant. In leading a group of youngsters, overage vets, and draft rejects to the top, manager Luke Sewell saw his team outhit, outslugged, and outpitched by others. Victory came in the last days of the season when the Browns swept a four-game series with the Yanks at Sportsman's Park. Nevertheless, only some 500,000 fans showed up for the Browns' home games; a chronic disease of this team, attendance anemia would soon drive the Browns out of St. Louis. Meanwhile, they lost the World Series to the hometown Cardinals 4-2 and then fell to third place in 1945.

With the decimated Yankees out of contention, the final wartime race became a two-team struggle between the Senators and Tigers. Fortified by league-leading pitching from a staff that included four overage, knuckleballing starters, the Senators, who managed only 27 homers, lost by only a game and a half to manager Steve O'Neill's Tigers. A decisive factor was the war's ending, which enabled some returning veterans to come back, including slugger Hank Greenberg.

Despite having missed almost five seasons, Greenberg batted .311 with 13 homers and 60 RBIs. His presence not only helped win a pennant, but it also helped swell Tiger home attendance to 1,280,000. In World Series play, the Tigers beat the Cubs 4-3, although one writer, noting the shabby play, pronounced it a test of which team could first lose the Series.

In the National League the war years featured the dominance of the Cardinals, winners of three consecutive pennants. Draft-proof players and able replacements from Rickey's farms kept the Cardinal team strong in the years 1942–44. Rickey's 1942 departure to Brooklyn augured ill for the Cardinal future, however. For the present the Cardinals dominated the league with crushing aplomb. In each championship year they boasted league-leading hitting and pitching. Only the 1942 race was close; that year the Cards came from behind to win 106 games and edge the Dodgers by two. Once atop, they made a shambles of the next two races, beating the runner-up Reds by 18 in 1943 and the Pirates by 14½ in 1944. In World Series play the Cardinals crushed the Yankees 4-1 in 1942, bowed to the Yankees by the same count in 1943, then downed the Browns 4-2 in 1944. The Cards' comeuppance came in 1945 when the Cubs, bolstered by the midseason acquisition of pitcher Hank Borowy from the Yankees, beat them by three games. With Phil Cavaretta leading the league in hitting, and Cub pitchers ahead in ERA, the Cubs won what was to be their last pennant to this day. In World Series play they extended their losing skein by falling to the Tigers in seven games.

AUSTERITY BASEBALL

Bracketed by the booming 1920s and the burgeoning post–World War II years, major league baseball endured belt-tightening austerities brought on by the Depression and war. Although low points plumbed in 1933 and in 1943 brought losses for most teams, baseball survived these bleak years far better than many other industries. If falling attendance limited income, still only one team, the Phillies, went bankrupt. When owner Jerry Nugent went under in 1943, the National League bought the club for $50,000. The club was resold to lumberman William Cox, who was ousted for improprieties after three months. Mercifully, at that point DuPont executive Robert Carpenter bought control; under his ownership the Phillies prospered. Meanwhile, the Braves and Browns came close to bankruptcy.

In the case of the Braves, financial help came from contractor Lou Perini; however, in 1953 he would move the team to greener pastures in Milwaukee. A similar uprooting was to befall an American League sickling, the Browns, who were harried by pinch-penny ownership and unable to compete against their hometown rivals, the Cardinals. In 1941 the Browns' owners sought to move the team to Los Angeles. Indeed, the outbreak of war nixed what could have been the first major league franchise shift since 1903. Although the Browns finished the war years in St. Louis, in 1953 they were sold to a Baltimore syndicate; the following year they entered the American League lists as the Baltimore Orioles.

comed the extra income from radio. Belatedly recognizing radio's hold on the nation, owners shed lingering fears that free baseball shows would cripple live attendance. Windfall income of $100,000, which sponsors paid for the 1934 World Series broadcasts, was shared equally and converted many owners to radio. When it came to broadcasting seasonal games, however, the policy was to each owner his own contracting. Naturally, this policy further advantaged teams located in metropolitan areas, where attendance strength already gave them an advantage. By 1939 most clubs reaped additional income by selling home-game radio rights. That year such income totaled more than $800,000; of this sum the Giant contract of $110,000 was the largest, and the Cardinals' $33,000 pact was the smallest.

Of course, few at this time expected that income from an electronic medium would one day top that from live attendance. Indeed, radio never did, but television would. In the late 'Thirties and early 'Forties, television's potential stirred the imagination of some; television displays were a popular sideshow at the New York World's Fair of 1939–40, and a few set owners enjoyed the few sports shows that were telecast thereafter. But not much airtime went to baseball telecasts, and any prospect of a breakthrough was stayed by the onset of the war.

Not surprisingly, some baseball writers worried about competition from radio sportscasters. As purveyors of baseball information, radio sportscasters like Mel Allen, Red Barber, Ty Totten, and Arch McDonald became popular figures. So did some ex-players, notably Jack Graney, Dizzy Dean, Harry Heilmann, and Waite Hoyt. Although few realized it, they were showing the way to a time when ex-players, as television sportscasters and color commentators, would ply careers as lucrative as those of their playing days.

Baseball writers were well advised to worry about such budding competition. At this time, however, few major changes affected baseball's newspaper dimension. Coverage was extensive and broad-based, involv-

Commissioner Landis in a characteristically belligerent pose during a negotiating session. (Courtesy Dennis Goldstein)

ing papers large and small. Editorial competition resulted in stylish features, fancy photographic work, and statistical innovations. Yet, on the whole, baseball writers comported themselves as they had in the 1920s; even the clichés hardly had changed. One critic, sports editor Stan Woodward, blasted the stylized product and sorted writers into three tendentious schools. The "gee whiz" school glamorized games and players; the "aw nuts" school belittled the same; the "on the button" school stressed routinized factual accounts. Although writers might occasionally dabble in each, no school reflected a fresh approach. That some ball clubs subsidized writers at this time supported a charge that objective, critical, colorful writing was in short supply.

The same criticism applied to most books and magazines devoted to baseball at this time; worshipful, bowdlerized accounts were the rule. Of course, baseball profited by all the free coverage. Indeed, the game was boosted by doting biographies of stars like Lou Gehrig, popular team histories, and the flood of celebratory articles. *The Sporting News* still provided complete weekly coverage and informed criticism of all levels of pro ball. During World War II, publisher J. G. Taylor Spink gave the game and his organ a boost by distributing thousands of copies of *The Sporting News* free of charge to servicemen.

More publicity for the major league game came with the year-long celebration of the game's accepted centennial in 1939. Although both baseball's 1839 birthdate and its invention by Abner Doubleday are mythical, baseball benefited by the celebration. As part of the hoopla, the Baseball Hall of Fame at Cooperstown, New York, was opened and the first stars enshrined. The Hall's museum began to attract thousands of devoted fans each year. After 1946, baseball scholars started to journey to the Hall's library when Ernie Lanigan became the first official baseball historian. A zealous compiler of statistics, Lanigan inspired others, including Lee Allen, his successor, and Sherley C. Thompson and Hy Turkin, who in 1944 began work on an authoritative *Encyclopedia of Baseball.* Since first publication in 1956, this compendium has served as a valuable source of statistics and records of campaigns and player performances.

When comparative records are obtainable, they show this era yielding to none in fielding heroic players. Although mighty Ruth played his last game in 1935 and was admittedly irreplaceable, sluggers like Ott, Greenberg, and Foxx stirred fans. Likewise, when Hornsby retired in 1937, fans regarded the Waners, DiMaggio, Williams, and Musial as worthy successors to this versatile hitter. Indeed, fans still speak reverently of Ted Williams's .406 batting mark of 1941, of DiMaggio's 56-game hitting streak of that year, and of Greenberg and Foxx's 58-homer seasons of this era.

Among the great teams of baseball history, only a later generation of Yankees topped the four world titles hung up by the 1936–39 Yankees. That performance ranked manager Joe McCarthy among the all-time great managers.

Nor did the umpiring profession stagnate. At this time umps benefited from a ruling that increased game crews to three men for each seasonal game and four for World Series games. Bill Klem supervised National umps, and Tom Connolly directed American arbiters. Owing

Connie Mack, owner-manager of the Athletics, briefs pitcher Pete Mitchell about keeping his pivot foot on the rubber, at 1940 spring camp in Anaheim, California. Forced to retire in 1950 after a half-century at the helm of the A's, the "Tall Tactician" sold his franchise in 1953 and died three years later. (Courtesy Charles Burkhardt)

to rivalry between them, the two leagues differed noticeably in the way plate umps positioned themselves and in the adoption of protective equipment by plate umps. Connolly urged American League umps to wear the external inflated mattress that the National League's Klem disdained, favoring an inner shield worn beneath the coat. Although umpiring became more uniform in general, colorful individuals still stood out; at this time the varying styles of umps such as Dolly Stark, George Magerkurth, Beans Reardon, and Lee Ballanfant added flavor to games.

In many ways, major league baseball demonstrated its resilience in these trying times of global depression and conflict. During the war all games were preceded by the playing of the national anthem, a patriotic gesture often done before but which now and afterwards became required ritual. Who could gainsay that this ritual strengthened the mystic notion that baseball was the national game? And if tangible demonstration of the game's service to the war effort was sought, it was evidenced by club policies of admitting servicemen free, by sales of war bonds at games, by gifts of bats and balls to servicemen, and, above all, by the military service of so many stars, whose normal careers were irretrievably interrupted along with those of millions of others.

Of course, countercurrents of unrest rose up and demanded corrective action. Most glaringly, baseball's unwritten policy of refusing to admit black players was being hotly challenged. During the war, even Latin Americans who were recruited had to be of light complexion. Thus, black players still played in segregated major leagues, although not for much longer. Had promoter Bill Veeck, Jr., had his way in 1943, he would have purchased the Phillies and added black players. Veeck's bid was rejected, however, some said because of Landis's stubborn support of segregation. In any event, when Landis died in 1944, resistance to baseball integration seemed to be dying too. Still, few expected the wall to crumble within a mere two years.

Landis's passing also freed owners to assume full and open control of the game's policy-making. True, Landis's vaunted influence was less than supposed, but as long as he held the commissioner post, he imposed his views on matters such as farm systems, player sales, and the negotiation of World Series radio rights. With his passing, owners never again allowed themselves to be saddled with an overbearing commissioner.

Still, owners kidded themselves if they thought their troubles would end with the war's end. As attendance rose in 1945, income rose, bringing demands from players for higher pay. Indeed, salaries of players and umps had been frozen during the war, making demands for redress understandable. Consequently, when returning war vets showed up in 1946, owners were confronted by a militant spirit. Some players talked of union action, and some threatened to jump to a rival Mexican league for better pay. Peacetime may have seemed wonderful in its bright prospect for baseball as usual, but when accompanied by problems such as these, it was a good bet that the game would take a different tack.

BEYOND THE PALE: THE BLACK MAJOR LEAGUES

AS THE TWENTIETH CENTURY DAWNED, THE STRUCture of professional baseball in America resembled a formidable pyramid topped by the lordly major leagues and with lowly Class D leagues forming the base. Dubbed "organized baseball" by officials, the pyramid encompassed all professional leagues recognized under the new National Agreement and by the newly formed National Association of Professional Baseball Leagues. Indeed, membership in the "OB" structure was both a status symbol and a necessity because unrecognized leagues were treated as outlaw circuits. As such, they were fair game for roster raids, and their personnel ran a risk of being blacklisted. Such pressure was enough to persuade one formidable outside circuit, the thriving Pacific Coast League, to seek an early accommodation with organized baseball.

But if repentant outlaw leagues might obtain official grace and admission into organized baseball, a strict color barrier forced black players and teams to play ball beyond the pale of organized baseball. By 1901 the exclusion of black players and teams from organized baseball was firmly set; indeed, it was part of the post–Civil War web of caste-like

Bud Fowler, a black player, with his teammates of the Keokuk, Iowa, team in 1885. As noted in the vignette "Beneath the Majors," minor league teams showed less racial prejudice than the majors, until the minors also succumbed to pressure to discriminate. (Courtesy John Thorn)

Cuban Giants, originally organized by black Long Islanders. These Giants attributed their success in scheduling games against white clubs to their pretense of hailing from a Caribbean island. (Courtesy Schomburg Center for Research in Black Culture, The New York Public Library)

customs and laws that forced black Americans to live segregated lives. In the universe of professional baseball, segregation forced aspiring black players into their own separate world. Compared to organized baseball, the black baseball world was less organized, less profitable, less heralded, and far less visible. Nevertheless, black teams and leagues made solid contributions to the growth of American baseball and ultimately to the integration of organized baseball.

Historically, black ball players, in company with all other black Americans, experienced decades of unequal treatment. Segregated institutions existed in American communities with black populations long before the Civil War, but the full force of inequality struck black Americans in the years following a restoration of home rule to the conquered southern states and a decline in wartime idealism in the North. Although black Americans were ostensibly equal to whites under the Fifteenth Amendment to the Constitution, after 1876 a web of exclusionary customs and state and local laws, rationalized by white supremacy and social-Darwinian ideologies, barred blacks from participating with whites in many basic areas of life.

In the world of baseball, black teams and players were formally excluded from the National Association of Base Ball Clubs; then in 1871–75 they were informally excluded, by "gentlemen's agreement," from participating in the National Association of Professional Base Ball Clubs. This exclusionary "gentlemen's agreement" also kept blacks out of the National League; although National League clubs took no formal action to bar black players, no *known* black player played in the National League from 1876 until 1947.

This is not to say that no black players played major league ball prior to Jackie Robinson's much heralded debut in 1947. Before being hounded out, two black brothers, Moses and Welday Walker, played major league ball in 1884 with the Toledo club of the American Association. Moreover, some black players may have broken through the major league color barrier by "passing" as white players. Among several suspected of "passing" over the years were catcher Vincent ("Sandy") Nava, who played with the National League's Providence team in 1882–84 and with Baltimore of the American Association in 1885–86; outfielder George Treadway, who played with the National League's Baltimore, Brooklyn, and Louisville teams in 1893–96; Cuban outfielder Armando Marsans, who played with four major league teams in 1911–18; Cuban infielder Rafael Almeida, who played with the National League's Cincinnati team in 1911–13; Cuban infielder Ramon Herrera, who played with the American League's Boston team in 1925–26; and Cuban outfielder Roberto Estallela, who played with three American League teams in 1935–49. Obviously, the attempt to impose a monolithic standard of racial classification based on skin color was sorely tried by the presence of dusky Cubans and native Americans.

Although excluded early from major league ranks, black players fared better with some of the emerging minor leagues. Not until the late 1890s did encroaching racial barriers shut down these havens, and as long as opportunities existed a handful of black players, including at least twenty in 1887, played integrated professional ball. Among the best of these players were the versatile Bud Fowler, second baseman Frank Grant, and pitcher George Stovey. In 1887 these men were starring in the International League when that circuit's officials voted

Philadelphia Giants of 1906, an early all-black team organized in response to Jim Crow practices. (Courtesy *Pittsburgh Courier* and Ronald A. Smith)

in midseason to ban all black players. Over the next five years other minor leagues did the same, so that by 1892 only a few Afro-Americans played on. The descending color barrier also ousted two black teams, the New York Gorhams and the Cuban Giants, which had been competing in the Middlestate League in 1889–90. In 1898 the last black team to compete in a league with white teams, the Acme Colored Giants, dropped out of the lowly Pennsylvania Iron and Oil League. By then an 1896 U.S. Supreme Court decision (*Plessy v. Ferguson*) had upheld the "separate but equal" doctrine allowing state and local laws to impose segregated facilities in public accommodations. Whether or not the scope of that ruling extended to professional baseball operations, the fact was that by 1896 there existed two separate worlds of professional baseball in America—white and black.

The two segregated professional baseball worlds had been developing for a long time. As early as 1867 two all-black clubs, the Philadelphia Excelsiors and Brooklyn Uniques, were playing outside the pale of the amateur National Association. Professional black teams did not appear until 1885, however, when a team of waiters from the Argyle Hotel of Babylon, Long Island, became the first full-salaried black team. The following year this team became the Cuban Giants; the Giants label derived from the famous National League team, and the Cuban label was adopted in hopes of luring paying customers with the promise of seeing exotic Caribbean performers. To this end the Cuban Giants for a time even babbled in gibberish while on the field. In reality, the team attracted fans by dint of good play. Playing as an independent team in 1887, the Cuban Giants defeated strong white teams and were scheduled to play a postseason exhibition series with the Association champion St. Louis Browns. But the Browns' players rejected what might have been a lucrative matchup. Over the years 1889–91 the Cuban Giants were enrolled in a series of white minor leagues, but each year the league folded. Thereafter, the Cuban Giants reverted to the status of an independent team, the best of several such black teams of the nineteenth century.

Hilldale Club, winners of the Eastern Colored League, competed in the first Negro World Series against the Kansas City Royals of the Negro National League. The Royals won the Series by five games to four. (Courtesy Schomburg Center for Research in Black Culture, The New York Public Library)

DEN BANTOP   WINTERS   CURRIE   LEE   CARR   C.JOHNSON   J.JOHNSON   RYAN   MACKEY   ALLEN   CAMPBELL   LEWIS   THOMAS   COCKRELL   B.RIGGS

But the vaunted supremacy of the Cuban Giants was never tested in an all-black league. In 1887 six independent black teams had launched such a league, but poor financing doomed this National League of Colored Base Ball Clubs after a month of play. Thereafter, no black professional leagues appeared until the early years of the twentieth century. In 1907 the International League of Colored Baseball Clubs surfaced, followed in 1909 by the New England Colored League and the Chicago Baseball League. But like the 1887 venture, these three leagues died aborning. Thus, most black pro teams played exhibition games against other black teams, white professional teams, and occasionally against major league opposition.

For all the rigors of barnstorming and gypsy-like travel, the number of black pro teams increased. By 1906 no fewer than fourteen black teams bore the name Giants, inspired by the famous Cuban Giants and by John McGraw's acclaimed National League team. Playing independently, black teams roamed the South, Midwest, and East. In the South, play was limited to contests against black teams, but elsewhere games with white pro teams were arranged by booking agents. For black players, the pay was a fraction of what white professionals got, but the money exceeded that of the average black working man.

Although no black leagues existed, the best of the black independents contended annually for the "colored championship of the world." Records of these encounters are spotty, but in 1902 and 1907 playing manager Solomon ("Sol") White's Philadelphia Giants claimed the title. In 1903 pitcher Andrew ("Rube") Foster hurled the Cuban X Giants to the title. Then, during the 'Teens, Foster organized and managed the Chicago American Giants to a string of colored world championships. As the best black team of that decade, Foster's Giants attracted large crowds. In these years Foster nursed a dream, shared by Sol White, who also wrote the first history of black baseball, of forming a black major league. Moreover, both men hoped that, by dint of hard work and stellar play, the best black teams would one day be integrated into the ranks of organized baseball. Although the latter dream never came to pass, Foster and White successfully launched a black major league in 1920.

More than mere dreamers, White and Foster in their playing years ranked among the top stars of black baseball. White was an excellent infielder, and Foster, in a 1902 late-season exhibition game against the Philadelphia Athletics, outpitched Rube Waddell and thereafter wore the nickname of "Rube." In the years following, other stars—such as John Henry Lloyd, a hard-hitting infielder, and "Smokey Joe" Williams, a power pitcher—emerged. Lloyd, who once batted .475 in a season, was touted by some as the best hitter of his era, barring none, and Williams was dubbed "the Black Mathewson." In exhibition contests against major league clubs, Williams repeatedly validated the comparison. On two occasions he outpitched Walter Johnson, and in 1915 he shut out the reigning National League champion Phillies.

In these years good black players earned additional cash and glory playing in Cuba, where baseball had caught on ever since the 1880s. Beginning in the early 1900s, some of the better Cuban players played in America, where they also encountered racial discrimination. How-

John Henry ("Pop") Lloyd, slugging shortstop and one of the early superstars of black baseball. Shown here at the peak of his career in 1918, when he joined the Brooklyn Royal Giants as their playing manager at the age of thirty-four. (Courtesy Schomburg Center for Research in Black Culture, The New York Public Library)

COLORED
BASEBALL & SPORTS
~ MONTHLY ~

Vol. 1 - No. 1   NEW YORK, SEPTEMBER 1, 1934   Price 15c

C. THOMAS, C. JENKINS, C. SPEARMAN
Three Shining Lights in Colored Baseball.

THE ONLY PUBLICATION OF ITS KIND IN THE WORLD

ever, black Americans who played winter ball in Cuba received good pay and were treated as equals. In these years black players played alongside some white major leaguers in Cuba. Some white players grew to appreciate the skills of black players. Such a lesson was drubbed into the Detroit Tigers in 1910 when they played a twelve-game exhibition series in Cuba. Playing against black Americans and Cubans, they lost seven games, tied one, and won four.

In 1920 Rube Foster's dream of launching a black major league run by black organizers came to pass. Fully aware of the great migrations that swelled black communities in the northern and midwestern regions, and buoyed by the popularity of his Chicago American Giants, Foster called a meeting of leading black clubs to discuss forming a league. Ten years earlier, squabbling black clubs had rejected a proposal to form a Negro National League, but this time Foster's arguments carried the day. In February 1920 the Negro National League took shape by enrolling clubs from Chicago, St. Louis, Pittsburgh, Cleveland, Kansas City, and Philadelphia. Except for owner J. L. Wilkinson of the Kansas City Monarchs, all club operators were black. Wilkinson was welcomed because he had successfully promoted an "All-Nations" team, whose ranks included a nucleus of black players along with American Indians, Japanese, and a few white players. Indeed, Wilkinson's Monarchs proved to be one of the strongest and stablest clubs in the history of the Negro majors.

The Negro National League suffered from a looseness of organization forced on it by circumstances. The playing schedule called for each team to play sixty championship games, but some teams played twice that many exhibition games. For most players, year-round play was the norm, making for arduous travel by trains, buses, and autos. Because black players were frequently barred from public accommodations, they often ate, slept, and dressed in their conveyances. Seasonal salaries ranging between $125 and $300 a month—$400 and more for stars— were augmented by winter ball. Happily, black fans, stimulated by black newspaper coverage, provided encouraging support; indeed, black baseball stars became heroes to black fans, especially when black teams defeated white professional teams in exhibitions, as they did more often than not. Such support from fans partially compensated for an almost total lack of black baseball coverage by the nation's leading newspapers and sporting journals. Certainly, one of the cruelest effects of segrega-

Right:
Speedy outfielder James ("Cool Papa") Bell once stole 175 bases in a season as a black major leaguer. Bell played in the 'Thirties with the Pittsburgh Crawfords, a team judged by some to be the best in black major league history. Bell has been elected to the Hall of Fame. (Courtesy Schomburg Center for Research in Black Culture, The New York Public Library)

Opposite:
This short-lived journal was launched by publisher Nat Trammell in 1934, with a strongly pro-integration editorial stance. Clint Thomas, shown on the left, was a star of the Black Yankees. When Thomas was honored by citizens of Ashland, Kentucky, in 1979, the occasion led to a movement to establish a Negro Baseball Hall of Fame in that town. (Courtesy Schomburg Center for Research in Black Culture, The New York Public Library)

tion in baseball, as in other areas of achievement, was the invisibility imposed by such silent treatment. As a result, most white fans knew little or nothing of the feats of black major league players.

But support of the Negro National League was strong, so much so that in 1923 a second black major league, the Eastern Colored League, appeared. Its arrival allowed for a dual major league structure with a Negro World Series. The first Negro World Series was played in 1924, ending with the National champion Kansas City Monarchs defeating the Eastern champion Philadelphia Hilldale team in a ten-game series. Superior pitching by Monarch aces Wilbur ("Bullet Joe") Rogan and José Mendez ("the Black Cuban") made the difference. The games returned only $300 to each winning player; this disappointing outcome was to plague all future Negro World Series encounters.

Though black fans gave slim support to World Series matches, they delighted in the performances of black baseball stars. In this decade veteran heroes such as "Pop" Lloyd and "Smokey Joe" Williams were joined by offensive stars as talented as James ("Cool Papa") Bell, "Mule" Suttles, and Oscar Charleston and by pitchers of the caliber of "Cannonball" Dick Redding and Leroy ("Satchel") Paige. Such stars enthralled black fans, especially when they defeated major league teams in exhibitions. They did so with such embarrassing frequency that

Pittsburgh Crawfords, champions of the Negro National League in 1935, posed beside their tour bus. (Courtesy Schomburg Center for Research in Black Culture, The New York Public Library)

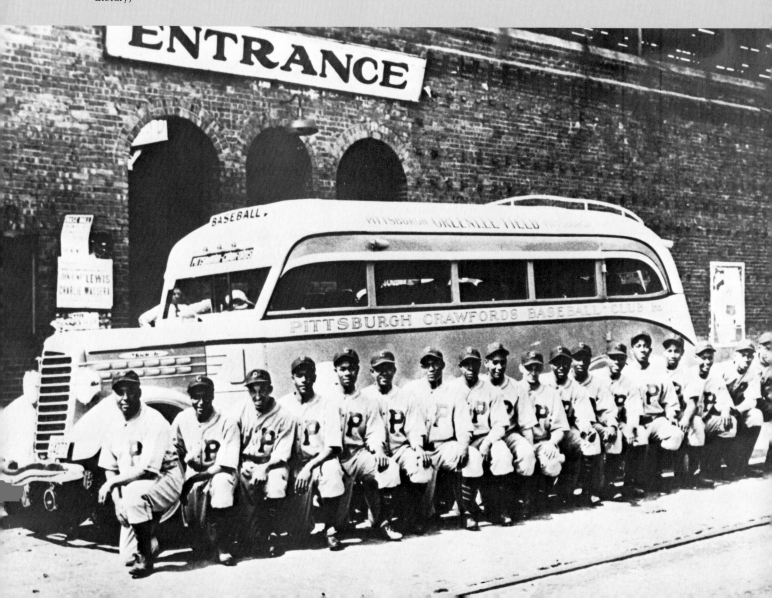

Above: Josh Gibson, star of the Pittsburgh Homestead Grays, demonstrating batting technique to young fans in 1943. (Courtesy Dennis Goldstein)

Right: Antonio Ruiz, star Cuban pitcher for the Cincinnati Clowns in 1943, when they played in the Negro American League. Usually unaffiliated barnstormers, the Clowns combined stunts with serious baseball. They became the Indianapolis-Cincinnati Clowns in 1944 and later the Indianapolis Clowns. (Courtesy Schomburg Center for Research in Black Culture, The New York Public Library)

Commissioner Landis ordered major league teams to wear special uniforms when engaging in exhibitions with black teams. By vaguely depicting the white major league teams as "All Stars," Landis hoped to avoid unfavorable comparisons. But fans of all stripes were attracted to such games. For black fans, victories scored by their heroes inspired beliefs in equality that black youngsters eagerly sought to realize in their play. Consequently, black schools, colleges, social clubs, and industrial workers groups organized teams and leagues, thus providing a reservoir of eager young talent.

In the late 1920s, however, dreams of future diamond glories were dimmed by the collapse of the black majors. In 1926 Foster's illness and retirement posed a leadership crisis for the black majors. For a time the baseball boom continued, as two minor leagues, the Negro Southern League and the Texas-Oklahoma-Louisiana League, joined the professional ranks. But by 1928 the boom became a bust. In 1928 the major Eastern Colored League collapsed, and the following year financial troubles affected the Negro National League. In 1930, as the onrushing Depression took its toll, Foster died; at least he was spared the agony of watching his beloved Negro National League fold up in 1931.

The collapse of the Negro National League ended the first phase of black major league baseball. But, after a one-year hiatus, a new breed of black promoters launched a second phase of the black majors. Heading the movement to restore the black major leagues was Gus Greenlee, a Pittsburgh numbers-game operator with a strong interest in baseball. Since 1930 Greenlee had sponsored a black pro team, the Pittsburgh Crawfords. Naming his team after a local black social club, Greenlee determined to make it the best in Pittsburgh. In 1932 Greenlee built his own stadium at a cost of $100,000 and recruited star players like Leroy ("Satchel") Paige, Josh Gibson, Oscar Charleston, Judy Johnson, and Cool Papa Bell to beef up his team. Greenlee also encouraged numbers operators in Newark, New York, Philadelphia, and Baltimore to back pro teams. In company with the rival Pittsburgh Homestead Grays, these teams formed the nucleus of the revived Negro National League, which commenced play in 1933.

In the years 1933–36 Greenlee's Crawfords reigned as the best black team ever assembled; a number of observers rated the team better than

Left: Satchel Paige, pitcher for the Kansas City Monarchs, and Josh Gibson were already legendary when they posed for this pregame photo in 1944. (Courtesy Dennis Goldstein)

Right: Roy Campanella in the early 'Forties as catcher for the Baltimore Elite Giants, a team he joined in 1937 at the age of fifteen. His catching ability and .353 batting average led him to a regular position with the Dodgers in 1948 and eventually to the Hall of Fame. (Courtesy John Thorn)

some white major league teams. With the Crawfords as the circuit's centerpiece and with some teams playing in rented major league parks, the Negro National League prospered. A popular Greenlee innovation was the staging of the annual East-West All-Star game. Played each summer from 1933 to 1950 at Comiskey Park in Chicago, the East-West All-Star game became the highlight of the season for the players and a major social event for fans. The first game drew 20,000 spectators, and by the 1940s throngs of 50,000 flocked to the spectacle.

In 1937 Greenlee's numbers operation was broken by police action. Financially weakened, and deserted by defecting stars, Greenlee saw his stadium razed in 1938 and his team dropped from the league. But the Negro National League was sturdy enough to withstand the passing of Greenlee. Indeed, black major league baseball received a powerful boost in 1937 when J. L. Wilkinson, the owner of the Kansas City Monarchs, formed a second major league, the Negro American League, with teams based in the South and Midwest. A resolute innovator, Wilkinson had kept his Monarchs afloat as an independent club by mortgaging his own home to pay salaries and by operating as his own booking agent. With a strong team behind him, Wilkinson persuaded teams from St. Louis, Chicago, Memphis, Atlanta, Jacksonville, and Birmingham to join his Negro American League. With frequent replacements, it lasted until 1950—two years longer than the second Negro National League, which folded in 1948.

The restoration of the dual major league system lent strong structural support to black baseball. Teams played scheduled championship games; the champions of each major league contended in the Negro World Series; and the East-West All-Star game, with fans voting for the star performers, solidified the major league enterprise. However, the number of championship games played by a team seldom exceeded sixty; as ever, most teams played far more exhibition games, and good players continued to venture to Latin America for additional paying opportunities. This second phase of black major league ball saw some teams renting major league parks. The New York Yankees, for example, received as much as $100,000 a year from such rental. Night ball was a popular innovation, and some teams carried their own portable lighting apparatus on road trips. Good managers and equipment were commonplace. Fans responded especially to the players, who often developed flashy styles of play, augmented at times by pregame clowning. But competition was serious, and fans admired the players as able professionals, frequently placing them on a heroic plane with black entertainers.

A powerful example to downtrodden American blacks, black baseball stars inspired both North American and Latin American blacks to seek membership in the professional ranks. Indeed, beginning in the 1920s, Latin American blacks played in the Negro majors. In turn, American black stars played often in Latin America, where they helped to popularize professional baseball in Cuba, Puerto Rico, Panama, Venezuela, the Dominican Republic, and Mexico. Playing alongside natives of these countries, black Americans enjoyed equal treatment. Meanwhile, white American professionals, who sometimes played alongside blacks in Latin America, became unwitting pioneers in the coming integration of North American professional baseball.

Monte Irvin, who returned from military service in 1946 to resume his career as a slugging outfielder for the Brooklyn Eagles of the Negro National League. Because of his stellar fielding and .373 batting average during eleven seasons with the Eagles, Irvin became a New York Giant in 1948 and was elected to the Hall of Fame in 1973. (Courtesy John Thorn)

The end of the black majors came shortly after Jackie Robinson, a reserve with the Kansas City Monarchs, was signed by Branch Rickey in 1945. In 1946, while Robinson starred with the Dodgers' Montreal farm club, the Negro majors enjoyed their best year financially. But the end of the black majors followed with devastating suddenness. The following year, when Robinson joined the formerly all-white majors, owner Wilkinson anxiously watched as Kansas City fans journeyed to St. Louis to sit in segregated sections and watch Robinson in his major league debut with the Dodgers. That year Wilkinson's attendance and that of other black teams fell alarmingly, while black fans turned to watching newly integrated major league games. For black owners, what followed was a financial nightmare; as losses at the gate mounted, good players were snapped up by big league scouts at bargain prices. In 1947 Newark lost $22,000, and in 1948 Wilkinson's Monarchs folded. The Negro National League collapsed in 1948, followed two years later by the Negro American League.

In retrospect, the integration of the white major leagues was a disaster for black major league operators and for most of the players. Had the late Rube Foster had his way, the integration of professional baseball would have come by having entire black teams join organized baseball's major and minor league ranks. Instead, individual black players were singled out. The result was that veteran black stars like Josh Gibson, Willie Wells, Cool Papa Bell, Ray Dandridge, and Gene Benson were passed over by big league scouts seeking more "educable" younger men like Robinson, Larry Doby, Hank Aaron, Roy Campanella, Willie Mays, and Don Newcombe. Thus, many black profession-

Indianapolis Clowns in the mid-1950s. Their barnstorming antics are described in the vignette "Beneath the Majors." (Courtesy Dennis Goldstein)

Mayor Vincent J. Murphy of Newark greets William Bell, manager of the Newark Eagles, at the opening of the Eagles' 1948 season in the Negro National League. That season proved to be the last both for the Eagles and for their league, although the Negro American League continued to play through the 1950 season. (Courtesy Schomburg Center for Research in Black Culture, The New York Public Library)

als found themselves abruptly cast adrift and forced to seek some other line of work. Moreover, the piecemeal pattern of integration in the majors was slow; not until 1959 did every major league team field at least one black player.

For a hundred or more black players, the integration of the majors was a traumatic event. Added to the curtailment of their playing careers was the trauma of being forgotten. Because the Negro majors had always operated beyond the pale of organized baseball, records of black players had never been listed in official compilations of organized baseball. Only in recent years have sports historians moved to set the record straight by studying the spotty data on the black majors and piecing together and evaluating the performances of star players. In this enterprise few have labored more diligently than the Negro Baseball Committee of the Society of American Baseball Research. Thanks to their efforts and those of other baseball historians, the Baseball Hall of Fame by 1982 had enrolled eight stars from the black majors, including Rube Foster. Further recognition of the significance of the black majors in American sporting history came in 1979 when the community of Ashland, Kentucky, became the proposed site for a future Negro Baseball Hall of History. Meanwhile, business leaders have annually sponsored a reunion of black players at Ashland. Thanks to such efforts, the survivors of the thinning ranks of the half-forgotten stars of the black major leagues will come to know how important their efforts were both to the history of baseball and to the history of their country.

FROM FIELDS TO PARKS TO STADIUMS AND DOMES

BASEBALL WAS FIRST PLAYED ON FIELDS OF VARIOUS *kinds: pastures, town squares and commons, military drill fields and parade grounds. When organized clubs began in the 1840s, they often called the locations of their diamonds "fields," as in the case of Hoboken's famous Elysian Fields, depicted in Chapter 1. Chicago teams used a fancier handle in referring to Dexter Park, while the New York Giants favored the earthy-sounding Polo Grounds, shown in Chapters 2 and 3.*

Before the Civil War a number of baseball organizations began erecting permanent structures to accommodate fans and players. An example was Baltimore's Pastime Club, which built expensive grounds with seats, fences, and clubhouse. After the Civil War, when entrepreneurs saw the commercial possibilities in paid admissions and refreshment sales at ball games, they started providing more seats and other conveniences for fans. Diamonds with grandstands became generally known as "parks."

As early as 1867 the Washington Nationals had a park surrounded by a ten-foot fence and shaded on the north side by roofed stands. Alfred Henry Spink, who later founded The Sporting News, *organized a group of St. Louis businessmen in 1875 to back the construction of Sportsman's Park.*

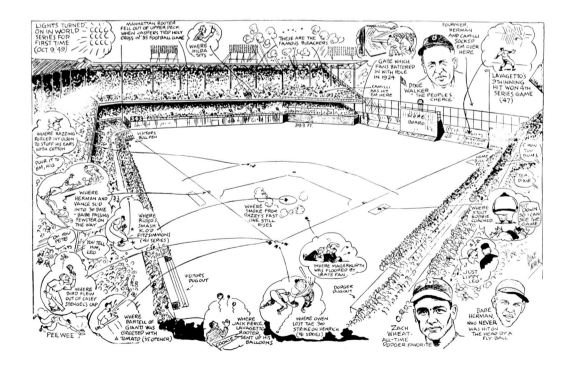

This park, with a capacity of 1,600 spectators, was the future home of the Browns and Cardinals. One of the first modern ballparks, with an all-steel grandstand and a capacity of 35,000, was Shibe Park in Philadelphia, depicted in Chapter 4. Opened in 1909, Shibe Park was home to the Athletics until 1955, and also to the Phillies from 1938 to 1969. Other famous parks were Fenway, home of the Boston Red Sox, and Comiskey, home of the Chicago White Sox. For some reason, five leading National League teams stayed with old-fashioned lingo: the Braves with Braves Field, the Cubs with Wrigley Field, the Dodgers with Ebbets Field, the Phillies with Baker Field, and the Pirates with Forbes Field.

In 1923, when the owners of the New York Yankees provided a 74,000-seat home for their powerhouse team, they emulated Roman emperors and collegiate football powers by calling it a "stadium." The "house that Ruth built," as described in Chapter 5, was on the Bronx side of the Harlem River opposite the Giants' Polo Grounds on the Manhattan side. Earlier, the Senators occupied Griffith Stadium, while the Tigers renamed their home as Briggs Stadium. Today, twenty of the twenty-six major league clubs have their homes in stadiums. Only the Giants, White Sox, and Red Sox remain at home in "parks," and the Cubs are the only club to call a "field" their home. In tune with the times and in response to local weather, the Houston Astros, Minnesota Twins, and Seattle Mariners are at home under "domes."

In the following pages, the present home of every major league club is depicted, sometimes in relation to the surrounding metropolis and sometimes accompanied by parking facilities, a necessity of the 1980s. All the photographs were graciously supplied by the respective clubs. Preceding the current photographs—for the sake of comparison and nostalgia—are cartoon drawings of two legendary sites that no longer exist: Ebbets Field and Griffith Stadium. The Polo Grounds can be seen in the photograph of Yankee Stadium, while Sportsman's Park is depicted in Chapter 6.

Opposite:
Ebbets Field, Brooklyn. Gene Mack's Hall of Fame Cartoons, Major League Ball Parks. (Copyright 1950, Gene Mack, Courtesy Eugene G. McGillicuddy, Jr., *Boston Globe*)

Below:
Griffith Stadium, Washington, D.C. Gene Mack's Hall of Fame Cartoons, Major League Ball Parks. (Copyright 1950, Gene Mack, Courtesy Eugene G. McGillicuddy, Jr., *Boston Globe*)

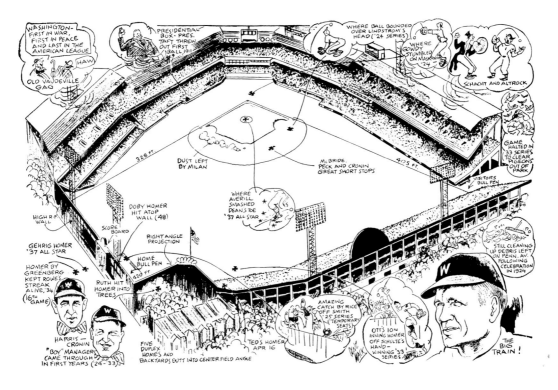

FROM FIELDS TO PARKS TO STADIUMS AND DOMES   209

Atlanta-Fulton County Stadium, home of Atlanta Braves.

Wrigley Field, home of Chicago Cubs.

Riverfront Stadium, home of Cincinnati Reds.

Houston Astrodome, home of Houston Astros.

Dodger Stadium, home of Los Angeles Dodgers.

Montreal's Olympic Stadium, home of Montreal Expos.

Shea Stadium, home of New York Mets.

Veterans Stadium, home of Philadelphia Phillies.

Three Rivers Stadium, home of Pittsburgh Pirates.

Busch Stadium, home of St. Louis Cardinals.

San Diego Stadium, home of San Diego Padres.

Candlestick Park, home of San Francisco Giants.

Memorial Stadium, home of Baltimore Orioles.

Fenway Park, home of Boston Red Sox.

Anaheim Stadium, home of California Angels.

Comiskey Park, home of Chicago
White Sox.

Cleveland Stadium, home of the
Cleveland Indians.

Tiger Stadium, home of Detroit Tigers.

Royals Stadium, home of Kansas City Royals.

County Stadium, Milwaukee, home of Milwaukee Brewers.

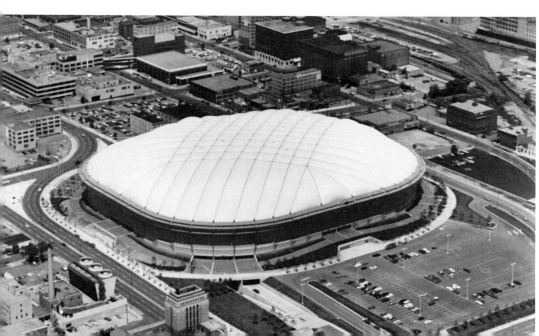

Metrodome, home of Minnesota Twins.

Oakland Stadium, home of Oakland Athletics.

Yankee Stadium, home of New York Yankees. (Note Polo Grounds, former home of New York Giants, across Harlem River.)

Kingdome, home of Seattle Mariners.

Arlington Stadium, home of
Texas Rangers.

Exhibition Stadium, home of
Toronto Blue Jays.

EXPANSION AND ELECTRONICS, 1946–1986

PROSPERITY AND OPTIMISM CHARACTERIZED THE *United States from V-J Day in August 1945 until midcentury, providing ideal conditions for big league baseball. American optimism was only slightly grazed by the Korean War of 1950–53—despite substantial casualties and the nation's first negotiated peace settlement since the War of 1812—while American prosperity was unwounded. From 1953 until the end of the 'Fifties, indeed until 1963, the mood of the country was largely upbeat, and the economy was expanding. Then came the cyclonic 'Sixties, a time of storm and stress for the nation but merely of growing pains for baseball, followed by the 'Seventies, when baseball soared while the United States tried to regain its equilibrium. The 'Eighties so far have been a decade of reexamination of fundamental assumptions affecting both the nation and the national game.*

Like a spring thaw, the end of World War II unleashed sweeping changes that profoundly altered major league baseball. Foremost among them were the game's racial integration, the decline of central cities, the impact of television, the expansion of the leagues, the unionization of players, the salary revolution, the growing talent shortage, and the competition from rival sports. Most of these problems were interconnected, and each of them challenged the acumen of owners during the forty-one seasons from 1946 through 1986.

In recent times professional baseball, more than most other institutions, has seemed to realize the American ideal of the "melting pot." By the 1960s clubs accepted players from groups that some pundits called "unmeltable ethnics." In 1947, seven years before the U.S. Supreme Court struck down segregation in the public schools, big league baseball broke the racial barrier. Dodger President Branch Rickey began the process by signing Jackie Robinson and assigning him to the Dodgers' Montreal farm club in 1946. The following year Robinson joined the Dodgers, where his exploits soon paved the way for scores of black American and Hispanic players to follow.

Postwar demographic factors gave both smiles and frowns to ball clubs. The nation's 150 million citizens, a number that an ongoing baby boom would swell to more than 200 million by 1970, had increasing leisure time and pocket money. Real wages in the United States doubled between 1938 and 1970, and Americans spent three times as much for recreation in 1950 as they had in 1940—a whopping $11 billion, which soared to $18 billion by 1960 and to $40 billion in the late 'Seventies. Cities continued to grow, but suburbs grew much faster, along with automobile ownership. This growth gave some pain to club owners, whose parks had been built when typical fans used trolleys or subways. Ten new parks were opened in the 1960s, most near highways and surrounded by parking lots—all of these costly establishments funded wholly or partly with city, county, state, or federal tax dollars.

The flight to the suburbs was combined with a population shift from the older industrial cities to new urban centers, especially in the West and South; this in turn led to an accelerating movement of franchises. In 1953 the first franchise shift in a half-century occurred when the Braves moved from

Boston to Milwaukee; the latest came in 1970 when the Seattle Pilots moved to Milwaukee. By 1985 rumors of possible franchise moves swirled about Pittsburgh, Cleveland, and the current Seattle club. In other responses to demographic shifts, the big leagues expanded from eight to ten teams in 1961 and to a dozen each in 1969. When the American League unilaterally expanded to fourteen teams in 1977, the dual major league pattern was skewed. In 1985 the National League seemed ready to restore the balance by adding two teams, while restive clubs in both leagues were licking their chops over promising new sites like Denver, Miami, New Orleans, and Phoenix. Habit-bound fans thought expansion might be out of hand. Indeed, a number would accept the wry comment of political scientist Robert H. Salisbury that "as long as there were 16 major league baseball teams, none west of St. Louis or south of Washington, American society held together. You could still count on things." Despite his dim view of expansion, Professor Salisbury concludes: "If we do attain a better social balance, however, it will be the calming effects of the summer game, not tax reform, that does it."

Baseball's calming effects were valuable at the many times after World War II when American society seemed in danger of being pulled apart by external or internal forces. The Cold War against Communism was frustratingly resistant to simple solutions, particularly when it heated up to the shooting stage in Korea and Vietnam, and therefore divided Americans. Resistance to the struggle for racial equality and social justice—culminating in assassinations of national leaders—was equally divisive. Revelations of corruption at high places in government, business, education, labor, journalism, and even religion—of which Watergate was only a prime example—eroded the trust that holds American society together. But there stood organized baseball, something you could still count on. Big league baseball symbolized the American dream, where pure ability prevails despite race, creed, color, or social origin. Expansion actually widened the influence of the dream, even across the border into Canada by the franchise route and into Latin America via player recruitment, thereby giving a living example of the One World ideal. Corruption had not tainted baseball since the Black Sox scandal of 1919–21, although some observers in the 'Eighties feared that widening revelations of drug abuse could become the worst scandal ever. Best of all, the continuity of baseball's rules, techniques, organizations, and customs—despite relatively limited expansion and modernization—was reassuring to Americans on the sociopolitical right, left, and center.

Although baseball's postwar changes were more than skin-deep, they have not made the game's familiar countenance unrecognizable. While many clubs have departed from pinstriped flannel, their uniforms stay with the basic knickers, knee-length stockings, and visored caps. Batting helmets and improved protective gear for catchers, as well as for umpires, enhance baseball's safety without reducing its excitement. Larger gloves make one-handed catches easier but do not eliminate fielding skill. Whippy, tapered bats still require talented hitters, and there are prohibitions against excessive gimmicks like bats with inserted rubber, cork, or mercury. Even if the new cowhide ball (replacing the traditional horsehide) is livelier, pitchers have learned new tricks to cope with batters. Stylistically, baseball stayed with the "big bang" offensive introduced by Babe Ruth in 1920, but pitchers armed themselves with varied deliveries, and managers effectively deployed relief-pitching specialists. A widened strike zone was tried in 1963–68 but was dropped because it gave an undue advantage to pitchers. The biggest rule change was made by the American League in 1973 when it authorized a designated hitter to bat for the pitcher, but the National League has stuck with the old rule, giving fans scope for some lively comparisons. Players' specialized talents also are used by modern managers in a way that approaches platooning, though far from the all-out platoon system adopted by football. Professional baseball's guild-like quality has been demonstrated by two economists, David N. Laband and Bernard F. Lentz, whose research shows the extraordinarily high percentage of big league ball players whose fathers were major or minor leaguers. The vast majority of rookies, of course, still come from families never before represented on the diamonds of the national game.

Television unquestionably has increased the percentage of Americans of all ages and both sexes who "follow" professional baseball, at least during a tight race or series or when some star attracts their interest—much as TV has widened the audience for "happenings" in music, politics, war, science, or religion. Many of these new electronic fans, or quasi fans, never will go to a big league ballpark, but some will. And some may transfer their TV-inspired baseball interest to Little League or Babe Ruth League, school or college, semi-pro or sandlot, or even minor league contests. Some of television's effects on baseball seem clearly positive; some seem clearly negative; and all are clearly debatable. Only one fact is obvious: Although baseball may be essentially the same as ever, its place in American society has changed radically in the Electronic Age.

On the positive side, televised games fetched ever-increasing revenues, which by 1984 exceeded ballpark ticket sales. Although live attendance dipped alarmingly in the 1950s and 1960s, it soared to new highs after 1975. (Some experts argue it would be even higher without TV—a bit like arguing that pie sales would be higher if ice cream had not been invented.) On the negative side, television stimulated the growth of rival sports, threatened baseball's stability by stimulating franchise shifts and league expansion, impelled owners to make costly changes in the staging of games, exacerbated the talent shortage, damaged the minors, and encouraged player militancy. (Here again the pie/ice cream comparison is apt.) The obvious question is not whether organized baseball can live with TV but how it can best do so.

The big leagues' increasing talent scarcity after World War II resulted from conditions fostered, if not created, by television: league expansion, player specialization, and competitive inter-sport recruitment. A host of talented athletes was needed to staff the burgeoning professional leagues in football and basketball, with their specialized individual players and platoons, along with the expanding national game. Baseball's traditional recruiting grounds, the sandlot leagues, were disappearing, while baseball remained a minor sport at many schools and colleges. Scouting could discover talent, and farm systems could develop it, but neither could create it. By the 1960s, therefore, clubs were spending millions on college baseball scholarships and summer leagues. In the spring of 1965, emulating pro football, the baseball leagues initiated free-agent drafts of promising high school and college ball players. Although the draft system shared the talent, it contributed to the escalation of bonuses and salaries. Unlike football and basketball, baseball's owners and managers believed rookies needed at least three years' seasoning in the minors—not to mention the minors' screening process, which only the fittest (or most determined) survived. But the minor leagues suffered a shocking decline in the 'Fifties; according to statistics compiled by writer Leonard Koppett, the 400 major leaguers of 1950 were chosen from 9,000 minor leaguers, whereas the 600 major leaguers of 1975 were picked from only 3,000 minor leaguers. Minor league officials blamed the majors for expanding into their territories, for indiscriminately drafting minor league players, and above all for upstaging minor league games with big league broadcasts and telecasts. Forced to act, the major leagues in the 'Sixties voted to subsidize the minors under the Player Development Program, which stabilized the feeder circuits; by 1985 the minors included 21 leagues and 184 teams. Since minor league players lacked bargaining power, either individually or collectively, their pay and working conditions lagged ever farther behind those of the majors. Although some clubs introduced belated reforms in their farm systems— notably the White Sox in 1967 and the Yankees in 1977, followed by the Dodgers and Phillies—the organized big league players paid scant attention to their "bush league" brethren.

Militant organization and bargaining by the Major League Players Association were intimately tied to the postwar boom in electronic media coverage. In 1946 club owners tamed the newly formed American Baseball Guild in part by granting pensions to over-five-year men and—most significantly—pledging to fund 80 percent of the costs with radio and television income. When the owners tried to abolish the pension system in 1953, the Players Association was born, rising to maturity in the 'Sixties as TV income skyrocketed. On three occasions player walkouts erupted, including the fifty-day strike of 1981 and the two-day strike of 1985. The winning of salary arbitration, and in 1976 of free-agent rights for six-year veterans, circumvented the reserve clause and contributed to awesome salary escalation. Comparative *figures tell the tale: In 1970 only twenty stars earned salaries of $100,000 or more; in 1980 the average annual player salary was $185,000; and in 1985 the average was $360,000!*

A major issue in the 1985 strike was the question of the owners' profit or loss. The owners first produced figures showing collective losses of $65 million per year, later reduced to $43 million, whereas the players alleged that owners were in fact making a profit of $9 million. Accounting professor George Sorter, who interpreted the figures for the owners, concluded that "each figure was legitimate" but that "each also described something different." He further concluded that, if he confined costs and revenues to those directly related to baseball operations, he would arrive at "a $27 million total loss for all 26 teams—roughly a $1 million average loss per team." Professor Sorter then drew this lesson from his findings: "There must be psychic returns that make people want to own ball clubs. The critical question is whether these psychic returns will continue to be sufficient to compensate for large and growing financial losses." The professor has given all baseball lovers food for serious thought.

7
POSTWAR PROSPERITY AND PROGRESS

BLESSED WITH VICTORY AND PEACE, AMERICANS OF 1946 understandably viewed the future with optimism. And why not? The prospects of abundance for most of the nearly 150 million citizens—a number due to swell to 179 million by 1960—were already apparent and glowing brighter. Stimulated by war production, unemployment stood at a mere 2 percent in 1946. Although the rapid demobilization of millions of soldiers posed a serious threat to employment, the menace was deflected by the G.I. Bill of Rights. A brilliant piece of legislation, the bill subsidized education and housing for returning members of the armed forces. In all, more than 2 million opted for higher education, an influx that not only boosted colleges but soon established the college degree as an essential passport into higher-level jobs. Likewise, the housing boom ignited by the bill's low-cost loans galvanized the economy. An inspired solution to the problem of reintegrating returning vets into the economy, the $14.5 billion cost of the program more than proved its worth as an economic pump-primer.

Thus primed, the American economy gathered strength from other forces. An unprecedented marriage and baby boom increased demand for housing, autos, and television sets. Indeed, television took the nation by storm; by 1959, 77 percent of all households had sets. With stunning speed, television viewing became the most popular leisure outlet, with sports subjects among the most favored programs. While television spearheaded the revolution in American leisure outlets, the leisure trend gained strength from declining work hours and rising family incomes. With 37 percent of American families enjoying incomes of over $7,500 a year by 1960, there was ample time and money for leisure diversion.

Of course, nettles also grew in the American abundance garden. Internally, the nation worried about creeping inflation, a soaring divorce rate, and the bugaboo of economic recession. Such fears were exacerbated by pressures from repressed minority groups that demanded a share of material blessings. Externally, the nation was learning that its status as a leading world power was a mixed blessing. With fearful suddenness the Soviet Union and China replaced prostrate Germany and Japan as threats. When the Soviet Union became a nuclear power, its growing might instilled a climate of fear in America of the 1950s. In its wake this fear evoked a Cold War mentality; arms buildups, military drafts, and campaigns against disloyalty or "subversion" were by-products. In 1950 fear of Communist expansion involved America in a

Albert Benjamin ("Happy") Chandler, national commissioner during baseball's transitional years between World War II and the Korean War. A successful politician in Kentucky, Chandler showed more courage than political skill as commissioner in 1945–51. (Courtesy John Thorn)

Top: Connie Mack III and his father, Roy Mack (in fedora), leave Broad Street Trust Company in Philadelphia in 1954, after selling the Athletics to a Kansas City group. This was one of five franchise moves of 1953–58. (Courtesy Charles Burkhardt)

Bottom: Jackie Robinson in action in 1953, at the height of his ten-year major league career. (Courtesy Ronald A. Smith and National Baseball Library, Cooperstown, New York)

United Nations "police action" against the Soviet client state of North Korea. The ensuing Korean War lasted until 1953; North Korean expansion was halted, but Red China emerged as a formidable bastion of Communist strength. After a brief respite, Cold War tensions increased in 1957 when the Soviet Union launched a space satellite; in retaliation America launched a major effort to narrow "the knowledge gap" in space programs and missile weaponry.

Yet, for all the grating internal and external fears, life in postwar America was bullishly optimistic. It was a time when many Americans aspired to good jobs, suburban domesticity, and the diversions of leisure. For pro-sports promoters these were giddy times; booms exceeded busts, especially for major league baseball, but rival sports like pro football, basketball, and hockey also gained ground. Although such competition posed small threats to baseball's preeminence until the 1950s, it was no time for standpatters. To boldly reach out and grasp opportunities for new baseball promotion was something smarter owners did once the first tide of prosperity washed over the game and receded.

For four years baseball's old order bathed in unprecedented prosperity. Beginning with the 1946 season, major league attendance rose to a record 18.8 million, soaring to 20.3 million in 1947 and to 21.3 million in 1948. But then the wave crested; after falling to 20.4 million in 1949, attendance sank to 17.7 million in 1950 and to 16.6 million in 1951. The same pattern engulfed the minor leagues, which rebounded from a near-disastrous 10.6 million overall attendance in 1945 and soared to 32.7 million in 1946. There followed three halcyon years during which attendance averaged 40 million, but by 1951 a sickening reversal dropped minor league attendance to 27.5 million.

That attendance at pro baseball games should boom so mightily, actually outpacing the nation's population growth, then bust dramatically, sent pundits scurrying for explanations. Certainly one explanation was the radio and television boom, blamed by Rickey for making a free show of games. By 1950 most major league clubs had local radio and television contracts, allowing games to be aired into their hinterlands. For the majors, revenue derived from these sources cushioned the impact of falling attendance, but the minors gained no such benefit. On the contrary, broadcasts converted minor league fans to major league ball. Staggered by this blow, the minors absorbed another crusher when five transplanted major league teams dislodged minor league teams from their established sites. Then, hard after these moves, came the major league expansion of the 1960s. The minors never recovered from such blows; instead, these proving grounds of future major league players survived in weakened form, becoming ever more dependent upon subsidies from major clubs. As for the black major leagues, they collapsed in the wake of major league baseball's integration; by 1950 the black leagues had virtually disappeared.

Another explanation for baseball's postwar decline took note of the growing popularity of other leisure outlets, including rival sports. Buoyed by television exposure, such sports grew mightily, posing a serious threat to baseball's dominance by the 1960s.

Yet another explanation faulted baseball's hidebound, traditional fifty-year-old format for failing to keep up with changing population

Four Red Sox heavy-hitters of 1946: from left, Ted Williams, outfield; Bobby Doerr, second base; Dom Di-Maggio, outfield; Vern Stephens, short-stop. (Courtesy Pat Reilly and National Baseball Library, Cooperstown, New York)

trends. Noting demographic shifts showing new population centers ripe for major league ball, a few shrewd owners uprooted their teams and moved to such sites. By 1958 five such moves took place. Although the sixteen-club format survived in this era, such moves indicated that true expansion was not far off. Thus, when the National League's Boston Braves, Brooklyn Dodgers, and New York Giants respectively occupied Milwaukee, Los Angeles, and San Francisco, while the American League's St. Louis Browns and Philadelphia Athletics transferred to Baltimore and Kansas City, the breakup of the old format was imminent. Still, the old guard resisted taking the expansionist plunge. Indeed, the final step was forced on them; the shove came in 1959 when outside promoters, pushing a rival major league, persuaded the majors to expand lest this menacing Continental League seize the choicest new sites.

In these tornado years other challenges equally momentous confronted major league promoters. Of these, none was more dramatic than the racial integration of the game. Undermined by anti-discrimination laws and policies, segregationist barriers began to crumble. An obvious target of postwar egalitarians was major league baseball's "unwritten law" barring black players. Thus excluded, black players played in segregated leagues, including major circuits like the Negro National League, which produced outstanding stars. Although constantly pressured to admit such stars, the white majors and minors resisted. While he lived, Commissioner Landis upheld restrictive racial policies, and after Landis's 1944 death, some owners pursued the same course. In Branch Rickey, however, they met a determined opponent. Declaring that integrated baseball was not only right but potentially profitable, Rickey electrified the baseball world of 1946 by signing up black infielder Jack Roosevelt Robinson of the Kansas City Monarchs and assigning him to the Dodgers' Montreal farm club.

Rickey's bold move opened the curtain on an American morality play with Jackie Robinson cast as the hero. Handpicked for his athletic prowess, as well as academic and military credentials, Robinson was coached and cautioned by Rickey, who urged him to shrug off slurs and slights and to concentrate on proving himself on the diamond. Responding brilliantly, the handsome, twenty-six-year-old Robinson starred at Montreal and a year later was summoned to the parent Dodgers as their first baseman. That year Robinson carried the hopes and fears of black players and fans on his broad shoulders. Despite

A trio of 1947 Yankees interviewed by sportswriter John Drebinger of the *New York Times:* from left, Joe DiMaggio, Joe Page, Specs Shea. (Courtesy *New York Times*)

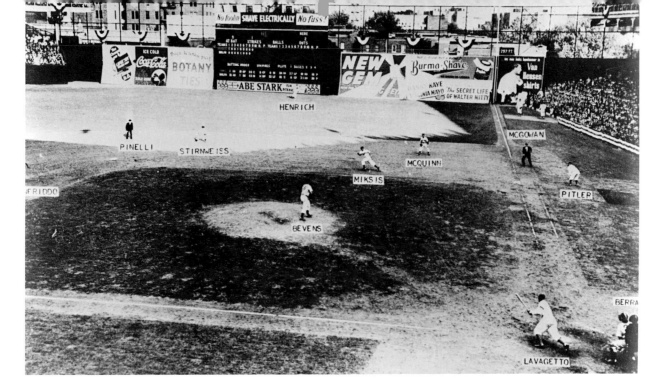

harassment by some players, fans, and owners, Robinson had the powerful support of new commissioner A. B. Chandler and a sympathetic tide of public opinion. In his first season Robinson won National League Rookie-of-the-Year honors; in his ten-year career, his leadership and attainments won him a place in baseball's Hall of Fame. More important, Robinson shone as one of the symbolic leaders who shaped baseball's changing course from 1946 to this day. As baseball's egalitarian pathfinder, he opened the doors for scores of black American and Hispanic players, whose outstanding play validated the wisdom of Rickey's noble experiment.

If Robinson's 1947 initiation spotlighted baseball's racial integration, a growing scarcity of young recruits helped to speed the process. To the astonishment of many baseball men, who counted on ex-players returning from war service to provide a talent surplus, many ex-servicemen failed to qualify. Of 300 returning G.I.'s in Rickey's 1946 Dodger camp, only a handful succeeded, and it was the same elsewhere. Faced with a growing talent shortage, clubs hired more scouts, who competed for promising youngsters by offering lavish bonuses. The "bonus baby" era of scouting lasted until 1965, and its high costs proved to be divisive. Since the bonus bidding favored richer clubs, others looked to the Negro leagues or to Latin America for cheaper prospects. By 1947, however, Rickey already was combing this source of talent; having divined the coming postwar talent shortage early, his scouting staff took the lead in signing black players and in corralling white youths and Hispanics. Hence, when the Robinson experiment succeeded, the Dodgers quickly summoned more black players. Other teams, including the Indians, Giants, and Braves, followed suit, but they were dwarfed by the scale of Rickey's latest farming operation. Ironically, the Yankees, who concentrated on young white players while pursuing a watch-and-wait policy on public reaction to blacks and Hispanics, racked up more world titles than did Rickey's Dodgers.

Dodger Cookie Lavagetto breaking up Yankee Bill Bevens's near-miss at becoming the first no-hit pitcher in World Series history. In the ninth inning of the fourth game of the 1947 Series, with two out and the Yanks ahead 2–1, Lavagetto doubled on Bevens's second pitch to drive in the winning Dodger runs. (Author's Collection)

Lou Boudreau, player-manager of the Indians, on the dugout steps in 1948. A Hall of Fame shortstop, he had a fifteen-year career batting average of .295. (Courtesy Mike Andersen)

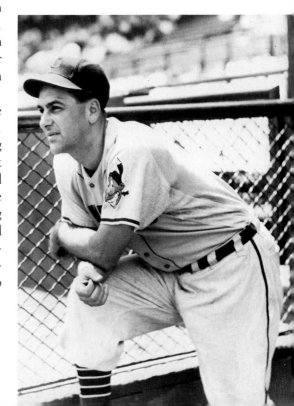

Strong pitching by bespectacled right-hander Paul ("Dizzy") Trout and Harold ("Hal") Newhouser helped the Tigers to a world championship in 1945 but could not take the Detroiters to the top again in the 'Forties and 'Fifties. Newhouser exceeded twenty victories for the fourth time in 1948, when the Tigers finished fifth. Trout slipped after 1946 from his fast pace of the early 1940s. (Courtesy Michael Mumby Collection)

Meanwhile, the bonus craze ignited the vexing problem of envious veterans. Eyeing the big bonuses paid to untried youths, veteran players demanded higher salaries. In 1946 this unrest was exploited by Mexican league promoters who made big pay offers to players who would jump to Mexico. A few did so and were blacklisted by Commissioner Chandler; however, a retaliatory lawsuit threatened to reverse this harsh piece of baseball law while also threatening the reserve clause. From 1950 to 1956 that clause was also menaced by a congressional subcommittee probe of baseball's position in respect to antitrust laws. Although no punitive legislation resulted, union activity by organized players in 1946 sowed seeds that three decades later circumvented the reserve clause and blossomed into an unprecedented salary revolution. Although the 1946 union threat aborted, it won the players some important concessions, including pension rights. To be sure, the players of this time had only a weak union, but under strong leadership in the 1960s the union became a potent force for boosting benefits and salaries.

Finally, any list of postwar problems must include the age-old dilemma of competitive imbalance among teams. In the past, powerful clubs always claimed an inordinate number of championships. For a brief time the Postwar Era held out hope that competitive balance might now be achieved. So it seemed in the years 1946–48 as three different teams in each major league won pennants. This hope was ruthlessly shattered in each league, however, by the rise of two of the most powerful dynasties in major league history.

YANKEE DOMINATION OF THE AMERICAN LEAGUE, 1946–1960

After a three-year power struggle during which the Red Sox, Yankees, and Indians each in turn won single pennants, American League teams bowed to the Yankee overlords as they achieved domination for ten of the next twelve seasons. Establishing an unprecedented pennant monopoly, the Yankees embellished their mastery by capturing seven world championship titles.

While Yankee power glorified the American League in these years, the fact was that no American team but the Yankees won a World Series in 1949–60. For Yankee lovers this was heady stuff, but the ensuing imbalance hurt the American League. Internally, the damage showed in falling attendance for most American clubs; externally, it was evidenced by superior National League attendance and offensive performances. What's more, by boldly occupying the most lucrative sites in the franchise moves of the 1950s, National League carpetbaggers scored another coup over the Americans. Nevertheless, when it came to the annual test of strength between the two leagues, usually it was the American League, represented by the Yankees, that unfurled the Series banner.

In 1946 there was little hint of such domination in the offing. Buoyed by the euphoria of peace and by the return of war vets, optimism surged among teams. On paper the Tigers, Red Sox, and Yankees all looked like major contenders. The new Yankee owners seemingly regarded their newly installed lighting system as a beacon for guiding the team to a pennant as well as for luring more fans to night games.

The Yanks collapsed ignominiously, however, finishing a distant third. As the team foundered, manager McCarthy quit, complaining of ill health and a breakdown of team discipline. Nor did the world champion Tigers fare well, finishing second and 12 games off the pace.

Instead, the Red Sox romped to an easy victory, winning 104 games. The pennant was the first for owner Yawkey, who had spent lavishly for years; for long-suffering Sox fans it was the first pennant since 1918. Returning slugger Ted Williams led the attack; his .342 batting, 38 homers, and 123 RBIs ranked him second to the leader in each of these categories. Johnny Pesky and Dom DiMaggio also topped .300 as manager Cronin's team led the league in batting. Dave ("Boo") Ferris (25-6) and Tex Hughson (20-11) were formidable pitchers. Nevertheless, when the Red Sox met the Cardinals in the 1946 World Series, they lost the hard-fought seven-game match.

Over the winter the Red Sox management considered swapping Williams for Joe DiMaggio of the Yankees. Had the deal gone through, Williams's 1947 Triple Crown batting (.342, 32, 114) would have been lost to the Sox. Still, Williams's virtuoso performance was too little to atone for faltering pitching. As the Sox fell to third, the Tigers repeated their second-place finish, but they lagged 12 games off the Yankee pace. Regrouping under manager Bucky Harris, the Yanks won 97 games. DiMaggio, batting .315 with 20 homers and 97 RBIs, led the Yankees to league-leading honors in batting and homers; the Yanks also fielded a superb pitching staff that included rookies Frank ("Specs") Shea and Vic Raschi, recently acquired veterans Allie Reynolds and Bobo Newsom, and reliefer Joe Page. Thus fortified, the Yankees beat the Dodgers in a memorable World Series, highlighted by Yankee pitcher Bill Bevens's abortive bid to pitch the first World Series no-hitter. The Yankees lost that game but won the deciding seventh game on Page's relief pitching.

Charles Dillon ("Casey") Stengel, Yankee manager from 1949 through 1960, a dozen years in which he sat out only two World Series. (Courtesy New York Yankees)

Joe DiMaggio beating the throw against the Senators in a late-season game in 1949. Injured for half the season, DiMaggio led the Yanks in a close pennant race thereafter. (Courtesy Michael Mumby Collection)

Victor John Angelo ("Vic") Raschi, whose 21–10 pitching helped the Yanks win a world championship in 1949. Joining him were Allie Reynolds (17–6), Tom Byrne (15–7), and Ed Lopat (15–10). (Courtesy New York Yankees)

Back on top of the world, the Yankees faced a resurgent Red Sox team. Now managed by ex-Yankee pilot McCarthy and fortified by two pitchers and a shortstop acquired from the Browns, the Sox mounted a blistering attack. So did the Indians, whose ranks included the American League's first black player, Larry Doby, and aging Satchel Paige, a legendary black pitching genius. For a time the A's also contended, but they faded in September. So did the Yanks in the closing days of that month, but the Indians and Red Sox finished in a dead heat. A sudden-death playoff game at Boston settled the issue, the Indians winning 8-3. For owner Bill Veeck's Indians, whose creative promotions attracted a record 2 million-plus home fans, it was the first pennant since 1920. Playing manager Lou Boudreau's .355 batting led the team; Doby batted .301, and ex-Yank Joe Gordon's 32 homers paced a league-leading offensive. Among the pitchers, starters Bob Lemon and ex-Yank Gene Bearden each won 20, Bob Feller won 19, and Paige posted a 6-1 record. Thus fired, the Indians burned the Boston Braves in the World Series, winning easily, four games to two.

Astonishingly, another eighteen seasons would pass before any American team but the Yanks hoisted a World Series banner. In that span the Yanks raised nine, each new banner attesting to their monopolistic rule. The Yankee reign began in 1949 when they won the first of a record five successive world titles. In this enterprise they were aided by general manager George Weiss, who was freed to ply his genius in trading and developing players. At Weiss's instigation, Casey Stengel, a veteran manager, was hired as the pilot. Never before a winner in the majors, manager Stengel now had the best talent he had ever known. The great DiMaggio, though aging and injury-hobbled, was the superstar; such was his lofty stature as team leader that it incited Stengel's jealousy. Along with DiMaggio, Stengel had half a dozen able outfielders, enabling him to platoon the best, depending on the game situation. It was the same with the infield, where only Phil Rizzuto at short was a fixture. Four able starting pitchers—Raschi, Reynolds, Ed Lopat, and Tom Byrne—were backed by reliefer Page. And in young Larry ("Yogi") Berra, Stengel had a promising catcher.

In a furious duel with McCarthy's Red Sox, the Yankees won the 1949 pennant by a single game. Although outhit, outslugged, and outpitched by others, the Yanks were bolstered by DiMaggio's brilliant deeds. Sidelined for half the season by injuries, DiMaggio returned in time to lead the team to three victories over the Sox in a crucial series. Thereafter, he batted .346 with 14 homers and 67 RBIs; that and Page's great relief work led the Yankee attack. Even so, help was wanted, and Weiss got it by acquiring slugger Johnny Mize from the Giants. Not till the last two days of the season was the issue settled; then the Yankees twice downed the Red Sox at home to win. After that achievement, the Yanks dispatched the Dodgers, winning the Series four games to one.

In the summer of 1950 Americans were jolted out of peacetime complacency by the outbreak of the Korean War. Although confined to a faraway peninsula and waged on a limited scale, the conflict lasted three years and reestablished the military draft. Under continuing international tensions, the draft endured until 1973; while it lasted it posed a threat to future baseball campaigns. The 1950 race was little affected, however; among the Yankees, aging and injuries (especially to DiMaggio) and shaky pitching were more troublesome. Hard-pressed by the Red Sox, who batted .302, and by the Tigers and Indians, the Yanks were bolstered by Mize's 25 homers and 72 RBIs and by late-season pitching brilliance from rookie Ed ("Whitey") Ford, who logged a 9-1 record. By winning 98, the Yanks beat out the Tigers by three and the Sox by four. They capped the victory by sweeping the Phillies in the World Series.

The following year, inroads by the military draft added to the Yankees' aging and injury woes. The draft took Ford, and age told on DiMaggio and the pitchers. But the farm system supplied promising replacements in infielder Gil MacDougald, pitcher Tom Morgan, and outfielder Mickey Mantle. Ticketed as DiMaggio's successor, young Mantle later starred; in 1951 he saw limited duty but batted .267 and showed power. Thus renewed, and bolstered by good pitching and Yogi Berra's MVP performance, the Yankees won the championship by five games over the Indians. Nor did the "miracle Giants" upset the Bronxites in the Series; after dropping two of the first three, the Yanks swept the next three, winning the finale on Bob Kuzava's redoubtable relief pitching.

Getting Kuzava had been the work of Weiss the trader; in 1952, as the Yanks sought a fourth world title, more help was needed to replace the departed DiMaggio and the injured Mantle. Responding, trader Weiss acquired outfielder Irv Noren from the Senators, then summoned young Billy Martin from the farm system. Recovering from injury, Mantle batted .311 with 23 homers and 87 RBIs to pace the team's league-leading attack, which was augmented by league-leading pitching. Though harried by the Indians, the Yanks matched the Tribe's September surge, holding on to win by two games. Then for a fourth time they faced the Dodgers. With each team swapping victories, a seven-game Series struggle ensued. However, the Yanks took the finale, again on Kuzava's sterling relief work.

Having tied their own record of four straight world titles, the Yankees eyed an unprecedented fifth. With pitcher Ford back from military duty, and youngsters Mantle, Martin, and MacDougald all battle-tested, the 1953 Yanks won easily. Breaking fast, they won 11 of their first 14 and in June reeled off 18 straight wins; thereafter, despite adversarial hassling and heckling, they coasted, winning by 8½ games over the Indians. Now only the Dodgers barred the way to a record five straight world titles, but this enemy fell in six games; by banging 12 hits in 24 at-bats, Martin starred for the Yankees.

In retrospect, 1953 was a watershed year for major league baseball. By moving to Milwaukee, the Braves upset the traditional format, and before the year was out, the Philadelphia A's moved to Kansas City as another breakaway franchise. Such moves inspired later carpetbaggery and signaled a coming era of expansion. Moreover, 1953 saw the Korean War end; it had not been a total war, but the loss of key players had hurt teams. Although the draft continued, at least the promise of peacetime campaigns was heartening.

Remaining to be exorcised was the Yankee bugaboo, a seemingly

John Robert ("Johnny") Mize, hard-hitting first baseman, who starred for the Cards in the 'Thirties, the Giants in the 'Forties, and the Yanks in the 'Fifties—less three seasons of military service. His forty-three timely pinch-hits helped the Yankees to five successive world championships in 1949–53. (Courtesy New York Yankees)

No Tomorrow at Ebbets

Dodgers' 1952 Series loss to the Yankees inspired this wry cartoon in the *Brooklyn Eagle*. (Courtesy National Baseball Library, Cooperstown, New York)

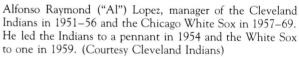

Alfonso Raymond ("Al") Lopez, manager of the Cleveland Indians in 1951–56 and the Chicago White Sox in 1957–69. He led the Indians to a pennant in 1954 and the White Sox to one in 1959. (Courtesy Cleveland Indians)

Edward Charles ("Whitey") Ford, phenomenal Yankee pitcher of the 'Fifties and 'Sixties. After a promising 1950 start, Ford spent two years in military service, then returned in 1953 for thirteen great seasons. He was 18–6 in 1953 and peaked at 25–4 in 1961. (Courtesy New York Yankees)

of Red Sox star Ted Williams, who bowed out of baseball with a homer in his last time at bat in 1960, these departures were signs of a dawning new era.

The same wistful dream of a new era of competitive balance that teased postwar American League teams also enthralled National League partisans. Indeed, over the first few peacetime seasons, a new National champion appeared each year before the Dodger dynasty took command. Although far less triumphant than the Yankees, the Dodgers' postwar compilation of seven pennants, three near-misses, and two world titles was dominant. No other contender came close; among other National winners, the Braves captured three pennants and a world title, the Giants took two pennants and a world championship, and the Cardinals, Phillies, Pirates, and Reds were one-shot winners who collectively accounted for two world titles.

That the Dodgers so speedily dispatched the Cards as National powers resulted from Branch Rickey's acumen. A dispute with owner Sam Breadon in 1942 ended Rickey's Cardinal career and sent him to Brooklyn. There, as general manager, he built the efficient Dodger farm system, which by 1946 controlled twenty-five minor league teams. By recruiting young players and pushing racial integration, Rickey shaped the course of baseball's continuing evolution and laid the groundwork for the Dodger dynasty that flowered so brightly in the 1950s.

The first harvest came in 1946 as the Dodgers rose up to deadlock the Cardinals. Rickey additions like outfielder Carl Furillo, infielder Eddie Stanky, and catcher Bruce Edwards joined established Dodger stars like

Cleveland's stellar pitching trio of 1954: from left, Bob Lemon, Mike Garcia, and Early Wynn. Lemon and Wynn have been elected to the Hall of Fame. Wynn moved to the White Sox in 1958 and helped win their 1959 pennant. (Courtesy Cleveland Indians)

Above left: Don Larsen winning the fifth game of the 1956 Series at Yankee Stadium with a no-hitter. In this scene the Yankee right-hander has just scored his final strike. (Courtesy Dennis Goldstein)

Above right: Don Larsen of the Yankees delivering his last pitch, a strike, to register the first no-hitter in World Series history. Larsen's fourteen-year career record was not spectacular, but he performed admirably under pressure, chalking up a 4–2 record for five World Series. (Courtesy New York Yankees)

Below: Al Gionfriddo of the Dodgers robbing Joe DiMaggio of a homer in the 1947 World Series. (Author's Collection)

Dixie Walker, Pee Wee Reese, and Pete Reiser in manager Durocher's lineup. Meanwhile, the Cardinals still drew on the Rickey legacy. Manager Eddie Dyer admitted as much as his Cardinals led the league in pitching, fielding, and batting. Leading the attack, outfielder Stan Musial (.365) won the batting title, the second of seven this superstar would own by the time he retired in 1963, and outfielder Enos Slaughter led the league in RBIs. Still, the Dodgers tied the Cards and forced the first championship playoff in National League history. The Cardinals easily won this best-of-three encounter and went on to beat the Red Sox in a seven-game World Series. Pitcher Harry Brecheen's three victories, the last a timely relief job in the finale, and Slaughter's bold base running in the finale established this pair as Series heroes.

Cardinal fans were fated to wait eighteen seasons before cheering another winner, however. In 1947 the Dodgers grabbed headlines with Rickey's precedent-shattering Jackie Robinson experiment. As the first black to play in the white majors in this century, Robinson was inserted at first base. Although much maligned, he won powerful support and proved his worth by .297 batting and by leading the league in stolen bases. Robinson won Rookie-of-the-Year honors, and with Walker and Reiser batting in the .300s, and pitcher Ralph Branca posting 21 wins, the Dodgers defeated the Cardinals by five games. A crowning tribute to Rickey, the victory was tainted by defeat at the hands of the Yankees, who won a seven-game Series struggle.

No immediate sequel followed the Dodgers' storied 1947 season. In a major overhaul, Rickey dealt veterans Walker and Vic Lombardi to the Pirates for pitcher Elvin ("Preacher") Roe and infielder Billy Cox, and signed star catcher Roy Campanella from the Negro leagues. With promising youngsters also on hand, the team suffered when manager Durocher, reinstated after his 1947 suspension, left to manage the Giants. Under interim manager Burt Shotton, the 1948 Dodgers managed a third-place finish. The Dodger fade-out enabled the Boston Braves to scale the heights by 6½ games over the Cardinals. Managed by former Cardinal skipper Billy Southworth, the Braves led the league in batting and pitching. However, the pitching staff was overly dependent upon aces Johnny Sain and Warren Spahn. Picked to lose in the World Series, the Braves fell to the Cleveland Indians in six games.

The predicted collapse of the Braves in 1949 raised the curtain on the postwar Dodger dynasty. Like the Yankees, who began their reign that year, the Dodgers led all National contenders for the next five years. Yet, compared with the Olympian Yanks, the Dodger dynasts were all too human. As the Yankees were winning five world titles, these Dodgers would win three pennants, lose two by narrow margins, and fail to raise a single Series banner.

Curiously enough, these rival dynasties began by winning their 1949 championships by the same thin margin. As the Yankees' 97-57 record edged the Red Sox by a game, so the same record carried the Dodgers to a single-game win over the Cards. The Dodger team, later to be dubbed the "Boys of Summer," was Rickey's handiwork. Managed by Shotton, the revamped team fielded a regular infield of Gil Hodges, Robinson, Reese, and Cox; Furillo and Snider were outfield stalwarts; Roy Campanella did most of the catching; and fireballing Don Newcombe, signed from the Negro National League, was an immediate pitching star. With Robinson (.342) leading the league in batting and winning MVP honors, the Dodgers led the league in homers, stolen bases, and fielding. But because the Cards led in pitching and batting, the contenders battled until the last day. The narrow victory highlighted Brooklyn's season, as the Dodgers again lost to the Yankees in the World Series. The two teams first swapped shutouts, but the Yankees swept the next three games.

Indeed, the Dodgers lost considerably more the following year. A festering power struggle between co-owners Walter O'Malley and Branch Rickey ended with O'Malley forcing Rickey out by season's end. Some observers blamed this struggle for the team's sluggish performance. Be that as it may, the Dodgers contended till the last day, though for most of the season they trailed the Phillies. Long the league doormats, the Phils were strengthened by such bonus babies as pitchers Robin Roberts (20-11) and Curt Simmons (17-8), outfielder Richie Ashburn, and catcher Stan Lopata. Dubbed the "Whiz Kids," manager Ed Sawyer's youthful team led by 7½ games in early September. Then they swooned; crippled by the loss of Simmons to the military draft, they saw their lead dwindle under a Dodger charge. Leading by one game, they faced the Dodgers at Ebbets Field in a must-win final game. With Roberts pitching against Newcombe, a strong throw by Ashburn cut down a potential Dodger winning run in the ninth, enabling the Phillies to win in the tenth on a three-run homer by Dick Sisler. The victory sent them into the World Series, but the Yankees swept them aside in four games.

That effort finished the Phillies as postwar contenders. With O'Malley in full control, the Dodgers regrouped under manager Chuck Dressen; turned loose, they threatened to tear the league apart in 1951. In early August they held a 13½-game lead over the Giants, who then mounted a charge. Managed by Leo Durocher and captained by shortstop Al Dark, the Giants won 37 of their last 44 games to tie the Dodgers. Although outhit and outslugged by the Dodgers, the Giants got league-leading pitching from a staff that boasted two 23-game winners in Sal Maglie and Larry Jansen.

To settle the 1951 championship, the Dodgers and Giants met in a three-game playoff series. At Brooklyn the Giants won the opener, but

Top: Stanley Frank ("Stan the Man") Musial, elected to the Hall of Fame for his twenty-two years as a Cardinal superstar. He batted .256 in four World Series. (Author's Collection)

Bottom: Enos Bradsher ("Country") Slaughter, who batted .291 in five World Series. In 1938–53 he played for the Cards, and in 1954–59 for other clubs. (Courtesy John Thorn)

Warren Spahn (left) and Johnny Sain, pitching aces of the Boston Braves in 1948. Spahn was 15–12 that year but thereafter averaged more than twenty annual victories for the Braves over a dozen seasons. Sain was 24–15 in 1948 but had only one more great season. (Courtesy Braves Baseball Club, National League)

at the Polo Grounds the Dodgers pummeled the Giants in the second game; in the third the Dodgers held a 4-1 lead going into the last of the ninth. Then, to the utter astonishment of the packed house and 95 million radio and television fans, the Giants rallied to win on outfielder Bobby Thomson's three-run homer. An electrifying victory, it glorified the Giants and branded the Dodgers as chokers. Indeed, it seems almost blasphemous to relate that the heroic Giants, after winning two of the first three games in the World Series, fell to the Yankees in six games.

To their credit, the chastened Dodgers flexed their muscles and captured the next two National League pennants. Bolstered by rookie pitcher Joe Black's 15 wins and as many saves, and by Furillo's league-leading batting, the 1952 Dodgers beat back another Giant counterattack to win by 4½ games. Then they battled the Yanks through seven games before losing the World Series. Shrugging off that loss, the 1953 Dodgers won 105 games, thirteen better than the rising Milwaukee Braves. Now as champs they took their league-leading honors in batting, homers, and fielding against the Yankees for a fifth time, but the results were the same. This time the Yankees won the Series in six games.

By now, five years of domination by the Yankees was sapping the morale of other contenders. Mercifully, a lull was nigh; in 1954 both Yankees and Dodgers slipped. In the Dodger camp, a contract dispute had O'Malley replacing manager Dressen with Walter Alston. Virtually unknown, the quiet Alston was a Dodger farm system manager. Although his appointment was jeered at, he stayed on for twenty-three seasons and became the winningest Dodger manager. But Alston's 1954 debut was inauspicious; worse, he was upstaged by Durocher, who drove the Giants to a five-game victory over the Dodgers. Back from military

Seven Dodger greats of 1949 and the 'Fifties: from left, Carl Furillo, Jackie Robinson, Roy Campanella, Pee Wee Reese, Duke Snider, Preacher Roe, Gil Hodges. (Courtesy Dodger Baseball Club, National League)

duty, outfielder Willie Mays batted .345 with 41 homers and 110 RBIs; Mays's brilliance, plus league-leading pitching from the likes of Maglie, Johnny Antonelli, and Hoyt Wilhelm, sparked the Giants. Then, to deepen Dodger gloom, Durocher led his dark-horse team to an astonishing Series victory over the awesome Cleveland Indians. The Giant sweep was a crusher; pinch-hitter Dusty Rhodes was a hitting star, and Mays's electrifying catch of a long drive that damped a Cleveland rally made him the fielding star.

Understandably crestfallen, the Dodgers saw their fortunes at last turn upward. Rallying again, the aging boys of summer mounted a furious assault in 1955. Leading the league in homers, batting, and pitching, they clinched the pennant in early September; the Dodgers left the second-place Braves 13½ games back at the end and buried the Giants, who responded by sacking Durocher. Among the Dodger heroes, Newcombe's 20-5 pitching shone, as did Campanella's .318 batting and 32 homers, which won him his third MVP award. Matched against their Yankee tormentors in the Series, the Dodgers felt old doubts as the Yanks won the first two games; but, playing at home, the Dodgers stormed back with three wins. After the Yanks tied the series, Johnny Podres shut them out 2-0 in the finale, aided by a clutch catch of a fly ball by outfielder Sandy Amoros. The victory was Brooklyn's first Series conquest in this century.

At this point, the National League's two consecutive Series victories signaled the rising power of the senior circuit. Other Nationals were flexing muscles, however, and in 1956 the Braves and Reds pressed the Dodgers hard. In edging the Braves by a game and the Reds by two, superb pitching by Newcombe (27-7) and timely wins from old Sal Maglie, acquired from the Giants in midseason, carried the day. In the Series, however, the vengeance-minded Yanks had the last word. In what was to be the last battle of this intra-urban rivalry, the Yankees reversed the 1955 script. This time they lost the first two, then came back to win three, the last being a perfect game pitched by Don Larsen. Then, after the Dodgers rallied to tie, the Yankees won the finale.

Owner O'Malley's shrewdly staged move to Los Angeles ended the local rivalry. By the end of 1957, the Dodgers quit Brooklyn; O'Malley also persuaded Giant owner Horace Stoneham to join him by staking a claim in San Francisco. These moves stirred a hornet's nest of protest from outraged Gothamites. The furor over these departing carpetbaggers swelled, inspiring a menacing third major league movement in 1959. It was this threat that pushed major league baseball into the Expansion Era.

The Dodgers' final Brooklyn season was joyless. With Robinson gone and Reese, Campanella, and Newcombe fading, the glory years of the summer boys were at an end. Into the power vacuum rushed the 1957 Braves, a well-balanced team managed by Fred Haney. Strong contenders since 1953, they now were ready. Their ranks included superstars like Warren Spahn, a versatile left-handed pitcher destined to win 363 games; slugger Hank Aaron, destined to break Ruth's lifetime homer mark; and slugging third baseman Eddie Mathews, destined for Hall of Fame membership. In 1957 Spahn's 21 wins led all National pitchers; Aaron led in homers and RBIs; and Mathews added 32

Don Newcombe, ace Dodger pitcher in 1949–57, with time away for Korean War service. In his first season he was 17–8; in 1955, when the Dodgers were world champs, he was 20–5; and in their pennant-winning season of 1956, he was 27–7. (Courtesy Dodger Baseball Club, National League)

Phillies of 1950, National League champions. (Courtesy The Phillies)

homers. Backed by pitchers like Lou Burdette and Bob Buhl, and hitters like Joe Adcock, Bill Bruton, and rookie phenom Bob ("Hurricane") Hazel, who hit .403 in 134 at-bats, the Braves topped the Cardinals by eight games. Pitted against the Yanks in the Series, they beat those feudal lords in seven games—with Burdette, a Yankee cast-off, posting three pitching victories. Thus, the Braves, who drew 2 million paid admissions along the way, became the first breakaway franchise to raise a World Series banner.

In 1958, as the Dodgers and Giants trekked westward, the Braves won again. Their pitching, strengthened by rookies Joey Jay and Carlton Willey, was headed by Spahn's and Burdette's combined 42 wins. League-leading pitching was blended with league-leading batting, fronted by Aaron (.326, 30, 95). It was enough to lap the rising Pirates by eight, but not enough to take the Yankees. The Braves' zenith came when they won three of the first four Series games, but the Yanks swept the last three to win.

The defeat ended the Braves' dynastic pretensions. In 1959 they looked like repeaters, but the Giants and Dodgers barred the way. In September the Giants collapsed, but the Dodgers stayed the course. Winning 13 of 14 in late September, Alston's men drew even and forced another playoff. It was the third of this era for the Dodgers, and this time the Dodgers won. Larry Sherry's relief work saved the opener, and the next time out Furillo's key hit helped nail down the Dodger win. For the Dodgers, who led the league only in fielding, while batting a weak .257, it was a gritty triumph. Astonishingly, they had risen from seventh place in 1958 to win in 1959. Among the few veterans from the former glory years were Hodges, Snider, Podres, and Gilliam; other-

Leo Ernest Durocher, manager of the Giants in 1948–55 after managing the Dodgers in 1939–48 and before managing the Cubs and the Astros. (Courtesy John Thorn)

Robin Evan Roberts, who pitched for the Phillies in 1948–61, leading the National League for four straight years in games won. He was elected to the Hall of Fame for his nineteen-year record of 286–245. (Courtesy John Thorn)

Bobby Thomson of the Giants hitting the winning home run against the Dodgers in the 1951 National League playoff series at the Polo Grounds. (Courtesy San Francisco Giants)

Opposite top:
Robert Brown ("Bobby") Thomson, Scottish-born outfielder for the Giants in 1946–53, being congratulated by teammates for his pennant-winning homer. A dependable hitter, he racked up thirty-two homers in 1951. (Courtesy San Francisco Giants)

Opposite bottom:
Jackie Robinson stealing home against the Chicago Cubs in 1952, when the Dodgers took the pennant. (Courtesy Los Angeles Dodgers)

Right: Dodger infield of 1952: clockwise, Jackie Robinson, second; Gil Hodges, first; Roy Campanella, catcher; Billy Cox, third; Pee Wee Reese, shortstop. (Courtesy John Thorn)

Below: Jackie Robinson stealing home against the Yanks in the 1955 World Series, helping the Dodgers to their first world championship. (Courtesy Los Angeles Dodgers)

Edwin Lee ("Eddie") Mathews, who helped the Milwaukee Braves to a 1957 world championship with 28 doubles, 32 homers, and 94 RBIs. (Courtesy Milwaukee Braves)

Sandy Amoros of the Dodgers catching Yogi Berra's line drive in the sixth inning of the seventh game of the 1955 World Series, squelching a Yankee rally. (Author's Collection)

wise it was a rebuilt team. As such, it was good enough to capture the World Series from the White Sox. A record 270,000 home fans saw the Dodgers sweep three games at the Los Angeles Coliseum, a converted football field that served as the team's temporary quarters. Those wins and reliever Sherry's heroic saves carried the Dodgers to victory in six games.

As the Postwar Era faded, so did the Dodgers, who fell to fourth in 1960. Now the Pirates battled the Braves for the championship. Although Rickey was no longer associated with the Pirates, his rebuilding efforts had transformed a chronic loser into a contender. Led by manager Danny Murtaugh, the Pirates fielded the brilliant outfield trio of Roberto Clemente, Bill Virdon, and Bob Skinner; second baseman Bill Mazeroski and shortstop Dick Groat anchored the infield; Bob Friend, Vernon Law, and reliever Roy Face provided formidable pitching. Led by Groat (.325) and Clemente (.314), the Pirates batted .276. After besting the Braves by seven games, they battled the Yanks in a memorable World Series. Although thrice pummeled by top-heavy scores, they won in seven games; Mazeroski's homer in the tenth inning of the finale was the crusher.

Not for another decade would Pittsburghers recapture the joy of 1960. By then, baseball's eight-club format was a faded memory of an era ending in 1961. Although Clemente's .351 batting led all hitters that year, the slumping Pirates fell to sixth, two notches below the Braves. With the pennant up for grabs, the Reds and Dodgers moved up. When the struggle ended, it was the Reds, pennant-starved since 1940, who held the heights. Managed by fiery Fred Hutchinson, the Reds were outmatched in every important category. Still, they batted .270 and poled 158 homers, with outfielders Vada Pinson (.343) and

Frank Robinson (.323, 37, 124) leading the attack. In a tight race they bested the Dodgers by four games, but the Reds were no match for the Yankees in the Series. Even with mighty Mantle sidelined, the Yankees won easily, four games to one.

Watching the Yankees notch yet another Series victory was a familiar humiliation for National partisans, but a new era was dawning. Although the prospect of an expanded league was fraught with uncertainties, the rising power of the National League, evidenced by superior attendance and performance records, afforded high hopes for future success in the unfolding Expansion Era.

Indeed, the growing power of the National League was a hallmark of the Postwar Era of major league history. Throughout the 'Fifties the senior circuit's superiority showed in offensive stats. In perpetuating the "big bang" style, National sluggers rewrote old seasonal homer marks by their bombardments. Averaging 1,100 homers a season in the 'Fifties,

POSTWAR ERA HIGHLIGHTS

The first world championship for the Brooklyn "Bums" was memorialized in a cartoon by Willard Mullin, who created this and other mythic sports characters for the *New York World-Telegram and the Sun.* (Courtesy National Baseball Library, Cooperstown, New York)

only in 1960 did they fail to outsmite Americans, whose homer output averaged less than 1,000 a season. At the same time, National hitters outhit Americans ten times, and for good measure, National base stealers outran American speedsters eleven times. Only in pitching performances did Americans lead, posting better ERAs seven times.

Black stars played an important part in tilting the balance of power in the Nationals' favor. More heavily recruited by National clubs, most of the hundred blacks who played in the majors by 1960 wore National League uniforms. Following in Jackie Robinson's footsteps, black stars

Roberto Clemente, who led the National League in batting averages four times in his eighteen-year career with the Pirates. (Courtesy Pittsburgh Pirates)

William Stanley ("Bill") Mazeroski celebrating his 1960 Series-winning homer for the Pirates against the Yankees. Although never a great hitter, Mazeroski came through in the clutch, averaging .400 in league playoffs and .308 in World Series. (Courtesy Pittsburgh Pirates)

like Campanella, Banks, Aaron, and Mays won their spurs by prodigious hitting. After Robinson became the first black batting champ in 1949, Mays won the 1954 title, and Aaron took honors in 1956 and 1959. As the National League's first black homer king, Mays's 1955 effort was followed by Aaron and Banks, who accounted for three of the

Selva Lewis ("Lew") Burdette, whose pitching played a big part in the Braves' 1957 Series victory and 1958 pennant. His 1958 percentage of .667 (20–10) topped the National League. (Courtesy John Thorn)

Ted Williams, who, with Joe DiMaggio and Stan Musial, was one of the three superstars of the postwar era. (Courtesy Herman Seid)

ever. Although much pummeled, starters maintained their high status by such adaptations as employing a variety of deliveries, by better training and conditioning programs, and by the aid of a 1958 ruling that enlarged the strike zone to include the area between a batter's armpits and the top of his knees. Among the great starting pitchers of this era, lefty Warren Spahn became the winningest southpaw of all time. A zealous student of his craft, Spahn had a repertoire that included a fastball, curve, slider, screwball, change-up, and sinker, as well as an excellent pickoff move to first base. A gifted fielder and competent hitter, Spahn lasted until 1965, when he owned 363 wins, 63 shutouts, and two no-hitters. Although nobody matched Spahn, burly Early Wynn won 300 games, Robin Roberts won 286, Ford won 236 and posted a winning percentage of .690, Feller won 266 games, ancient Bobo Newsom won 211, Bob Lemon won 207, and Jim Bunning topped 200 by winning over 100 games in each major league. Of these masters, all but Newsom and Bunning are in the Hall of Fame.

Certainly such redoubtable hurlers were needed at this time to keep alive the flickering myth that pitching was 90 percent of a game. On the contrary, as the big bang style reached its apogee, it seemed as if hitters had taken over. Compared with past eras, this one produced more homers, more strikeouts, and fewer stolen bases. As sluggers flailed away, exemplars like Joe Adcock and Ernie Banks each clouted four homers in single games, and in 1955 Dale Long homered in eight straight games. Moreover, pinch-hitting specialists like Dusty Rhodes, Johnny Mize, Jerry Lynch, and Forrest ("Smoky") Burgess tormented pitchers; of this lot, Burgess pinch-hit safely 145 times in the years 1946–67.

Abetted by increasing television exposure, postwar hitters were glamorized; however, their glory paled by comparison with the fortune-favored generations that followed. For one reason, the public of this era seemed to take a dim view of money-hungry players. The pioneering attempts at unionization produced a backlash of hostility that branded players as spoiled mercenaries. Especially was this judgment hung on bonus babies, as those untried youths who were paid $4,000 or more for signing big league contracts were dubbed. Not surprisingly, envious veteran players also damned these fortunate youths.

Yet, it was the veteran players whose unionist activities of 1946 stirred greater wrath. Foreshadowing a coming storm, players of 1946 demanded higher pay, fringe benefits, a pension plan, and relief from such harsh rules of baseball law as the reserve clause and blacklists. Indeed, the blacklist was used against a few Mexican League jumpers that same year. One of them, Danny Gardella, sued, however, and by a 2-1 decision the Second U.S. Circuit Court of Appeals granted him a trial. Fearful of its consequences, the owners settled out of court: Gardella got $60,000, and the commissioner granted a general amnesty to other jumpers. Meanwhile, other players were rallying behind Robert Murphy, an experienced labor relations lawyer, who organized the American Baseball Guild. Backed by federal labor laws and recent legislation protecting the job rights of ex-servicemen, the guild threat prompted owners to grant a minimum salary of $5,000, spring-training expense allowances, a restriction on salary cuts, and limited severance

DiMaggio family gathered when their most famous member was honored at Yankee Stadium before his 1951 retirement. (Courtesy Dennis Goldstein)

pay. Along with a promise of a pension to come, these concessions blunted the 1946 strike threat and reduced the guild to company union status.

In 1953, however, when owners delayed action on the pension plan, player representatives hired lawyer J. Norman Lewis and regrouped as the Major League Players Association. The following year Lewis won an increase in the minimum salary to $6,000 and the promise of a pension for any player with five years of big league service. Nothing was done about the reserve clause, which the U.S. Supreme Court upheld that year in its Toolson decision; essentially, the Court held that any change in the clause must come via congressional action. But the House of Representatives' two subcommittee inquiries produced no remedial legislation. Moreover, the owners in 1958 refused to consider Lewis's request that 20 percent of baseball revenues go to player salaries. That quixotic bid was Lewis's last major effort; in 1959 the players ousted him. Although the Postwar Era ended with the Players Association in disarray, the organization survived; its great achievement thus far was securing a pension plan to be funded by national radio and television revenue. Beyond that, players still elected representatives who kept alive the flickering fire of collective bargaining.

Unfortunately for this generation of players, the harvest of their militant moves was reaped by later generations. For now, as pitcher Sal

Above left: Joe Black, who won 1952 Rookie-of-the-Year honors for his 14 wins and 15 saves—a large contribution to the Dodgers' pennant. (Courtesy John Thorn)

Above right: Casimir James ("Jim") Konstanty, who won the 1950 National League MVP Award for his role in the Phillies' capture of a pennant. He never again came close to that season's record of 16 wins and 22 saves, though he did win 7 and save 11 for the 1955 pennant-winning Yankees. (Courtesy John Thorn)

Maglie put it, the owners got all the money. Although that was an exaggeration, the fact was that 75 percent of player salaries of this era ranged between $10,000 and $25,000. While this was good money for the times, only a few stars received as much as $50,000 a year, and only a handful reached the exalted $100,000 zenith.

Ironically, while some critics scolded these players as mercenaries, others derided them as colorless conformists who lacked the raucous spirit of past generations. If indeed this generation of players was more close-mouthed than others, there were good reasons for their reticence. Minority groups, for instance, were demanding and winning respect. By 1958 nearly a hundred blacks and some eighty Hispanics wore big league uniforms. Also, there were more college-educated and married men in the ranks; when only thirty bachelors were counted late in the era, Rickey blessed the marriage trend for instilling more serious behavior. Still, some faulted the trend; some managers blamed marriages for disrupting team unity with wifely cliques and complaints. Player marriages undoubtedly suffered by long absences, sudden uprootings, and fears of infidelity; on the latter point observers noted no lessening in the numbers of "baseball Annies," or diamond camp followers.

Certainly, team unity undermined marital togetherness. As ever, a team was a tightly knit community whose members shared a unique language and the usual fears of being traded or cut. As always, making the majors required intense dedication; at this time the average player spent six years learning his trade in the minors, and the average stay in the majors was less than five years. Players also faced increasing strains caused by the greater number of night games; more hectic travel schedules, which included air travel to distant western cities; and more specialized roles as players. The strategy of platooning players speeded the specialization trend, as managers more freely substituted pitchers, fielders, and hitters to cope with game situations. Among pitchers, relief specialists were used more frequently, and more batters became switch-hitters.

Equipment changes also contributed to a changing style of play. In this era improved fielding averages were credited to bigger gloves, with two breaks, replacing old single-pocket gloves. Likewise, the plenteous home runs owed much to lighter, narrowly tapered bats and the use of more new balls in games; as a result, a team might use a thousand dozen balls in a season. Also, a rule requiring hitters to wear protective helmets emboldened batters. Yet, for the most part, playing rules changed little; the 1950 rules recodification did little more than redefine the strike zone, restore the sacrifice fly rule, and revise qualifications for batting champs. At this time a few new awards were instituted to honor splendid performers. By the end of the decade each league gave a Most Valuable Player Award for the best all-round player, a Cy Young Award for the best pitcher, and a Fireman of the Year Award for the best relief pitcher.

The old ballparks still served in this era, but a 1958 rule took note of an incipient new park building boom and ordained that new parks must conform to standard minimum distances of 325 feet from home plate to the right and left field fences. Meanwhile, older parks changed; except for Wrigley Field in Chicago, all sported lights for night ball. Inside some parks electronic scoreboards displayed information and erupted noisily to celebrate home team homers. To add to the entertaining atmosphere, concessionaires hawked greater varieties of food, drink, and souvenirs. These remunerative sales were welcomed, as was the money from television contracts; by 1960 television revenue annually added $19 million to club coffers.

By now, new owners were running most clubs. As old-guard owners sold their interests to wealthier newcomers, at prices as high as $5.5 million, the newcomers tended to be wealthy businessmen who lacked baseball expertise. For this reason, most delegated authority to general managers and other staff experts. Thus, most clubs now resembled small-scale corporate organizations, with more powers accruing to general managers and much less to field managers. Some general managers sought reputations as brilliant traders. For instance, Frank Lane swung some five hundred player trades during his peripatetic career, but his flashy deals never matched the consummate genius of Rickey or Weiss.

Of course, real power was wielded by owners. As in the past, each insisted on controlling his own franchise. Such individualism, combined with each league's independence, made it difficult to enact uniform policies for the greater good of baseball promotion. Nor could the baseball commissioner make major decisions or set policies. On the contrary, a commissioner's powers were sharply limited, so that major decisions now came from an oligarchy of assertive owners, including O'Malley and Dan Topping of the Yankees. Such men wielded inordi-

Hoyt Wilhelm, who had been a fair starter for the Giants but became a consistently effective reliefer for the Orioles and White Sox in the late 'Fifties and the 'Sixties. (Courtesy Gordon Miller)

Above left: Al Kaline's first day in uniform in 1953, as a nineteen-year-old "bonus baby." Here he is being reassured by Tiger manager Fred Hutchinson. Kaline's twenty-two-year record of 3,007 hits and a .297 batting average won him a place in the Hall of Fame. (Courtesy Michael Mumby Collection)

Above right: Danny Gardella, who jumped to the Mexican League in 1946, successfully defied "organized baseball's" blacklist. (Courtesy Dennis Goldstein)

nate power through their membership on the Executive Council and were regarded as the most powerful men in baseball.

As a result, the commissioner's status sank to that of a mere hireling. When Landis's successor, A. B. Chandler, attempted to assert himself by disciplining players, owners, and managers, he was sacked before the end of his first term and was succeeded in 1951 by Ford Frick, who accepted his subordinate role. For the next fourteen years Frick passively presided over major changes that transformed the game. These included increased television coverage, franchise moves, inroads from rival sports, and deterioration of the minor leagues.

From a thriving network of 59 leagues and 7,812 players in 1946, by 1964 the minor leagues shrank to 19 leagues and 2,448 players. For this shrinkage, television and radio broadcasts of major league games and the popularity of rival sports and leisure activities were blamed. Whatever the cause, the majors now faced a talent shortage problem that, combined with an alarming decrease in the number of independent minor league promoters, forced the majors to subsidize the minor leagues.

Fully as menacing as the talent shortage problem was television's impact upon the game. Like a two-faced Janus, television added to team coffers and cultivated new fans with one face, while doubtlessly contributing to lower gate attendance with the other. An alarming 1950–54 slump in live attendance prompted some owners to propose a limit on televised games or at least measures to make the video shows less attractive than live games. But the lure of dollars easily trampled such Luddite proposals; indeed, the strength of a city's television market became a major consideration in future expansion moves.

Obviously, there was no downing television; at this time TV viewing was the nation's most popular leisure outlet and as such threatened to upstage newspapers and radio. As big-city daily newspapers declined in numbers, the survivors still devoted 15 percent of their news space to sports. While rival sports vied with baseball for news space (even in *The Sporting News*), baseball held its own. However, a changing trend in baseball journalism now tended to give less attention to the full description of games and more to analysis, features, and problems regarding the game. While writers still followed teams, they no longer accepted subsidies from them. Changing editorial policies, aiming at getting more objective and critical accounts, denied writers such perquisites and also cramped the cliché-ridden, worshipful style of some veteran wordsmiths.

At this time the varying styles of baseball writing included the flowery eloquence of Frank Graham and Arthur Daley, the gossipy outpourings of Dick Young, the realistic probes of Milt Gross, and the sprightly cartoons of Willard Mullin. As ever, New York City was baseball journalism's mecca, and Red Smith of the declining *Herald Tribune* was acknowledged as the most influential force in American sportswriting. A master of informed and critical prose, the eloquent Smith credited editor Stan Woodward for honing his skills. As a foremost advocate of the probing, objective style of coverage, Woodward became editor of

Brooks Robinson as a nineteen-year-old rookie during the 1956 season, beginning his brilliant twenty-three-year career with the Orioles. (Courtesy Dennis Goldstein)

the fledgling *Sports Illustrated* weekly, where he inspired a pride of younger imitators.

If baseball writing managed to adapt to the challenge of television, radio baseball was swamped by the new medium. Although radio contracts helped some major league clubs during the Depression and war years, others held out until 1946, when profits from local contracts and shares of national broadcasts converted all. However, this brief radio boom quickly gave way to the onslaught of television. While radio broadcasts continued, the medium became subordinated to television. As Americans of the 'Fifties rushed to buy television sets, television producers dangled attractive contract offers. Since each club was free to negotiate its own local contracts, the revenue was unevenly distributed. Yet there was no gainsaying the importance of this revenue source: In 1950 television income totaled $2.3 million; in 1956, $6.2 million; in 1960, $12.5 million. Such sums included local revenue and increasing national revenue from the sale of World Series and All-Star game rights, which were shared equally. Thus, as baseball entered its Expansion Era, television was a major catalyst of the changes that dramatically transformed the game.

8

THE EXPANSIVE 'SIXTIES

BASEBALL IN THE 'SIXTIES FOLLOWED THE REVOLUtionary course set in the 'Fifties. Following the first franchise shift in fifty years, when the Braves moved to Milwaukee, big league membership rolls by 1969 reflected American population trends—especially the flight to the suburbs and to the Sunbelt. Following the major leagues' breaking of the color barrier in 1947, the number of black players grew to one of every five major leaguers in 1960 and continued in the 'Sixties toward one of every four. Following halting steps toward unionization in 1953, a revived Players Association started major leaguers on their ascent toward the super-salaries of super-entertainers. Following an uneasy liaison with television in the 'Fifties, big league baseball by the mid-1960s was one of TV's pampered darlings, raking in millions for broadcast rights. To be sure, TV revenue was unevenly distributed among the clubs and was in large part a trade-off for declining ballpark attendance, especially in the minors. The depressed state of the minor leagues exacerbated a major league player shortage, as did competition with other sports, which shared fickle TV's affection.

Ranged alongside the strident issues that divided and buffeted America of the 1960s, baseball's growing pains of that decade seem petty. Externally, Cold War tensions mounted. In 1962 the Cuban missile crisis stirred a brief but chilling threat of war with the Soviet Union; by 1964 Soviet expansionism involved the United States in a frustratingly indecisive nine-year war in Vietnam. This conflict not only cost 50,000 American lives but also divided the citizenry. Bitter debates about the war sharpened differences over such issues as sexual liberation, the "generation gap," women's rights, and racial equality. Such debates at times reached fever pitch, as during the summers of 1964 and 1967 when race riots erupted in some major cities, or during the aftermath of the assassinations of the Kennedy brothers and Martin Luther King.

Despite the nation's travail, the 'Sixties were good years for most Americans. Unemployment throughout the decade averaged only 3.4 percent and the average annual wage for all workers topped $8,000, staying well ahead of inflation. As ever, work, family life, and leisure enjoyment were the focal concerns of most citizens. On the side of leisure, various activities, including participatory sports, grew in popularity, but watching television kept the top spot it had gained in the 'Fifties.

Certainly, television contributed mightily to the growth of big sports; televised sporting events were the most popular of the varied programs.

Walter O'Malley, expansive owner of the 'Sixties, who moved the Dodgers from Flatbush to Chavez Ravine. (Courtesy Los Angeles Dodgers)

In catering to the growing public appetite for more, producers profitably aired a variety of participant and team sports. Such exposure fueled a national sports mania, but the popularity of so many different sports made it apparent that sports in general, rather than any single sport, had become the nation's leading pastime.

For major league baseball promoters, this eclectic trend was disturbing. As television spurred the growth of rival team sports, baseball's lofty position was threatened. Even more disturbing was the popularity of rival pro sports in newer urban areas that as yet were unserved by major league baseball teams. None too soon, baseball men countered this threat by expanding in 1961–62. Yet more was required, so 1969 saw another expansion round, followed by yet another in 1977. From today's perspective such moves seem natural, inevitable, and assuredly profitable, but to tradition-bound baseball men of 1960, the first expansion move was a fearful step forward.

WALTER O'MALLEY, EXPANSIONIST

As it turned out, expansion revitalized the major league game. Still, baseball leaders had to be prodded, and the necessary push was provided by adventurous owners like Walter Francis O'Malley. As owner of the National League's prosperous Brooklyn franchise, O'Malley had gained control in the early 'Fifties. After ousting Rickey, whom he regarded as a dangerous rival, O'Malley soon established himself as the most powerful of baseball owners. In establishing his power O'Malley took advantage of the disarray among top levels of the baseball establishment. For this vacuum, one might cite the declining powers of the baseball commissioner. When Landis's successor, Commissioner Albert B. Chandler, tried to assert power, O'Malley joined the 1950 move that ousted

Bowie Kuhn, commissioner from 1968 to 1984, who made the following comment about O'Malley's stature: "I respect it, but don't bow to it. We think alike." (Courtesy Office of the Baseball Commissioner)

him and brought in the compliant Ford Frick in 1951. Frick served two seven-year terms and was succeeded first by William ("Spike") Eckert, who lasted only till 1968, then by Bowie Kuhn, who served until 1984. Such successors to Landis were Merovingians, fully subservient to owners. As policy makers, owners seldom agreed on anything. Characteristically individualistic and contentious, the successor owners of the Postwar and Expansion eras were no exceptions. Moreover, as old-guard owners passed on, including five in 1959 alone, their successors were often inexperienced in baseball matters and occupied with outside business interests.

But the plump, jowly, cigar-smoking O'Malley was a notable exception in his zealous devotion to baseball. Born to wealth, the canny O'Malley had earned degrees in law and engineering, skills that served him well when he invaded the Los Angeles area. In planning the move, O'Malley used his memberships on key baseball committees, including the powerful Executive Council, to clear the way. In 1957 he stunned the baseball world by announcing his intention to move the Dodgers to Los Angeles, in company with owner Horace Stoneham, whose Giants would move to San Francisco. The news ignited a firestorm of criticism and prompted a congressional inquiry. However, O'Malley coolly informed a congressional subcommittee that the moves had the approval of his colleagues and that neither the commissioner nor the National League president opposed the plan. O'Malley's *fait accompli* silenced those probers, though not his Brooklyn critics. Indeed, many bridled at O'Malley's remark, "If I'm going to be a carpetbagger, I might just as well carry the satchel."

No pioneer trekking westward was ever so sure of success when he got there. O'Malley's Los Angeles deal allowed him to purchase three hundred acres of land and its mineral rights at a cheap price; in addition, the city of Los Angeles agreed to build access roads to the park that

O'Malley financed and owned. Thus, four years after playing in a converted football stadium, the Dodgers occupied the new $20 million Dodger Stadium that was O'Malley's monument. Thenceforth, till his death in 1979, O'Malley prospered as no owner ever did. An astute promoter, his attendance records were unmatched; equally impressive were his revenues from concessions, from television, and from the ancillary development of his surplus acreage. As baseball's *éminence grise*, O'Malley was conceded to be the most powerful of owners—the shaper of policies and manipulator of commissioners. And the crowning achievement that ranked him among the great shapers of the past thirty years of baseball history was his role as baseball's expansionist.

BASEBALL'S FIRST EXPANSION ROUND, 1961–1962

More than any previous act of carpetbaggery, O'Malley's westward move shoved baseball into the Expansion Era. The 1958 enfranchisement of Los Angeles and San Francisco whetted the appetites of other growing urban areas for major league ball. In 1959 the menacing Continental League promised to sate such hungers, but O'Malley persuaded major league owners to torpedo the threat by absorbing two Continental franchises. Thus, Houston and a New York replacement were admitted to the National League in 1962. In return for relocating in New York, however, the Nationals were forced to allow the Americans a foothold in Los Angeles. Although this compromise was anathema to

Sandy Koufax of the Dodgers completing one of two no-hitters he pitched against the Giants in the 'Sixties. (Courtesy Los Angeles Dodgers)

Willie Mays in action. Mays set so many batting records during his twenty-one seasons with the Giants, 1951–72, that he was elected to the Hall of Fame six years after retiring. (Courtesy San Francisco Giants)

O'Malley, he responded by making life unbearable for his competitors. Forced to compete with the popular Dodgers, the well-financed Los Angeles Angels drew poorly playing in a minor league park. Nor did their lot improve when O'Malley admitted them as tenants in his new stadium. After a few years of O'Malley's exploitative treatment, owner Gene Autry welcomed an offer to quit Los Angeles for nearby Anaheim, where his renamed California Angels soon prospered.

Baseball's first expansion movement was a political victory for the National League. By adding Houston and New York, the Nationals gained a pair of stable outposts. In New York the Mets astonished observers by drawing huge crowds in the face of five seasons of incredible ineptitude. Meanwhile, the American League expansion took on the proportions of a major blunder. In taking the plunge a year ahead of the Nationals, the Americans were outfoxed by O'Malley in Los Angeles and saddled with a weak expansion team in Washington. The Washington transplant was forced on the league because owner Cal Griffith insisted on moving his original Washington Senators to Bloomington, Minnesota, where they played under the name of the Minnesota Twins. That move provoked such bitter outbursts that the Americans were forced to plant a team in Washington. There the new Senators languished for eleven seasons, until removal to the Dallas–Fort Worth area gave that franchise new life as the Texas Rangers.

Some of the problems that cropped up in the wake of this first expansion round suggested that another round would soon follow. For one, the ten-team, 162-game format made for nine seasonal losers in each league; in all but the closest races such a situation was sure to evoke public apathy. For another, more promising sites still clamored for major league ball, a temptation to some restive owners. First to succumb were the owners of the Milwaukee Braves, who moved their team to Atlanta in 1966. That move enraged owner Charles Finley of the Kansas City Athletics; Finley had eyed the Atlanta location for himself, but his fellow owners had blocked the move. Two years later, having alienated Kansas City fans in the meantime, Finley won approval to move his club to Oakland, where his new site encroached on the territory of the nearby Giants. The controversy caused by the relocation of the A's was overshadowed, however, by protests and lawsuits from Kansas City and Milwaukee interests. To blunt these suits, major league owners promised to put expansion teams into these abandoned cities. Thus, baseball's ten-team format was fated to be upset by a new round of expansion coming in the near future.

Willie McCovey, regular first baseman for the Giants from 1960 through 1973. He led the National League in homers thrice in the 'Sixties. (Courtesy San Francisco Giants)

THE NATIONAL LEAGUE ASCENDANT, 1962–1968

The seven campaigns waged under the 1962 format furnished satisfying proof to National League moguls that theirs was the more powerful circuit. Paced by O'Malley's Dodgers, the National League outdrew their rivals by more than 16 million paying customers. In addition, the Nationals won four of the seven World Series clashes and seven of eight All-Star games, consistently outhitting and outrunning American players. In seven of the eight seasons, National batting averages topped the best of the Americans, and every year the leading National hitter

outdid his junior-circuit counterpart. It was the same in base stealing, as National speedsters led in bases stolen seven times. Only in homers and pitching did Americans shine, six times outslugging and four times outpitching (with lower ERAs) their rivals.

But this dramatic turnabout in baseball's power balance was not yet evidenced by 1962. In preparing for their first expansion campaign, National contenders were weakened by the loss of reserve players sold via an expansion draft in order to stock the new Houston and New York teams. After paying hefty initiation fees, which established clubs divided, each newcomer was permitted to draft unreserved players from the rosters of established teams. Such players could be bought at a fixed price for all, but since established teams could reserve their best twenty-five players, this was a dubious opportunity. Not surprisingly, the new-comers finished far behind; the Mets lost a horrendous 120 games, but the surprising Houston Colt-45s managed an eighth-place finish.

Nevertheless, the draft stripped established teams of able reserves and thus proved to be a factor in the 1962 campaign. Teams with good farm systems, like the Dodgers and Giants, more easily recouped losses caused by the expansion draft. Although the doughty Reds bettered their previous gait, their 98 wins earned them only third place. During most of the season Alston's Dodgers led, propelled by Don Drysdale's league-leading pitching, outfielder Tom Davis's league-leading hitting, and Maury Wills's record-breaking 104 base thefts. But the hard-hitting Giants hung tough; they led the league in batting, with four .300 hitters and Willie Mays's league-leading slugging (49 homers). In the September stretch, when the Dodgers lost their last four games, the Giants drew even. The deadlock forced the fourth postseasonal playoff series in National League history. Having been in the three previous playoffs and having lost two, the Dodgers were naturally skittish. True to form, they lost again. Playing before a stunned home crowd, the Dodgers lost the decisive game when their relievers blew a 4-2 lead by yielding four runs in the ninth. This eerie repeat of the 1951 scenario also haunted the Giants, however. As in 1951 their victory sent them against the Yankees, and once again they lost, but only after seven hard-fought games. The Giant defeat came on the final play of the seventh game when Willie McCovey's line shot was gloved by the perfectly positioned Yankee second baseman, Bobby Richardson.

The loss marked the zenith of Giant fortunes; although they finished second five times, the Cardinals and Dodgers divided the next six pennants. In 1963 there was no stopping the well-armed Dodgers. At last, lefty Sandy Koufax attained his long-awaited stardom. Although plagued by painful arthritis in his pitching arm, Koufax won 25 and led all hurlers in strikeouts and ERA. Behind him his mates batted a paltry .251, but Davis won another batting title, and Wills, who batted .302, led in bases stolen. After topping the Cardinals by six games, Alston's

Two outstanding Cardinals during the team's glory years of the 'Sixties: outfielder Curt Flood (*top*) and veteran infielder Red Schoendienst. (Courtesy Gordon R. Miller)

pitchers held the vaunted Yankee hitters to a mere .171 average as they swept the Bombers in the World Series.

Koufax turned in another masterful year in 1964, but the Dodgers finished sixth, 13 games back. In this wide-open race the lowly Phillies used Jim Bunning's and Chris Short's pitching and Richie Allen's hitting to seize the lead. Moving into September they led by 6½ games; they then collapsed, lost 10 straight, and opened the way for the Cardinals. The St. Louisans had been given up for dead; their manager, John Keane, had even contracted to manage the Yankees in 1965. But they astounded everybody by winning 28 of their last 39 games to edge the Reds and Phillies by a single game. In winning for the first time since 1946, the Cards led the league in hitting; the pacesetter was Lou Brock, a recent Cub acquisition, who batted .348 as a Cardinal and whose 43 steals set him on a record-breaking course. Joining Brock, outfielder Curt Flood and first baseman Bill White each topped .300, and third baseman Ken Boyer led the league in RBIs. Among the pitchers, Ray Sadecki won 20, Curt Simmons won 18, and Bob Gibson, rising to stardom, won 19. With Keane ticketed to manage the Yanks in 1965, there was some question about the propriety of his managing against the New Yorkers in the 1964 Series. The Cardinals silenced critics, however, by beating the Yanks in seven games.

Superstitious observers might have seen this Cinderella victory as a harbinger of the changes that beset baseball in 1965. Their impact ranged from the positive, as in the opening of Houston's all-weather Astrodome; to the ambivalent, as in the appointment of William Eckert, a little-known former Air Force general, to the commissionership; to the menacing, as instanced by the new rookie draft or the general decline in batting. The recent batting decline served notice that the always precarious balance between pitching and hitting was again out of whack. The new free-agent (rookie) draft was touted as a remedy for the chronic talent shortage problem; henceforth, top high school and college prospects would be pooled and drafted in turn by all major clubs.

For the Cardinals, the immediate future presaged two years of futility; for ex-Cardinal manager Keane, his fate was to preside over the collapse of the Yankee dynasty. But for the Dodgers, the future held two years of championship glory. In reaping the first fruits, the 1965 Dodgers won by two games over the Giants as the Cards fell to seventh place. This year league batting slumped to .249, the Dodgers contributing a .245 team effort. Pitchers Koufax and Drysdale carried the team with 49 wins, however. Needing extraordinary help, the Dodgers got it in the aftermath of an ugly brawl that marred one of their duels with the Giants. For cracking Dodger catcher John Roseboro's head with a bat, Giant pitching ace Juan Marichal was suspended for eight games. It cost Marichal two pitching starts that might have made the difference. The

Another duo of superlative players for the 'Sixties Cardinals: outfielder and base-stealing leader Lou Brock (*top*) and ace pitcher Bob Gibson. (Courtesy Gordon R. Miller)

Richie Allen, a strong hitter for the Phillies in 1963–69 and again in 1975–76. Despite his effectiveness, Philadelphia "boo birds" objected to his independent manner and made his life miserable. (Courtesy Paul H. Roedig)

champion Dodgers made the most of their victory by beating the Minnesota Twins in the World Series. The dogged Twins held out for seven games, but Koufax nailed down the title with a three-hit shutout in the decisive game.

As Dodger saviors, Koufax and Drysdale now determined to make O'Malley pay well for their services. Certainly, the money was there, as Dodger attendance had topped the two-million mark for a seventh straight year. Acting on a lawyer's advice, the pair staged a joint holdout, each pledging to sign only if the other was satisfied. Although O'Malley fumed, the tactic worked; signing the duo cost the owner over $200,000. Although this coup hinted at a coming salary revolution, that eventuality owed more to Marvin Miller's emergence as director of the Major League Players Association.

With their stars back in orbit, the Dodgers repeated as champs by an even narrower margin. In eking a 1½-game win over the Giants, the light-hitting Dodgers got 27 wins from Koufax and 14 wins and 21 saves from reliefer Phil Regan. It was too little to carry the World Series; matched against the Orioles' gifted young hurlers, the Dodgers scored two runs in the first game and none thereafter. In a Series marked by impotence, the Dodgers, batting .142, were swept by the .200-hitting Orioles.

That decline was an early symptom of a general batting famine that stalked the majors over the next two seasons. Ever since 1963, when rule makers raised the strike zone, pitchers had turned supermen. In 1967 the average ERA among major league pitchers was 3.30, low for recent times, but in 1968 hurlers lowered the mark to 2.98, an effectiveness rate unmatched since 1919. Naturally, this produced abysmally low batting averages; from a sick .242 in 1967, major league averages dipped to a dismal .237 in 1968, an all-time hitting futility record.

A predictable casualty of the hitting famine was the 1967 Dodgers, who batted a ludicrous .236 and played without the great Koufax. Although at the peak of his brilliant career, the star hurler retired rather than risk further damage to his arthritic arm. As the Dodgers sank, the well-balanced Cardinals winged to the heights on .263 team batting and the brilliant pitching of Bob Gibson and reliefer Joe Hoerner. Once atop the league, the Cardinals roosted there for the 1967–68 seasons, each time lapping the Giants by at least nine games. Leading the Cardinal attack in these years, outfielder Brock twice led the league in steals; outfielder Curt Flood twice topped .300; catcher Tim McCarver led the league's receivers; and Bob Gibson, recovering from a 1967 injury, posted a glittering 1968 ERA of 1.12 on 22 wins.

In World Series play, manager Red Schoendienst's men defeated the "miracle" Red Sox in seven games in 1967. Brock's .414 batting plus seven steals and Gibson's three victories with 26 strikeouts were standout performances. The following year, however, the Tigers clouted the Cards off their perch. Down three games to one, the Tigers fought back, winning the finale in St. Louis 4-1. Flood misjudged a fly ball in the seventh inning to open the gates to the winning rally.

The 1968 campaign marked the end of the first phase of expansion. When the National League resumed hostilities the following year, there would be two new franchises—the San Diego Padres and Montreal

Expos. Bewildered fans also would have to get used to seeing the twelve clubs arrayed in two divisions, East and West. After playing 162 games, the winners of each division would meet in a best-of-five playoff test to determine the league champion. At the same time, rule makers took a swipe at the hitting problem. Pitchers now had to cope with mounds lowered to ten inches and a strike zone reduced to the area between a batter's knees and his armpits. Thus, as the decade waned, the National League embarked on a bold new course, trusting that the fans would follow.

THE STRUGGLING AMERICAN LEAGUE, 1961–1968

Outdone by their National rivals both in recent gate receipts and in comparative records, the struggling junior circuit in 1961 sought to gain an edge by expanding to ten teams one year ahead of their rivals. Alas, the attendance edge was fleeting, and the new American franchises, Washington and Los Angeles, ran into formidable problems. For one, the inept new version of the Washington Senators, who replaced the Minnesota-bound originals, languished in the nation's capital. Hampered by mismanagement and poor attendance, these Senators became the league's sick man until invigorated by removal to Arlington, Texas, in 1971. As for the Los Angeles Angels, they were upstaged by the Dodgers and driven eventually to move to nearby Anaheim, where a new park and new identity as the California Angels turned them into a formidable, if luckless, contender.

Along with these new misfortunes, American League contenders still faced their merciless Yankee overlords. Now managed by Ralph Houk, the perennial champs not only snapped up the first four pennants under the new format, but they continued to attract 40 percent of the entire league's annual attendance. By now it seemed as if the Yanks would rule forever. In 1961 the Yankees' "M & M" boys, as Roger Maris and Mickey Mantle were dubbed, smashed 115 homers and drove in 270 runs. That year Maris's 61 homers broke Ruth's seasonal record, though an asterisk in official records reminds fans that it took the moody outfielder 162 games to do what the Babe did in 154. With lefty Whitey Ford's 25 victories leading the league's pitchers, the hard-hitting Yanks (240 homers) romped to an eight-game victory over the Tigers and crushed the Cincinnati Reds in the World Series four games to one.

Jim Bunning of the Phillies making his last pitch in a perfect game against the Mets on June 21, 1964. Bunning was very effective for the Phils in 1957–63 after nine seasons with the Tigers. (Courtesy Dennis Goldstein) million behind the Nationals, it was a sober reminder of the ability of strong Yankee teams to stimulate attendance. In short, a sick Yankee team infected the entire league.

Wide-open races marked the final American campaigns of the early Expansion Era. In 1965 the Twins rushed into the power vacuum, winning by seven over the White Sox. Piloted by Sam Mele, the Twins led the league in hitting, fronted by outfielder Tony Oliva's league-leading .321 batting. Boasting sluggers like infielders Harmon Killebrew and Don Mincher and outfielders Bob Allison and Jim Hall, and sturdy pitchers like Jim Grant (21-7), Jim Kaat (18-11), and reliefer Al Worthington (21 saves), the Twins won 102 games. Assisting manager Mele were two ex-Yanks, pitching coach Johnny Sain and infielder coach Billy Martin. The brain trust nearly did it. Matched against vaunted Dodger pitchers Koufax and Drysdale in the Series, the Twins battled through seven games before succumbing to Koufax's final shutout.

The following year pitcher Kaat won 25 games, and slugger Killebrew poled 39 homers, but the Twins lost to the Baltimore Orioles. Ironically, another ex-Yankee, Hank Bauer, skippered the Orioles, whose 1966 lineup also included ex-Yankee outfielders Russ Snyder and Curt Blefary. They hit well, but the big Bird was ex–Cincinnati Red outfielder Frank Robinson, whose .316 batting, 49 homers, and 122 RBIs won him a rare Triple Crown. Slugging first baseman John ("Boog") Powell and slick-fielding third baseman Brooks Robinson also topped 100 RBIs; this made life easy for young pitchers Dave McNally, Jim Palmer, Wally Bunker, and Steve Barber. Against the Dodgers in the Series, however, the Birds were installed as underdogs; seldom were forecasters so totally wrong. After Oriole hurler Moe Drabowsky relieved McNally in the third inning of the first game and nailed down a victory with shutout relief and 11 strikeouts, the Dodgers' doom was sealed. Not another run did the Dodgers get, as Palmer, Bunker, and McNally all fired shutouts and allowed only 14 hits in a stunning sweep.

It was to be a one-year perch for the Birds; in 1967 injuries and a hitting slump snared them. As the Orioles slipped to sixth, the White Sox, Twins, Tigers, and Red Sox fought it out. Few expected the complacent Red Sox, a team that had gone twenty-one seasons with no pennant, to win, but they did—by a single game over the Twins and Tigers. Piloted by Dick Williams, a hard-driving, no-nonsense rookie manager, the Red Sox overcame the tragic loss of slugger Tony Conigliaro. A victim of a gruesome beaning, the young outfielder's promising career was ruined. For the nonce, however, outfielder Carl Yastrzemski's Triple Crown performance (.326, 44, 127) and first baseman George Scott's .303 batting with 82 RBIs paced the league-leading offensive for the Sox. Jim Lonborg's 22 pitching wins also led the league and fronted a staff that otherwise needed every one of reliefer John Wyatt's 20 saves. A brilliant September stretch drive allowed the Sox to pull off their "little miracle." But afterwards, like their 1946 forebears, these Sox ran afoul of the Cardinals and lost by the same count in the World Series—4 games to 3.

The following year the hitting famine savaged the majors; for the Americans the "Year of the Pitcher" was devastating, as hitters aver-

Elston Howard, consistent heavy-hitter for the Yankees from 1955 until 1967, reaching .348 in 1961. Howard divided his time between outfield and backstop position until 1961, when he became first-string catcher. (Courtesy New York Yankees)

aged a horrendous .230. Incredibly, only one batter among Americans, Yastrzemski, topped .300, and his .301 took batting honors. But "Yaz's" effort was too little to save the pitching-poor Sox from finishing 17 games off the pace.

To the fore in 1968 leaped the Detroit Tigers, whose last view from the heights had come nearly twenty-five years earlier. This year a league-leading homer barrage atoned for the Tigers' anemic .235 team average. Outfielders Willie Horton and Jim Northrup joined with first baseman Norm Cash and catcher Bill Freehan to lead the attack. But the brightest star was the fun-loving, controversial pitching whiz, Denny McLain. By winning 31 games on a 1.96 ERA, this right-hander broke the 30-win barrier for the first time since the 'Thirties. That feat accounted for nearly a third of the team's 103 victories. In the World Series, however, McLain's stablemate, lefty Mickey Lolich, was the savior. A 17-game winner in the regular season, Lolich won three in the Series, including the decisive seventh game at St. Louis. Yet no Series victory came harder than that one. With his team down three games to one, Lolich kept hopes alive by pitching a gritty 5-3 win. Then McLain finally won a game on a 13-1 laugher, but Lolich nailed down the comeback by holding the host Cards in the finale to five hits and winning 4-1. It was a near thing; a misplayed ball by a Cardinal outfielder made the difference and tarnished Bob Gibson's record-breaking Series feat of fanning 35 Tigers.

Bolstered by this unexpected turn of fortune, the American League geared for the plunge into a second expansion round. When the league resumed hostilities in 1969, it did so under an East-West divisional format that included new teams with strange totems. It was all rather puzzling to fans, but anyone who thought that once this shock was over baseball would settle down was deluded; the near future decreed more shocks to come.

Harmon Killebrew, reliable slugger for the Minnesota Twins throughout the 'Sixties. He led the American League in homers five times and in RBIs twice during that decade. (Courtesy Minnesota Twins)

Perhaps baseball owners of 1966 were too distracted by slumping attendance or by the hornet's nest of protest stirred by the Milwaukee Braves' carpetbagging move to Atlanta to pay close attention to their deteriorating relations with players. The owners were soon to pay a heavy price for years of shortsightedness. It was as if the owners of 1966 had been sitting atop an active volcano whose eruption was nigh and whose force was bound to raise players to positions of power and wealth.

For 1966 was the year that organized players installed Marvin Miller as executive director of their moribund Major League Players Association. Time's passing revealed the significance of that move, since Miller fashioned the Association into a collective bargaining agency that won unprecedented concessions from owners. Indeed, by the time Miller retired in glory in 1983, the players benefited from a soaring salary escalation that sent *average* salaries of that year to $241,000. What's more, the 1983 season saw nineteen stars ink contracts worth *at least* $750,000 a year. Yet, this dazzling achievement was not the centerpiece of Miller's seventeen-year stewardship; that attainment was circumventing the reserve clause, where Miller played a key role in the

MARVIN MILLER, EMANCIPATOR

momentous arbitration decision of 1975. For such successes Miller takes a place alongside Jackie Robinson and Walter O'Malley as one of the great trio of innovators that reshaped baseball's postwar history.

Surely, players of 1966 felt the need for a leader of Miller's stripe. Following the collapse of the American Baseball Guild in 1946, the cause of organized players was becalmed in a sea of company unionism; the period of immobility continued for a dozen years after the Major League Players Association was formed in 1954. After brief displays of militance at its inception, the Association foundered under the leadership of Judge Robert Cannon of Milwaukee. Although Cannon donated his services to the Association, his cozy relations with owners, along with his reported hopes of becoming the game's commissioner, belatedly persuaded player representatives that the judge was part of their problems. Stirred by the Association's nearly empty treasury, by fears that their pension program was in danger, and by suspected discrimination against Association activists by some owners, player representatives moved to jettison the judge. Acting on advice from Professor George W. Taylor of the University of Pennsylvania's Wharton School, player reps Robin Roberts and Jim Bunning asked Marvin Julian Miller to become the Association's paid director.

In 1965 the forty-eight-year-old, dapper, slightly built Miller was secure in his post as research director of the United Steelworkers Union, but he accepted the call. An experienced labor negotiator and well informed in the intricacies of U.S. labor laws, Miller determined to shape the Association from a semi-paternalistic organization into a tough bargaining group. It was no easy task. First he had to sell himself to players, including some who distrusted mustaches; but Miller did so by touring training camps in the spring of 1966, explaining his plans and fielding questions. Although hampered by aroused owners who branded him a labor goon, Miller won the players' confidence; by a count of 489-136 they voted him in. In July he was installed in his $50,000-a-year position and was given an additional $100,000 to establish an office. If some players groused at having to pay dues of $350 a year to finance all this, they soon changed their tune.

From the outset Miller forced owners to follow established labor laws. When outgoing director Cannon advised Miller to sign a moral turpitude clause requested by owners, Miller blandly struck it out, saying, "Judge, have you ever heard of the Constitution of the United States?" Soon thereafter, owners felt the lash of Miller's snappy rhetoric, especially when he ventured the opinion that "owners are unnecessary." For owners, being obliged to follow labor laws chafed; as a start, when they balked at deducting dues from player salaries, Miller invoked the check-off law to make them do so. In speedily welding the Association into a formidable power, Miller scored a dazzling string of successes that won him the solid support of the players. Such solidarity was Miller's greatest delight; in 1974 he exulted over the fact that all 600 major league players were Association members.

The key to Miller's success was in forcing owners to bargain collectively and formally. During his tenure, his negotiations produced five formal contracts hammered out in sessions with owners' representatives John Gaherin and, later, Ray Grebey. Called Basic Agreements, these

James Lee ("Jim") Kaat, a dependable pitcher for the Twins from 1962 through 1972. His twenty-three-year career record was 278-234. (Courtesy Minnesota Twins)

contracts spelled out policies on pension funding, minimum salaries, working conditions, the use of arbitration panels to adjudicate contract and salary disputes, and the right of players to employ agents to negotiate salaries. Although Miller scored victories in all these matters, the arbitration concession proved to be the weapon that negated the hated reserve clause. The victory came in 1975 when Dodger pitcher Andy Messersmith, after playing that season without signing a contract, asked arbitrators to free him to sell his services anew. Arguing that he had met the terms of his contract, which had given the club a year's option on his services, Messersmith won his point. The arbitration panel of Miller, Gaherin, and professional arbitrator Peter Seitz voted 2-1 in Messersmith's favor. A portentous decision, when upheld in federal courts it became the precedent for all player contracts. Although Miller in 1976 accepted a compromise limiting the renegotiation privilege to six-year veterans, this decision led to the annual re-entry draft auction, which soon sent all salaries skyward.

If circumventing the reserve clause was the capstone of Miller's successes, he insisted that "the most important thing was the growing maturity of player leadership" that "came through their reactions to a series of crises." The first three Basic Agreements centered on pension reforms, which the owners stubbornly contested. The first agreement, in 1967, increased minimum salaries and expanded the pension system somewhat. In 1969 the second agreement came after players threatened a strike to extend pension coverage; confronted by a solid array of players, the owners backed down and made concessions. When the third agreement was pending in 1972, the owners balked at sweetening the pensions more; solidly united, the players staged a thirteen-day strike and won further concessions, including the right of players with two years of service to seek binding arbitration in salary disputes.

In 1976 the pending fourth Basic Agreement was stalled when owners, embittered over the Messersmith decision, staged a lockout of training camps. The resulting compromise on eligibility for the re-entry draft already has been noted, but the owners also raised the issue of compensation. Alarmed at the spiraling salary trend, the owners refused to negotiate a fourth agreement unless the players agreed to compensate any owner who lost a player in a re-entry draft; the owners wanted compensation in the form of an established player, but they settled for a choice in the rookie draft. When the owners revived their demand in 1980, it threatened to cause a strike that was delayed until 1981 by a cooling-off period. The 1981 strike hit players hard financially, but they held firm. While the owners won a limited victory on the compensation issue in the fifth Basic Agreement, the players' concession failed to halt the rising salary trend.

A pair of high-flying Robinsons among the Orioles: Brooks (*top*) played twenty-three seasons for Baltimore, most of them superbly. Frank (*center*) had a half-dozen strong years for the Orioles, 1966–71, and later managed the Indians and Giants. (Courtesy Baltimore Orioles)

Bottom: David Arthur ("Dave") McNally, a strong pitcher for the Orioles in the late 'Sixties and early 'Seventies. His fourteen-year career record was .607, and he was .600 in five league championships and .667 in four World Series. (Courtesy Baltimore Orioles)

If "power to the people" was a forlorn slogan of American protest groups during the stirring 'Sixties, in baseball at least it had some meaning. To major league players Miller was the emancipator, the "Players' Commissioner," who realized the dashed hopes of union-minded predecessors like John Ward. Although a bitter owners' spokesman derided a suggestion that Miller be voted into the Hall of Fame with the snide rejoinder that only through the janitor's entrance would that happen, to Expansion Era players Miller was already enshrined in their Hall of Fame.

THE 'SIXTIES STYLE

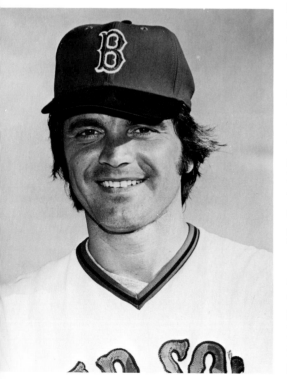

Anthony Richard ("Tony") Conigliaro, who led the American League in homers in 1965, his second season with the Red Sox, but whose career declined after he was beaned in 1967. (Courtesy Boston Red Sox)

Miller's impact on the player salary front owed much to the militant spirit amidst his constituents. Inspired by the reformist sentiments loosed in the 'Sixties, this generation of players seemed like a new breed—bolder, more individualistic, and more assertive than those of past eras. Even before Miller appeared on the scene, some had lashed out at repressive disciplinary measures; for the most part they understood the power of unified action. Harnessing such strength and guiding it was Miller's task; hiring Miller in defiance of hostile owners was the masterstroke delivered by this emergent new breed.

If Miller needed guidelines for his reformist course, these were supplied by some assertive players. For daring to pen two revealing books that criticized owners, general managers, and field managers amidst iconoclastic descriptions of his life in baseball, pitcher Jim Brosnan had been branded as a troublemaker. However, Brosnan's bold stand encouraged pitcher Jim Bouton to publish some of his grievances, including his losing salary negotiations with the Yankees. At the end of the decade Bouton bared these and other observations in even more naturalistic style than Brosnan's. When *Ball Four* hit the stalls in 1970, its candid revelations appalled the baseball establishment. But when called to account by Commissioner Kuhn, Bouton was joined by Miller, whose reminders of free-press rights blocked any punitive action.

While other players voiced various grievances, the most strident complaints centered on salaries. By the mid-1960s the salary issue had become a potential time bomb. Despite increasing baseball revenue from television, the minimum salary in 1966 stood at $7,000, as it had for a decade, and the average annual salary was $17,000. Only superstars like Mays and Mantle drew salaries of $100,000 or more by 1965. Moreover, players still had to bargain individually with GMs or owners, who refused to reveal what other players were getting. Thus, bargaining sessions were usually mismatches; most often, players were worsted by smooth-talking GMs like Emil ("Buzzy") Bavasi of the Dodgers, who boasted of saving O'Malley $2 million by beating down player demands.

Now signs of a turnabout were evident. Shortly before Miller took office in 1966, Dodger pitching aces Koufax and Drysdale scored a portentous coup. By staging an unprecedented joint holdout for $100,000-range salaries, they forced O'Malley to treat with Koufax's lawyer, who threatened to sue O'Malley in the federal courts if the owner invoked the reserve clause. This medicine worked, and the players won; meanwhile, Boston pitcher Earl Wilson forced his club to bargain with a

Carl Michael ("Yaz") Yastrzemski, a consistent performer for the Red Sox for twenty-one seasons starting in 1961, but a superstar in the 'Sixties.(Courtesy Boston Red Sox)

hired agent, lawyer Bob Woolf. Doubtlessly, these precedent-setters cleared the way for all players to hire bargaining agents, as many did by the end of this decade.

Little victories like these foretold the coming storm on the salary front. That other reforms would follow was hinted by Ken Harrelson's 1968 coup. A journeyman player with the A's, Harrelson was attuned to the "hippie" style of the 'Sixties, which he flaunted with his garish clothes, long hair, and candid utterances. Such affectations affronted owner Charles Finley. In the aftermath of a stormy incident involving a teammate's misconduct, Finley fired the manager and suspended Harrelson. Outraged, Harrelson publicly called Finley a "menace to baseball" and threatened to lead a team strike. For that, Harrelson was fired, but Finley rued this rash act. An unfair labor practice complaint that Miller filed with the National Labor Relations Board forced Finley to reinstate Harrelson. This defused the strike threat. As for Harrelson, whose ouster freed him from reserve clause obligations, he sold himself to the Red Sox and pocketed a $75,000 signing bonus!

A trio of hungry Tigers of 1968: (top) Denny McLain, (center) Mickey Lolich, (bottom) Bill Freehan. (Courtesy Detroit Tigers)

These isolated curtain-raisers revealed the plot of the great drama to come. When it played in the 1970s, the drama featured a spiraling salary revolution that cast most players as plutocrats, but nonetheless ready to strike for more privileges. When the players succeeded in freeing themselves from reserve clause constraints and arbitrary discipline codes, they incurred a lot of wrath from some owners and some fans, as well as some envious gusts from retired veterans. Sadly for some players whose careers ended during the 1960s, they too joined the ranks of the envious. Like Moses, their lot was merely to glimpse the promised land. By 1970 Miller's first two Basic Agreements raised minimum salaries to $13,000; that year the average player salary hovered around $25,000, and the ranks of $100,000-a-year plutocrats numbered about twenty. While this was an astounding increase over the $9,000 average salary of 1954, the salary spiral was just beginning; by the mid-1970s the average salary stood at $100,000.

Ken Harrelson, who tangled with owner Finley of the Athletics in 1968, the year the team was being moved to Oakland. The unconventional Harrelson was with the Red Sox and Indians briefly till the end of his nine-year career. (Courtesy Boston Red Sox)

In other ways this generation stood out as a different breed. Better paid and defended than players of past eras, they were also more numerous, more highly educated, more outspoken, more likely to be married, and better trained and doctored. The first round of expansion upped their numbers to 500, and the chronic shortage of young talent raised their market value. In 1965 the talent shortage led owners to invoke a free-agent (rookie) draft system. To staff the shrinking minor leagues, the majors subsidized minor league teams. They also eyed southern and western colleges as prime sources of recruits. Baseball was a year-round sport at such schools, and from their teams players sometimes joined the majors. This trend, combined with the continuing national thirst for higher education, accounted for the relatively large number of college-educated players in major league ranks. The increasing number of married players also mirrored a national trend, as did the growing divorce rate. At this time some critical observers blamed the mix of higher education and player marriages for spawning selfish and less dedicated players; defenders, however, applauded the new breed's tough-minded defense of individual freedom.

Their equipment also set this generation of players apart. Now in general use, brightly painted batting helmets complemented trimmer, flashier uniforms that were increasingly being made of double-knit materials; in time, gaudy color combinations would have fans forgetting the traditional baggy flannels. Such costumery befitted players who were more in the public eye. Credit television for molding players into national celebrities. By the end of this decade 94 percent of the nation's households had television sets, and the rush to acquire color sets was on. What television viewers seemed to crave was entertainment, and baseball, with its diet of night games and players in the role of celebrities, was helping to satisfy the tastes of viewers.

Yet, in the main, these players acquitted themselves well on the field. From a batting perspective this was a time of extremes. In 1962 hitters smashed 3,001 homers, a record output of nearly one a game. But only six years later hitters impotently swung for the lowest batting averages in living memory, while the homer percentage hit a fifty-year low. By way of compensation, fans were treated to virtuoso performances by hurlers like Koufax, Marichal, and Gibson; indeed, the passing of time saw this brief era raise up all-time-great pitching stars. Meanwhile, pitching dominance accounted in part for a revival of base stealing; at this time base stealers doubled the 1950 low figure for that art when only 20 steals were accomplished per 100 games.

One of the hallmarks of this decade was the splendid offensive performance of black and Hispanic players. At this time more than 20 percent of major leaguers were black, while Hispanic players accounted for nearly a hundred more. If some reactionaries saw varieties of complexion as a threat to the game's popularity, none could fault the virtuosity of darker-skinned stars.

Certainly, the fact that the National League housed a greater number of black stars was a factor in its offensive predominance. Over the years 1962–68 black stars won six of the seven National batting crowns, including three by Roberto Clemente, two by Tommy Davis, and two by Matty Alou. Meanwhile, all seven homer titles went to blacks, including three by Mays, two by Aaron, two by Willie McCovey, and

BASEBALL AND ETHNIC INTEGRATION

Charles Finley, right, who found that ball players can be stubborner than the A's mule mascot, and Casey Stengel. (Courtesy Oakland Athletics)

one shared by Aaron and McCovey. In addition, black stars took five of the National's seven MVP crowns in this period.

A lesser trend was under way in the American League, where prior to this time no black player had ever won a batting title or an MVP award. Now three batting titles went to blacks (two by Tony Oliva and one by Frank Robinson), and MVP awards went to Robinson, Elston Howard, and Zoilo Versalles. Robinson, who became the first player to win MVP awards in both major leagues, was the unanimous choice for the 1966 award by dint of a Triple Crown performance.

Such achievements raised up two black demigods. An emergent new trio of superstars included black outfielders Willie Mays and Hank Aaron. Each had established his slugging credentials in the 'Fifties. Now at the pinnacle of his glory, Mays, who was voted "Player of the 'Sixties" by *The Sporting News*, took aim at Ruth's vaunted lifetime homer total of 714. Although he fell short, upon retiring in 1973 he had clouted 660 homers on a .302 lifetime average and was a member of the exclusive 3,000-hit club. As the flashy Mays spent his strength, durable Hank Aaron mounted his own stubborn, plodding assault on Ruth's Olympian mark. In these years he steadily narrowed the gap and drew within one homer at the close of the 1973 season. Then, early in 1974, he electrified the baseball world by blasting his 715th at Atlanta. When he retired, he had raised the new mark to 755, had batted .307, and had joined the 3,000-hit club.

By then the third member of the new top trio was an established star. A hustling dervish of a player, Pete Rose joined the Reds in 1963, the year Musial played his last game. There was irony in that, as Musial then held the National League record for total hits (3,630), which Rose later broke. No slugger was this hell-for-leather white player, but Rose was a versatile infielder-outfielder and a switch-hitting virtuoso. After winning Rookie-of-the-Year honors in 1963, Rose landed the first of his three batting titles in 1968. Thenceforth, he kept up a furious pace, including tying Keeler's National League mark of hitting safely in 44 consecutive games. All this won him *The Sporting News* accolade of "Player of the 'Seventies." Nor did he stop there; in 1981 he passed Musial's hit total. Then, with élan unslowed by the weight of more than forty years, in 1985 the veteran broke Ty Cobb's "untouchable" record of 4,191 lifetime hits.

Just below the top threesome was black Panamanian Rod Carew. In 1967 Carew was a rookie with the Minnesota Twins, but he later eclipsed the exploits of teammate Tony Oliva to land seven American League batting titles.

While no player of the 1961–80 era surpassed the deeds of these lordly batsmen, other hitters won patents of nobility. At this time aging sluggers like Ed Mathews, Ernie Banks, Duke Snider, and the ailing Mickey Mantle retired with numerous homers—enough to assure each a place in the Hall of Fame. As these stars flickered out, a new galaxy of sluggers—including Harmon Killebrew, Willie McCovey, Billy Williams, Frank Robinson, and Frank Howard—shone forth. In this first expansion period, Killebrew hit 313 homers; McCovey, 242; Robinson, 216; Howard, 202; and Williams, 201. In the years 1963–70 Williams set a new National record by playing 1,117 consecutive games with the

Mickey Mantle hanging up his uniform for the last time at the end of the 1968 season, after eighteen years of stardom. The Yankees later retired his number. (Courtesy New York Yankees)

Cubs. Nor should the name of Roger Maris be forgot; like a flashing comet he illuminated the American League's first expansion season by poling 61 homers to break Ruth's seasonal record. Also at this time two American Leaguers, Carl Yastrzemski and Frank Robinson, notched back-to-back Triple Crowns. Yastrzemski's followed hard after Robinson's 1966 effort; an awesome achievement, these consecutive masterpieces bolstered sagging American League morale. But not for long; the following year the hitting famine ravaged the league, enabling Yastrzemski to win the batting title with a modest .301 mark.

Coping with the hitting famine was a problem facing both leagues; in the National League a base-stealing revival helped. When the National League expanded in 1962, Maury Wills of the Dodgers reigned as prince of thieves. That year his 104 swipes set an all-time seasonal mark; by 1965 he had led National stealers five straight seasons. At this point a new claimant arose, as Cardinal Lou Brock won the next three crowns. As the new monarch, Brock went on to erase Wills's seasonal record and also the all-time marks of Cobb and Billy Hamilton; this achievement, plus membership in the 3,000-hit club, won Brock a place in the Hall of Fame.

PITCHING PYROTECHNICS

Yet, for the most part, the hitters and stealers—even matchless fielders like Brooks Robinson of the Orioles, who glittered as the best all-round third baseman of all time—were overshadowed by pitching virtuosos. In fact, one must go back half a century for a comparable decade when pitchers fanned so many batters, posted so many 20-victory seasons, hurled so many perfect games, or attained such stardom as in these 'Sixties.

Pete Rose, a rising superstar of the 'Sixties and still going strong in the 'Eighties. (Courtesy The Phillies)

At this time such postwar holdovers as Spahn, Wynn, Ford, and Roberts ended their brilliant careers and awaited Hall of Fame transfiguration. Of this quartet, Spahn and Wynn became the thirteenth and fourteenth members of the exclusive 300-victory club; Spahn's 363 wins enshrined him as baseball's winningest left-hander. Yet, so many new stars arose that the passing of titans like Spahn hardly dimmed the skies. Brightest of the new stars were ace starters Koufax, Drysdale, Gibson, Gaylord Perry, Steve Carlton, Jim Palmer, Juan Marichal, Tom Seaver, Denny McLain, Ferguson Jenkins, Phil and Joe Niekro, Jim Hunter, Nolan Ryan, Jim Kaat, and Jim Bunning. Among them, Perry would join the 300 club in 1982, Carlton in 1983, and Seaver and Phil Niekro in 1985. Gibson, who won 251 games and fanned 3,117, dominated the 1968 "Year of the Pitcher" when he posted a 1.12 ERA and fanned a record 35 batters in the World Series. Not to be outdone, McLain dominated American League hurlers; his 31–6 record broke the 30-win barrier for the first time in thirty years. Also in that year Drysdale reeled off a record 58⅔ shutout innings.

It was a decade of dazzling pitching performances. Now at his peak, the "Dominican Dandy" Juan Marichal used his baffling assortment of deliveries to win 243 games and assure his Hall of Fame spot. Koufax, battling crippling arthritis, won three Cy Young awards to secure his niche. Bunning and Perry became the first hurlers since Cy Young to win a hundred games in each major league. Three flingers—Bunning, Koufax, and Hunter—hurled perfect games; in all of baseball history there had been only eight such masterpieces before. Ryan spun the first of his record five no-hitters and, along with Perry and Carlton, broke Walter Johnson's all-time strikeout record in the 1983 season. Indeed, these new stars fanned batters at such a rate that fans of this decade were seeing fifteen pitchers whose names would eventually be listed among the twenty all-time leading strikeout masters.

Just as sparkling were the relievers; now the "bullpen revolution" they wrought had every team depending on a varied relief corps. A "Fireman of the Year" Award instituted in 1960 honored these specialists, as did the custom of awarding statistical "saves," which relievers found useful as bargaining chips at salary-negotiating time. In this decade Wilhelm retired, having appeared in more games than any other pitcher and having won more games in relief (123) than any other, although Lindy McDaniel's 119 was close. Although no reliever of this decade topped Roy Face's 18–1 log of 1959, Dick Radatz and Ron Perranoski each won 16 in a season; moreover, Barney Schultz and Tom Dukes each tied Face's record of pitching in nine straight games.

Alas for the dominant pitchers, for their near perfection made them targets of penalties. As their mastery lowered average runs scored per game from eight in 1963 to seven in 1968, attendance, like batting, hit a low point. Alarmed at the attendance loss, officials elected to boost batting by penalizing pitchers. In analyzing the batting famine, officials blamed their liberal 1962 decision that raised the strike zone; that, plus better gloves, more sophisticated defenses, the bullpen revolution, and the versatile deliveries that nearly every pitcher armed himself with, were cited as causes. To bring back fans it was decided to narrow the

Rodney Cline ("Rod") Carew, who racked up a .332 career batting average during a dozen seasons with the Twins and three with the Angels. (Courtesy Minnesota Twins)

strike zone and to lower pitching mounds. This medicine worked for a brief time, but within a few years a renewed pitching resurgence required new nostrums to balance this ever-unstable equation.

A new ballpark building boom furnished some impressive stages for these players. In this decade ten new parks opened their gates, of which seven were in the National League. Because of the 1958 rule ordaining that new parks must conform to minimum distances from home plate to the outfield fences, the new parks tended to look alike, with fan-shaped playing fields set inside a bowl-like structure, surrounded by acres of parking lots, and generally located in a suburban area.

A celebrated new departure was Houston's Astrodome, an enclosed, air-conditioned bowl that opened to extravagant plaudits in 1965; some touted it as one of the world's wonders. Erected at a cost of $31 million, the Astrodome inspired imitators in the 1970s with its conquest of weather. Oddly, a major drawback led to another innovation; when it was discovered that grass would not grow in the roofed Astrodome, the problem was overcome by carpeting the field with synthetic "Astro-turf." Although scorned by purists, synthetic grass was widely adopted within a decade. Although critics hotly debated its impact on hitting and fielding, the product's weather advantages were obvious. Soon, newly developed water-sucking machines enabled clubs with synthetic carpets to play games that would formerly have been canceled because of wet grounds.

With the debatable exception of O'Malley's Dodger Stadium, all new parks were constructed at public expense. Ranging in costs from $14.5 million to $31 million, these outlays were burdensome and controversial. In persuading local citizens to approve stadium bond issues, proponents dazzled them with visions of jobs and revenues to come from the so-called "multiplier effect" that such parks would bring to the economy. Although the promise proved illusory, so strong was the glamor attached to landing a major club, or the fear of an extant one leaving town if ill-housed, that public financing powered this latest park building boom. At this time erratic attendance figures furnished ammunition for both sides of stadium-financing debates. With more new parks than its junior rival, National League attendance twice bettered American by more than 4 million. After luring a record 15 million fans in 1966, however, National attendance sagged to 11.7 million in 1968, a figure that barely topped the rising American League attendance.

The attendance decline excited fears that major league baseball might be losing its hold on sports-minded America. Indeed, the majors' 23 million total attendance of 1968 was only three million above that of 1960, when only sixteen clubs performed. The ominous specter of attendance decline sent the baseball establishment scurrying for explanations and possible remedies. No easy explanations were vouchsafed; counting the possible causes required all one's fingers. External causes like television, rival sports, and the disruptive summer riots of these years were cited, along with internal factors like the unwieldy ten-club

PROBLEMS AND PORTENTS

Sandy Koufax showing his explosive style. (Courtesy Los Angeles Dodgers)

format, the hitting decline, the prominence of black stars, and the lack of an outstanding superstar to match towering figures that now appeared in rival sports.

One senses a gloomy undercurrent of discontent among baseball men who grappled with such problems. In his 1964 farewell speech, retiring commissioner Frick warned that the game faced an image problem. Instead of baseball's being perceived as a sport, he argued that television and money-hungry people were fast making fans see the game as a commercialized entertainment. Coming from Frick, who had done nothing to avert such a come-about, the words smacked of hypocrisy. Nor did Frick's successors, William Eckert or Bowie Kuhn, do much more; at best, their words supported the owners' positions and prompted hot retorts from critics.

By 1968 the attendance problem and the hitting famine loomed as more immediate threats to baseball's success. In linking these problems the obvious solution seemed to call for reviving hitting through rule changes. As it turned out, this forthright approach worked well enough. After brushing aside some radical proposals—such as shortening the distance between bases, increasing the size of balls, restricting the number of night games, or alleviating hectic travel schedules—rule makers of 1968 simply opted to penalize pitchers by lowering mounds and narrowing the strike zone. The remedy worked better in the National League than it did in the American; hence, in 1973 the junior league's moguls unilaterally adopted a designated-hitter rule. Astonishingly, having designated batters hit for pitchers also worked well. As hitting and attendance surged upward in the 1970s, prophets of gloom were silenced. But other critics rightly directed attention to other problems threatening the game.

For one, the militant unionism of the players was blamed for disenchanting fans, undercutting managers, and infecting umpires with the same virus. Indeed, field managers steadily lost status and disciplinary power, and their importance as strategists was much questioned. As always, managers were often fired, but now they were more likely to become scapegoats and blamesakes for team misfortunes. Nor did owner Phil Wrigley help matters when he staged his quixotic experiment in replacing the field manager with rotating coaches. After several seasons this scheme was judged a failure. Bad as such blows were, the cruelest cut for harried managers must have been to watch their status sink as that of their archenemies the umpires rose. Inspired by the players' successful unionism, in 1969 all umpires joined the Major League Umpires Association. In less than a decade strikes launched by this strong Association won for umps pay increases, benefits, and protection beyond the wildest dreams of their downtrodden forebears.

To the delight of unionists, the gloomy opposition forecasts that rising player salaries would alienate fans and bankrupt clubs were not borne out. On the contrary, fans seemed to be enchanted by player plutocrats and by some of the more controversial player-characters of the time. Thus, Denny McLain's suspension and reinstatement following revelations of his involvement with gamblers created less stir than did his declining pitching effectiveness. Also, Jim Bouton's irreverent books became best-sellers and inspired more of the same from like-

Roy Face, outstanding Pittsburgh reliever of the late 'Fifties and early 'Sixties. (Courtesy Pittsburgh Pirates)

minded characters such as Joe Pepitone and Bo Belinsky, who turned out even earthier confessions. Indeed, the popularity of such decorum-defiers lent substance to exiled owner Bill Veeck's contention that baseball had need of more colorful characters.

That members of minority groups were freer now to express themselves was still uncertain. At this time a few critics suggested that the rising numbers of black and Hispanic players might account for the attendance decline. Such fears stemmed from certain tremulous reactions to militant black protest movements taking place in the 'Sixties; some black groups were blamed for inciting ugly riots in several cities, and the separatist demands of black extremists resulted in reactionary backlash. Of course, the great majority of black Americans opted for integration and lawful reforms. Especially did black players choose the integrationist course. While some players rightly protested continuing incidents of discrimination and were joined by some social critics, including those whose studies suggested that some teams imposed quotas on black players, in the main black players shared in player gains. Nor did any open rifts pit black players against white players during these strident years. That racial discrimination lingered in more subtle forms was voiced by stars like Bob Gibson, Hank Aaron, and Roberto Clemente. At this time black faces were missing from the ranks of umpires, field managers, and coaches. But not for long; within a few years these omissions were being remedied. On the whole, by emphasizing winning games over other issues, baseball transcended the racial storms of these years. As Ernie Banks somewhat over-optimistically put it, "In baseball the only race is to beat the throw."

In the 1960s the exaggerated fear of too many blacks in team lineups masked the larger problem of finding enough able recruits to man the teams. As manager Ted Williams explained in 1967, baseball no longer got the best athletes; hence, good player-development programs were wanted. It was a succinct statement of the game's talent scarcity problem. Bolstered by television exposure, rival team sports like football, basketball, hockey, and soccer gained powerful fan support, as did individual sports like tournament tennis and golf. At the grass-roots level, young scholastic athletes increasingly took to these; hence, at many schools and colleges, baseball was becoming a minor sport, and the once-ubiquitous summer sandlot leagues were shrinking in numbers.

Even more alarming was the shrinking number of minor leagues to fewer than twenty by 1960. To prop up the survivors and to cope with the talent shortage problem, the majors in 1962 voted to reclassify and subsidize the minor leagues. Under the Player Development Plan the majors agreed to sponsor and subsidize a hundred minor league teams. Three years later the owners voted to share the dwindling numbers of young prospects. In establishing the free-agent (rookie) draft, the owners adopted a procedure that had long been damned as "socialistic." The procedure curtailed free-enterprise scouting by pooling the nation's top school and college prospects and holding annual drafts with each club making its choice in turn. Although the system is legally questionable, nobody has challenged the draft. It is also expensive; signing top draft choices requires hefty bonus payments, and in contrast to the football and basketball drafts that this procedure imitated, baseball draft-

Dick Radatz, reliable "fireman" for the Red Sox, 1962–65. (Courtesy John Thorn)

ees need an average of three years of costly seasoning in the minors. Now called "player development," this seasoning process has become the main function of the minor leagues; since some clubs are better developers than others, an element of free enterprise remains. Moreover, some independent minor league operators continue to thrive outside this system. Likewise, free-enterprise scouting still pays off. Latin America is a fertile ground; although the Cuban Revolution of 1959 barred one prime source of talent, scouts have uncovered future stars in areas like the Dominican Republic, Panama, and Puerto Rico. However, any hopes of recruiting good Japanese players died in this decade; instead, Japan fielded its own flourishing major leagues and even took to signing some American players.

Baseball faced a talent problem at this time because rival sports not only vied with baseball in wooing top young athletes, but also challenged baseball's mythic claim to being the national pastime. Some pundits now argued that Americans embraced sports in general rather than any single sport. Defenders of this position pointed to the $3 billion that Americans now spent annually for sports equipment and noted that participation sports were also vying with baseball.

Backed by hefty television contracts, rival team sports—especially football, basketball, and hockey—expanded their schedules and encroached on both ends of baseball's long season. Also at this time baseball stood to be upstaged by the lavish television coverage of the quadrennial Olympic games. In 1967 baseball faced a head-on challenge from a television-backed major soccer league. Poor ratings aborted this threat, but the steady growth of scholastic soccer programs threatened to renew activity on this front in the future.

Of all these threats, pro football posed the most formidable challenge. Indeed, Commissioner Kuhn's gridiron counterpart, Commissioner Pete Rozelle, provoked Kuhn's heated defense of baseball's preeminence. Although the debates between the two commissioners were ludicrous, baseball promoters were envious of pro football's profitable format, including lavish national television contracts that the member teams divided evenly. Significantly, in 1964 the rival American Football League landed a $30-million NBC television pact that enabled the circuit to challenge the lordly National Football League. The following year the upstart AFL gave all team sports a lesson in successful promotion when the New York Jets signed quarterback Joe Namath to a multi-year $427,000 contract. That coup made both the league's reputation and Namath's. The flashy Namath became a national celebrity who ranked somewhat below prizefighter Muhammad Ali, who commanded million-dollar purses. Baseball promoters of the time could only envy such stars and hope for a day when one of their own became a national idol.

When that day came, television clearly would create the idol. Certainly, television was the catalyst that ignited America's sporting explosion. Watching televised sports had become America's favorite leisure pastime. For baseball, rising television revenue inspired franchise shifts and expansion, raised the values of clubs, made celebrities of players, and pushed player salaries upward. On the negative side, some owners blamed television for slumping gate attendance, and a few tried to ban

Bat Day at Connie Mack Stadium in June 1968, before the Phillies moved to Veterans Stadium. This crowd-pleasing gimmick was photographed for the *Philadelphia Bulletin*. (Courtesy Photojournalism Collection, Temple University Libraries)

improved television technology that promised to give viewers a better show than ballpark fans got. Overall, however, television created new baseball fans and nationalized the major league game. Nevertheless, owners clung to their local television policy, allowing shared network contracts only for World Series games, All-Star games, and a limited number of nationally televised seasonal games. While this policy kept baseball from sharing multi-million-dollar national television contracts on the scale of pro football, baseball's television revenue increased steadily. Helping to boost this revenue was a new policy of entrusting network contract bargaining to a committee of owners assisted by a professional adviser. This procedure now replaced the much-criticized policy of leaving such matters to the commissioner.

That one day soon television would carry baseball to undreamed of financial heights was as yet dimly perceived. At this time nobody dared predict that by 1984 television revenue would surpass paid attendance; yet, baseball's television revenue rose from $19 million in 1964 to $25 million in 1967 and showed no signs of peaking. At this time, too, television revenue was raising the value of franchises; in these years the sale of the A's fetched $3.9 million, and the Yankee sale netted more than $11 million. Also, expansion franchises that sold for $2 million in 1961–62 were pegged at $5.6 million by the American League and $10 million by the National in the upcoming 1969 expansion round. Nor was there any shortage of buyers; would-be owners vied to buy in and become instant celebrities. Other motives for buying into baseball included the advertising boost the game might give to the owner's outside business interests, the generous tax advantages that existed at this time, and the likelihood of recouping one's outlay from television income.

Of course, the television revolution raised some serious problems. For one, organized players demanded a share of the bonanza. For another, television producers threatened to reshape the game by urging innovations like nocturnal World Series games and other format changes. Some local television announcers were accused of hyping games and shilling for owners who had the power to hire and fire them. Television also transformed baseball's traditional relationship with the sporting press. Under pressure from television, big-city newspapers declined in numbers and readership. Although this trend was partly offset by increasing numbers of suburban newspapers, surviving newspapers adapted by expanding their advertising columns and reducing news columns. By now, news was being presented in magazine-like fashion. Because television news services usually beat newspapers on fast-breaking stories, a new journalistic style emerged. Such a style stressed probing, interpretive analyses of news events. In baseball reporting the trend showed in the new style of "chipmunk journalism." Such reportage had writers focusing less on the outcomes of games and more on issues surrounding baseball. While old-style writers still covered games, readers of baseball news were reading more probing accounts of issues like salary and labor disputes, team morale problems, players' off-field lives, criticisms of owners and officials, and clubs' handling of hot issues like racism and sexism. Topics like these were served up by new-style "chipmunks," whose output soon became a controversial issue for baseball insiders.

Such problems as television, unionism, soaring salaries, and threats from rival sports plagued baseball in the 1960s and showed no signs of lessening. Nevertheless, baseball owners voted to add four new teams for the upcoming 1969 season. If this latest expansion move seemed to be a radical break with tradition, it proved to be a wise move. With a new format calling for two divisional races in each major league, followed by intra-league playoffs and the World Series, the new plan proved more popular than the two ten-team races it replaced. Accompanied by remedial action to end the hitting famine, this new format triggered an attendance boom. Although strikes and unprecedented salary increases accompanied baseball's move into popular and prosperous uplands, the game's remarkable resilience gave the lie to pundit Marshall McLuhan's gloomy forecast that the game was doomed because "baseball is too individual a sport for the new age."

9
THE SOARING 'SEVENTIES

TOWARD THE END OF THE STORMY 'SIXTIES, AMERI-can optimism received a needed boost when the nation's astronauts made the first manned moon landing in the summer of 1969. That boost was welcome, since American optimism continued to be sorely tried in the 'Seventies.

On the side of foreign relations: The end of the Vietnam War in 1973 brought little relief, as new trouble spots erupted around the globe. Overseas, frustrations culminated in 1979 with the seizure of the U.S. embassy in Iran by fanatical nationalists and with the invasion of Afghanistan by Soviet forces. The American military draft ended in 1973 but was revived on a standby basis five years later. The global arms race continued to be both costly and worrisome.

On the domestic side: A vice president, a president, and top presidential aides resigned in 1973–74 after being charged with various crimes. In that same period, the nation suffered the sharpest recession since the 1930s and began to experience "stagflation"—inflated prices combined with stagnated economic growth. Marriages were delayed, and the birth rate fell. By the end of the 'Seventies some gloomy forecasters warned Americans to lower their expectations, saying the age of abundance was over.

Despite these national headaches, the United States continued to be a healthy environment for sports. America's population grew from 204 million in 1970 to 226.5 million in 1980, thanks largely to a falling

Three "Miracle" Mets of 1969, first expansion team to win a World Series: pitchers Jerry Koosman (*left*) and Tom Seaver (*right*) and shortstop Bud Harrelson, a steady defensive player. (Courtesy New York Mets)

death rate. The percentage of retirees rose, as did the adequacy of pensions. Both employed and retired Americans contributed to a boom in recreational spending, which rose from $18 billion to $40 billion during the 'Seventies.

BASEBALL'S MOONWALK

Top: A trio of Mets celebrating their 1969 Series victory over the Orioles: pitcher Jerry Koosman, catcher Jerry Grote, and third baseman Ed Charles. (Author's Collection)

Bottom: Bill Mazeroski, Pirate second baseman, showing his form at the age of thirty-two, during the 1969 season. Here he forced out Del Maxwell of the Cardinals and threw for the double play. (Courtesy Newman-Schmidt Studios, Pittsburgh)

Any thought that baseball might swap its traditional dual major league structure for some version of pro football's divisional system struck horsehide fundamentalists as the rankest kind of heresy—a prospect about as likely as men walking on the moon. Yet the 1969 season called for just such a format. In taking the expansion plunge for a second time, owners voted to add two more clubs to each league, raising major league membership to twenty-four clubs. Moreover, each major league was subdivided, roughly on a geographical basis, into Eastern and Western divisions. Although the skewed playing schedule retained the 162-game format, each team would play intra-divisional opponents eighteen times and outsiders twelve times. After finishing the regular schedule of games, the two divisional winners would meet in a playoff series to settle the issue of league championship. Afterwards, the league champs would settle the world championship in the usual way, although the Series would be delayed until late in October.

In playing out this scenario in 1969, four newcomers with strange-sounding totems joined the lists. The American League's Eastern Division housed six familiar teams (Tigers, Orioles, Indians, Red Sox, Yanks, and Senators), but the Western Division fielded such strangers as the Oakland A's (formerly the Kansas City A's), Kansas City Royals, and Seattle Pilots; the latter pair were expansionist teams composed initially of expansion draft cullings. For its part the National League opted to put a newcomer in each division. In the East the Montreal Expos added an international flavor, as the Canadians joined with the Cubs, Cards, Pirates, Phillies, and Mets. In the West the San Diego Padres became the league's third California franchise and were aligned with the Dodgers, Giants, Braves, Reds, and Astros.

Defenders of this revolutionary expansion format touted its competitive advantage over the former ten-team system, which made for two winners and eighteen also-rans. Supporters counted on the lure of four divisional races to sustain fan interest. Fans, they said, would crow over a divisional championship, even if the winner lost the league championship playoff. What's more, a divisional winner would get to fly a pennant; as for losing teams, it was argued that under the new system the worst any team could finish was sixth—better by far than tenth! Such sleight-of-hand logic failed to impress some critics, who lambasted the plan as a money-making scam foisted by television interests. To muffle such charges, fledgling commissioner Bowie Kuhn consolingly (and erroneously) predicted that the majors would undertake no further expansion for at least ten years. His words failed to satisfy one jaded writer, who predicted (also erroneously) that the combination of greedy promoters and striking players would so alienate fans as to make the game extinct by 1980.

Gloomy forecasts like that one were accompanied by alarums over a players' strike that threatened to end the new experiment before it started. Strike clouds gathered when contract talks leading to a second Basic Agreement broke down over the issue of more money for the players' pension fund. To force the issue, Miller recommended that no player sign a 1969 contract until the matter was settled. In support of Miller, five hundred players planned to quit the spring-training camps, but Kuhn nipped the threat by persuading owners to resume bargaining. A resulting second Basic Agreement sweetened the pension pot and allowed four-year veterans to qualify for pensions. Extending till December 1971, the agreement promised three seasons of peace on the labor front.

Although Neil Armstrong's July moonwalk temporarily upstaged the critical 1969 baseball season, the spotlight quickly swung back to baseball—where an ill-starred team, emerging from a black hole of futility, bid fair to stage baseball's equivalent of a moonwalk. The unlikely heroes of this unfolding drama were the New York Mets of the National League. Abject doormats since joining in 1962, this team's best claim to fame was a large and loyal following who showed up despite the Mets' penchant for losing often by "doing dumb things." Prior to 1969 their record stood at 394 wins and 737 losses, and true to form, they again lost their season opener in 1969.

Early on, it appeared that this mixed crew of aging vets and promising youngsters was going nowhere in the National League East. Although Met hitters produced only a .242 average, manager Gil Hodges

Manny Sanguillen, Pirate catcher in 1969–76, demonstrating his prowess in a season game against the Astros. (Courtesy Pittsburgh Pirates)

had a fine pitching staff headed by young Tom Seaver, whose 25-7 record led the league. For most of the season the Mets trailed the Cubs, who looked like sure bets to land their first pennant since 1945. But the Cubs faded in September, while the Mets won 38 of their last 49 games; the momentum carried them to 100 wins and an eight-game margin in the East. This highly publicized "impossible dream" was the sports story of 1969, easily eclipsing the hot Western Division race, which the Braves won by three games over the Dodgers on the strength of .258 team batting paced by Hank Aaron's 44 homers.

Given little chance against the heavy-hitting Braves in the playoff series for the National League championship, Met hitters exploded for 27 runs while sweeping the stunned Braves. Pitted against the American League's formidable Orioles, the Mets seemed likely to end their drama on a tragic note. Under sophomore manager Earl Weaver, the Orioles had made a shambles of the American Eastern race, winning 109 games and lapping the Tigers by 19 games. Paced by sluggers Boog Powell and Frank Robinson, the Orioles compiled a .265 batting average that included 175 homers; besides, the pitching staff boasted a pair of 20-game winners in Mike Cuellar and Dave McNally and owned the league's best ERA. In the playoff for the American League title they faced the Twins, winners by nine games over the A's in the Western Division. Weaver's men swept manager Billy Martin's good-hitting team in the playoff. Going into the World Series, the high-flying Orioles rode the heady current of a 14-game winning streak.

Under the circumstances, who could blame Baltimore papers for cackling that the end of the Met miracle was nigh? So it seemed when the host Orioles, behind pitcher Cuellar, breezed to a 4-1 opening-game win. Then came the turnabout; the next day the Mets squared matters behind Jerry Koosman's two-hit pitching. Action then shifted to Shea Stadium, where 56,000 Metomaniacal fans inspired the Mets to blank the Orioles 5-0 behind pitchers Gary Gentry and Nolan Ryan. Ahead two games to one, the Mets won again as Seaver's gritty ten-inning hurling, assisted by a pair of acrobatic catches by outfielder Ron Swoboda, avenged the ace pitcher's opening-game defeat. Now, only

From left, George Lee ("Sparky") Anderson, who managed the Reds to four pennants and two world championships between 1970 and 1976, with two of his stalwarts, Johnny Bench and Pete Rose. (Courtesy Cincinnati Reds)

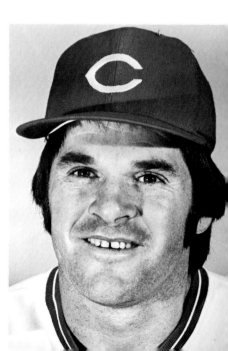

one more win was needed, and the Mets got it in dramatic style. Overcoming a three-run deficit, the Mets drew even in the sixth; then, aided by two errors, they scored the winning runs in the eighth.

The final out released a tornado of fan emotions; a joyous riot ensued that saw some delirious Metophiles ripping up clods of Shea soil for fetish keepsakes. For a week Metomania gripped Gotham and spread over the land, creating a legend that tickled the fantasies of ordinary souls. Within six months a dozen hastily written books celebrated the event; the enshrined players were deluged with endorsement offers. Sadly for the Mets, it was more than they could handle. By kindling jealousies, fans destroyed team unity. Thus, as in a Greek tragedy, the heroes fell to earth in 1970. But the hoopla over the Met moonwalk made a roaring success of baseball's expansion experiment. National League attendance jumped by 3 million in 1969 and continued upward through the 'Seventies. Such sturdy support sent baseball stock soaring. As attendance touched new peaks, so did the popularity of televised games, which added more revenue. With only slight setbacks, such as the brief player strike of 1972, the boom continued.

Spearheading baseball's boom decade, the National League averaged over 16 million paid admissions a year; in 1970–76 it outdrew its American rivals by some 24 million tickets. This decisive advantage came despite resurging American League homer power and the junior circuit's four Series victories. What counted more were the National's five new parks that opened their gates in this decade. Two housed the expansion Padres and Expos, who faced formidable challenges of building winning teams from scratch. Of this pair, the Padres foundered at first, before coming under the spirited ownership of hamburger king Ray Kroc. Even if National attendance gained little from the early Padres, it got a powerful shove from the new parks that housed the Pirates, Reds, and Phillies. In company with the Dodgers, whose return to power midway in the decade set all-time attendance records, these teams formed powerful dynasties that monopolized divisional races and dampened idealistic hopes that the new divisional format would usher in an age of competitive balance. On the contrary, save for the 1973 season, when another miracle Met team won out, these four teams defended National honor in nine World Series matches.

These four mini-dynasties monopolized the divisional races of 1970–80. During those eleven seasons the Pirates and Phillies won ten Eastern Division races; in the West the Reds and Dodgers accounted for nine. By winning six divisional titles apiece, the Eastern-based Pirates and Western-based Reds were the dominant teams. These two antagonists were evenly matched; in their four battles for league championships, each won two. Moreover, each won two World Series titles.

The first round of hostilities between the Pirates and Reds came in 1970. As if to baptize their new Three Rivers Stadium, the Pirates handed Pittsburgh fans a divisional flag that year. With only Mazeroski and Clemente on hand from their 1960 world champs, new Pirate faces included outfielders Matty Alou, Willie Stargell, and Al Oliver; infield

CAMPAIGNS OF THE 'SEVENTIES: THE NATIONAL LEAGUE

Daniel Edward ("Danny") Murtaugh, manager of the Pirates for fifteen seasons from 1957 through 1976, including two World Series years. (Courtesy Pittsburgh Pirates)

Wilver Dornel ("Willie") Stargell, hard-hitting outfielder and first baseman for the Pirates during an entire generation, 1962–81. (Courtesy Pittsburgh Pirates)

Joe Morgan, second baseman for the Cincinnati Reds in the 'Seventies. (Courtesy Cincinnati Reds)

regulars included Bob Robertson, Dave Cash, Gene Alley, and Richie Hebner; and catcher Manny Sanguillen handled a fair pitching staff that was heavily dependent upon reliever Dave Giusti. With Giusti saving 26 games and Clemente batting .352, manager Danny Murtaugh's Pirates' 89 victories topped the Cubs by five games to win the Eastern crown. By batting .270 the Reds tied the Pirates' team effort, but the Reds had more punch—a league-leading 191 homers. Along with speed on the base paths, the versatile Red assault had Cincinnati fans jamming new Riverfront Stadium to cheer their "Big Red Machine." Managed by George ("Sparky") Anderson, the Reds boasted a trio of .300-plus hitters in outfielders Pete Rose and Bob Tolan and first baseman Tony Perez. They also had baseball's best catcher in Johnny Bench; in 1970 his .293 batting and league-leading 45 homers and 148 RBIs won Bench MVP honors. While the starting pitching staff was weak, Anderson successfully deployed relievers Wayne Granger, Clay Carroll, and Don Gullett. The Reds won easily in the West.

In the first playoff clash between these titans, the Reds swept the Pirates to land the 1970 league championship. But the World Series was another story. Paired against the resolute Orioles, who still smarted from their 1969 humiliation at the hands of the Mets, the Reds lost the first two games in Cincinnati and went on to lose the world title in five games.

What soon became the Reds' chronic problem—poor pitching—contributed to their fourth-place finish in 1971. Into the breach rushed the Giants and Dodgers. Riding an 11-game lead compiled in June, the Giants led all the way, but a horrendous September slump allowed the Dodgers to come within a game at the end. In eking out a narrow victory in the West, manager Charlie Fox's Giants got stout pitching from Juan Marichal and Gaylord Perry; it was needed to overcome an anemic .247 team batting average bolstered by 140 homers. Outfielder Bobby Bonds led the hitters with a .288 batting average, 33 homers, and 102 RBIs. These Western champs were overmatched by the Pirates. Essentially the veteran 1970 team, Murtaugh's men pounded a league-leading 154 homers on .274 batting. Again Clemente led the attack, this time with .341 batting; joining him, Stargell batted .295 and led the league in homers. With Giusti saving 30 games, the Pirates' 97 wins topped the runner-up Cardinals by seven games in the East. In the playoff for the league title, the Pirates performed as expected; after losing the opener in San Francisco, they swept the next three games.

For all their firepower the Pirates were underdogs in the 1971 World Series. The American League Orioles carried a 14-game winning streak into the fray, which for the first time called for night games. Although critics attacked this surrender to television powers, the nocturnal games proved very popular. What fans saw was a storied Pirate comeback; after losing two games in Baltimore, the Pirates swept three at home and went on to win in seven games. Once news of the final victory hit Pittsburgh, a hundred thousand revelers went on a riotous tear. Dubbed the "Big Buc Binge," its destructive violence was followed by eight seasons of serenity before the Pirates won again.

Indeed, National contenders were fated to lose the next three Series matches to the powerful Oakland Athletics. For a time there was the alarming threat that the first of these might not come off. In the spring of 1972 a breakdown in contract negotiations triggered a player strike. Before it was settled the walkout curtailed spring training and canceled some seasonal games. In the National League the shortened schedule had no bearing on the outcome of divisional races. In the East the Pirates, now managed by Bill Virdon, romped to an easy 11-game victory. League-leading hitting was fronted by five .300 hitters, including Clemente, who joined the 3,000-hit club; what's more, the pitching staff managed a 2.81 ERA. In the West, meanwhile, the Big Red Machine rolled to a 10½-game win over the Houston Astros, whose general manager helped the Reds by dealing them second baseman Joe Morgan. In time Morgan would win two MVP awards as a Red, but this year Bench's homer-hitting took the honor; his long blows and Rose's steady hitting compensated for shaky starting pitchers, who completed only 25 games. By saving 37 games, reliever Clay Carroll won the Fireman of the Year Award. Given little chance against the Pirates, the Reds fought hard. Down two games to one in the playoff series, they rallied to win the league title; the winning run was scored in the final game on a wild pitch by a Pirate reliefer.

The victory sent the clean-shaven Reds against the Oakland A's, whose mustaches and garish uniforms had critics sneering that they resembled "hippies." But when the taut seven-game struggle ended, the longhairs had beaten the Red Machine. To the horror of baseball purists, the hairstyle adopted by the A's spread to other clubs. Still seen as a symbol of protest, long hair became a bone of contention in baseball even as many ordinary American males also adopted the style. But critics of 1973 were more horrified by the American League's unilateral adoption of the designated-hitter rule, which the National League rejected.

Certainly, the National League could have benefited from some extra hitting in 1973. The East was woefully weak; overall its six teams compiled a 470-500 won-loss record. Stunned by Clemente's tragic death and pitcher Steve Blass's ineffectiveness, the Pirates fell to third. Even so, their 80-82 record left them only 2½ games out; still closer were the Cards with an 81-81 record. The winners by a narrow margin were the Mets. Now managed by Yogi Berra, these "miracle Mets" batted a lowly .246 and smote only 85 homers. Pitching saved them, as Tom Seaver led the league in wins, strikeouts, and ERA, for a dominating Cy Young performance. George Stone contributed 12 wins, and reliever Tug McGraw saved 25 games. Few expected the Mets, a team with a measly 82-79 record, to prevail against the powerful Reds in the playoffs. In their hard-fought Western campaign the Reds came from 11

During the 'Seventies shortstop Dave Concepcion was one of the spark plugs in Cincinnati's "Big Red Machine." (Courtesy Cincinnati Reds)

Steve Blass, who pitched strongly for the Pirates from 1966 through 1972, but then faded. (Courtesy Pittsburgh Pirates)

Two newsmaking managers of the 'Sixties and 'Seventies: (*top*) Earl Sidney Weaver of the Orioles and (*bottom*) Lawrence Peter ("Yogi") Berra of the Yankees and Mets. Weaver led the Birds to four pennants and a world championship between 1969 and 1979. Berra's Yanks won a pennant in 1964, and his Mets took one in 1973, though both lost in the Series. (Courtesy Baltimore Orioles and New York Yankees)

games back to overhaul the Dodgers. Rose's batting led the pitching-poor Reds; his .338 mark won him MVP honors. Although batting only .254, the Reds bashed 137 homers and led the league in bases stolen. Nevertheless, in their showdown with the Reds, the New Yorkers took league honors by winning three of the five games.

That a team with so skimpy a record as the Mets' might go on to become world champs was one of the criticisms voiced against the divisional system. Indeed, the Mets very nearly did win the Series; at one point they led the A's three games to two, but the A's won the last two to quash "the impossible dream." Barely had purists stopped shivering over that brush with fantasy when they were confronted by baseball's switch from horsehide to cowhide balls. Dire predictions of a 1974 hitting surge never came off, however. Instead, fans responded enthusiastically to Aaron's 715th homer and to Brock's record-setting 118 stolen bases. Along with tight divisional races, these feats dimmed the cowhide ball controversy.

In the 1974 Eastern race the Mets dutifully faded to fifth, while the Pirates reasserted their authority. Piloted once more by their now-ailing talisman Murtaugh, the Bucs foundered in the early going. Then league-leading hitting, paced by Stargell, Oliver, and Richie Zisk, powered a surge that carried them to a 1½-game victory over the Cardinals. Almost as close was the Western tussle between the Reds and Dodgers. Led by veteran manager Alston, the Dodger "Mod Squad" now fielded the most durable infield of all time: Steve Garvey, Davey Lopes, Bill Russell, and Ron Cey. First baseman Garvey's solid hitting (.312-21-111) won MVP honors, while the Cy Young award went to reliefer Mike Marshall, who appeared in an astonishing 106 games, winning 15 and saving 21. Such feats enabled the Dodgers to edge the Reds by four games. Dodger balance told in the championship playoffs; opening at home they snatched the first two games and went on to win three games to one. Pitted against the bickering Oakland A's in the World Series, the solid Dodgers looked like good bets to win. However, the A's split the first two games played at Los Angeles, then swept three games at home to land a third straight world title.

Nobody at the time knew it, but 1975 was a watershed year for baseball. For one thing, the A's lost their brief monopoly on world titles. But far more portentous was the overturning of the reserve clause that Dodger pitching ace Andy Messersmith precipitated by refusing to sign his 1975 contract. After playing the 1975 season without a contract, Messersmith argued that he had fulfilled his 1974 contract's one-year option clause; thus, he claimed the right to sell his services in the open market. An arbitrational panel agreed, and so did the federal court that ruled on the owners' appeal. That decision implied that any player might do the same. Within a year, although the right was restricted to six-year vets, other stars were doing the same; the resulting spiraling salaries ushered in the new era of player plutocrats.

In the years following the inauguration of the re-entry draft in 1976, news of player movements at times upstaged pennant races. Not that there was much to say about National League races of 1975–76. Cincinnati's Big Red Machine trampled opponents; in 1975 manager Anderson's relentless Reds won 108 games to lap the runner-up Dodgers by

Henry Louis ("Hank") Aaron, Braves outfielder in 1954–74, hitting his 715th homer to break Babe Ruth's lifetime record. The event took place on April 8, 1974, at Atlanta Stadium. (Courtesy Atlanta Braves)

Shortstop Bill Russell of the 'Seventies Dodgers. (Courtesy Los Angeles Dodgers)

20 games. The Reds' offense was brutally efficient with its .271 team batting, 124 homers, and league leadership in stolen bases. Little Joe Morgan's batting (.327-14-94) won MVP honors, while Rose, Ken Griffey, and George Foster also weighed in with .300-plus batting. In the playoffs they faced the Pirates, who had beaten the rising Phillies by 6½ games. Although young Dave Parker (.308-25-101) appeared as Clemente's promising successor, he and his Pirate mates were swept in the playoffs. The victory sent the Reds into the Series against a powerful Red Sox team. In a classic duel that stretched over seven games and attracted some 75 million television viewers for the final contests, the Reds won the decisive game in Boston.

The Reds continued their mastery in 1976, the year the nation celebrated its two hundredth birthday and the National League feted its centennial. A lockout of spring-training camps by owners, embittered by the Messersmith decision, marred baseball's celebration, but a compromise settlement saved the season. When play commenced, the Reds spared no rivals; their 102 wins carried them to a 10-game victory over the Dodgers in the West. Now at the height of their power, the Reds led the league in hitting, homers, RBIs, fielding, bases stolen, and attendance. Again Morgan won MVP honors, and this time outfielder Cesar Geronimo joined Rose, Griffey, and Foster in clouting .300. In the East, meanwhile, the Phillies unleashed a trio of .300 hitters in outfielders Jay Johnstone, Garry Maddox, and Greg Luzinski; such hitting plus a league-leading 38 homers by third baseman Mike Schmidt and a 20-victory performance by pitcher Steve Carlton helped the Phillies oust the Pirates by nine games in the East. But the jittery Phillies bowed to the Reds in three straight games, and the resurgent Yankees fell even harder in the World Series, losing to the Reds in four straight. In the wake of this second straight Series conquest, some compared the Reds with the 1927 Yankees. Although the comparison was presumptuous, the fact was that no National team but the Reds had won consecutive world titles since 1922.

In the absence of external intervention, the Reds in 1977 bid fair to continue their dominance. Unhappily for Cincinnati, an outside force was at hand; the newly adopted re-entry draft allowed six-year vets to auction their services, and pitcher Don Gullett snapped at a hefty Yankee offer. His loss, and a questionable trade that sent slugger Tony Perez to the Expos, weakened the team; not even the midseason acquisition of ace pitcher Tom Seaver from the Mets saved the Reds from the Dodger juggernaut. Now managed by Tom Lasorda, the Dodgers had only one .300 hitter, Reggie Smith, but the team led in homers and pitching ERA. It was enough to bury the Reds by 10 games. In the East, manager Danny Ozark's Phillies repeated. This time they led the league in batting; Carlton's 23 wins led league pitchers, and Schmidt and Luzinski combined for 77 homers. However, the Phillies, after splitting the first two playoff games in Los Angeles, lost in two straight games at home. Now only the Yankees barred the Dodgers' way, and this latter-day generation suffered the fate of past Dodger teams, losing the World Series four games to two.

Except for an even greater Dodger humiliation, the 1978 season repeated this scenario. In a season-long duel with the Reds, who were inspired by Rose's record-tying 44-game hitting streak and the star's entry into the 3,000-hit club, the Dodgers eked out a 2½-game victory. Again Dodger pitching and power hitting made the difference. While this struggle raged, an even closer one took place in the East, where the Phils won by a game and a half over the Pirates. League-leading fielding offset the Phillies' mediocre pitching and batting. This was of little avail against the Dodgers in the playoffs. After winning the first two games in Philadelphia, the Dodgers won the match three games to one. Handed a Series rematch with the Yankees, whose comeback victory in the American League was the sports story of the summer of 1978, manager Lasorda sought to inspire his charges by dedicating their effort to their late coach, Jim Gilliam. Striking early, the Dodgers took the first two games, but the Yankees swept the next four to win; it was another glittering addition to the Yankees' miracle season.

Stunned by that loss, Dodger hopes of coming back in 1979 received another crusher in the loss of ace pitcher Tommy John to the re-entry draft. In August 1979 the elder O'Malley died; his last days were soured by declining attendance and his team's faltering effort. As the Dodgers withered, the Astros and Reds battled for the Western title. Off to an early lead, the Astros were backed by intimidating pitching from towering J. R. Richard and knuckleballer Joe Niekro; Niekro won 21, while Richard's 18 wins produced more than 300 strikeouts and the league's best ERA. But strong pitching failed to atone for mediocre batting; after July the Astros played only .500 ball. As Houston struggled, the Reds methodically closed the gap. On the last day, the tight race ended with the Reds up by 1½ games. The unexpected triumph was the Reds' sixth in this decade, but it came without help from Pete Rose or manager Anderson. The popular Anderson had been sacked for losing in 1978, and the lionized Rose had joined the Phillies via the re-entry route after the club refused to pay him a superstar's salary. Thus, despite the victory, embittered fans stayed away; paid attendance in 1979 fell by 175,000, blighting the effort of manager John McNamara and the heroic efforts of pitcher Tom Seaver (16 wins) and surviving Big Red Machine vets.

With the Phils in 1979, the affluent exile Rose batted .331, but except for slugger Mike Schmidt (45 homers, 114 RBIs) and pitcher Carlton (18 wins), the other Phils were humdrum. After an early-season burst, they fell back, leaving the field to the Pirates and Expos. These well-matched rivals fought to the end before the Pirates won by a game. Managed by Chuck Tanner and straw-bossed by veteran Pops Stargell, who chose the team's battle hymn (the rock song "We Are Family") and who led the team in homers, the Pirates developed a

The 'Seventies Dodger infield also included first baseman Steve Garvey. (Courtesy Los Angeles Dodgers)

Two mainstays of the durable Dodger infield of the 'Seventies were second baseman Davey Lopes (*top*) and third baseman Ron Cey (*bottom*). (Courtesy Los Angeles Dodgers)

crushing offense. Recently acquired infielders Tim Foli, Bill Madlock, and Phil Garner each hit above .290; outfielder Dave Parker hit .310; and fellow outfielder Omar Moreno stole 77 bases. The pitching was vulnerable, but 52 saves by Pirate relievers aided the starters. Growing stronger as the season waned, the Pirates, led by Stargell, swept the Reds in the playoffs. Next came a rematch with the Orioles in the Series. Since their 1971 meeting neither team had scaled championship heights, but memories of the Pirate comeback victory haunted the Orioles. This time the determined Orioles struck harder; shrugging off cold weather, they took a commanding three-games-to-one lead and poised for the clincher that never came. Instead, the Pirates rallied to sweep the next three games, with the redoubtable Stargell leading the assault.

Hardly had baseball fans comprehended Pittsburgh's storied win than a menacing strike threat clouded the upcoming 1980 season. At issue was the re-entry draft; for the past four seasons these annual auctions had boosted salaries astonishingly. The trend appalled owners, furious at receiving only an untried prospect as compensation for any star player lost to the drafts. Although owners no longer hoped to restore the reserve clause to full power, they wanted an able player as compensation for anyone lost in a draft. In pressing this demand as essential to any new Basic Agreement, they flung a take-it-or-else gauntlet at the organized players. When neither side budged, the deadline of May 23 seemed likely to mark the beginning of a great strike. Mercifully, an eleventh-hour decision to keep talking and to extend the old Basic Agreement saved the season.

Although played in the eye of a gathering hurricane, the 1980 season was a memorable one. In the East, manager Dallas Green rallied his aging, high-salaried Phils to a stirring victory over the injury-ridden Expos and the slumping Pirates. By winning 21 of their last 28 games, including two of three crucial Montreal games, the Phils squeaked to victory. Carlton's 24-9 pitching won the Cy Young Award; Schmidt took MVP honors for his .286-48-125 stickwork; and the team batted .270. Equally dramatic was the Western struggle, in which the Astros, Dodgers, and Reds fought it out. At the end, only 3½ games separated the trio, with the Dodgers and Astros deadlocked. The Dodgers managed the tie by beating the Astros at home in the last three games; for the Astros that was a crusher, but the team was used to dealing with adversity. For instance, when ace pitcher J. R. Richard suffered a stroke, pitcher Verne Ruhle came off the disabled list and won 12 games. Re-entry acquisitions Joe Morgan and Nolan Ryan helped; Morgan hit well in the stretch, and Ryan (toiling under a million-dollar-a-year contract) kept the team afloat. In the sudden-death playoff for the Western title, Joe Niekro's pitching carried the team to a 7-1 win over the Dodgers.

More drama marked the 1980 championship playoff series. The Phils won the opener at Philadelphia, but they lost the next two outings. Then, with some 60 million television fans watching action from the Astrodome, the Phils rallied to win two. In the nail-biting finale the Phils came back from a 5-2 deficit; routing Ryan, they tied the game and won it in the tenth inning. The victory sent the Phillies into the

World Series for the first time in thirty years. Never yet a world champion, the Phils stole a march on the Kansas City Royals by winning the first two games at home. Then they swooned and lost two, but rallying swiftly, they took the last game played in Kansas City and then won a 4-1 game at home to nail down the banner. The joyous outpourings of fans from the "city of losers" were fated to be short-lived. In the desolate season that followed, the memory of 1980 went glimmering amidst the rancor of the great strike.

In the American League, expansion's first fruits left a bitter aftertaste in official mouths. Attendance in 1969 was a bust; the two American additions increased attendance over 1968 by less than a million, while National attendance jumped by more than 3 million. The disparity soon grew worse; by 1971 the attendance gap between the two majors widened to more than 5 million, in the National's favor. In addition, the Americans absorbed another humiliating blow when the newly admitted Seattle Pilots went bankrupt. Fortunately, a Milwaukee buyer moved the club to that city at a cost of $10 million. Unfortunately, 1971 saw another disruption when the mismanaged Washington Senators were shifted to Arlington, Texas, and became the Texas Rangers.

By now, owners were learning that moving franchises around could be risky. Each of these latest moves evoked lawsuits. To avoid a court battle with Seattle interests, American owners in 1977 handed Seattle a new expansion team, soon dubbed the Mariners. At the same time,

CAMPAIGNS OF THE 'SEVENTIES: THE AMERICAN LEAGUE

Mike Marshall, great reliever of the 'Seventies, emerging from the bullpen and jogging to the mound. Marshall served the Dodgers well in 1974 and 1975 after starring for the Expos and before starring for the Twins. (Courtesy Los Angeles Dodgers)

the Americans admitted the Toronto Blue Jays. As a result of this awkward, unilateral expansion, the American League offers fourteen teams to the National's twelve. From the start it also has meant adopting a skewed schedule, but it has enabled the American League to take and hold the lead in annual attendance statistics.

Yet another bold step helped the American League attain parity with the National in offensive statistics. It came in 1973 when the Americans unilaterally adopted the designated-hitter rule, aimed at ending the chronic hitting famine. Unlike the National hitters, who benefited from the 1969 pitching restrictions, American hitters still foundered; in 1972 American batting was a puny .239. As a remedy, the ploy of allowing a DH to bat for a pitcher worked. In 1973 averages jumped by 20 points and never fell below .250 thereafter.

Such bold ventures had National League officials deriding their American colleagues for making a mockery of the game. What counted, however, was that the Americans gained a questionable sort of parity. But, like the National League, the American circuit lacked competitive balance. In the years 1970–80 four teams reaped most of the divisional titles. In the East, manager Earl Weaver's powerful Orioles won five divisional titles and four times finished second; that record made the Birds the winningest major league team of the decade. However, the Orioles were challenged by the reviving Yankees, who captured four Eastern titles. It was the same story in the West, where the Oakland A's snagged five divisional flags before yielding to the Kansas City Royals, who took four.

The omnivorous appetites of these four teams allowed few leftovers. Among exceptions, the Minnesota Twins rode their 1969 momentum to stage another victory romp in the West in 1970. In lapping the rising Oakland A's, the Twins used league-leading hitting, led by Rod Carew, Rich Reese, and Tony Oliva, with slugger Killebrew weighing in with 41 homers and 113 RBIs. Unfortunately for the Twins, the Orioles also repeated in the East. Thrashing the runner-up Yankees by 15 games, the Orioles batted .257; Frank Robinson's .306 led, augmented by Powell's 35 homers and 114 RBIs and Brooks Robinson's 94 RBIs and masterful third base play. In addition, the Birds had the league's best pitching; Cuellar and McNally each won 24, Palmer added 20, and reliever Pete Richert saved 25. Such versatility was too much for the Twins, who were swept in the championship playoffs. That victory sent the Orioles into the World Series against the Cincinnati Reds. Burning to avenge their 1969 humiliation, the Birds unleashed a 50-hit barrage led by Brooks Robinson, who also frustrated the Reds with his fielding. The lopsided four-games-to-one victory restored Oriole honor, but manager Weaver never won another world title.

In spite of aging stars and flagging attendance, the Orioles repeated in 1971. Young outfielder Merv Rettenmund batted .318 to pace the hitters; aging Frank Robinson, in his last Oriole season, batted .281 with 28 homers and 99 RBIs. While the Birds led the league in hitting, the loudest plaudits went to the league-leading pitching staff, which boasted four 20-game winners in McNally, Palmer, Cuellar, and Pat Dobson. In the West, meanwhile, the Oakland A's rose to test Weaver's veterans. A controversial team, the A's were owned since

Manuel Rafael ("Manny") Mota, Dodger outfielder and pinch-hitter from 1970 to 1980. Mota led the National League in pinch-hits in 1974 and holds the career record for pinch-hits. (Courtesy Los Angeles Dodgers)

1961 by maverick Charles Oscar Finley, who defied many a baseball convention in his zeal to win. In boosting his team in his earlier years in Kansas City, he improved the stadium, concocted zany promotional stunts, hired and sacked a string of managers and GMs, and decked his players in green and gold uniforms. When none of these devices attracted large crowds, Finley cast about for greener pastures. Before quitting Kansas City for Oakland late in 1967, Finley warred with local fans and fellow owners. Cheering Finley's departure, Senator Stuart Symington of Missouri opined that "Oakland is the luckiest city since Hiroshima."

Ironically, Oakland also failed to produce anticipated high attendance. The city was located so close to the Giants' San Francisco lair that both teams fed off the same hinterlands. Moreover, Finley's methods also alienated Oakland fans. Yet, Finley combined genius with his erratic abrasiveness. His contempt for managers, GMs, scouts, and other experts was based on personal experience that persuaded him that he knew as much. Certainly none could fault his skill at spotting, signing, and developing young players. By 1968 he had nursed a dozen promising youngsters at a cost of less than $1 million in bonuses, but much more in their schooling. In 1969–70 his young team finished second in the West; from 1971–75 they ruled the West, extending their conquests to include a skein of three straight World Series victories that remains an unmatched feat of the expansion era.

In 1971 the A's were managed by Dick Williams, the toughest and best of Finley's string of foremen. The young outfield of Rick Monday, Joe Rudi, and Reggie Jackson hit hard; such was Jackson's élan as a homer hitter that he soon became baseball's leading celebrity. In the infield Mike Epstein temporarily held first base, but Dick Green, Bert Campaneris, and Sal Bando were solid fixtures. The pitching staff included Vida Blue, Jim Hunter, Jim Odom, and superb reliefer Rollie Fingers; backing them, Gene Tenace became a durable catcher and utility man. Once unleashed, the 1971 A's won 101 games and routed the runner-up Kansas City Royals. In the 1971 league championship duel, the Orioles swept the A's, giving the Birds a 14-game winning streak as they entered the World Series against the Pirates. The Orioles won the first two in that struggle, but they lost the next three and ultimately the world title in a seven-game battle.

For the next three years American League fortunes rode with Finley's controversial A's. Needing another pitcher, Finley got a good one when he pried lefty Ken Holtzman from the Cubs. In the strike-torn season of 1972, Holtzman won 19, compensating for Blue's ineffectiveness. Blue lost his edge after a bitter salary wrangle with Finley. Victors by 5½ games over the White Sox, Finley's team now sported long hair and mustaches (for which he paid each man $300). Their Eastern rival was the Tigers, whose half-game victory over the Red Sox resulted directly from the strike-skewed schedule. Manager Billy Martin's Tigers won the Eastern title by virtue of winning one more game than the Bostonians. The puny .237 Tiger batting average was laughable, but pitchers Mickey Lolich and Joe Coleman together won 41 games to help the cause. Picked to lose against the A's, they did so, but only after carrying the struggle to the five-game limit. Reggie Jackson was a casualty of

David Gene ("Dave") Parker, Pirate outfielder, who batted over .300 for five straight seasons in the 'Seventies, as well as .345 in the 1979 World Series. (Courtesy Pittsburgh Pirates)

Greg Luzinski, hard-hitting Phillie outfielder, in an altercation with Bill Greif, pitcher for the San Diego Padres, during the 1975 season. Photograph in the *Philadelphia Bulletin*. (Courtesy of Photojournalism Collection, Temple University Libraries)

that grueling playoff; because an injury sidelined him, the A's were installed as underdogs to the Reds in the World Series. Catcher Tenace took charge, however; his three homers and other key hits paced the A's to a four-games-to-three victory. It was a near thing, as the A's nearly blew a three-games-to-one lead. In the end Oakland's relief pitchers made the difference.

After scaling the championship heights in 1972, the A's held the pinnacle for the next two seasons. Their 1973 triumph was another close call. Mounting a diversified attack that included .260 team batting, 147 stolen bases, and 40 wins from pitchers Hunter and Holtzman, the A's beat the Royals by six games in the West. Leading the attack, Jackson batted .293 and led the league in homers and RBIs. Manager Williams also used the designated-hitter rule to advantage, getting 81 RBIs from Deron Johnson. However, Weaver's rebuilt Orioles won more impressively in the East. Their eight-game romp over the Red Sox was wrought by outfielders Rich Coggins, Don Baylor, and Al Bumbry. Coggins and Bumbry topped .300, as did DH Tommy Davis; Davis's .306-7-84 effort was the best so far by this new breed of specialists. Oriole pitching was sound: Palmer's 22 wins earned him another Cy Young Award, young Doyle Alexander won 12, and aging vets Cuellar and McNally combined for 35 wins. The playoff between the A's and Orioles went the limit, but Hunter's two victories told for the A's. Hard after that ordeal, the A's faced the unthreatening Mets and very nearly lost the World Series to a team that had barely played .500 ball during its season. Down three games to two, the A's rallied to win in seven games. The close call eroded team morale; Finley nearly ignited a mutiny by attempting to fire an erring infielder, and at the end of the Series manager Williams resigned, citing Finley's meddling.

Oakland's internal strife escalated in 1974. Finley's choice of Al Dark to succeed Williams didn't help; unbeloved by players and harried by Finley, Dark caught flak from all sides, despite claiming to behave like a born-again Christian. For his part, Finley berated his manager, his players, and his fans, the latter for not showing up in sufficient numbers. Still, the A's won in the West, beating out Martin's Texas Rangers by six games. Bando, Jackson, and Rudi combined to drive in more than 300 runs; Hunter's 25-12 pitching led the league, while Fingers saved 18 games. In the East the Yankees, goaded by new owner George Steinbrenner, were stirring. For much of the season the Yanks or the Red Sox looked like winners, but in September the Orioles rallied from an eight-game deficit. Winning 27 of 33, they topped the Eastern Division by two games. The Birds' .256 batting was paced by DH Davis, and Cuellar's 22 wins paced the pitchers. In the playoff series the Orioles won the opener but lost the next three. Two of Oakland's victories were shutouts, and the A's won the decisive game by dint of one hit, Jackson's double. The easy victory failed to unite the team, however; it was a bickering team that manager Dark led against the Dodgers in the World Series. Nevertheless, the A's won handily, four games to one. Three wins came by 3-2 scores, with the relief corps bailing out starters as they had in all previous Oakland Series wins.

Events now conspired to end Oakland's skein of three straight world titles. In December 1974 an arbitrational panel supported Jim Hunter

Tim McCarver, Phillie catcher, collides with Tom Hutton, Phillie first baseman, while going after a foul pop-up during a 1976 season game against the Giants. Photograph in the *Philadelphia Bulletin*. (Courtesy Photojournalism Collection, Temple University Libraries)

in his salary dispute with Finley. Freed to sign with another club, Hunter chose the Yankees and signed a five-year contract worth $2.8 million. Losing this ace was a crusher to the A's, but during the 1975 season Blue, Holtzman, and Fingers took up the slack; offensively, Claudell Washington and Jackson supplied power enough to lead the team to a seven-game win over the Royals. However, the balance of power was shifting eastward, where the Red Sox and Orioles had battled all season long. Mounting a .275 batting assault, the Sox won by 4½ games. Rookie outfielder Fred Lynn's .331-21-105 effort snagged both MVP and Rookie-of-the-Year awards. Another rookie, outfielder Jim Rice, added a .309-22-102 effort, and catcher Carlton Fisk batted .331. With a good corps of starting pitchers to boot, the Red Sox thrashed the A's in three straight games to capture the league championship. The Red Sox nearly crowned their campaign with a World Series win over Cincinnati's Big Red Machine. The tense struggle went the limit and drew record television ratings. Down three games to two, the Sox tied the Series on Fisk's twelfth-inning homer. In the finale the Sox led 3-0, but they lost to the rallying Reds on a ninth-inning bloop single.

All too soon the drama of the 1975 Series was overshadowed by renewed hostilities between players and owners. The arbitration decision in the Messersmith case prompted enraged owners to stage a lockout of spring-training camps in 1976. Triggered by the lack of a new Basic Agreement, the "owners' strike" cast a small shadow on the nation's bicentennial celebrations, of which the National League's centenary was a part. Happily, a compromise saved the season; summer negotiations produced a new Basic Agreement that conceded the right of six-year veterans to auction themselves anew in annual re-entry drafts beginning in the fall of 1976.

Thus, the 1976 season became the last to be played under the old,

Walter Emmons Alston (*top*), Dodger manager from 1954 through 1976, including seven World Series years, with his successor, (*bottom*) Thomas Charles Lasorda, who seems destined for a similar record. (Courtesy Los Angeles Dodgers)

restrictive reserve clause. Since that measure had been introduced by the National League back in the 1870s, its circumvention lent a touch of irony to the celebrations of the National League's centennial. Indeed, the team whose owner would spend the most money on re-entering free agents now rose to power in the American League East. Since 1973 the Yankees had been owned by a group headed by shipping executive George Steinbrenner, who soon made his leading presence felt. Wealthy, egotistical, and imperious, Steinbrenner had a penchant for meddling in team affairs that rivaled Finley's. By contrast, Steinbrenner spent lavishly on players, besides impetuously hiring and firing executives and managers; such tactics revived the Yanks and made good the owner's brash promise to land a championship within five years. As opprobrious as his methods was his indictment for illegally donating to President Nixon's campaign fund, for which he drew a brief suspension from Commissioner Kuhn. But Yankee fans forgave and forgot in their delight over their team's resurgence.

In 1976 the Yankees reoccupied Yankee Stadium, which had been refurbished at a cost of more than $100 million of public monies. After three seasons of exile at Shea Stadium, the returning Yankees had the opportunity to crown their return with a centennial season victory. Under manager Billy Martin, their combative, outspoken leader, the team met the challenge. Revamped by the chief owner's spending, plus canny trades made by harried general manager Gabe Paul, the team was solid. In the outfield Lou Pinella, Mickey Rivers, and Roy White had proven talent; the infield of Chris Chambliss, Willie Randolph, Fred Stanley, and Graig Nettles was sound; catcher Thurman Munson's defensive skill and .302 batting won the MVP award; and Jim Hunter, Ed Figueroa, and Dock Ellis were formidable starting pitchers, backed by ace reliefer Sparky Lyle with 23 saves. A .269 team batting average, fortified by Nettles's league-leading 32 homers, won over the Orioles in the East.

As the Yanks came back, the expansionist Kansas City Royals ended Oakland's five-year Western monopoly. Ensconced in a new stadium, manager Whitey Herzog's Royals batted .269, paced by third baseman George Brett's league-leading .333 batting; Brett nosed out teammate Hal McRae by a single point. Still, the A's died hard, losing by 2½ games. Rightly fearing the upcoming exodus of his veterans to the re-entry draft, Finley had sold Jackson and Holtzman and was about to peddle others when Kuhn voided the deals. Finley's deals took their toll, but new manager Chuck Tanner found able replacements and employed a running attack that netted 341 stolen bases. A brilliant stratagem, it was too little to stave off the Royals. In the playoffs the Royals fought the Yankees to a standstill before falling to Chambliss's ninth-inning homer in the final game. That blow touched off a riot, as joyous Yankee fans swarmed their field, some snatching pieces of the stadium turf as fetishes. That was the Yankee summit; Cincinnati's Big Red Machine ambushed Martin's men in the World Series, winning in four straight games.

Blooded in these battles, the Yanks recovered to win all honors in 1977–78. The first re-entry draft enabled Steinbrenner to beef up his team for 1977, and the owner made the most of the opportunity. For

$8.5 million in long-term salaries he signed pitcher Don Gullett and slugger Reggie Jackson; other deals landed pitcher Mike Torrez and shortstop Bucky Dent. If Steinbrenner's splurge evoked gibes about buying pennants, his money talked. Although the charismatic Jackson clashed with manager Martin, the slugger's .286-32-110 batting paced the team's offensive of .281 batting and 184 homers. Among the starting pitchers, Ron Guidry won 16, while reliever Sparky Lyle's 13 wins and 26 saves took Cy Young honors. In a tight race the Yanks edged the Orioles by 2½ games. In the West, Herzog's Royals had easier going, beating the Rangers by eight games. George Brett and Al Cowens led the Royals' .277 batting assault. In the playoffs, the Royals seized a 2-1 lead in games, but the Yankees overcame the Royals' home park advantage; after tying the matches, the Yanks won the finale on a timely three-run rally. Now only the Dodgers barred the way, but the Yanks dispatched those old rivals in six games. Jackson was the Series hero; his three consecutive homers in the decisive game had home fans screaming, "Reggie! Reggie! Reggie!" In the afterglow a "Reggie" candy bar appeared, lending more luster to "Mr. October's" towering image.

For an encore the 1978 Yanks treated their fans to one of the most amazing victories in baseball history. Although Steinbrenner's latest re-entry market plunge landed reliever Richard ("Goose") Gossage, the faltering Bombers at one point trailed the slugging Red Sox by 13 games. As the Yanks foundered, the harried Martin lashed out at his chief tormentors, calling Jackson a liar and Steinbrenner a convict. For that bit of insubordination, Martin was sacked; yet so lustily did Yankee fans cheer their fallen pilot, at a July Old-Timers Day fest, that Steinbrenner recanted and promised to recall Martin in the near future. Meanwhile, Bob Lemon skippered the team; Lemon's calm demeanor, plus a providential Gotham newspaper strike that shut off gossipy reportage, worked wonders. Better still, injured vets returned to action, enabling the Bombers to stage a counterattack. By massacring the Red Sox in two late-season meetings, the Yanks closed in. At season's end the rivals were tied. In the sudden-death Eastern playoff game, homers by Dent and Jackson powered a 5-4 win at Boston. Winning pitcher Guidry finished with a gaudy 25-3 record that easily took Cy Young honors. The Yankee comeback drama eclipsed the Royals' third straight Western conquest. Although they won by five games over the Angels, the Royals were no match for the stampeding Yanks. After splitting the opening games at Kansas City, the Yanks scored 6-5 and 2-1 victories to clinch the league title. In the World Series the Dodgers snatched two home victories, but the Yankee team of destiny swept the next four. The Yankee miracle season of 1978 was the zenith of American League fortunes; over the next four years the fates smiled on the Nationals.

Despite Steinbrenner's latest re-entry draft spending, during which he netted pitchers Tommy John and Luis Tiant, the Yanks collapsed in 1979. Savaged by injuries and shocked by catcher Munson's tragic death in a plane crash, the Yankees finished fourth in the East. Weaver's Orioles easily distanced the hard-hitting Milwaukee Brewers in 1979. Ironically, three ex-Yankees—pitchers Scott McGregor and Tippy Martinez and catcher Rick Dempsey—boosted the Birds, who

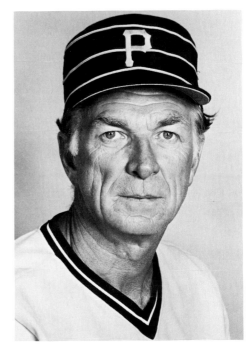

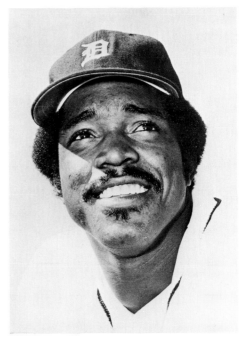

Top: Charles William ("Chuck") Tanner, Pirate manager from 1977 through 1981, including the 1979 world championship season. (Courtesy Pittsburgh Pirates)

Bottom: Ron LeFlore, whose league-leading steals helped keep the Expos in the 1980 race, until he broke his wrist. In 1978 he had led the American League in stolen bases for the Tigers. (Courtesy Detroit Tigers)

Bob Boone, first-string catcher for the Phillies after 1972, catching a "foul tip" fired from a special mortar during 1979 spring training. Boone chalked up three runs and four RBIs in the 1980 Series. Photograph in the *Philadelphia Bulletin*. (Courtesy Photojournalism Collection, Temple University Libraries)

also got a Cy Young performance from pitcher Mike Flanagan (23 wins). If the Orioles won without recourse to re-entry auctions, the Angels' Western victory owed much to owner Gene Autry's lavish bidding. Since joining the league in 1961, Autry had spent $15 million on star players. In 1979 first baseman Rod Carew signed a $4 million extended contract. Among the team's high-priced starters, only third baseman Carney Lansford was a homegrown product. One expensive acquisition, outfielder Don Baylor, shrugged off injury and took over as DH, where his .296-39-139 performance won MVP honors. Although the Angels staggered much of the way, they won the West by three games over the Royals. In the playoff, however, the Western plutocrats lost to the Orioles by three games to one. Matched against the Pirates in the World Series, the Birds snatched three of the first four and seemed likely to avenge their 1971 licking at the hands of the Bucs. But the resurgent Pirates swept the last three games to hand snake-bit manager Weaver his third Series loss.

Baseball's sprightly 'Seventies closed under the ominous threat of an impending player strike. What the owners demanded was compensation in the form of a big league player for any club losing a player to the re-entry draft. Under the expiring Basic Agreement all they got was an extra choice in the rookie draft. When the Players Association spurned this "giveback," negotiations for a new labor contract broke down. Only a last-minute agreement to extend negotiations saved the 1980 season.

Ron Reed, Phillie reliefer, who was credited with a save in the 1980 World Series along with Tug McGraw's win plus two saves. Photo by Paul H. Roedig. (Courtesy John Thorn)

Mike Schmidt demonstrating the power that contributed a .381 batting average, with six runs and seven RBIs, to the Phillies' 1980 Series victory. (Courtesy The Phillies)

Stephen Norman ("Steve") Carlton, Phillie left-hander, who led the National League three times in games won between 1972 and 1980, and who won two games in the 1980 Series. (Courtesy The Phillies)

Ted Williams, a former superstar who managed the Washington Senators in 1969–71 and in their first season as the Texas Rangers in 1972. AP Wirephoto. (Courtesy Texas Rangers)

With the strike threat postponed, the Yanks and Orioles locked in a fierce struggle for 1980 Eastern honors. Another lavish splurge in the re-entry mart added pitcher Rudy May and slugger Bob Watson to the Yanks. Managed by Dick Howser (who had succeeded Lemon and Martin after the 1979 debacle), the Yanks squandered a big lead in September. For a week they clung to a half-game lead, but then they rallied to top the East in the final week. By contrast, the Royals waltzed to victory in the West. Manager Herzog was gone, replaced by Jim Frey, who installed newcomers Willie Mays Aikens at first base and Dan Quisenberry to front-line relief duty. Quisenberry saved 33 games and Aikens drove in 98 runs, while Brett hit for a lofty .390 average to take MVP honors. What's more, outfielder Willie Wilson batted .326 and stole 79 bases. It added up to a 14-game romp over the runner-up A's, managed now by the peripatetic Martin. By beating the Yankees eight of twelve times this season, the Royals signaled what their old tormentors were going to get in the playoffs. Opening at home, the Royals whipped the Yankees 7-2 and 3-2; then they completed a sweep by downing the Yanks on Brett's three-run homer off Gossage in New York. Incensed by the blowout, Steinbrenner cashiered Howser. The victory sent the Royals to the World Series against the Phillies. Neither team had ever won a world title, but the Phillies' drought was nearly a century old. Brett's indisposition doubtlessly hurt the Royals, as the Phils snatched the first two games and went on to win in six. Thus, for a second year, the Americans suffered defeat; however, this comedown paled before the upcoming humiliation endured by both major leagues in the "dishonest season" of 1981.

THE TELEVISION DEMIURGE

In the 1970s increasing television revenue helped push player salaries upward in spite of a shaky national economy. Now, more than ever, watching televised sports was the favorite pastime of Americans. In company with other televised sports, baseball benefited from improving video technology, such as instant replays, isolation shots, and better deployment of cameras. Aided by improved sportscasting, including commentaries from ex-players, video baseball came of age. As a result, some observers claimed that television fans saw more than ballpark fans did, and one market researcher declared that the television audience was now the backbone of baseball's fandom. Moreover, such claims were supported by rising ratings of televised games; such ratings meant more revenue from commercial sponsors, which in turn continually raised the revenue that the clubs got from network and local television contracts. By 1980, 30 percent of baseball's annual gross revenue of over $500 million came from television.

The rising tide of television cash was felt at the beginning of the decade. In 1971 Commissioner Kuhn negotiated a four-year $70 million network package; in 1976 the owners' television committee signed a new $92 million four-year pact; when that expired another four-year pact fetched $110 million. Since network income was shared equally, by 1980 each team's annual cut came to $1.8 million. A tidy sum, it might have been much larger if owners had not clung to their policy of allowing each owner to negotiate his own local television pact for his team's seasonal games. For this reason, network packages were limited to World Series games, All-Star games, league championship playoff games, and selected games of the week. To be sure, local television sales brought additional revenue, but vast differences in local television markets meant bonanzas for some clubs and pittances for others. Besides widening the gap between rich and poor clubs, the policy also resulted in idiosyncratic programming: Some teams televised most of their games; others, like the Dodgers, televised very few. By the mid-1970s some $31 million annually flowed to club coffers from local pacts. Of this total, a hefty $6.3 million went to the most favored Montreal Expos, while the least fortunate Kansas City Royals got only $500,000 a year. This sort of disparity prompted some have-not clubs to plump for exclusive, shared network contracts. In buttressing their argument, they cited the hefty $5-million-a-year windfall that each NFL football team received from network contracts. Still, there was some justification for continuing the local contracting policy. By the 1980s local television markets would become the fastest growing part of commercial television. On the horizon, moreover, was the promise of more television revenue from the growing cable television industry.

Of course, there was a menacing side to baseball's lucrative affair with television interests. Cassandras foresaw the ruination of live attendance, but the burgeoning attendance boom of this decade belied this fear. After holding near the 30-million mark in 1973–75, annual attendance set new highs in each of the succeeding five seasons. In 1980 attendance hit 43 million; then, after slumping to 26 million in the strike year of 1981, it surged to 45 million in 1982.

Other videophobes warned of meddlesome television producers turn-

Milwaukee Brewer Paul Molitor slides safely into home. At the end of 1986, Molitor had played nine seasons with the Brewers and had accumulated a total of 231 stolen bases. (Courtesy Milwaukee Brewers)

Baltimore Oriole pitching aces during their 1969–71 pennant-winning seasons: Mike Cuellar (*left*) and Jim Palmer. (Courtesy Baltimore Orioles; Jim Rowe)

ing the game into a staged entertainment. Some cited the nocturnal World Series games as a sellout to television's powers of darkness. Not seldom, cold weather plagued these night games, but soaring television ratings warmed club owners. Nevertheless, baseball officials were well advised to keep a critical eye on producers; some producers wanted to limit the playing schedule to long weekends, and some proposed increasing the league championship playoff series from five to seven games.

Baseball's anti-television forces also attacked talkative sportscasters, accusing local commentators of shilling for home teams, and network sportscasters like Howard Cosell of shilling for themselves. Others wondered if the presence of television moguls like Gene Autry, Ted Turner, and John Fetzer among owners' ranks might herald a day when most clubs were owned by television interests. One mighty threat evaporated in this decade, however; in 1973 the giant CBS network sold the Yankees to George Steinbrenner's combine.

For good reason television baseball was a focal point of strident criticism in these years. Some critics feared that players were gaining too much in cash and glory. That organized players had a stake in network television revenue was firmly established now. Indeed, since 1971 Marvin Miller continually urged that the Players Association be permitted to participate in network contract negotiations. Although this petition was denied, the cash and glory that rained upon television-blessed players at this time caused many minds to boggle.

Soaring annual salaries told the dazzling tale. At the dawn of the 'Seventies observers marveled at $1 million team payrolls and the fact that half a dozen stars commanded $100,000 annual salaries. But this was only the beginning of the salary revolution. Average annual salaries climbed from $38,000 in 1971 to $52,000 in 1976, to $75,000 in 1977, to $90,000 in 1978, to $100,000 in 1979, to $185,000 in 1980, and into the $200,000 range thereafter. The great gains after 1976 resulted from the re-entry draft system, adopted in the wake of the Messersmith decision. Beginning with the first re-entry draft in 1977, these annual player auctions produced frenzied bidding by owners. After the first draft, the twenty-four free-agent players had won a total of $25 million in contracts; Reggie Jackson led with a five-year contract at $580,000 annually. Owner bidding continued its skyward trend throughout the decade. In 1978 Vida Blue took first place at $850,000 per year, and Nolan Ryan snared the first million-dollar annual salary in 1979. Indeed, that year saw top baseball stars earning more than their counterparts in football, basketball, hockey, tennis, and golf. A widening "ripple effect" also made lesser plutocrats of ordinary players. Moreover, the salary arbitration rights won by Miller in 1973 added to the ripple effect as arbitrators, taking cues from salaries won in re-entry auctions, upgraded those of petitioning players.

Obviously, Miller's victories at bargaining tables enabled players to gain heftier chunks of baseball's increasing revenues. Equally obvious was the fact that the soaring salaries were more than owners wanted to give, but lacking a united front and fearing conspiracy suits if they tried to fix salaries, owners found themselves in the vulnerable position of bidding against one another for star players. Some owners with limited financial resources blamed high-rolling colleagues like Steinbrenner and Autry for bidding salaries to forbidding heights. Reflecting such sentiments, Commissioner Kuhn's state-of-the-game messages annually forecast bankruptcies unless salaries came down. As of 1980, however, no such calamity had occurred. Nevertheless, the growing chasm between rich and poor clubs was alarming. By 1979 the top payrolls had reached $4 million per club, whereas the Twins took last place with only $1.9 million in salaries. No wonder that Twins owner Cal Griffith, the only owner still dependent on baseball income for his livelihood, lamented bitterly. However, his players, and those playing for other conservative owners, lamented just as keenly their lack of a high-rolling owner.

In addition to salaries exceeding those of corporation executives and easily topping that of the nation's president, players enjoyed a lucrative pension plan and such fringe benefits as payments to widows, life insurance, and medical and dental coverage. No wonder envious critics called them pampered, but Miller defended his charges' affluence. He did, however, lash out at player agents who took up to 10 percent of a player's salary for negotiating his salary contract. In Miller's judgment 4 percent was the fair limit. Owners agreed, but their resentment extended to salary arbitration and re-entry draft procedures. Thus, owners' attempts to roll back their own concessions and to clamp a lid on rising salaries precipitated the 1981 strike and the ensuing climate of mutual suspicion.

Pitcher Rollie Fingers, who helped power the Oakland Athletics to three straight world-championship seasons, 1972–74. (Courtesy Oakland Athletics)

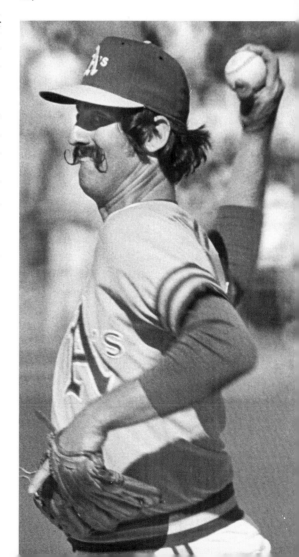

The lavish benefits enjoyed by the new breed of players were dispropor-
tionate to their playing. Although this decade saw its share of glittering
performances, overall productivity was mixed. After 1970, when homer
hitting averaged 90 per 100 games, distance hitting tailed off; by 1980
it had sagged to 60 per 100 games. The decline was more pronounced
in the National League, where batting averages after 1973 also lagged
behind those in the American League. In the years 1969–82 overall
batting averages hovered about the .255 mark; this bettered standards

PERFORMANCE OF
THE PLUTOCRATS

Two Oakland Athletic pitching aces
during their 1972–74 world-championship seasons: Ken Holtzman (*opposite*)
and Vida Blue. (Courtesy Oakland
Athletics)

Reggie Jackson (right) in an earnest discussion with A's manager Al Dark. (Courtesy Oakland Athletics)

Jim Rice, who helped the Red Sox win the 1975 pennant and later led the American League in homers in 1977 and 1978. (Courtesy John Thorn)

of the feeble 'Sixties, but not those of the Postwar Era. For their part, pitchers' ERAs were above those of the 'Sixties. On the positive side, fielding averages rose slightly and base stealing soared. At this time speedsters like Lou Brock and Rickey Henderson pushed thefts from 40 per 100 games in 1970 to 80 per 100 by 1980. In 1974 Brock stole a record 118 and went on to break Cobb's lifetime total.

At this time two unilateral moves by the American League lent a counterfeit note to that league's leadership in homers and hitting. One was the American's 1977 mini-expansion; the addition of two clubs naturally swelled seasonal homer totals. The other was the league's adoption of the designated-hitter rule in 1973. Prior to that move National hitters outbatted Americans for nine consecutive seasons. However, the ploy of allowing a DH to bat for a pitcher raised American batting averages. After a three-year trial period the rule was made permanent in 1976, but it remains controversial. Nevertheless, eight years under the rule saw it evolving into a major offensive weapon. At first, aging, slow-footed sluggers like Rico Carty, Tom Davis, and Tony Oliva served, but they were replaced by younger, speedier specialists groomed in the minors, where the DH system was first employed in 1969. Despite the popularity of the DH rule in the American League, the National League refused to adopt it and insisted that it be used only in alternating years in World Series play. Some critics thought that American League managers were disadvantaged in the off-years since American pitchers were inexperienced hitters and American managers were less skilled at deploying pinch-hitters. Moreover, some critics faulted the DH rule for "burning out" starting pitchers, arguing that American managers tended to keep starters in the game longer.

Luis Tiant, who won eighteen games for the Red Sox as a starting pitcher during the 1975 season and two games in the World Series. (Courtesy Boston Red Sox)

For their part, pitchers in the 'Seventies never matched the gaudy ERA mark of 1968. The 1969 rule that narrowed strike zones and lowered pitching mounds helped to push ERAs well above the 3.50 mark in these years. To compensate, pitchers used varied deliveries with telling effect; strikeouts were plentiful, so much so that by 1974 eight of the ten batters on the dubious all-time list of most times struck out hailed from the Expansion Era. Among strikeout artists, Nolan Ryan and Sandy Koufax averaged better than one whiff an inning, while Gibson, Seaver, and Sam McDowell edged that mark. The fire-balling Ryan broke Koufax's seasonal mark of 383 strikeouts. By now, able relief pitchers were as important as starters to a team's success. Inspired by Hoyt Wilhelm, who retired at age forty-eight in 1972 after having set records for most games pitched in relief (1,018) and most games won in relief (123), baseball's "bullpen revolution" was now completed. In the 'Seventies highly paid "short men," imbued with "killer instincts," were deployed late in close games to get essential outs. Among the best were Mike Marshall, Rollie Fingers, Tug McGraw, Sparky Lyle, Goose Gossage, and Bruce Sutter. The peerless Fingers notched three Fireman of the Year awards. Marshall, who appeared in 106 games in 1974, saving 21 and winning 15, was a Cy Young winner, as was Lyle, winner of 13 and savior of 26 with the 1977 Yankees. The fireballing Gossage set a record for reliefers by fanning 151 batters in 1977.

Thurman Lee Munson, outstanding catcher for the Yankees from 1970 until his tragic death in 1979. (Courtesy New York Yankees)

Thanks to the pitching restrictions, hitters were better able to cope with such formidable adversaries. Continuing a trend of the Postwar Era, black players sparked batting offensives. Indeed, the National League's preeminence in the 1970s owed much to its greater recruiting of Afro-American and Hispanic players. Baseball's black tide crested in 1974, when 26 percent of the active players were blacks, and fell to 20 percent by 1979. Nevertheless, black hitters stood out among offensive leaders; in stolen bases blacks or Hispanics led each major league in every season since 1953.

As Mays and Aaron ended their glorious careers by the mid-1970s, Panamanian Rod Carew seized the spotlight by winning six American League batting titles; his .388 mark of 1979 was the highest since the war. Among the most recent members of the 3,000-hit club were black players Aaron, Mays, and Brock. Moreover, in this decade a dozen MVP awards (six in each league) went to black stars, including two to Joe Morgan. By now the list of all-time leading homer hitters included six blacks. Aaron led, of course, but Mays (660) was third and Frank Robinson (586) was fourth. Robinson became the first black to manage teams in both major leagues. Black pitchers also stood out: The phenomenal left-hander Vida Blue won both the American League's MVP and Cy Young awards in his first full season (1971), matching Bob Gibson's achievement in the National League in 1968; J. R. Richard won 74 games in four seasons, fanning over 300 batters in 1978, before a stroke felled him two years later.

Hispanics also excelled; by the 'Eighties they made up 10 percent of the playing ranks. Hailing mainly from Puerto Rico, the Dominican Republic, Panama, Venezuela, and Mexico, they endured the same lingering race prejudice as Afro-Americans because of their typically dark complexions. That, plus differences in language and lifestyle, confronted Hispanic players with many challenges. In 1972 the great Roberto Clemente became an international hero following his tragic death while on a mercy mission to aid Nicaraguan earthquake victims. Swiftly voted into the Hall of Fame, Clemente had impeccable credentials, including 3,000 hits, twelve Golden Glove awards, four batting titles, and a lifetime .317 average. More than those attainments, his courageous struggle to win respect for Hispanic players memorialized him as the Latin American Jackie Robinson.

Among Hispanic stars, Manny Mota set a new all-time pinch-hitting record by rapping out his 145th hit in 1979. Pitcher Juan Marichal, who retired in this decade, was voted into the Hall of Fame. Shortstops Dave Concepcion and Bert Campaneris starred in these years, but no shortstop surpassed Luis Aparicio's feats; the little Venezuelan retired in 1970, having compiled the best fielding mark and the most assists by any shortstop. Following Aparicio's example, Concepcion was the most versatile shortstop in the National League, and Campaneris five times led the American in stolen bases. Such feats won respect for Hispanic players. Although immigration quotas restricted the number of players hailing from foreign countries (Puerto Rico, as a U.S. commonwealth, was not subject to quotas), scouts eagerly sought the best, and clubs now strove to ease adjustment problems. Belatedly, some clubs honored Latin American stars with dedicatory games, but more significant was

Graig Nettles, who joined the Yankees as third baseman in 1973, after three seasons with the Twins and three with the Indians. His spectacular fielding helped the Yanks win the 1978 World Series. (Courtesy New York Yankees)

Amos Otis of the Royals, Western Division leaders, batting against the Milwaukee Brewers in an August 1976 season game. (Courtesy Ronald A. Smith)

Ron Guidry, star pitcher for the Yankees in 1977–80. His 25–3 record, with a 1.74 ERA, led the American League in 1978. (Courtesy New York Yankees)

Paul Molitor, hard-hitting second baseman for the Brewers in the late 'Seventies and 'Eighties. (Courtesy Milwaukee Brewers)

Rod Carew joined the Angels in 1979, and in 1985 joined the elite 3,000-hit club. (Courtesy California Angels)

Angels pitcher Nolan Ryan being interviewed by ABC sportscaster Bob Uecker in July 1979. (Courtesy American Broadcasting System)

the $800,000 annual salary that Rod Carew received from the Angels in 1978.

Given the mighty presence of Afro-American and Hispanic players, it was fitting that the two ethnic strands joined in the most celebrated baseball star of the 'Seventies. In the TV age, baseball needed a dominant personality to hold its own against national idols from other sports, such as pugilist Muhammad Ali, quarterback Joe Namath, and basketball star Julius Erving. Reginald Martinez Jackson was baseball's answer; he is a black American, but his father's line can be traced to Latin America, and he speaks both Spanish and English. Intelligent and outspoken, Jackson proclaimed himself to be "the best in baseball. . . . No one does as many things as well as I do." This was bluster; Jackson was an above-average batter and an average fielder. But homer hitting was his forte, and nobody delivered the big bang with more élan than he. From 1967 to 1980 he averaged 30 homers a year, and he topped the 500 mark in the 'Eighties. What's more, Jackson was a winner who played with ten divisional champions and five world champions, and who appeared in eight All-Star games. His booming homers led *Time* and *Sports Illustrated* to hail him as baseball's "Superduperstar" in 1974. In the first re-entry draft he was the most coveted prize; he signed a five-year Yankee contract for a record $2.9 million. Although

Howard Cosell, ABC sportscaster from the 'Sixties into the 'Eighties. (Author's Collection)

Left: Joan Payson, who owned the New York Mets during the Expansion Era. Currently the Cincinnati Reds are owned by a woman, Marge Schott. (Courtesy New York Mets)

Right: Marvin Miller, executive director of the Major League Players Association, telling the news media that a strike would be inevitable if the owners did not meet the demands set forth by the players' executive board. This news conference took place in Tampa on February 25, 1981. Photo by Bill Creighton of United Press International. (Courtesy *The Sporting News*)

his Yankee years were strife-ridden, New York media exposure caused the nation's fans to recognize his face and his number, 44. Responding, this crowd-pleaser blasted key homers in the Yankee Series victories of 1977–78. Always quotable, the controversial Jackson may not have been the best player of this decade, but he was baseball's greatest celebrity since the days of DiMaggio and Williams. With Jackson showing the way, black stars reaped fair shares of the cash and glory that blessed the new breed.

Along with the large contingents of black and Hispanic stars in the 1970s, the United States continued to produce outstanding homegrown players from its white melting pot. That fact was hardly surprising in a nation where the white majority has had a baseball tradition for a century and a quarter and where newcomers encourage their sons to play the national game. Forty-seven of the 1,147 players on major league rosters in 1980 were the sons of former major leaguers, according to a book by economists David Laband and Bernard Lentz. That is an astonishing four out of every hundred! Many more major leaguers were the sons of onetime minor leaguers—as many as 68 percent, Laband and Lentz estimate. Clearly, there are professional baseball families in North America.

The ascendancy of pitchers, both starters and relievers, in the 'Seventies already has been noted. One example clinches the point: Jim Palmer, the best pitcher of the 1970s, won 20 or more games in each of seven seasons. Yet some men still hit hard. When Harmon Killebrew retired early in this period, having slugged his way to fifth place on the all-time homer list, Mike Schmidt of the Phillies took on the slugging mantle. The right-handed-batting Schmidt won five National League homer titles and two MVP awards, besides being a fine fielding third baseman. Although no other white slugger matched Schmidt, Johnny Bench, Dave Kingman, and Gorman Thomas each won a pair of homer crowns. Of this trio, Bench was in a class by himself. The best catcher of the 'Seventies, he won ten Golden Glove awards and set records for homer and RBI production by catchers. Although Bench excelled, it was an age of great catchers; receivers like Carlton Fisk, Thurman Munson, Ted Simmons, and Gary Carter would have been standouts at any time.

Other white infielders of the 1970s were noted for both talent and durability. As the 'Eighties dawned, first baseman Steve Garvey was approaching Bill Williams's National League record for straight games played, having hit better than .300 six times since 1973. Paul Molitor of the Brewers was becoming the new king of second basemen. Among shortstops, veteran Larry Bowa owned the best fielding average, but the spotlight was moving to the more versatile Robin Yount. If no third sacker matched the fielding of Brooks Robinson, Schmidt, Graig Nettles, and George Brett were worthy successors. The most celebrated white star of this era was Pete Rose; at the beginning of the 1980s this fortyish hustler was close to Stan Musial's National League hit record and within sight of Ty Cobb's lifetime record. Although Rose sneered at Father Time, Carl Yastrzemski announced that 1983 would be his last season; Yaz had rapped his 3,000th hit and 400th homer in 1979. Other outfielders in a class with the great black and Hispanic pickets were Fred Lynn, Bill Buckner, and Joe Rudi.

Given the cash and glory that blessed players of this time, it mattered little if a player was classed as great or adequate. Ably defended by their Association, players of the 'Seventies were more assertive, better doc-

Rickey Henderson, who set a new American League seasonal record of one hundred steals while playing outfield for the A's in 1980. (Author's Collection)

tored, and better equipped than their forebears. Improving training and sports medicine techniques extended playing careers and allowed a score of fortyish players to perform ably. Union "protectsia" accounted for the assertiveness, best glimpsed through candid interviews, revealing biographies, and the effective use of arbitrational panels, which players resorted to when threatened by peremptory discipline. Their equipment now included special shoes for playing on artificial surfaces, garishly colored uniforms and batting helmets, bigger gloves, and improved catcher's equipment to enhance mobility. That they now swung Louisville Slugger bats made in Indiana at cowhide balls no longer incited complaints. Improved coaching techniques, augmented by radar guns, advanced scouting reports, and diagnostic films, helped to dispel fear of failure; while fear of injury always remained, fear of peremptory dismissal was diminished by many long-term contracts now awarded.

REAPERS OF THE WHIRLWIND

Dave Kingman, a slugger often traded in the 'Seventies because of his low batting average and high salary demands. He hit 270 homers for five teams, including the Mets, during the 1970s. (Courtesy New York Mets)

Although most club owners still cultivated the image of gentlemen sportsmen, most were businessmen who sought to boost their enterprises and their social status by their baseball investments. Despite a 1977 *Forbes Magazine* opinion that baseball was a poor investment, no owner at this time went broke in baseball. Even as they lost tax shelter advantages, rising television revenues and franchise values compensated. When put up for sale in these times, clubs fetched good prices. In 1976 the Giants went for $8 million; in 1977 the Red Sox brought $16 million; in 1979 the Mets sold for $21 million; in 1980 the A's went for $12.7 million. Elite clubs like the Dodgers and Yankees reportedly spurned offers of $50 million or more. When the American League added two new teams in 1977, the franchises were snapped up at $6 million apiece, the total being equally divided among the established clubs. At this time baseball's revenue situation stirred bullish reactions. In 1977 gross annual revenues reached $263 million. Although unevenly divided, such monies included ever more money from equal shares of network television fees.

Of course, rising player salaries vexed owners. Have-nots among them envied pro football's owner unity, which afforded equal division of hefty television revenue and which held down player salaries and prevented costly re-entry draft auctions. By comparison, baseball owners lacked unity; unevenly involved, some were absentee owners who delegated authority to executives. Some, like Charles Finley, Ewing Kauffman, Peter O'Malley, George Steinbrenner, and Edward B. Williams, were assertive types, but they seldom united in common cause. Left leaderless by the passing of Walter O'Malley, owners were victims of their own independence. Their disunity evoked scorn and mockery from critics, among whom a television mogul suggested sarcastically that each owner be subject to psychological testing and be licensed. Belatedly in 1980 owners united against players, but by then the players' position was too strong to yield to frontal assault.

If owners at times looked like anachronisms, their commissioner system seemed to have lost its meaning. The latest holder of the post, Bowie Kuhn, resembled the African king whose magical powers no

Two top reliefers of the 'Seventies: Tug McGraw (*left*) of the Mets and Phillies, Bruce Sutter of the Cubs and Cards. McGraw was credited with 25 saves in 1973, when the Mets won a pennant, and with 20 season saves and a Series win plus two saves for the world champion Phillies in 1980. Sutter led the National League with 37 saves for the Cubs in 1979 and 28 in 1980, then moved to the Cardinals. (Courtesy John Thorn)

longer made the winds blow. Appointed in 1969, Kuhn tried to be assertive, but his wings were clipped. Instead of extending Kuhn's powers, the owners excluded him from executive decisions and television contracting; in the all-important area of negotiations with organized players, Kuhn was sidelined. Nor did Kuhn dare to invoke baseball law against players, lest he incur lawsuits. What's more, the independent status of each league barred Kuhn from extending his powers. Thus, when the American League unilaterally adopted its DH rule and expanded to fourteen clubs, Kuhn could do nothing, clearly proving that the commissioner was merely the mouthpiece of his employers. Kuhn's annual state-of-the-game messages attacked players' escalating salaries, but Miller derided such complaints as annual poor-mouth speeches. Fans, writers, and players also sniped at Kuhn, who, like Dickens's Mr. Turvydrop, sought vainly to maintain his dignity amidst the sallies. Sometimes Kuhn struck back; some players were fined, and two popular ex-stars, Mays and Mantle, were barred from any baseball connection because they were employed by gambling casinos. But actions against players ran the risk of grievance procedures by their Asso-

Reggie Jackson as a Yankee "Superduperstar" from 1977 to 1982. (Courtesy New York Yankees)

ciation. Moreover, the least credible of all Kuhn's acts were his occasional sallies against maverick owners like Finley, Ted Turner, and Steinbrenner.

Commissioner Kuhn shared his status-deprived lot with field managers. Sniped at from all sides, managers saw their authority and credibility sink to the pits. Long-term contracts that dwarfed any manager's gave top players tremendous advantage over their foremen. Worse still, the assertive new breed of players questioned disciplinary codes, training regimens, and even managerial tactics. Owners also undercut managers; Finley publicly scorned them and fired a dozen. The same was true of Steinbrenner, who sacked Martin and Lemon twice. By now, blaming the manager for team failure was accepted doctrine; general managers also used managers as scapegoats, while writers and fans accepted the sacrificial heads of scores of managers as evidence of remedial action.

Yet some doughty managers survived and kept alive the importance of the field commander role. In this decade Walter Alston retired; his twenty-one years at the helm of the Dodgers was unsurpassed by any contemporary. His successor, Tom Lasorda, sought to control his men by stressing the Dodger "family" mystique. Most managers used conciliatory tactics to control their players; among postures they adopted were those of cheerleaders, teachers, or guidance counsellors. Hard-nosed disciplinary codes were generally ineffective against this generation of union-backed players. Thus, Sparky Anderson lamented that only rookies responded to strict discipline and that soon they became dissenters. Still, the notion of a manager's essential role in a team's victory march survived. In 1976 a spectacular demonstration of a manager's worth saw the Pirates pay Finley $100,000 plus an able catcher to obtain the services of manager Chuck Tanner. But so many managers were hired and sacked that by 1980 Weaver, Gene Mauch, Tanner, and Lasorda were the reigning deans.

The old Napoleonic tradition survived in such personalities as Dick Williams, Billy Martin, and Earl Weaver. From 1968 to 1980 the flinty Weaver was the winningest active manager in baseball. A zealous master of rules, tactics, and strategy, Weaver imposed his system throughout the Oriole network. Pitching development was his forte, and Weaver also deployed all his players. Nervous, combative, and excitable, Weaver harried umps, bullied malingerers, and won the grudging loyalty of his men. His closest rivals, Williams and Martin, were similar in style. Their winning ways had players generally accepting their autocratic mannerisms. Hard-driving Williams won three American League pennants and drove the A's to two world titles. Although his effectiveness was conceded, his clashes with owners made him a peripatetic manager. Martin was even more unyielding; although he won divisional titles with the Twins, Tigers, Yanks, and A's, his clashes with owners made him the most traveled manager of this time. Yet, few faulted his leadership ability or his mastery of tactics and strategy. Openly resentful of the sunken status of managers, Martin probably voiced the sentiments of all managers when he urged owners to give baseball helmsmen the same high pay and power as pro football coaches.

If Martin wished to include the right to upbraid umpires in his plea, he was too late; those officials now possessed too much countervailing power. Like the players, umps were shielded by a powerful union. In 1969 attorney John Reynolds brought all major league umps under the protective umbrella of the Major League Umpires Association. The following year he called a one-day strike that won bargaining rights for the Association; the first resulting formal contract raised average umps' salaries to $21,000. After Reynolds retired in 1972, the Association foundered under the controversial leadership of John Cifeli; even so, the average salary rose to $31,000 at the time of Cifeli's 1978 ouster. A resurgence of power followed the appointment of Richard G. Phillips, a hard-driving Philadelphia lawyer. This new director staged a brief strike to renegotiate the existing contract; although this was stayed by an

Maury Wills, a fine all-around player in the 'Sixties and early 'Seventies, met rough going as a manager in 1980–81. Taking the helm of the Seattle Mariners four years after the club was launched, Wills was unable to find smooth sailing in the face of a low salary scale, low attendance, and low TV income. (Courtesy Seattle Mariners)

injunction, Phillips circumvented the court order by persuading umps to sign no contracts for 1979. That move cleared the way for a successful strike that had umps walking picket lines until May 18. It ended when owners yielded to widespread complaints over the officiating of inadequately trained substitutes. The resultant new contract exalted the status of umpires. In addition to a salary schedule that ranged from $22,000 to $50,000, umps won improved expense allowances, freedom from arbitrary dismissals, two weeks of paid vacation, and a guarantee of forty-five paid days in the event of a player strike. Such gains emboldened umps; a few vented their pent-up ire against old antagonists in published books, while abusive players, managers, and owners faced stiff penalties. Such power for umps was an astonishing turnabout; some wags now speculated over what might befall fans who yelled, "Kill the Ump!" That umps could also become television celebrities was another new wrinkle; two of them, Ron Luciano and Jim Honochick, did so.

THE CHANGING FACE OF BASEBALL'S FANDOM

Dire forecasts that fans would oppose the aggrandizement of players and umpires were quashed by soaring attendance and television ratings. Indeed, the high-salary trend exerted a magnetic effect on fans, who turned out in increasing numbers. As live attendance passed the 40-million mark in 1979 and continued upward, doomsayers lamely argued that live attendance back in 1949 had topped 60 million. But that old figure counted minor league attendance, which had become a casualty of the television and expansion eras. By 1980 attendance figures confirmed the major league game as a truly national spectacle. Given the great popularity of television baseball, however, it was now abundantly clear that the electronic medium was the key to the game's profitable future. To be sure, 1980 still showed gate receipts counting for the lion's share of baseball revenues, with concession sales adding substantially. Such figures supported the old shibboleth that baseball's fate was at the gate. Now clubs regarded a million paid admissions a year as essential; two million was excellent; bliss was a three-million annual gate, which so far only the Dodgers had attained.

New parks spurred attendance; by the 'Eighties the latest building boom had run its course, highlighted by the American League's all-weather edifices in Seattle and Minnesota. Although parks built since 1958 conformed to minimum outfield distance standards, variations in parks affected team performances. Some disparaged Aaron's homer record because Atlanta Stadium was reputed to be a homer launching pad.

To lure more fans into parks, clubs now hired promotional experts. Emulating the legendary owner-promoter Bill Veeck, they used a variety of giveaways, including free bats, balls, caps, jackets, and the like for kids; adults were potlatched with free panty hose, T-shirts, and the like. Cheap beer nights became tabooed, however; the notorious Cleveland beer riot of 1974 resulted in a forfeited game. Likewise, Veeck's scheme of pitting rock music fans against disco rivals fomented a Chicago riot. Still, promoters pushed varied entertainments in their zeal to fill seats; canned music, fireworks, orchestrated cheering, and clowns attired as totem animals were standard fare in all parks. Baseball's best lure, however, was its low ticket prices; averaging less than five dollars, baseball tickets were the cheapest of the spectator sports. Even so, the entertainment lure persisted. As ever, some fans devised their own entertainments, including ubiquitous signs (some with insulting gibes), streakers, the well-endowed "Morganna the Wild One's" kissing assaults on players, the "boo birds" of Philadelphia, the "bleacher bums" of Chicago, and the notorious Los Angeles aeronaut who once bombed Dodger Stadium with flour sacks. In company with pickpockets, missile hurlers, drunks, and assorted show-offs, such exuberant fans impelled alarmed promoters to beef up security forces.

Indeed, large crowds both delighted and appalled promoters. Most promoters still clung to the "bad animal" theory of crowds, and some paranoids judged fans of these years to be the worst ever. Some critics blamed promoters for over-stressing entertainment; others cited a host of explanations, including a supposed decline in national morality, television's stimulus to violence, and the changing character of ballpark neighborhoods. In truth, nobody knew much about ballpark fans; attempts at understanding included Kuhn's scheme of allowing players to fraternize with fans before game time, and club efforts at improving relations with minority groups and with neighborhood residents.

Fan excesses notwithstanding, baseball's sturdy growth was owed to its enormous and varied fandom. If television fans were becoming the backbone of the game's supporters, other fan subcultures—like newspaper fans, radio fans, souvenir collectors, table game buffs, statistical

"Phillie Phanatic" (Dave Raymond) seems to amuse umpire John Kibler at a 1979 game. A 'Seventies fad called for clubs to hire clowns as cheerleaders and chief hecklers, arousing mixed emotions in serious fans, players, and umps. Photo by DiMarco for the *Philadelphia Bulletin*. (Courtesy Photojournalism Collection, Temple University Libraries)

freaks, and organized researchers—were the sinews of the body. Among the latter, the North American Society for Sports History and the Society for American Baseball Research were organized in 1973; while NASSH's membership was professorial, SABR's eclectic ranks approached 3,000 by 1980. Each year SABR staged national and regional meetings and published a wide range of articles in its journals, monographs, and popular magazine. At this time, too, a spate of histories, biographies, statistical compilations, novels, movies, and magazine articles sated ravenous public appetites for baseball information. These varied outpourings both inspired newspaper writers and offended them by poaching on the turf they long had regarded as their own.

In adapting to such competitors, as well as to the encroachments of sportscasters, sportswriters served up inside stories of the game. Although some old-guard scribes scorned this new style as "chipmunk journalism," most adopted the new approach. Hence, newspaper fans feasted on probing accounts of labor troubles, legal issues, salary trends, and troublesome matters like racism, sexism, and drug abuse in the world of baseball. Not seldom, gossipy probes into players' lives affected team morale and heightened tensions among players, managers, and owners. Martin's troubles with Steinbrenner and Jackson and Finley's clashes with all constituencies were cases in point. Fear of poison-pen writers led some players to refuse interviews; as of 1980 pitcher Steve Carlton set a record of having granted only a single interview in five years. Overall, the vast and varied literary outpouring fueled the baseball boom. What the torrent of publications revealed was the strength of baseball's hold on many segments of the American public. It was a strength that would be tested and strained in the great strike of 1981.

A T ITS BEGINNING, ORGANIZED BASEBALL IN AMERICA received the enthusiastic backing of college students. Within a year of the 1857 founding of the National Association of Base Ball Players, students at Harvard and Princeton organized baseball clubs and played games against National Association teams. Two years later, in 1859, the first intercollegiate baseball game saw Amherst defeat Williams by a score of 73-32. Since the game was played under "Massachusetts rules," with thirteen men on a side, and had other atavistic features, some historians have dismissed the event as insignificant to the history of baseball. Be that as it may, soon afterwards intercollegiate games were played under the "New York rules" adopted by the National Association in 1857. Thereafter, the "New York game" rapidly became the dominant form of baseball in America.

College baseball was booming when the Civil War put a damper on activities. After 1865, however, college campuses were caught up in the postwar baseball boom. Not only were eastern colleges such as Harvard, Yale, and Princeton involved, but clubs were formed on campuses as far west as Kansas and Wisconsin and as far south as the University of Virginia. These collegiate ball clubs began as student-initiated activities and continued under student control until the turn of the century. By then college officials were gaining control over such student activities. Officials' concern over rowdyism at games, games conflicting with

BELOW THE SALT: COLLEGIATE BASEBALL AND OTHER AMATEUR FORMS

"Base Ball Match" between Harvard and Yale in August 1867, sketched by an artist for *Harper's Weekly*. (Courtesy John A. Lucas and Ronald A. Smith)

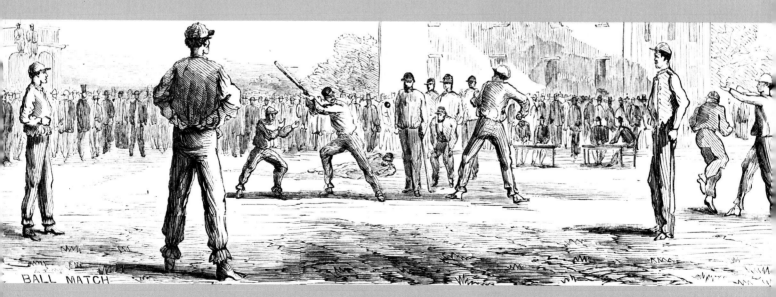

BALL MATCH

328   BELOW THE SALT

classes, eligibility of players, and the status of coaches prompted efforts to integrate intercollegiate sports with academic programs.

The formative years of intercollegiate baseball were dominated by eastern colleges. From 1865 to 1870 Harvard, Yale, and Princeton ranked with the strongest of National Association teams. Especially Harvard—in the spring of 1869 the Crimson student team embarked on a two-week road tour of Pennsylvania and New York, on which they defeated the powerful Philadelphia Athletics among other victims. That year also saw Harvard fall to the all-conquering Cincinnati Reds by a 30-11 score. The following year the Harvard club entrained upon a forty-three-day, twenty-five-game tour extending as far west as St. Louis. During this campaign Harvard posted a 17-8 won-lost record, compiled against National Association powers like Troy, Chicago, and Philadelphia. Again that year the Crimson club lost to the Cincinnati Reds, but this time only after the Reds staged a last-inning rally. Overall, Harvard's formidable showing in the late 1860s provided a powerful stimulant to the rise of intercollegiate baseball.

By the 1870s baseball had become the most popular team sport at colleges, but in the absence of organized leagues, most teams played intramural games or contended against outside clubs. In these years Harvard and Yale played twice as many games against outsiders, including professional clubs, as they did against other colleges. Belatedly, in 1879, the major eastern college clubs moved to establish a league called the American College Base Ball Association. Members included clubs from Harvard, Yale, Princeton, Brown, Dartmouth, and Amherst. The league was plagued with problems, including the lack of a fixed playing schedule and a continuing debate over player eligibility. Because the ACBBA took no stand on the eligibility question, Harvard immediately stirred a fuss when it fielded two graduate students. The eligibility issue also caused a furor during the championship game between Brown and Yale. In that crucial game, Brown used pitcher Lee Richmond, who had recently hurled a no-hit game for the professional Worcester club against the Chicago club of the National League. When Richmond pitched Brown to the 1879 ACBBA championship, Yale protested that he was a professional. Not surprisingly, the issue of player eligibility came under hot debate at the fall meeting of the league. Because no rule existed to bar professional players, Brown's victory was sustained, though henceforth pro players were to be ruled ineligible. But the question of playing graduate students was not resolved. Refusal to come to grips with that matter prompted Yale's representatives to quit the meeting, and the 1880 ACBBA season was boycotted by Yale. Al-

J. Lee Richmond, who pitched winning games for both Brown and the professional Worcester team in 1879. In 1880, while still a Brown student, he pitched the first perfect game in major league history for Worcester, which had joined the National League. (Courtesy Brown University Archives and Ronald A. Smith)

Opposite:

Top: Harvard team of 1867. (Courtesy Dennis Goldstein)

Bottom: Oberlin College team in the late 1870s. The Walker brothers, Moses Fleetwood (seated and numbered 6 by the photographer) and Welday Wilberforce (standing and numbered 10), are recorded as the first blacks in college baseball and in the majors. "Fleet" and Welday Walker played for Toledo in the American Association during the 1884 season, before being hounded out of "organized baseball" by bigots like "Pop" Anson. (Courtesy John A. Lucas and Ronald A. Smith)

Harvard versus Dartmouth at Hanover, 1882. (Courtesy Dennis Goldstein)

though the knotty problem of eligibility, including a workable definition of professional players, was never resolved, the league survived for eight seasons; in those years Yale returned to become the dominant team. In 1887 the ACBBA broke up when Harvard, Yale, Princeton, and Columbia formed their own league, forcing Amherst, Brown, Dartmouth, and Williams to form another conference.

Meanwhile, other colleges organized intercollegiate leagues. During the late nineteenth century, college baseball leagues, mostly organized at the state level, cropped up in all sections of the land. In the 1880s the Western Conference was organized as a regional circuit of midwestern college teams, but full conference play did not begin until 1895. At first, the universities of Michigan and Chicago dominated play; then, in 1907–17, after Michigan dropped out, the University of Illinois ruled the league.

By the turn of the century, although baseball still prevailed as the most popular intercollegiate team sport, the game obviously faced a serious climatic problem. Because baseball is a warm-weather game, the colleges' summer recesses threatened the sport's future dominance. The same problem affected the high school programs that developed during the twentieth century. Unless colleges or schools happened to be located in climates favoring spring and fall play, nature conspired against the sport. Moreover, this same climatic problem aggravated the issue of player eligibility. During summer vacations many college players played semi-professional and professional baseball. Often, good players got sinecure jobs at resorts, where they did little else but play ball for money raised by dividing gate receipts at games. Upon returning to their colleges, such players reverted to amateur status in their own

Sandlot game in Washington, D.C., 1918. (Courtesy French Collection, Library of Congress)

minds and in the minds of their partisans. New intercollegiate sports, notably football and basketball, also were confronted with the issue of professionalism.

By 1905 intercollegiate football was overshadowing baseball at many colleges. That year the National Collegiate Athletic Association was organized, and from the start the conducting of football games dominated deliberations. Although intercollegiate baseball steadily lost standing to football and basketball, it continued to be embroiled in debates over amateurism versus professionalism. This issue was never satisfactorily resolved, but the NCAA did manage to bring intercollegiate sports under the control of college administrations. By 1929 most intercollegiate sports programs were controlled by college physical education departments, with most of the coaches holding faculty status.

As rival team sports steadily gained popularity, baseball by the 1930s became a minor sport at many colleges. Moreover, at California colleges where strong baseball programs existed, coaches complained of losing key players to professional teams. On top of these woes came Depression-forced cutbacks in college sports programs; in the ensuing budgetary cuts, baseball programs often were among the first to go. By 1938 the status of intercollegiate baseball was so low that Branch Rickey voiced concern when addressing that year's NCAA convention. Strong college programs, Rickey told the delegates, were vital to the health of the game in general and to the major leagues in particular.

Yet, the low point in the sinking fortunes of college baseball was still to be plumbed; the bottom was touched during World War II. In 1945 the newly formed American Association of College Baseball Coaches received a sobering report. That year, of 682 colleges polled, only 242 played intercollegiate baseball. But 1945 was the nadir of the college baseball decline. Within a year the G.I. Bill of Rights triggered a lasting boom in college attendance and, concurrently, in all college sports programs.

Early in the postwar boom, college baseball underwent a revival. Interest in intercollegiate baseball surged in 1946 when the NCAA successfully sponsored an East-West College All-Star game. Encouraged by that coup, the NCAA staged the first College World Series to decide the national intercollegiate baseball championship. From the start the College World Series was a popular spectacle. First hosted in 1947 by Western Michigan University, within a year the classic outgrew this modest habitat and was moved to Omaha, which became the perennial host city. By the 1980s capacity crowds regularly jammed Omaha's Rosenblatt Stadium, and Series games were also aired on national television. Today the College World Series is the centerpiece of expanded intercollegiate baseball competitions sponsored by the NCAA. Under NCAA sponsorship, college teams and leagues are grouped into three divisions, according to school size and the judged strength of the leagues. Although College World Series competition is limited to Division I schools, the NCAA also sponsors tournaments for Division II and Division III teams. In addition, the National Association of Intercollegiate Athletics sponsors an annual tournament for small colleges unaffiliated with the NCAA.

No other college tournament matches the color and spectacle of the College World Series. Each year thirty-six teams are chosen to compete: twenty-four Division I conference champions plus twelve teams selected at large. Regional playoffs trim the field of entries to eight teams, which journey to Omaha each June for double-elimination play to determine the national champion. Teams from California and Texas won the first four of the College World Series. Since then teams from colleges in Sunbelt states have continued to win most titles. Blessed by favorable weather that allows teams to play a hundred or more games a year, Sunbelt colleges in Arizona and California won fourteen of the fifteen titles between 1968 and 1982. By 1982 the big winner was coach Rod Dedeaux's University of Southern California team, boasting of eleven World Series titles. With more than twelve hundred coaching victories, the veteran Dedeaux currently leads all Division I coaches. But Cliff Gustafson of the University of Texas (with thirteen Southwestern Conference pennants in his first fifteen seasons), Jim Brock of

Left: Quarterfinal action in 1981 Little League World Series at Williamsport, Pennsylvania. Batter from Barrington (Illinois) Little League, which won 6–5, hits against the National Little League of Escondido (Calif.). (Courtesy Little League Baseball®)

Right: A player from the winning quarterfinal team grounds out to the shortstop in the 1981 Little League World Series. Representing the South, the Belmont Heights Little League of Tampa (Florida) defeated the Federal Little League of Stamford (Connecticut) and went on to the championship game, which they lost 4–2 to Tai-Chung (Taiwan). Dwight Gooden of the New York Mets is a graduate of the Belmont Heights Little League. (Courtesy Little League Baseball®)

Coach Ron Fraser (*top*), of the University of Miami Hurricanes, and two of his team's trio of 1986 players drafted by the majors. Outfielder Greg Vaughn (*middle*) went with the Milwaukee Brewers system; pitcher Dan Davies was drafted by the Cleveland Indians. Miami teams coached by Fraser have won the College World Series twice in the 'Eighties. (Courtesy Sports Publicity Department, University of Miami)

the University of Arizona, and Ron Frazer of the University of Miami are formidable rivals.

By 1982 Miami baseball teams had won over nine hundred games for Frazer. A gifted coach, Frazer is also a promotional genius. To boost his program at Miami, Frazer in 1965 started charging admission to games, a risky innovation for a college sport where traditionally attendance and revenues have been negligible. Frazer lures fans by dint of promotions like dollar bill scrambles, giveaways, and lotteries that pay off in imaginative prizes. So successful have been Frazer's ploys that as of 1982 he could boast an annual $350,000 operating budget for his baseball program. By then, other intercollegiate baseball programs were supported by generous budgets, good playing facilities, and enticing scholarships for promising recruits. Indeed, major college baseball powers now scout high school and American Legion games in quest of able recruits.

Although the resurgence of intercollegiate and interscholastic baseball owes much to first-rate coaching and lavish financing, it has also drawn increasing support from the major leagues. Such support is a recent trend and stems directly from the talent shortage problem; it was a chronic postwar talent shortage that helped cause the shrinkage of the minor leagues. By the 1960s the major leagues addressed the problem by taking the drastic steps of adopting the annual rookie draft and subsidizing virtually all the surviving minor leagues. In addition, major league player-development specialists were obliged to abandon ancient prejudices against college ball players, including the myth that college graduates were too old to be considered as viable major league prospects. Nevertheless, in the early years of the annual rookie drafts, player developers still harbored a preference for high school players, although since 1977 most of the nine hundred amateur players selected in the drafts have been from college teams. In this selection process, baseball programs at four-year colleges are protected by a rule that bars the signing of a college player until he completes his junior year or turns twenty-one years of age. However, Sunbelt-based junior colleges with strong programs remain vulnerable to major league drafts; for junior colleges this is a vexing problem.

Certainly the growing preference by major league scouts for college players has raised the status of college baseball programs. Any doubts about the importance of colleges as talent suppliers to the major leagues have been dispelled by comparative statistics showing a steady increase in the number of major league players with college backgrounds. In 1938 only 11.6 percent of active major leaguers had attended college, but the percentage rose to 27.6 by 1946 and soared to nearly 50 by 1961. As of 1982, 72.8 percent of American-born big league players had college backgrounds. Moreover, beginning in the 1980s no fewer than ten major league teams were expending most of their annual rookie draft choices on college players. Still, it should not be supposed that college baseball programs are displacing the minor leagues as major league talent developers. On the contrary, few college ball players have ever made the jump from college baseball to major league lineups. Unlike college football or basketball players, college baseball players are regarded by major league developers as unfinished products who require minor league seasoning. Indeed, some major league talent developers fault college teams for using aluminum bats, which are blamed for inflating slugging performances at the college level of play.

Professional baseball recruiters might fault college players for lack of polish, but there is no gainsaying the importance of intercollegiate baseball as a major source of professional talent. From the earliest days of major league baseball to this day, college-trained players have starred in the big leagues. At the dawning of major league history, a former intramural baseball player at Notre Dame, Adrian Anson, went on to star in the National Association and the National League, where he captained the Chicago White Stockings until his retirement in 1897. Another nineteenth-century great, John Ward, had played baseball at Penn State. Other nineteenth-century major league standouts included ex-collegians Lee Richmond (Brown), who hurled the first perfect game in the majors; Lou Sockalexis (Holy Cross); and Dave Fultz and Fred Tenney (Brown). During the early years of the twentieth century, the galaxy of college-nurtured major league stars included Eddie Collins (Columbia), Jake Stahl (Illinois), Christy Mathewson (Bucknell), Eddie Plank (Gettysburg), Hal Chase (Santa Clara), and Duffy Lewis and Harry Hooper (St. Mary's). The majors' golden years of 1920–40 fielded such former college stars as George Sisler (Michigan), Lou Geh-

Rick Raether, All-American relief pitcher of the University of Miami, who in 1986 set a new four-year collegiate record for saves, with 37. Raether helped Miami to a College World Series victory in 1985. After graduation he joined the Tulsa farm club of the Texas Rangers. Photo by Ken Lee. (Courtesy Sports Publicity Department, University of Miami)

rig (Columbia), Frankie Frisch (Fordham), Riggs Stephenson (Alabama), Charley Gehringer (Michigan), Pinky Higgins (Texas), Joe Sewell (Alabama), Joe Dugan (Holy Cross), Jim Tabor (Alabama), and Whit Wyatt (Georgia Tech). During the postwar era the expanding list included standouts like Jackie Robinson (UCLA), Robin Roberts (Michigan State), and Lou Boudreau (Illinois). And among the plenteous college-bred stars of recent times are men like Reggie Jackson (Arizona State), Steve Garvey (Michigan State), Tom Seaver and Fred Lynn (Southern Cal.), and Kirk Gibson (Michigan State).

Besides providing a steady flow of talent to the majors, college base-

At the 1985 College World Series, Will Clark of Mississippi State was called safe by plate umpire Richard Zivic, though University of Texas catcher Robbie Byers nearly had him out. Photo by Chris Young. (Courtesy *Omaha World-Herald*)

336   BELOW THE SALT

ball has made other contributions to the diamond game. Innovations of the early years such as the catcher's mask and curveball pitching have been attributed to college players. Moreover, Oberlin and Harvard pioneered in the racial integration of the game. From Oberlin came the Walker brothers, who became the first blacks to play in the majors, while Harvard in 1904 dared to buck prevailing racist taboos by playing black shortstop Clarence Matthews. Yet, in the postwar integration of their major conferences and tournaments, the colleges lagged behind the major leagues, where there were a hundred black players by 1960. As late as 1961, according to a study by Harold H. Wolf, some colleges would not admit black players or compete against teams that did so.

On another front, however, colleges are credited with helping to spread baseball to Japan and to Latin America, where today the passion for baseball rivals that of America. In Japan the baseball mania began at such colleges as Waseda University, where Japanese teachers brought the game from America; in Latin America, where American colleges have long participated in the Pan-American games, such competition spurred baseball's popularity in half a dozen Latin American countries. Indeed, today baseball is played in seventy-nine countries around the world, and among these, forty-seven countries have organized baseball federations.

Since 1961 the expanding global interest in baseball has had NCAA planners envisioning a global college world series. However, it is now more likely that this dream will be usurped by another—that of amateur baseball as a regular part of the Olympic games. This is the goal of the amateur U.S. Baseball Federation, which in 1984 succeeded in raising baseball to the status of an Olympic demonstration sport. Prior to 1984 baseball competition was presented as an exhibition sport in six Olympiads. Now raised to the status of demonstration sport, baseball is only one step away from becoming an established Olympic team sport. Thus, the prospect of quadrennial Olympic baseball competition now presents another major opportunity for amateur American ball players.

Obviously, trends such as these signify baseball's continuing growth and popularity. Today in America there are an estimated 20 million amateur players of all ages, with another 30 million American softball players. Such grass-roots support is vital to the continuing health of the major leagues. To sustain the interest, the major leagues now contribute over $500,000 a year to amateur baseball programs. Of this sum, nearly $285,000 goes towards sponsoring college and high school tournaments and summer college leagues. Another $236,000 goes to amateur organizations such as the U.S. Baseball Federation, the American Amateur Baseball Congress, the National American Baseball Federation, the All-American Baseball Federation, the American Legion Junior Baseball program, Pony League Baseball, Babe Ruth Baseball, and Little League Baseball. By wisely investing in amateur baseball programs such as these, the major leagues are insuring their own future success.

10

AFTERWORD: THE ENIGMATIC 'EIGHTIES

AMERICAN BASEBALL'S FUTURE SEEMED AS HARD TO predict in the mid-1980s as the future of the United States and the world. Prognostication is never easy, but the period 1981–86 brought a record number of mixed signals and disagreements among experts about the state of the nation and of the national game. Both seemed relatively healthy, but both shared symptoms of (take your choice) delayed growing pains or inevitable collapse.

The popularity of President Reagan when he was inaugurated at the beginning of 1981 was seen by some observers as a sign of revived American unity; yet, in the baseball sector, the following spring found big league owners and players locked in a bitter strike. The strike settlement failed to resolve fundamental differences. Owners held that the cost of player salaries and privileges made most franchises uneconomic, while many fans saw modern players as greedy plutocrats. Players claimed a right to a hefty share of revenue in the electronic age, while some fans applauded their heroes' success in "getting it while the getting was good."

The nation's economy recovered from a recession during the Reagan administration; inflation was reduced substantially, and Americans seemed more secure and confident in an unstable world. A host of experts and other citizens felt sure these favorable trends would persist, whereas an opposing multitude feared all such progress was illusory and would fizzle. Perceptions of organized baseball were equally mixed. Optimists were confident the national game would surmount such ailments as money-grubbing, drug-taking, and faltering leadership. Pessimists were equally certain the ailments were incurable. Regardless of their forecasts, both optimistic and pessimistic fans in record numbers took themselves out to the ballpark or tuned in to the old ball game.

THE GREAT STRIKE OF 1981

Any possibility that the cooling-off period might produce a strike-saving settlement faded with the old year of 1980. With the stroke of the New Year, the fateful deadline passed with no agreement; since both owners and players refused to budge on the issue of compensating owners for players lost in re-entry drafts, the time of talk ended and the time of strife began. Ostensibly, this impasse was the only barrier to a new Basic Agreement, but Miller suspected that the compensation issue masked a determined owner effort to bust the Players Association. In February, Ray Grebey, the tough-talking negotiator hired by the owners to bargain with the Players Association, flatly rejected a Miller proposal that eventually became the basis for settlement. Now Grebey was stonewalling, and the owners were girding for a strike. Besides piling up a $15 million war chest, the owners purchased $50 million worth of strike insurance from Lloyds of London. If the players walked out, the policy would reimburse owners $100,000 for each lost game for a period of six weeks. Since the Players Association would decide whether to strike or not, it could purchase no such insurance. When the owners invoked their compensation plan in February, the players found it unacceptable. By an overwhelming majority, they voted to hit the bricks on May 29, but they delayed action when a last-minute reprieve came via an unfair-labor-practice suit filed against the owners. A federal court threw out the suit and quashed this hope. A new deadline for striking was set by the Association for June 11, and when no agreement was reached, the strike began at the end of that day.

Once unleashed, the strike fed on pent-up emotions for fifty days. Although exceeded by the season-long strike of 1890, this one erased a third of the scheduled games. The walkout cost players nearly $30 million, but owners' revenue losses totaled nearly $116 million. What's more, the strike influenced the economies of major league cities already hit by the recession. Hotels, television stations, concessionaires, and stadium employees suffered losses. The strike also threatened baseball's image, as bewildered and disgruntled fans tried to make sense of the war of words waged in the media. Many fans blamed Miller and damned the pampered players, but some felt the owners had provoked the strike. One poll even showed fans supporting the players by a narrow margin.

Tempers flared at bargaining sessions as federal mediator Ken Moffett vainly tried to lead the disputants toward a settlement. Both Miller and Grebey hung tough, but when the lengthening strike threatened to shut down the entire season, pressures mounted to end it. Once the Lloyds policy ran out, the owners wavered and Grebey's power waned. As anxiety mounted, Miller fanned the owners' fears by raising the threat of players organizing their own major league, or at least using their coming freedom from contracts to jump their clubs. The salary-starved players put great pressure on Miller to settle, however. On the last day of July a compromise on the compensation issue was hammered out. Veteran players who qualified for re-entry drafts were to be classed into three categories based on the measured quality of their performances. Beginning with the 1981 re-entry draft, any club that lost a top-ranked player would get either a major leaguer or a seasoned minor leaguer as compensation. The compensation process would not directly penalize the club that signed a free agent, however; instead, a club seeking compensation would pick from a pool of players supplied by all clubs. This procedure blocked the owners' demand for direct compensation; the compromise cooled player fears of a possible ceiling on salaries that might have resulted from direct compensation. With this compensation agreement as its cornerstone, the new Basic Agreement was speedily adopted and lasted through the 1984 season. Among its other provisions, players were credited with time served while on strike and were granted a week's time to shape up before resuming the seasonal play.

Fernando Valenzuela, whose pitching helped the Dodgers to a world championship in 1981 and a division first place in 1983. (Courtesy Los Angeles Dodgers)

THE "DISHONEST SEASON," 1981

It was sportswriter Red Smith who harshly labeled the patchwork campaign that resulted as the dishonest season; it was a sentiment shared by many. Indeed, it might have been better to have ended the season on the day of the walkout rather than undergo play under the questionable format devised by Commissioner Kuhn's committee. What those worthies decided was to split the playing season so as to produce two winners for each division. The scheme made first-half-season victors of those clubs that happened to be leading their divisions on June 11. The second half-season began in August and followed the regular playing schedule from that point. While the split-season plan was not without precedent (having long been used by minor league teams and once by the majors back in 1892), it smacked of money-grubbing. Under the plan the first-half winners were ineligible to win the second half. If a team won both halves, it must then battle the second-place team of the second half in a playoff. The playoff series between the half-season winners would determine the divisional champs; those winners then would engage in the usual playoffs to settle the league championships; then the two winners would meet in the World Series. If this procedure confused fans, it also smacked of "hippodroming"; however, no one thought to resurrect that old-fashioned epithet and fling it in the face of Kuhn's committee.

Although many seem inclined to forget the 1981 playing season, it did produce winners and losers along with a complement of heroes, villains, and fools. It began on an optimistic note. Of fourteen players who went the re-entry route the previous fall, five came off with contracts worth at least $500,000; one of these, outfielder Dave Winfield, became the reigning plutocrat by signing a ten-year Yankee pact worth $20 million. Other coups sent salaries soaring. To retain stars like Phil Niekro, Andre Dawson, and George Brett, their owners made them millionaires. Outfielder Fred Lynn also became a millionaire when traded to the Angels, and a spate of trades also beefed up the Cardinals and the Brewers.

To some observers it was the impending strike that had teams battling like Kilkenny cats in the early 1981 going. Be that as it may, all divisional races were hotly contested and attendance ran high. Western National League fans warmed to chubby Fernando Valenzuela, a twenty-year-old Mexican pitching "phenom," who won his first eight games with an 0.50 ERA! Valenzuela's feats helped the Dodgers lead the Reds by half a game at strike time. In the National East, the Phillies rose to the top. Carlton's 9-1 pitching and Schmidt's 14 homers lifted them to a 1½-game lead over the Cardinals when the curtain descended. The Phillies' last game stirred their fans with Pete Rose's assault on the all-time National League hit record; just before strike time, Rose banged his 3,630th hit to tie Musial's record.

Fiercely contested races also marked the early American campaigns. In the East the slow-starting Yankees won 15 of their last 23 games to snatch a two-game lead over the Orioles at walkout time. Plutocrat Winfield led Yankee batters, but the most celebrated Eastern hero was pitcher Len Barker of the Indians, who hurled a perfect game, the league's first since 1968. Just as dramatic was the Western race, where manager Martin got his Oakland A's off with 11 straight wins. There-

Dave Winfield, who left the Padres to join the Yankees in 1981 for a ten-year contract estimated to be worth $20 million. (Courtesy New York Yankees)

after, Oakland's durable starting pitchers and the team's old-fashioned hit-and-run, base-stealing offense (dubbed "Billy Ball" by A's fans) had the A's 1½ games up on the Rangers at strike time.

After the long strike scuttled a third of the playing season, its settlement made first-half winners of these four teams. Since the four were disqualified from winning the second half, the Phillies, Dodgers, and Yanks played lackluster ball the rest of the way. Indeed, if overall records for each of these three clubs had counted, not one would have won a division title. Not so with Martin's A's, who played brilliantly and barely lost the second half to the Royals in the American West. However, the Royals' overall 50-53 record raised the specter of a losing team possibly becoming the world champs. Other horrors haunted the 1981 season. Cincinnati posted the best overall record in the majors, but because the Houston Astros beat the Reds by 1½ games in the second half, Cincinnati's only consolation was a homemade pennant that they defiantly raised. In the National East the Cards owned the best overall record, but they lost the second half by a mere half-game to the Expos. A schedule quirk allowed the Expos to play one more game, which they won. Likewise, the Orioles in the American East went unrewarded; they had the best overall record in that division, but they lost out to the Brewers in the second half. Small wonder then that suspicious fans turned away. Despite close second-half races, attendance and television ratings sagged in seventeen cities. Overall attendance was 22 million, but attendance per game was 2,000 less than in 1980.

At least the woeful season afforded some highlights. Rose got his record-breaking hit and took aim at Cobb's all-time hit record; Ryan of the Astros pitched a record-setting fifth no-hitter; veteran Gaylord Perry of Seattle notched his 297th pitching victory; Tim Raines of the Expos stole 71 bases; Schmidt of the Phils poled 31 homers and drove in 91 runs to win another MVP award; reliefer Rollie Fingers of the Brewers saved 28 games, with a 1.04 ERA, to win both Cy Young and MVP honors in the American; and Valenzuela's 13-7 pitching earned him both Cy Young and Rookie-of-the-Year honors in the National (although Seaver's 14-2 record with the Reds was baseball's best). Such feats contrasted starkly with other seasonal records. For example, seasonal batting titles went to Carney Lansford of the Red Sox (.336 on 399 at-bats) and to Bill Madlock of the Pirates (.341 on a mere 279 at-bats, only four above the minimum allowed for this year).

An even greater skepticism surrounded the eight winning teams that met in best-of-five playoff tourneys to determine the divisional championships. In the American West, the A's held the Royals to two runs and one extra base hit in sweeping their series. In the East, the Brewers and Yanks battled five games before the Yanks prevailed on three homers in the finale. Just as hard-fought were the National duels. In the East, Steve Rogers of the Expos hurled a 3-0 shutout in the fifth game to give the Canadians their first divisional flag. In the West, the Dodgers lost the first two games to the Astros but scored three straight victories to land the title. The plucky Dodgers then mounted another desperate rally in their battle with the Expos for the National League championship. After losing two of the first three games, the Dodgers shook off foul-weather effects to win the next two games at Montreal's

Gorman Thomas (*top*) and Robin Yount, whose strong hitting and fielding helped the Brewers to a pennant in 1982. (Courtesy Milwaukee Brewers)

Olympic Stadium. While these contenders fought their French and Indian war, the lordly Yanks dashed A's manager Martin's revengeful dream by sweeping Oakland.

The final chapter of the dismal season pitted the gritty Dodgers against their Yankee nemesis. Opening at home, the Yanks won the first two games. Then, for a third time in postseasonal play, the Dodgers rose from the dead; after snatching three single-run victories, the Dodgers buried the Yanks 9-2 before a shocked Yankee Stadium crowd. The comeback avenged what the Yanks had done to the Dodgers back in 1978 and was etched in record books along with Yankee reliefer George Frazier's dubious achievement of *losing* three Series games. Unhappily, the crassness of the "dishonest season" tainted the Dodger victory; mostly, 1981 seemed to be the season best forgotten.

THREE PROSPEROUS SEASONS, 1982–1984

To confound the doomsayers, the ill wind of baseball's dishonest season swiftly blew out, allowing the game to rebound to record heights of popularity. The resurgence came despite a national recession that in 1982 idled 10 million American workers; in bucking that trend, base-ball attendance jumped to a record 45 million, and the game's televi-sion ratings followed suit. What's more, pro football failed to keep pace with baseball's comeback; rather, in 1982 baseball benefited from the National Football League players' strike and from the United States Football League's challenge to the NFL monopoly. When the USFL began its radical experiment of staging spring and summer football in 1983, some feared that the games might affect baseball attendance. Not only did this not happen, but the USFL hurt the NFL by luring good college players into its ranks and by bidding football salaries upward. Finally, baseball players' fears that lower salaries might follow the strike of 1981 proved groundless; instead, the 1981–82 round of contract signings zoomed average annual salaries to $250,000. Among newly minted million-dollar-a-year plutocrats were Gary Carter, Ken Griffey, George Foster, Bill Madlock, and Mike Schmidt; each of these either signed with his former club or else benefited by being traded to a high-rolling club. Among those taking the re-entry draft route, Reggie Jackson signed with the Angels; thanks to the attendance clause in his new contract, Jackson became a million-dollar man in 1982.

This latest salary surge had many observers asking what the strike had been all about. Even the much-feared compensation plan looked like a paper tiger. Ironically, only one club got to pick from the player pool. When the Phillies signed White Sox reliefer Ed Farmer, the Sox as compensation picked a promising young catcher deposited in the pool by the Pirates. But if some critics questioned the wisdom of the players' strike, Miller defended it; in 1982 he also filed a grievance procedure against suspected owner evasions of players' free-agent rights. At the same time, some hundred players sought arbitration of salaries, but the vast majority of these petitions were settled before they reached the formal stage. Since most players seemed satisfied about their pay, this did not seem to be what the strike had been about. That the strike was a power struggle between owners and players was certainly true. If this was the key issue, then future struggles loomed over the division of increasing television revenue. As millionaire-player Dave Winfield put it during the strike: "Free agency and compensation aren't the only issues involved in our future and not the most important. Television and cable TV will be very important down the line. For what's at stake we may have to change the entire player-owner relationship as we know it." Be that as it may, the game's speedy recovery reflected boundless optimism over baseball's immediate future. Such confidence was borne out by the highly successful 1982 season. That year all divisional races were hotly contested, and hopes for competitive balance were fulfilled when no 1981 divisional winner repeated.

In the National East, the Cardinals, Phillies, Expos, and Pirates locked in a four-way race that ended with the Cards topping the Phillies by three games. Although manager Whitey Herzog's Cards bashed only 67 homers, they batted .264 and stole 200 bases. Leading the attack, ex-Phillie outfielder Lonnie Smith hit .307, scored 120 runs, and stole 68 bases; first baseman Keith Hernandez batted .299 with 94 RBIs; and outfielder George Hendrick hit 19 homers and drove in 104 runs. Starter Joaquin Andujar (15-10) headed a fair pitching staff that boasted the league's best reliever in Bruce Sutter (9 wins, 36 saves). In the West, the Braves, Dodgers, Giants, and Padres fought an even closer battle. Manager Joe Torre's Braves broke away fast, winning their first 13 games; but after setting that modern record, they slogged along at a 76-73 clip, barely enough to edge the Dodgers by a game and the Giants by two. Slugging by Dale Murphy, whose .281-36-109 effort won the outfielder the MVP award, plus third baseman Bob Horner's 32 homers and 97 RBIs, powered the Brave offensive. Yet, apart from leading the league in homers, the Braves were ordinary; their batting and fielding were mediocre. So was the pitching, but aging Phil Niekro (17-4) and reliever Gene Garber (30 saves) were brilliant exceptions.

By coincidence, the hotly contested American races had winners prevailing by similarly close margins. In the East, the explosive Brewers engaged in a three-way struggle with the Orioles and Red Sox, winning by a single game over the Orioles. Punfully dubbed "Harvey's Wallbangers," manager Harvey Kuenn's Brewers batted .279 and smote 216 homers, the most in the majors in 1982. Outfielders Gorman Thomas and Ben Oglivie combined for 73 homers and 214 RBIs, and infielders Cecil Cooper, Paul Molitor, and Robin Yount each topped .300 while combining for 80 homers. Shortstop Yount's herculean MVP performance saw him lead the league in slugging percentage, hits, total bases, and doubles, while winning a Golden Glove award; he missed winning the batting title by a point. Meanwhile, pitcher Pete Vuckovich won the Cy Young award for his 18-6 pitching, but the Brewer staff surrendered nearly four earned runs a game. Hence, ace reliever Rollie Fingers's 29 saves were indispensable; when arm trouble sidelined him in September, the Brewers barely staggered to victory. In the West, meanwhile, owner Autry's plutocratic Angels fought off the Royals and White Sox to win by three games. Acquiring slugger Reggie Jackson from the Yanks was a major coup; the aging celebrity smacked 39 homers to tie Thomas for the league lead. Swelling the Angels' .274

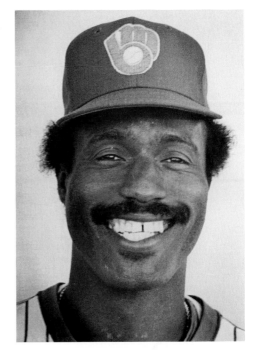

Ben Oglivie (*top*) and Cecil Cooper, two outstanding Brewers during their 1982 pennant-winning season. (Courtesy Milwaukee Brewers)

batting were first baseman Rod Carew (.319), infielder Doug De Cinces (.301), and outfielder Fred Lynn (.299); the Angels' 186-homer total was baseball's second best. The team's 3.82 ERA was the league's second best, but the Angels lacked dependable relief; hence, acquiring starter Tommy John from the sagging Yanks was a midseason godsend.

In the playoff for the American League championship, the Brewers defeated the Angels three games to two. In the National League playoff, the Cardinals dispatched the Braves in three games. Thus, the Cardinals and Brewers squared off in a Series match that shaped up as a classic test between the big bang style of the Brewers and the fleet-running, base-stealing style of the Cards. It took seven games to settle the issue, with Cardinal hitting and relief pitching finally deciding it. Reliefer Sutter won one and saved two games for the Cards, while the Brewers sorely missed their irreplaceable reliefer Fingers. After absorbing a 10-0 drubbing in the opener, the Cards won the next two games. Back came the Brewers with two home victories, but the Cards used their home advantage to square the Series. In the decisive game the Cards punched 15 hits off four Brewer pitchers to land their first world title in fifteen seasons. For American League

Greg Luzinski, who joined the White Sox from the Phillies in 1983 and helped take the Chicagoans to the American League playoffs. (Courtesy Chicago White Sox)

Steve Trout, White Sox pitcher and son of Paul ("Dizzy") Trout, longtime pitcher for the Tigers. (Courtesy Chicago White Sox)

partisans, this fourth straight Series loss, combined with a horrendous record of 19 losses in the past 20 All-Star games, made for an inferiority complex that was worsened by a sportswriter's pun that the major league game was becoming the "National's Pastime!"

Baseball history abounds with similar misguided judgments, however, and in 1983 American Leaguers determined to fling such gibes back at their detractors. For various reasons, including re-entry acquisitions, trades, and productive farm systems, neither league enjoyed a clear-cut advantage. Nor did any single team, as the divisional winners of 1982 learned to their humility. In 1983 the American League outhit and outhomered their National rivals, and for a change even won the All-Star game. When it came time for the fall showdown between the two leagues, the Americans rested their hopes on two new divisional winners.

One newly crowned divisional winner was the Western-based Chicago White Sox. Pennantless since 1959, the Sox long languished as also-rans at Comiskey Park, located in a run-down urban area. Under new owners Eddie Einhorn and Jerry Reinsdorf, who bought the club from Bill Veeck in 1980, a dramatic revival took place. The park was refurbished and ticket prices raised, but most of all, the team was beefed up. Over the winter the club purchased pitcher Floyd Bannister in the re-entry draft; prior to that, hefty cash outlays corralled slugger Greg ("Bull") Luzinski from the Phils and catcher Carlton Fisk from the Red Sox. A June trade landed second baseman Julio Cruz from Seattle. These additions strengthened a team that included promising pitchers La Marr Hoyt, Rich Dotson, and relievers Dennis Lamp and Salome Barojas. Rookie Ron Kittle joined Rudy Law and Harold Baines in the outfield, and Cruz anchored an infield that included first baseman Tom Paciorek, shortstop Scott Fletcher, and third baseman Vern Law. Welding the White Sox into a winning unit took time, but the woefully weak Western Division afforded plenty of that commodity. The defending champion Angels faded ignominiously, and no other rival played winning baseball. In mid-July manager Tony La Russa had the White Sox on top to stay; they went on to win the division title by 20 games over Kansas City, clinching it on September 17. The winning Sox batted only .262 but bashed 157 homers. Ron Kittle's 35 homers and 100 RBIs led the assault and won him Rookie-of-the-Year honors. Joining Kittle were Luzinski (32-95), Fisk (26-86), and Baines (20-99). Such power made life easy for the pitchers; burly Hoyt (24-10) won the Cy Young Award, Rich Dotson went 22-7, Bannister was 16-10, and relievers Lamp and Barojas saved 27. While some carping critics derided the Sox style of bombing their way to top-heavy wins in a forlorn division as "winning ugly," more than 2 million fans paid to see them and made a battle cry of the gibe.

It was a much tighter race in the American League East, a division some judged as the best in baseball. There, Baltimore, Detroit, New York, and Toronto all finished atop the fading 1982 champion Brewers, who sacked manager Kuenn. Again, owner Steinbrenner strengthened the Yankees with a spending spree; this one brought outfielders Don Baylor and Steve Kemp, plus pitcher Bob Shirley, to manager Billy Martin. The Yankee challenge faded ludicrously, however, in the aftermath of the notorious August "pine tar" episode. An umpire's decision to disallow an apparent game-winning homer struck by Royal George Brett, because he allegedly had too much pine tar on his bat, created a memorable brawl at Yankee Stadium. Later, however, the league president overruled the ump so that the Royals won the game. By season's end, the Yanks finished third and Steinbrenner fired Martin for a third time. Manager Sparky Anderson's rising Detroit Tigers contended most of the way, but in the September stretch drive the Orioles broke out to win by six games. Managed by freshman Joe Altobelli, who succeeded the great Earl Weaver, the Orioles' .269 batting ranked seventh in the league, but the Birds led in homers with 168. Sophomore shortstop Cal Ripken, Jr., son of an Oriole coach, played every game and took MVP honors on his .318-27-102 batting, and veteran first baseman Eddie Murray weighed in with a .306-33-111 effort. Altobelli's platooning in left field yielded a .291-35-130 offensive from John Lowenstein and Gary Roenicke, who shared that spot, and the late-season acquisition of veteran outfielder Tito Landrum added a .310 effort. As usual, Oriole pitching was strong; the staff's 3.63 ERA ranked second in the league. Rookies Mike Boddicker (16-8, 2.77 ERA) and Storm Davis (13-7, 3.59) complemented veterans Mike Flanagan (12-4, 3.30) and Scott

Mike Schmidt coming home for the Phillies in the 1983 National League playoffs against the Dodgers. The Phils took the pennant but lost the Series to the Orioles. (Courtesy The Phillies)

McGregor (18-7, 3.18). These starters were backed by reliefer Tippy Martinez, who won 9 and saved 21.

In the playoff for the league championship, the Orioles lost the opener to the White Sox but snapped back to win three straight by decisive 6-1, 11-1, and 3-0 scores. In the clincher Davis and Martinez combined on a 3-0 shutout capped by Landrum's tenth-inning homer. By landing a sixth American League flag in eighteen years, Baltimore carried the league's standard into the World Series.

The same fate that befell 1982 American League division champs was visited upon the erstwhile champion Braves and Cardinals of the National League. But the dethroning process was so fiercely contested that neither division race was settled until the final week.

In the West the Braves and Dodgers looked like the class of the league; moving into September, these rivals had been crushing Eastern foes and were dueling for division honors. When the Braves built a 6½-game lead in mid-August, they seemed likely to repeat as division champs, but a spate of injuries struck down key players. The cruelest of these came when third baseman Bob Horner broke his wrist; on top of this, three days later Horner's replacement went down with a sprained ankle. With slugger Horner (.303-20-68) lost for the season, homeric Dale Murphy's production tailed off as enemy hurlers "pitched around" him. Through it all, the Braves led in batting, and Murphy (.302-36-121) won a second straight MVP crown. The injury-depleted offense could not atone for weak pitching, however. To improve the pitching, the Braves bid high for the services of Ranger pitcher Rick Honeycutt, but the American League ace signed with the Dodgers. Getting Honeycutt was a defensive move for the Dodgers, whose pitching staff of Bob Welch, Fernando Valenzuela, Alejandro Pena, Burt Hooton, and relievers Steve Howe and Tom Niedenfuer was the league's best. In the end, Dodger pitching made the difference, as the staff's 3.10 ERA led the league. Offensively the Dodgers batted only .250, with no regular topping .300. Third baseman Pedro Guerrero (.298-32-103) and outfielder Mike Marshall (.284-17-65) led the attack, which sorely missed dependable hitters Steve Garvey and Ron Cey, now in alien uniforms. Garvey's replacement, the much-touted Greg Brock, batted only .224 but poled 20 homers. In the final weeks of the campaign, the Dodgers overtook Atlanta and won by three games.

In the East, meanwhile, a wide-open race had five teams contending into September. The defending world champion Cards batted .270, but woebegone pitching consigned them to fourth place, 11 games behind the Pirates, Expos, and Phils. For most of the campaign these perennial rivals fought to a standstill; at the halfway mark the Phils were in first place, despite being one game above .500. At that point the Phillies fired manager Pat Corrales and brought in general manager Paul Owens as his replacement. "Pope" Owens platooned his aging "Wheez Kids"; the roster now included four over-forty veterans (Pete Rose, Tony Perez, Joe Morgan, and Ron Reed). The Phillies managed only a .249 batting average with 125 homers, and only part-time outfielders Greg Gross and Joe Lefebvre topped .300. Slugger Mike Schmidt's 40 homers and 109 RBIs supplied most of the punch. Not until September, when Joe Morgan and Gary Matthews

Sparky Anderson, who managed the Tigers in their 1984 Series victory. Almost a decade earlier, in 1975 and 1976, he led the Reds to consecutive world championships. (Courtesy Detroit Tigers)

Alan Trammell, Tiger shortstop, named Most Valuable Player in the 1984 World Series, during his eighth season in the majors. (Courtesy Detroit Tigers)

broke out of slumps and when minor leaguer Len Matuszek came up to hit .275-4-16, did the Phils catch fire. The Phillies won 11 straight games and 21 of their last 25 to beat the runner-up Pirates by six games. Superior pitching made the difference; the Phils' 3.34 ERA ranked second to the Dodgers. Leading the staff was veteran John Denny, acquired from Cleveland in the off-season. Denny's 19-6, 2.37 won him the Cy Young Award; veteran Steve Carlton went 15-16 but topped the 300 mark in lifetime wins. Reliefer Al Holland's 25 saves won him the league's Fireman of the Year Award.

In the championship playoff, the Phillies faced their Dodger tormentors, who had beaten them eleven times during the season. However, the Dodgers were crippled by the loss of reliefer Steve Howe, suspended for drug abuse, and by an injury to starter Bob Welch. Playing in Los Angeles, the Phils won the opener 1-0 on stout pitching by Carlton and Holland and on a Schmidt homer. Then, following a 4-1 loss, the Phillies swept the next two games by identical 7-2 scores.

The victory sent the Phils against the Orioles in the 80th World Series. When the Phils won the opener in Baltimore 2-1 on Denny's pitching and homers by Maddox and Morgan, the American League seemed headed for its fifth straight Series loss. However, Mike Boddicker's three-hit pitching keyed a 4-1 victory to square matters. Then, when action shifted to Philadelphia, the Orioles swept the Phils by scores of 3-2, 5-4, and 5-0 to win the Series and restore some honor to the American League cause.

Now emerged the season of 1984, a year made ominous by the chimerical imagery of George Orwell. But if the nation was generally spared the fruits of the late novelist's bleak totalitarian forecast, some baseball teams might have blamed Orwell for their circumstances. Most prominent among the jinxed were the four division winners of 1983, all summarily dethroned by outsiders.

In the National League East, the defending champion Phils shed such aging stars as Rose, Morgan, and Matthews in favor of younger lights like Len Matuszek, Juan Samuel, and Von Hayes. But the Phillies' general manager blundered when he sent Matthews and Bob Dernier to the Cubs. The pair teamed with another ex-Phil, Keith Moreland, to form the Cubs' starting outfield. Matthews and Moreland combined for 30 homers and 162 RBIs, while Dernier stole 45 bases; Matthews also delivered 19 game-winning hits. However, it was another ex-Phil, second baseman Ryne Sandberg, who towered over everybody; brilliant fielding and hitting (.314-19-84 and 32 steals) won Sandberg league MVP honors. With Sandberg in the infield were Dodger castoff Ron Cey and the young first baseman Leon ("Bull") Durham. Cey's 25 homers and 97 RBIs and Durham's .279 batting, with 23 homers and 96 RBIs, powered the team. For good measure, manager Jim Frey got additional power from young catcher Jody Davis's 19 homers and 94 RBIs.

Shrewd trades by Cubs general manager Dallas Green, a former Phils manager and scouting director, turned the Chicagoans into offensive terrors and shored up a shaky pitching staff. An earlier deal by Green had landed the Phillies' Sandberg and Larry Bowa. Then, just as the 1984 campaign was under way, Green acquired pitchers Dennis Eckersley, George Frazier, and Rick Sutcliffe. All were needed, but Sutcliffe was the decisive acquisition. Pried from Cleveland, the towering bearded left-hander won 16 games and lost only once, a performance that won him the Cy Young Award. Sutcliffe, Steve Trout (13-7), and reliefer Lee Smith (33 saves) sparkled amidst a pitching staff that ranked tenth in the league. Manager Frey, who once piloted the Royals to an American League title, knit the Cubs into a contender. In late July the Cubs trailed the surprising Mets by 4½ games, but then the Cubs beat the Mets seven of eight times to take the lead. Once atop the East, they held the heights, winning by 6½ games over the Mets. The Mets were powered by Keith Hernandez, Hubie Brooks, and George Foster, but the talk of the league was their nineteen-year-old pitching phenom, Dwight Gooden, who won 17 and fanned 276. As for the Phils, they lost their last nine games and finished fourth. As scapegoats, manager Paul Owens was relieved, and batting coach Deron Johnson was fired even though his hitters led the league in batting. But such scapegoating failed to erase the stigma of the Phillies' ludicrous trades, which strengthened rivals and helped to crown the Cubs' Dallas Green as Executive of the Year.

For Phillies executives, small comfort came from watching the erstwhile champion Dodgers fall just as hard in the National League West. In the early going, pitching kept the Dodgers in contention, but weak hitting and a chronic third-base problem dropped them to fourth. Thus, Dodger fans also grumbled over front-office decisions that had earlier freed star infielders Cey and Steve Garvey to star with rival clubs;

Pete Rose making his 4,192nd hit on September 11, 1985, to break Ty Cobb's career record. (Courtesy Cincinnati Reds)

nevertheless, Dodger fans still showed up more than three-million strong. The Dodger collapse raised Atlanta's hopes, but once again these were dashed by slugger Bob Horner's injury jinx. Although Dale Murphy tied Mike Schmidt for league homer honors, the Braves' .247 batting dropped them to second. For this result, manager Joe Torre was fired.

The plight of the Dodgers and Braves opened the way for the San Diego Padres to scale the heights for the first time in their sixteen-year history. The Padres' 92-70 record was the only winning record by a Western team, and it was enough to win by 12 games. Death robbed owner Ray Kroc of the earthly delight of watching his team surge under manager Dick Williams. Prior to 1984 Williams's two seasons at San Diego had produced identical 81-81 records, but now his well-balanced team ranked fifth in pitching and hitting. One of Kroc's last acts was to acquire ex-Yankee reliever "Goose" Gossage, and it paid off with 25 saves. Gossage's work complemented that of starters Eric Show (15-9), Mark Thurmond (14-8), and Ed Whitsun (14-8). Offensively the Padres were paced by young outfielders Tony Gwynn and Kevin McReynolds; Gwynn's .351 batting led the league, and McReynolds weighed in with .278 batting, 20 homers, and 75 RBIs. Additional strength came from infielders, whose defensive work also sparkled. First baseman Steve Garvey batted .284 with 86 RBIs; second baseman Alan Wiggins stole 69 bases; shortstop Gary Templeton batted .257; third baseman Graig Nettles, the forty-year-old former Yankee star, contributed 20 homers and 65 RBIs. As his Padres rolled along, manager Williams did his part to ward off complacency. For fomenting a notorious beanball fracas in Atlanta, Williams was slapped with a $10,000 fine and a ten-day suspension. Yet nothing derailed the Padres nor stayed the enthusiasm of their supporters as attendance topped two million.

Williams's aggressive leadership was sorely tried during the playoff series for the league championship. As the series opened in Chicago, the Cubs took the opener 13-0 and followed with a 4-2 victory. With the Padres on the brink of extinction, they got a lift from a ruling by lame-duck commissioner Kuhn. If the Cubs won, Kuhn ruled, the first two World Series games must be played at night in the American League city because Wrigley Field had no lights. Daytime games on weekdays, according to the commissioner, would lose too much revenue, especially from TV. Kuhn's decision evoked protests from purists, while the battling Padres used it to gain a psychological advantage. When action shifted to San Diego, the Padres swept the next three games to claim the title. Never before in the history of the National League playoffs had a team rebounded in such fashion. What's more, Padre manager Williams now had the opportunity of becoming the first manager to win a World Series title in both major leagues.

Of course, Williams's Padres had to beat the American League contender. This was no easy prospect, as the American League East was baseball's strongest circuit. There in the spring the world champion Orioles were picked to beat off the challenging Blue Jays, Yankees, and Red Sox. Indeed, the Blue Jays finished second, and the Yankees, after a horrendous first half, rallied strongly to finish third ahead of the Red

Nolan Ryan, who continued to break strikeout records after joining the Astros from the Angels in 1980. (Courtesy Houston Astros)

Sox. This part of the script followed forecasts, but that the Orioles should wind up behind the Red Sox discredited soothsayers. To the surprise of many, the Detroit Tigers made a shambles of the Eastern race. Breaking away swiftly, the Detroiters led the pack from day one and never looked back; at one point their record stood at 35-5. Although Toronto once closed to within 3½ games, the inept Blue Jay bullpen failed to keep pace, losing 28 games. During the second half of the race, the Yankees outpaced the Tigers with a 51-29 gait, paced by the league-leading batting of young Don Mattingly (.343-23-110) and Dave Winfield (.340-19-100), but Detroit's margin was too great; at the end the Blue Jays trailed by 15 games and the Yankees by 17.

Detroit's 104 victories swelled the pride of the team's new owner, pizza king Tom Monaghan. In winning, the Tigers boasted the league's best pitching, with an ERA of 3.49. But effective starters Dan Petry (18-8), Milt Wilcox (17-8), and Jack Morris (19-11) were overshadowed by relievers Aurelio Lopez (10-1 with 14 saves) and Willie Hernandez. A timely acquisition from the Phillies, Hernandez became a legendary fireman. In 80 appearances the twenty-nine-year-old lefty won 9 and saved 32; in save situations Hernandez succeeded in 32 of 33 and posted a 1.94 ERA. For his heroics, Hernandez won both the Cy Young and Most Valuable Player awards. Offensively the Tigers batted .271, and their 187 homers led the league. Catcher Lance Parrish led the club in homers (33) and RBIs (98); center fielder Kirk Gibson batted .287, with 27 homers and 91 RBIs, and stole 29 bases; outfielder Chet Lemon weighed in with .287-20-76. Additional support came from infielders Alan Trammell (.314-14-69) and Lou Whitaker (.289-13-56). Backed by these stalwarts, the team's loquacious manager, Sparky Anderson, also had a shot at becoming the first manager to win World Series titles in both major leagues.

To accomplish that feat, Anderson first had to strike down the Western champs. For most of the season in that weakest of major league circuits, the honors were up for grabs. A vacuum opened early when the defending champion White Sox slumped to last place in league batting and finished in fifth place. Among the clubs rushing to the fore, the most surprising was Minnesota. Now under new ownership, the Twins led the division going into September. First baseman Kent Hrbek led the offensive with 27 homers and 107 RBIs, but in the September stretch five losses to Chicago and two to Cleveland, one of which saw the Indians rally from a 10-0 deficit, dropped the young Twins to a second-place tie with the California Angels; at the close, both contenders finished at 81-81, three games behind the Kansas City Royals.

The Royals' 84-78 record was the worst winning mark of any divisional champion since 1973 (except for the strikebound 1981 season). Yet it was a gritty triumph over formidable obstacles. Going into the race, team morale was battered by the loss of stars due to drug convictions, injuries, and retirement. Star outfielder Willie Wilson missed the

George Brett, Royal second baseman, who helped his team to a 1984 world championship with his .335 hitting. Brett batted .390 during the Royals' 1980 pennant-winning season. (Courtesy Kansas City Royals)

first 32 games because of a drug conviction; an operation sidelined star infielder George Brett for the first 33 games; veteran pitcher Paul Splittorff retired. Moreover, the bad situation worsened when midseason injuries ravaged the infield. Forced to go with younger players, including half a dozen rookie pitchers, manager Dick Howser saw his team lag eight games back at the halfway mark. Fortunately for the Royals, neither the Twins nor the Angels could pull away. In rallying his forces, Howser got 17 wins from young pitcher Bud Black and 44 saves from veteran reliefer Dan Quisenberry. Offensively the Royals batted .268: Wilson shook off the stigma of his conviction with .301 batting; DH Hal McRae batted .303; Brett batted .284; and first baseman Steve Balboni hit 28 homers. Among the newcomers who met the test, young outfielders Darryl Motley (.284) and Pat Sheridan (.283) became starters. Along with veteran Jorge Orta (.298), acquired from Toronto, manager Howser developed a formidable outfield. In the September stretch drive the Royals crushed the Angels and overtook the slumping Twins to win by 3½ games. But, in the playoff series, the Tigers swept the Royals.

The opening of the 1984 World Series sent the powerful Tigers to San Diego to meet the brown-and-yellow-clad Padres. The favored Tigers won the opener 3-2, but the next night the Padres rallied to even matters. It was the high-water mark for the Padres. When action shifted to Detroit, the Tigers swept the next three games by scores of 5-2, 4-2, and 8-4. In defrocking the Padres, Tiger hitters roughed up Williams's starting pitchers in shocking fashion; in the five games, Padre starters lasted a total of 10⅓ innings and were pummeled for 25 hits, 5 homers, and 17 runs. As a result, the Padres were behind in every game, and only stout middle-relief pitching kept the games close. Moreover, the Padres' offensive was weakened by the absence of

Yankee outfielder Rickey Henderson eyes a pitch from Red Sox ace Roger Clemens in this May 17, 1986, game played at Yankee Stadium. The Red Sox won the game handily and went on to win the American League's Eastern Division by 5-1/2 games over the runner-up Yankees. (N.Y. Daily News Photo)

McReynolds, who was sidelined by an injury. Tiger heroes included pitcher Jack Morris, winner of two games; Alan Trammell, whose .450 batting won him the Series MVP award; and Kirk Gibson, who twice homered in the final game. For Detroit manager Sparky Anderson, his glory was in becoming the first manager to have won world championship honors in both major leagues.

Piled atop the Orioles' 1983 victory, Detroit's victory boosted American League stock. The victory was soured somewhat, however, by rioting Detroit fans; their excesses resulted in one death, eighty injuries, forty incarcerations, and an estimated $100,000 in property damages. The Detroit riot was the latest of a string of post–World Series outbursts dating back at least fifteen seasons. In accounting for these destructive rituals, some social scientists blamed booze and drugs as precipitating factors; it was also noted that fans from victorious cities were more likely to indulge in riots than were the defeated. Perhaps, as one observer mused, the nation was entering an era of over-reaction to championship sporting events. But, short of increasing police forces or searching fans at the turnstiles for concealed booze, little in the way of effective new remedies was vouchsafed.

Shortstop Ozzie Smith, one of the mainstays of the 1985 pennant-winning Cardinals. Smith won a sixth straight Golden Glove Award in 1985. (Courtesy St. Louis Cardinals)

It would be tasteless to suggest that riotous climaxes gave evidence of the persisting vitality of major league baseball. Other less volatile indicators said as much, demonstrating that the game was riding a wave of popular success. Although seasonal attendance for 1984 fell some 800,000 below the record attendance of 1983, television ratings were good, and the current network television contract assured each club of $4 million before the first pitch of a season was tossed. Moreover, club owners of 1984 could gloat over the slumping popularity of the rival pro football game. The United States Football League, whose schedule directly competed with baseball's early-season games, was losing money. And the National Football League, whose measured popularity in television ratings had long exceeded baseball's, was losing ground. After peaking in 1981–82, the NFL's attendance and television ratings slumped, prompting television networks to seek rebates under the terms of their current $2.1 billion, five-year contract. For the reversal of pro football fortunes, some observers blamed overexposure on television, escalating player salaries, and lawsuits engendered by three recent franchise shifts.

But the fact that baseball faced similar troubles barred owners from chortling too much at their rival's discomfiture. Like the NFL, baseball faced a problem of too much television. In addition to national and local games, interloping transmissions by superstations showing games played by the Braves, Yankees, Mets, and Cubs had angry owners demanding remedial action against these invasions. Furthermore, baseball also faced a problem of restless franchises anxious to quit familiar haunts for richer pastures elsewhere. Among the discontented were Pittsburgh, Cleveland, San Francisco, and Seattle. Meanwhile, a committee of owners pondered the matter of expanding the major leagues to accommodate promising new sites. In November, this effort was agi-

BASEBALL'S PROSPECTS IN 1984

Outfielder Willie McGee topped the National League in batting in 1985 and won its Most Valuable Player Award as he helped to lead the Cardinals to the pennant that year. (Courtesy St. Louis Cardinals)

Darrell Evans, Giant and Tiger third baseman. In 1985, at the age of thirty-eight, Evans became the oldest player ever to lead the American League in homers, with forty for the season. (Courtesy San Francisco Giants)

tated by the vague threat from a rival major league, dubbed the North American Baseball League; its spokesman talked of planting teams in New York, Brooklyn, New Jersey, Washington, Indianapolis, Denver, Tampa Bay, New Orleans, and Mexico City. However, the league proved to be a deflatable trial balloon; any resemblance between this feint and that by the formidable Continental League of the late 1950s beggared comparison.

On the labor front, major league owners faced the pressing problem of agreeing to another costly contract. With the fifth Basic Agreement due to expire on the last day of 1984, negotiations for a new pact with Players Association representatives were nowhere near a settlement. At issue was the players' demand for a hefty share of the current $1.1 billion, six-year network television package, which the players wanted applied to their lucrative pension benefits. The players also sought to shore up the annual salary arbitration procedure, while the owners, correctly perceiving arbitration awards as a key to spiraling salaries, sought to restrict its use. A less volatile issue was the proposal to replace the annual re-entry draft with a policy allowing any team to negotiate with any qualified free agent. And the same hot issue that had triggered the 1981 strike, that of compensating clubs for players lost in annual free-agent auctions, showed signs of surfacing anew in the negotiations for the new Basic Agreement. Of course, the chief bone of contention between players and owners was soaring player salaries. In 1984 some twenty players drew salaries of a million dollars a year or more; at $1,989,875 Mike Schmidt of the Phillies was the reigning plutocrat of the moment. What's more, the average player salary of 1984 approached $330,000, while that of the highest-paid manager, Tom Lasorda, was $333,000.

AN OLYMPIAN COMMISSIONER?

Baseball's mounting problems, especially the possibility of another strike like the 1981 crippler, underscored the need for enlightened leadership. Club owners continued to dissipate their strength, however, by clinging to cherished traditions of independence. These traditions preserved an image of two independent and competing major leagues. Moreover, within each league each owner tended to rule each franchise as an independent fief. By contrast, National Football League owners, despite some mavericks in their ranks, presented an enviable united front under their policy of subordinating local interests to those of the league. In baseball, long-standing disunity between leagues and among owners went far to explain the impotence of baseball's commissioner. In September 1984 the lame-duck incumbent, Bowie Kuhn, finally quit his post. His sixteen years of service were celebrated with an elaborate but shammy farewell banquet attended by eight hundred guests. Acquiescent as always, Kuhn bade farewell, averring that he left with no real regrets and that baseball was one of the real jewels of American history.

The new commissioner, Peter V. Ueberroth, needed no introduction. Since March 1984, when he accepted the post, a combination of luck and adroitness had thrust him into the national limelight as the successful promoter of the attenuated 1984 summer Olympic games in

Los Angeles. As recently as 1979, this travel-agency entrepreneur was an anonymous American millionaire. Ueberroth's rise began when he accepted the post of president of the Los Angeles Olympic Organizing Committee. Promoting the 1984 summer games was no easy task; indeed, the last summer Olympics staged in the Western world, the 1976 Montreal games, had lost over a billion dollars. But Ueberroth met the challenge by organizing an army of assistants and by launching successful promotional campaigns. In 1982 he negotiated a $225 million television contract (contingent upon favorable ratings) and pried an additional $130 million from corporate sponsors. These widely publicized coups brought him to the attention of the baseball owners' search committee, and by early 1984 it was announced that the modishly handsome, forty-seven-year-old Ueberroth would succeed Kuhn as baseball's latest symbolic king.

At the time of the March announcement, Ueberroth was committed to finishing his task as promoter of the 1984 Olympiad. But in May word came that the Soviet Union and its Warsaw Pact allies would boycott the Los Angeles games. This shocking announcement clouded the future of the games and Ueberroth's soaring reputation as the able promoter. Indeed, the news came on the day that Ueberroth's latest promotional ploy, an eighty-two-day cross-country torchlight relay, was to begin. The plan required each torchbearer to pay $3,000 for the privilege of carrying the Olympic flame a single kilometer, and was intended to garner cash and glory for the upcoming games. The Soviet withdrawal threatened to make a mockery of the effort, but a wave of anti-Soviet sentiment ensued. The torchlight relay became a sustained media event and stimulated ticket sales. Once the games began the same enthusiasm continued, boosting television ratings as viewers delighted in the raft of medals that American athletes piled up against competition weakened by the absence of athletes from boycotting countries. In the aftermath of this successful coup, Ueberroth basked in the glory of a $155 million surplus. Moreover, public adulation made a national hero of Ueberroth, who by year's end was named "Man of the Year" by *Time* magazine and *The Sporting News*, which awarded him its $10,000 Waterford Trophy.

Ueberroth's popularity was still peaking when he assumed the post of baseball commissioner in October. Such was the aura surrounding the new incumbent that some observers speculated that the baseball post must surely be a stepping stone for bigger things for Ueberroth; others wondered if the charismatic Ueberroth would be too glamorous for the owners to abide. Indeed, Ueberroth's avowed intention to be a strong and independent commissioner was on record; earlier he had told reporters that, although he was no baseball man, he planned to bring his skills as a businessman and problem-solver to baseball. Ueberroth's skills were tested early by an embarrassing umpires' strike that disrupted the divisional playoffs. Acting as arbitrator, Ueberroth granted the umpires a $1.4 million package over three years, which raised the pay of umpires working postseasonal games and also gave an additional $720,000 to be shared by all umpires. In announcing his decision, Ueberroth lavishly acknowledged the importance of baseball's sixty umpires. For their part, the umpires responded by becoming stalwart Ue-

Freddie Lynn, Oriole outfielder, who was in the top dozen of American League hitters at the middle of the 1986 season. In 1975, in his first full season with the Red Sox, Lynn batted .331 and became the first player ever to win both Rookie-of-the-Year and MVP honors. (Author's Collection)

berroth supporters; one went so far as to name the lecture room at his training school "Ueberroth Hall."

Although Ueberroth's decision in the umpire strike did not sit well with the league presidents, who intimated he had usurped their powers, the new commissioner's honeymoon with his employers was at its height when he addressed the owners at the winter meetings in December. Speaking boldly, Ueberroth challenged the owners to solve baseball's knotty problems with him but warned them that he would not always share their views, in particular their opinions of the Players Association. Such candor, while generally praised, raised eyebrows and led to further speculation about the commissioner's ambitions. Indeed, when *Time* later named Ueberroth its "Man of the Year," the article mentioned a minor boomlet touting Ueberroth as a Republican presidential candidate. Such speculation was later scaled down to rumors about the possibility of Ueberroth's running for the U.S. Senate in 1986 against the California incumbent Alan Cranston. This was heady stuff, but Ueberroth's prospects depended upon his present ability to burnish his image by functioning as an activist baseball commissioner. Given the weakness of his largely ceremonial position, an activist image would have been hard to project in any case, and when buffeted by the problems of baseball's feverish 1985 season, Ueberroth at times seemed to be out of his element.

1985—A COMET OF A SEASON

Along with the more mundane reasons served up to explain the unprecedented events of the 1985 season, one might add the disruptive influences attributed by the superstitious to events like the return of Halley's comet. Indeed, 1985 was a tumultuous year in baseball, a year marked by peaks of glory and sloughs of despond.

Among the problems that darkened the 1985 season, none loomed more ominously than the threat of another players' strike. What made another strike appear likely was the continuing salary spiral that swelled the number of million-dollar-a-year players to thirty-six (including a dozen men above $1.6 million) and raised the average salary to $363,000. To cap the salary gusher, the owners' negotiating committee, headed by Lee MacPhail, zeroed in on the salary arbitration procedure, insisting that awards be limited to 100 percent of a player's former salary; moreover, the owners demanded that a player wait three years before qualifying for arbitration. But the Major League Players Association negotiators, headed by director Don Fehr and emeritus director Marvin Miller, held out for the present two-year qualification for arbitration and also demanded that a third of the national television and radio revenue, or $60 million a year, be added to the players' pension fund. With battle lines drawn over these and lesser issues, the prospect of a major strike darkened the 1985 season. To break the impasse, Commissioner Ueberroth persuaded the owners to open their books to back their oft-repeated claims of mounting losses. This tactic failed to budge either side, however, since both hired accountants who fell to challenging each other's figures. Thus, the owners' experts claimed losses of $43 million (later scaled back to $27 million) for 1984, while

Opposite:
Rising National League stars of the 'Eighties: Ryne Sandberg, second baseman for the Cubs (*top*); Dale Murphy, center fielder for the Braves. (Courtesy Chicago Cubs, Atlanta Braves)

the players' experts claimed the owners had actually profited by $9 million.

To make sense of these sharply divergent claims and to come up with a realistic assessment of the costs of baseball operations, the owners engaged George Sorter, professor of accounting, taxation, and business law at the New York University School of Business. In Sorter's judgment each side's claim was legitimate, but each side was describing something different. The owners' estimate included non-operating costs, such as interest expenses and depreciation of the value of a team's players. For their part, the players' figure of a $9 million profit for the owners was based on the "excess of current cash receipts over current cash disbursements." In preference to both claims, Sorter's research came up with a $27 million total loss figure for the twenty-six major league teams during 1984. Deferred player salary compensation—surely an operating cost—was a major factor contributing to the loss. This grim picture of an average annual loss of a million dollars per team suggested that the baseball industry as a whole was a losing venture. This was hardly news, since financial experts had been saying as much for decades. Nor was there news in Sorter's suggestion that "psychic returns" compensated owners for losses. But the critical question Sorter vouchsafed for baseball's future was a timely one: How long could psychic returns continue to "compensate for large and growing financial losses"?

As the two sides debated, fans reacted with a plague-on-both-houses attitude, though a *New York Times* poll of fans showed greater hostility towards the "greedy" players' cause. With no settlement in sight and a strike deadline set for August 6, Ueberroth tried to play the role of activist peacemaker. In June, Ueberroth managed to alienate both sides when he told some player representatives that the owner proposal to cap salaries was ridiculous and that owner reports of losses were exaggerated. Not surprisingly, the owners felt betrayed, while the players reacted with suspicion. On the eve of the strike, Ueberroth tried to head off a walkout by submitting a last-ditch proposal that neither side accepted and that Miller called amateurish. With no settlement in sight, the strike began on August 6, but two days later it ended. Obviously, neither side wanted a repeat of the crippling 1981 walkout. Hence, when the strike began, so did serious negotiations that quickly produced a compromise settlement. The new Basic Agreement extended through the 1989 season and was a bundle of compromises. The major issues were settled by the owners' agreeing to drop their salary-cap proposal, while the players agreed to the three-year waiting period (beginning in 1987) before a player could take a salary dispute to arbitration. The pension dispute was resolved by the owners' agreeing to contribute $196 million over six years to the players' pension fund. Such monies were to come from national radio and television revenue. The amount was significantly less than the one-third sought by the players, but it swelled the annual pension for a ten-year player to $91,000; under the old plan a twenty-year veteran received $57,000 a year. Since previously retired players, and of course minor leaguers, were excluded from the owners' latest largesse, this concession heaped new charges of greed on current players.

Those were the major issues resolved by the new agreement. Ironically, the compensation issue, which had provoked the great 1981 strike, was treated now as a minor issue. Under the new agreement, both the compensation plan and the re-entry draft were dropped. Henceforth, any team was free to negotiate with any qualified free agent, and clubs losing a quality free agent received no quality player in return. Among other minor issues, the minimum salary was raised to $60,000; the new seven-game playoff format for the League Championship Series (already in place for 1985) was formalized; and the National League was given a green light to expand by adding two new clubs. The speedy forging of a new labor contract spared baseball the agony of a protracted strike; only two days of scheduled play were lost, and the twenty-five games were easily rescheduled. Although credit for concluding the agreement was given by informed observers to negotiators MacPhail and Fehr, Ueberroth's dramatic announcement of the settlement won him unearned kudos. While the commissioner disclaimed any role in the negotiations, once again he wore the mantle of miracle worker.

Yet, hardly was the strike settled when another problem exploded over the baseball scene. As menacing as any strike, the rumbling scandal of players involved with illegal drugs threatened the game's image. To be sure, this problem had been brewing for several years and focused mainly on cocaine. In 1985 an estimated 20 million Americans illegally bought this euphoria-inducing but addictive and potentially deadly substance. An expensive habit, cocaine had become the drug of choice among many high-income Americans, including prominent entertainers and athletes. To meet demand for this product, by 1985 an estimated seventy tons were clandestinely produced and smuggled into an underground market, where profits from its distribution and sale ran into billions. Worse still, efforts by law enforcement agencies to stem the traffic or to punish dealers and users were woefully inadequate. Because of the low level of public outrage against cocaine consumption, users ran little risk of heavy punishment. Thus, America of the 1980s faced a national epidemic of cocaine abuse aggravated by widespread flouting of prohibitive laws.

That baseball players numbered among cocaine users was not news. In 1980 Ken Moffett of the Players Association estimated that 40 percent of the major league players were users, and in 1983 three Kansas City Royals were briefly jailed as convicted users. At that time Commissioner Kuhn suspended the three along with a few others, but the suspensions were either modified or overturned by arbitrators on appeal. When more cases of player abuse surfaced in 1984, representatives of the owners reached an agreement with the Players Association calling for the punishment of distributors but not of repentant users; the latter might escape punishment by agreeing to undergo rehabilitative treatment. Apparently, the owners were reluctant to lose the services of valued players. Moreover, when a club sought to get rid of a suspected user, other clubs willingly snapped him up, especially if he was a good player.

In 1985 Commissioner Ueberroth determined to take a stand on this issue. In May he ordered minor leaguers and non-unionized baseball employees to submit to urine-analysis tests for evidence of abuse. For this action Ueberroth was accused by some of creating a major issue of a problem that was already receding and of violating the civil rights of those targeted. The same critics accused Ueberroth of singling out cocaine while ignoring the broader problem of improper use of drugs, including cortisone, painkillers, amphetamines, and alcohol. Cynical observers also accused Ueberroth of grandstanding; by posing as an activist reformer out to cleanse the national game, they charged, he was really making future political capital. But, in August, revelations coming out of two federal court trials in Pittsburgh persuaded Ueberroth to step up his campaign. At the trials, six active major league players and one ex-player were subpoenaed as prosecution witnesses against two accused drug traffickers. Although granted immunity from prosecution, the player-witnesses were confessed users and customers of the accused. Placed on the stand, all seven admitted to having used cocaine, and in the course of testimony they named eleven other active players as users. The much-publicized trials resulted in convictions of the traffickers, while the player-witnesses were deservedly humiliated. Upon rejoining their teams, however, the players received sympathetic applause from many fans.

Press reaction was mixed; some writers favored forgiving the players, but others pronounced the episode to be the game's biggest scandal since the Black Sox revelation and urged suspensions. Ueberroth sided with the hard-liners. In a major speech loaded with jeremiads about the game's disgrace, he warned that baseball was on trial in the eyes of the public. In his peroration he declared that a corrective policy must be in place before the season ended. On September 24, he followed up his speech by sending letters to all major league players requesting that each man voluntarily submit to drug testing. What followed was a basic lesson in politics for the commissioner. When reporters sought factual proof for his contention that cocaine abuse among players was on the increase, or that fans were souring on the game, or that players truly were role models for American youth, Ueberroth could cite only personal impressions. Worse, his assertive stance placed the commissioner in direct conflict with the Players Association. Calling the commissioner's appeal a blatant attempt to make political capital, the Association's Fehr reminded the commissioner of two political realities—that pressure on players to take tests could be construed as violating their civil rights, and that any policy on the problem must be negotiated with the union. For its part, the Association pledged to help toward forging a policy that could include drug testing. But Ueberroth's deadline passed with no policy in place.

There were other instances when Ueberroth's assertive activism came a cropper. Over the winter of 1984 he announced his intention to resolve the long-standing designated-hitter controversy by polling fans. The Players Association reminded him, however, that this matter was a subject for labor negotiations and that the Association would defend the rights of designated hitters, a class of specialists of thirteen years' standing. Moreover, a recent decline in National League hitting seemingly had the senior circuit leaning towards adopting the American League rule. In March 1985, Ueberroth had his fingers rapped by a Cook County, Illinois, circuit judge, who ruled in favor of neighbor-

Three stars of the American League East in the mid-1980s: (*opposite, top*) Cal Ripken, Jr., Oriole shortstop; (*opposite, bottom*) Don Mattingly, Yankee first baseman; (*above*) Wade Boggs, Red Sox third baseman. Boggs led his league in hitting at midseason 1986, while Mattingly was number three. (Courtesy Baltimore Orioles, New York Yankees, Boston Red Sox)

hood residents seeking to block the installation of lights at Wrigley Field. To buttress the Chicago Cubs' contention that the lights were necessary, Ueberroth wrote a supporting letter in which he threatened to schedule any postseason games involving the Cubs at another park. Judge Richard Curry, in ruling for the residents opposed to Wrigley Field lighting, caustically commented that "the Cubs and the Commissioner of Baseball have lost their grasp on reality and perspective on values." By the end of Ueberroth's rookie year as commissioner, there was evidence that his charm did not give him seven-league boots. He was learning the bitter lesson that his baseball post was more a sticky morass than a stepping stone to high political office.

RECORDS BY THE SHEAVES

Wally Joyner, rookie first baseman for the California Angels, whose .300 hitting helped his team to get ahead of the Texas Rangers at midseason 1986. (Courtesy California Angels)

Fortunately for major league baseball, the comet year of 1985 furnished dazzling high points to compensate for its embarrassments. Fittingly, most of these stirring moments occurred on the playing fields, where splendid performances by individuals combined with close races to attract a record 48.8 million to the ballparks.

The eve of the 1985 season featured a titillating April Fools' Day hoax that may have been an omen telling of the uniqueness of the coming season. Concocted by writer George Plimpton, the article appeared in *Sports Illustrated* and told readers of the awesome feats of a young pitching "phenom" named Sidd Finch in the camp of the New York Mets. A strange, bizarrely intellectual character, Finch had never played baseball, but by dint of rigorous mental and physical discipline acquired while studying in Tibet, he had learned to throw a baseball 165 miles per hour with ease and accuracy! However, Finch was hard put to decide whether to pitch professionally, to become a professional French-horn player, or to return to the lamasery for further training! Plimpton's tongue-in-cheek yarn delighted many and fooled some, including a Florida newspaper editor who dispatched a reporter to cover the phenom.

As it turned out, baseball's 1985 season needed no fictional characters because real players rewrote enough records to satisfy the hungriest of figure filberts. Among the epochal achievements, none surpassed the interest stirred by Pete Rose's closely monitored pursuit of Ty Cobb's all-time hit record. When the season began, Rose needed 95 hits to break Cobb's record of 4,191. On September 11, the forty-four-year-old playing manager of the Cincinnati Reds struck the record-breaker off pitcher Eric Show of the Padres. A crowd of 47,000 fans in Cincinnati saw the historic hit, and millions of television viewers saw it via network-intercepted relays. Ironically, the record was set on the fifty-seventh anniversary of the last game Cobb played. To disparagers who belittled Rose's achievement (Rose batted 2,300 more times than did Cobb), Rose allowed, "I'm not the greatest hitter ever, I just got the most hits." And when President Reagan phoned his congratulations, Rose brashly chided, "You missed a good ball game tonight." By season's end Rose extended his record to 4,204 hits.

While Rose's feat was the peak, other towering achievements dotted the 1985 landscape. Five weeks before Rose's triumph, two veterans joined the company of immortals on the same day. On Sunday, August 4, at Anaheim, Rod Carew struck his 3,000th hit, against his former Minnesota team. The thirty-nine-year-old Carew became only the sixteenth member of the 3,000-hit club. Meanwhile, eastward across the land at Yankee Stadium, White Sox pitcher Tom Seaver beat the Yanks to become the seventeenth pitcher to notch 300 victories. On that day the forty-year-old Seaver's lifetime record showed 300 wins, 189 losses, and a 2.81 ERA. Nor was Seaver's the last such effort of 1985. At Toronto, on the last day of the season, Phil Niekro shut out the Blue Jays 8-0 to join the club. The forty-five-year-old Yankee's feat came after four abortive attempts and left him with a lifetime 300-250, 3.23 ERA record. Still another pitching landmark was set in July, when the great strikeout artist Nolan Ryan recorded his 4,000th career strikeout to move into a class by himself. Still possessed of an intimidating fastball, the thirty-eight-year-old Astro hurler fanned eleven Mets at the Astrodome. By the end of the 1985 season, Ryan, who five times had fanned 300 or more batters in a season, extended his Olympian strikeout mark to 4,083. And, to lend a touch of symmetry to the epic feats of 1985, Reggie Jackson of the Angels acted for the sluggers. Jackson's latest flurry of 27 homers raised his lifetime total to 530 and ranked him eighth on the all-time slugging list.

Meanwhile, as fading veterans authored these records, precocious youngsters served notice that the firmament would not lack new stars. Brightest of the young lot was pitcher Dwight Gooden of the Mets. In 1984, as a nineteen-year-old phenom, the rookie led the majors in strikeouts and posted a 17-9, 2.60 ERA record. That debut marked the right-hander among the five youthful prodigies of this century, but after Gooden's majestic 1985 season, he stood alone. Topping all major league pitchers, he posted a 24-4, 1.53 ERA record and struck out 268 batters. Gooden's brilliance overshadowed a trio of up-and-coming young hurlers. Bret Saberhagen of the Royals, only twenty-one, posted a 20-6 record; Tom Browning of the Reds was 20-9; and Orel Hershiser of the Dodgers, 19-3. Equally sparkling was the younger crop of hitters. Don Mattingly of the Yanks burnished his 1984 record by batting .324, with 35 homers and a major-league-leading 145 RBIs. Wade Boggs of the Red Sox topped the majors with a .368 batting mark, while Willie McGee of the Cardinals led National hitters with a .353 effort. Moreover, 1985 saw the debut of Cardinal rookie speedster Vince Coleman; the base-stealing comet stole 110 bases to lead all and to establish a new rookie record.

For artistry-minded fans such feats were enough, but for those who required a spicing of controversy there were other episodes. For instance, when the Yanks floundered early, Steinbrenner sacked manager Yogi Berra and recalled Billy Martin for a fourth stint as Yankee pilot. This time was as mercurial as the others. Martin rallied the Bombers, but late in the season he was involved in a barroom brawl with one of his pitchers. For this he was later fired again. Meanwhile, at Baltimore, the Oriole management lured Earl Weaver out of retirement in the vain hope that his past record of success and his umpire-baiting style would inspire the 1985 Orioles. On the fan front, some complained of longer commercials on network television broadcasts, and others faulted the

Kirby Puckett, center fielder for the Twins, who ranked fourth among American League hitters at the middle of the 1986 season, with a .339 average. (Courtesy Minnesota Twins)

plan to extend the League Championship Series playoffs to a best-of-seven-games format. Both these innovations were negotiated by Ueber-roth, and both added extra revenue; the extension of the playoffs brought in an extra $9 million.

Above all, baseball's comet year produced four sparkling divisional races, three of them undecided until the second-to-last day of the season. However, 1985 was a bleak year for would-be dynasts. Of the four hopeful repeaters from 1984, three were ousted and one, the Royals, posted the poorest championship record as winners of the lightly regarded American League Western Division.

At the start of the 1985 campaign there were reasons aplenty for picking the world champion Tigers to repeat. The year before, manager Anderson's team had romped to victory on the strength of league-leading pitching, hitting, and homer production. But in 1985 Detroit hitting slumped 18 points, and its pitching was bested by three rival clubs. The Tigers contended in the early going, but they faded in midseason and finished in third place, 15 games behind the division-winning Toronto Blue Jays. Ironically, that was the same margin by which the 1984 Tigers had lapped the runner-up Blue Jays. Toronto's surge to the top of the

Dwight Gooden, whose ten pitching victories helped the Mets to a commanding lead in the National League East at midseason 1986. In the American League East, Roger Clemens of the Red Sox helped to keep his team ahead with his dazzling string of fourteen victories. (Courtesy New York Mets)

American League's powerful Eastern Division, where the winner had gone on to win the league championship in nine of the past ten seasons, surprised many experts. A 1977 expansion team, the Jays had attracted little attention over the years. Even this year they were the poorest road attraction in the East, although 2.4 million home fans watched them play at Exhibition Stadium. This record was partly explained by their lack of any authentic star, with the possible exception of pitcher Dave Stieb. That the Jays rose so high so fast owed much to general manager Pat Gillich, a good judge of playing talent and a canny dealer. After stints with the Orioles and Yankees, Gillich joined Toronto, where in quick time he and N. E. Hardy built an effective minor league system that benefited from their scouting knowledge of Dominican Republic players. Such was Toronto's success in uncovering Dominican talent (an enterprise shared by Los Angeles, Pittsburgh, St. Louis, and Philadelphia scouts) that envious rivals voted to establish a general draft of Dominican Republic players in 1985. However, the Jays banked on this competitive advantage in 1985. Moreover, Gillich's canny use of the major league draft also helped strengthen the team. This draft was designed to free players from overstocked teams, and Gillich used it to snag players such as infielders Willie Upshaw and Kelly Gruber, outfielders George Bell and Lou Thornton, and pitcher Jim Acker. For each of these men Gillich paid the set price of $25,000, which the envious soon caused to be raised to $50,000. Gillich also used the trade route to land relief pitcher Tom Henke and infielders Rance Mulliniks and Damaso Garcia. Other Gillich deals strengthened the vulnerable Toronto bullpen, and an earlier key acquisition was pitcher Doyle Alexander, a Yankee castoff.

Tony Gwynn, Padre right fielder, whose .341 hitting was near the top of the National League at midseason 1986. (Courtesy San Diego Padres)

For the team's manager, Gillich had picked up Bobby Cox, whom the Braves had fired in 1981. Under Cox the young Jays steadily improved, finishing second in 1984. By 1985 Cox's young, closely knit team showed a remarkable balance of speed, pitching, batting, and defense. Over the winter the Jays improved a weak relief corps by acquiring Bill Caudill and Gary Lavelle, and in July Tom Henke was called up from the minors in time to save 13 games. Pitching was the key to Toronto's success. The staff's ERA of 3.29 was the league's best. Starters Stieb, Alexander, and Key combined for 45 victories and were backed by a relief corps that saved 47 games, with middle reliever Dennis Lamp posting an 11-0 record. Offensively the Jays ranked second in batting (.269) and in stolen bases (143). Although no regular batted .300, Jesse Barfield and Tony Fernandez each hit .289, Garcia hit .282, and Upshaw and Bell each hit .275.

By May 13, Cox had the Jays in first place, where they roosted the rest of the way. Their closest competitor was the rejuvenated Yankees. After floundering early, the Yankees surged under the resurrected Martin. Newly acquired center fielder Rickey Henderson (.314-24-72) led the league in stolen bases; Mattingly drove in 145 runs; and Dave Winfield batted .275-26-114. Overall, the Yankees batted .267 and topped Toronto's homer output by 18. Pitcher Ron Guidry (22-6, 3.27) regained his top form and led an improved pitching corps, including forty-five-year-old Phil Niekro, whose 16th victory was also the 300th of his long career. During the campaign the Yankees thrice surged from far behind to close within two games of the Jays, but each time they

Three top relievers of the 'Eighties: (*below*), Dave Righetti of the Yankees; (*opposite, right*) Rich ("Goose") Gossage of the Padres, a former Yankee with 257 saves and 96 wins by the end of his fourteenth season in 1985; (*opposite, left*) Dan Quisenberry of the Royals, who won his fourth consecutive Fireman of the Year Award in 1985. (Courtesy New York Yankees, George Brace, Kansas City Royals)

slumped thereafter. On September 30, they were five games behind, but then they closed to within two games. Then, on the second-to-last day of the season, Doyle Alexander beat his former Yankee teammates 5-1 to clinch the divisional title for the Blue Jays.

Just as hotly contested was the American League's Western Division race, where the California Angels and Kansas City Royals played a reprise of their 1984 duel. To be sure, observers of this low-rated division (some disparagers called it "the American League Worst") noted that in recent years only the Royals had played winning ball against Eastern contenders. Moreover, even if the Royals dominated the Western Division, having won the title in five of the past nine seasons, only once had they won an American League pennant. Indeed, neither the Angels nor the Royals showed offensive power in 1985. The Angels' .251 batting was the league's worst, and their pitching effectiveness was ranked fifth. By batting .252 the Royals barely topped the Angels, but the Royals boasted the league's second-best pitching. Given such modestly endowed contenders, it was understandable that the Western struggle was generally viewed as a sideshow of the great Eastern conflict. During the campaign Angel manager Gene Mauch fielded an aging team. Of the regulars, only outfielder Juan Beniquez batted .300; first baseman Rod Carew hit .280; and outfielders Brian Downing and Reggie Jackson combined for 47 homers and 170 RBIs to power the team, though Jackson slumped badly in the stretch. Starting pitchers Mike Witt, Don Romanick, and Don Sutton won 44 games, and ace reliever Donnie Moore saved 31. It was little enough, but Mauch's team clung to first place most of the way.

For their part, the dogged Royals were accustomed to battling from behind. They did so in 1984, overtaking both the Angels and the Twins, but then they were swept by the Tigers in the playoff. Indeed, veteran manager Dick Howser had yet to win a postseason game, and his prospects were not bright this year. From a respectable .268 team batting mark in 1984, Royal batting slumped to .252. But George Brett rebounded from a .284 mark in 1984 to a superb performance of .335, with 30 homers, 112 RBIs, and 16 game-winning hits. Burly first baseman Steve Balboni hit only .244, but his 36 homers drove home 88 runs. DH Hal McRae drove in 70, and second baseman Frank White drove in 69; 83 stolen bases by outfielders Willie Wilson and Lonnie Smith (acquired from the Cardinals in May) varied the offense. Two other regulars, catcher Jim Sundberg and shortstop Buddy Biancalana, contributed little offensively but provided solid defensive support. Atoning for the modest offensive was the fine young pitching staff, ably handled by the veteran Sundberg, whom the club had acquired from Milwaukee. Of the five starting pitchers, Bud Black, the winner of 17 games in 1984, slumped to 10-15, but the others took up the slack. Sophomore Bret Saberhagen, only twenty-one, posted a 20-6, 2.87 ERA record; Charlie Leibrandt, the oldest at twenty-eight, was 17-9, 2.69; youngsters Danny Jackson and Mark Gubicza each won 14. When timely relief was needed, Howser summoned Dan Quisenberry, the best short reliever in the league; in 1985 Quisenberry saved 37 games for the Royals. Over the first half of the season the Royals lost as many games as they won and trailed the Angels at the halfway mark by 7½ games.

But in August the team began winning regularly, and on September 6 they overhauled the Angels. The Royals briefly slumped in the stretch, but in the final week of play they won three of four games from the Angels. They clinched on the second-to-last day of the season; their 91-71 record was the poorest of any divisional winner, but good enough to top the Angels by one game. At this point the Royals' proudest boast was that they had repeated as winners, something no other team had done thus far in this decade.

In the National League, meanwhile, the comet season saw the dethronement of both 1984 division winners and a continuation of a current hitting drought. In 1985 only three teams, the Cardinals, Astros, and Dodgers, batted above .260, while five teams failed to match the lowly .251 mark of the American League Angels. Concern over this drought had some alarmists calling for the adoption of the DH rule, while others proposed penalizing pitchers. Indeed, the National League was more the pitchers' league. Compared with American League hurlers, who on average surrendered more than four runs a game, National pitchers allowed one run less per game. In the National League West, the Dodger pitching staff yielded the fewest earned runs of any team in baseball, and Dodger hitters posted the second-best batting mark (.261) in the league. Such prowess was too much for the defending champion Padres, who were outmanned on both fronts. In 1985 slumps, injuries, and personal problems plagued the Padres. Outfielder Tony Gwynn batted .317, well below his 1984 championship pace. No other regular topped .300, not even Steve Garvey, while outfielder Kevin McReynolds slumped to .234. The loss of second baseman Alan Wiggins, dispatched to Baltimore as a result of persisting drug problems, took its toll of the infield. A key injury sidelined reliefer Goose Gossage, who had managed to save 26 games. After contending briefly in

the early weeks, the Padres slumped to third place, finishing 12 games behind the winning Dodgers and 6½ back of the rising Cincinnati Reds. The sudden rise of the Reds brought added glory to playing manager Pete Rose, whose personal moment of glory came when he broke Cobb's hitting record. With young pitcher Tom Browning winning 20 games and veteran Dave Parker's resurgent batting (.312-34-125 RBIs), the Reds dogged the Dodgers through September, finishing 5½ games off the pace.

In winning by the widest margin of any 1985 divisional champion, the Dodgers relied on the best quartet of starting pitchers in the majors. Orel Hershisher, Bob Welch, Fernando Valenzuela, and Jerry Reuss accounted for 62 wins, while relievers Tom Niedenfuer and Ken Howell saved 31. What's more, the Dodger staff's ERA was the best in the majors. In support of this corps, Dodger hitters mounted a .261 attack, the second-best offensive in the league. Leading the onslaught were outfielders Pedro Guerrero and Mike Marshall and catcher Mike Scioscia. Guerrero hit .320 with 33 homers and 87 RBIs, Marshall's .293 batting included 28 homers and 95 RBIs, and Scioscia's .296 hitting drove in 53 runs. But manager Lasorda still faced a vexing infield problem. First baseman Greg Brock and second baseman Steve Sax were adequate at these positions, but shortstop and third base posed problems. The shortstop problem was solved by installing rookie Mariano Duncan, who fielded brilliantly but batted only .244. The third-base problem persisted until the end of August, when Lasorda acquired Bill Madlock from the moribund Pirates. At Pittsburgh the aging four-time batting champ was hitting a mere .251, but with the Dodgers the pudgy infielder hit .360 and sparked the club in the stretch. Although the Dodgers won handily, a late-season wrist injury that hampered Guerrero's batting swing augured ill for the playoff tests.

The question of which team would battle the Dodgers in the playoffs went unanswered until the last days of the season, when the torrid Eastern race was finally settled. At the opening of the Eastern campaign, the Chicago Cubs and New York Mets were odds-on favorites. In the early weeks the Cubs lived up to their promise, but later an incredible spate of injuries decimated their starting pitching staff. Forced to go with second-line hurlers, the Cubs' pitching effectiveness sank to a 4.16 ERA, second worst in the league. Nor did the hitters take up the slack. Although Cub batters led the league in homers, overall hitting slumped to .254. Thus, after a promising start, the team's dismal fourth-place finish mocked their management's frantic (and abortive) early-season attempt to install lights at Wrigley Field in time for the 1985 playoffs.

Meanwhile, the Mets lived up to their preseason expectations. With Dwight Gooden pitching sensationally, and newly acquired catcher Gary Carter batting .281 with 32 homers and 100 RBIs, the Mets contended all the way. First baseman Keith Hernandez batted .309, and outfielders Darryl Strawberry and George Foster combined for 50 homers. But Foster was a defensive liability, and the Mets missed shortstop Hubie Brooks, who went to Montreal in exchange for Carter; at Montreal, Brooks drove in 100 runs for the Expos. Still, with the league's third-best pitching and a respectable .257 batting attack, the

Mets waged a furious season-long battle with the Cardinals. The Mets won 98 games, three more than the Dodgers, but finished three games behind their unheralded opponents in the East.

Indeed, few preseason pundits had picked the Cardinals to win in the East. For one reason, the loss of ace reliefer Bruce Sutter in the free-agent draft appeared insurmountable. However, manager Whitey Herzog fashioned a four-man relief crew of Jeff Lahti, Todd Worley, and new acquisitions Ken Dayley and Bill Campbell that saved 39 games. Other timely acquisitions strengthened this unsung team. A brilliant trading coup brought pitcher John Tudor from the Pirates in exchange for outfielder George Hendrick. With the Cardinals, Tudor lost six of his first seven games, but he finished with 21 wins, 8 losses, and a 1.93 ERA, a record surpassed only by the great Gooden. Moreover, for a time, starter Joaquin Andujar rivaled Gooden, but after going 16-4 in the first half, Andujar won only five more, while losing seven. Overall, the Cardinal pitching corps ranked second to the Dodgers.

Other canny trades bolstered the Cards. A one-sided trade with the Giants landed slugger Jack Clark, who batted .281-22-87 for the Cards. When an injury sidelined Clark for 40 games, a deal with the Reds brought outfielder Caesar Cedeno to help take up the slack. With Clark at first, Tom Herr at second, the brilliant Ozzie Smith at short, and Terry Pendleton at third, the Cardinals had a solid inner defense. Cedeno strengthened an outfield that included Willie McGee, Andy Van Slyke, and the speedy rookie Vince Coleman. Coleman batted .267 but reached first base often. Once there, he was the league's prime base-stealing threat. In 1985 Coleman stole 110 bases, for a rookie record; the Cardinals' total of 314 stolen bases ranked among all-time seasonal efforts. With speedsters like Coleman and Ozzie Smith on base, the table was set for hitters McGee, Herr, and Clark. McGee's .353 batting won the league title, and he drove in 82 runs; Herr batted .302 and drove in 110 runs. Overall, the Cardinals led the league in batting and runs scored, and defensively the team committed the fewest errors of any club.

Such prowess was needed to fend off the Mets. In seasonal play the Cardinals never lost a game that they led going into the ninth inning. In early September there were four consecutive games when this resilient team rallied to overcome big deficits and win. Such pressure was too much for the Mets. In a late-season duel between these rivals, the Mets won three of four to close within two games, but afterwards the Mets swooned. In the last week the Cardinals clinched; their record of 101-61 was the best in baseball and topped the Mets by three games.

In the playoffs for the 1985 league championships, the divisional winners now faced best-of-seven-games tests, the same format as used in the World Series. The decision to extend the old best-of-five playoff format had been made by the owners, who chose to exercise their option under the terms of the current network television contract. Although television moguls were leery about the extension, the two hotly contested playoff struggles produced the highest television ratings of any playoff series thus far.

The National League playoff series opened at Dodger Stadium, where more than 3 million fans had paid to watch the Dodgers during the

Three pitchers who joined the exclusive 300-victory club in the 'Eighties: (*opposite top*) Gaylord Perry, who retired from the Seattle Mariners after winning his 314th game; (*opposite bottom*) Phil Niekro, who topped the 300 mark as a Yankee in 1985 and was still active as an Indian in 1986, at the age of forty-six; (*above*) Don Sutton, who capped his twenty-two-year career in 1986 by winning his 300th game for the Angels. (Courtesy Author's Collection for Perry and Niekro photos, California Angels for Sutton photo)

regular season. Playing before capacity crowds, the Dodgers won the first two games; in the opener Fernando Valenzuela outpitched John Tudor, whose last pitching loss dated back to July 20. But when action shifted to St. Louis, the Cardinals swept the next three games. Returning home for the sixth game, the desperate Dodgers mounted a 4-1 lead, but the Cardinals rallied behind Ozzie Smith's game-tying triple, which Clark followed with the decisive homer. For his batting feats, Smith was awarded the National League Championship Series MVP award.

Meanwhile, it took the full seven games for the American League championship drama to run its course. Opening at Toronto, the underdog Royals lost the first two games. When action shifted to Kansas City, the Royals won the third, but lost the fourth as pitcher Dave Stieb notched his second win for the Blue Jays. Down three games to one, the Royals won their final home game but faced the unlikely prospect of winning the final two games in Toronto. But the resilient Royals proceeded to do just that, winning the sixth game 5-3 behind the stout pitching of young Mark Gubicza, Bud Black, and Dan Quisenberry. For the crucial seventh game the Blue Jays called on Stieb to pitch with three days' rest. The Royals jumped on Stieb for two early runs, then scored four in the sixth, three coming on Jim Sundberg's bases-loaded triple. The 6-2 Royal victory was nailed down by pitchers Bret Saberhagen, Charlie Leibrandt, and Quisenberry. Indeed, during the playoff series Royal pitchers held the Jays to a lowly .225 batting average.

If there was any augury in the Royals' recent pitching statistics, it was missed by pundits who tended to install the Royals as miscast underdogs

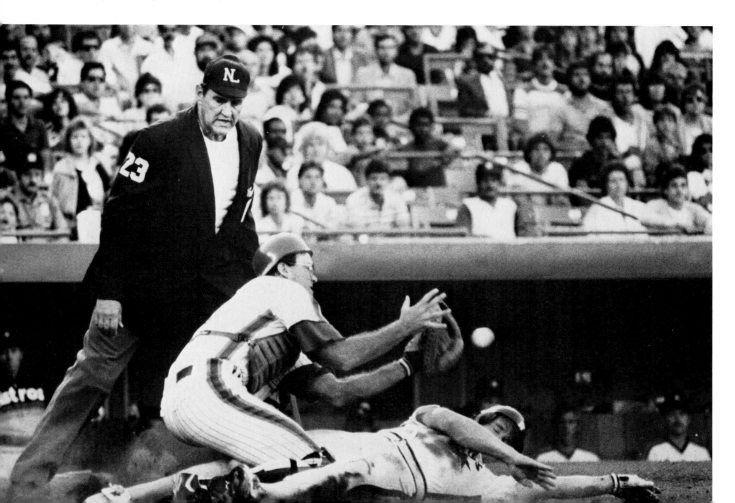

in the upcoming World Series test against the Cardinals. Except for George Brett, whose prodigious batting had powered his team in the October stretch drive for the divisional flag and most recently in the playoffs with his .370 batting, the Royals' offensive hardly compared with that of the Cards. Moreover, the alternate-year rule now barred the Royals from using DH Hal McRae. Thus, even though the Cardinals had lost the services of speedster Vince Coleman from a freak accident in their recent playoff series, the Royals appeared to be out-gunned. In this all-Missouri Series matchup, which locals dubbed the "I-70 Series" for the interstate highway that linked the two cities, the Cardinals were the heavy favorites. Indeed, when the Royals lost the first two games in their home park, the script seemed to be playing out as expected. At this point, history was against the Royals, since no team had ever won a World Series after losing the first two games at home. But this was the comet year in baseball, and blasted precedents were part of the scheme of things.

What followed was the stuff of baseball legend. The Royals won the third game in St. Louis, but they lost the fourth as John Tudor recorded his second victory, a sparkling 3-0 shutout. But this was the high-water mark of Cardinal fortunes, as the St. Louisans fell victim to the "Miracle of I-70." In the fifth game Danny Jackson scattered five hits as the Royals romped to a 6-1 victory. Returning home to Kansas City, the Royals were losing the sixth game by a 1-0 score going into the last of the ninth inning. At this point, with their backs to the wall, the Royals, aided by a controversial umpire's call at first base, scored two runs on Dane Iorg's pinch-hit single to square the Series. Then, in the decisive seventh game, the Royals jumped on Tudor early and went on to rout the Cardinals 11-0. It was a fantastic finish, and ironically the score matched that by which an earlier generation of Cardinals routed the Tigers in the seventh game of the 1934 Series. As the Cardinals read their grim destiny on the scoreboard, they turned testy. Pitcher Joaquin Andujar and manager Herzog were thrown out of the game for protesting calls. But 41,000 delirious Royal fans cheered their miracle workers.

In retrospect, the Royal victory was an incredible turnabout. The young Royal pitching staff—paced by Saberhagen, who pitched the deciding game and won the MVP trophy for his two victories—held the Cardinal hitters to a measly .185 batting average. Offensively the Royals batted a lusty .270. The Royal victory was the capstone of a year of extraordinary highlights in baseball.

1986—NEW FACES, OLD AND NEW PROBLEMS

Notwithstanding the brilliance of the comet season, 1986 was no time for clucking or preening. Despite all the heroics, the new attendance record, the comfortable television ratings, and the promise of four years of peace on the labor front, owners fearfully appraised the game's financial future. Nor was their sentiment merely another of the poor-mouthing laments ritually sounded at annual meetings, since this alarm was based on substance. Over the winter an alarming note was sounded in financial reports of the major television networks. The message por-

tended that a vital source of baseball funding was shrinking. At the end of 1985, reports from the three major networks showed sharply lowering profits. While CBS made a modest $10 million from its sports programming, that figure was offset by heavy losses reported by ABC and NBC. Worse, the reported losses came despite generally good ratings for network-televised baseball and football games.

For this shocking reversal in network revenue, a glut of sports programs was blamed, along with changing tastes of television viewers. By bankrolling other forms of programming, advertisers were discovering that they could reach targeted consumers just as effectively and with less cost. Hence, network sports-programming divisions no longer enjoyed a seller's market, and networks were cutting back on these branches. For major sports like baseball and football, this was shocking news; it seemingly meant the decline of a lucrative revenue source that had steadily increased since the 1970s. Because pro football owners derived 60 percent of their annual revenue from network television, they were more vulnerable than their baseball counterparts. But the prospect of landing another lucrative network contract in 1989 seemed bleak for baseball owners. Reacting to the grim news, Commissioner Ueberroth and pessimistic owners called for new tactics aimed at cutting spiraling salaries. But optimists, mostly rooted in Players Association councils, argued that television money would continue to flow from the exclusive purchases of major games by single advertisers or from revenue to come from paid-television programming. At least for the present, or until the current network television contracts expired in 1989, the prospects of belt-tightening austerities were deferred.

Thus, in 1986 player salaries continued to rise despite a noticeable lack of bidding by owners for the services of players in the latest re-entry draft auction. In the 1985 draft only three major stars—Kirk Gibson, Carlton Fisk, and Donnie Moore—were on the block. Surprisingly, no owner bid for their services, prompting charges of owner collusion against qualified free agents. All three came to terms with their former clubs, however, and each received a generous contract in the million-dollar or near-million-dollar range.

But if the latest re-entry draft failed to raise the stakes for the ten players involved, the thirty-five players who opted for salary arbitration kept the salary spiral going. By now it was widely recognized that arbitration awards had become the significant force fueling the high-salary trend. Since a player needed only two years in the majors to opt for arbitration, the generous awards pushed salaries of younger players sharply higher in the early stages of their careers. To arrest this trend, beleaguered owners had battled hard to add an additional year before a player might be eligible for arbitration. Having won this point in the 1985 negotiations, the owners could look to some relief in 1987, when the three-year eligibility rule took effect.

Meanwhile, salary arbitration awards continued to advantage players. Over the winter of 1986, some thirty-five players opted for salary arbitration, and even though the clubs won twenty of these cases, all players received substantial raises. Among the big winners, Orel Hershiser saw his salary climb from $212,000 to $1,000,000, while Bret Saberhagen went from $160,000 to $925,000. Among the losers, Wade Boggs failed to get the $1,850,000 he sought, but he still received $1,350,000, the largest sum yet awarded in a salary arbitration case. Of eight other players who had asked for $500,000 or more in arbitration and who lost their cases, the worst showing of any resulted in a $50,000 raise! Moreover, by threatening to go to arbitration, star players pried fat out-of-court settlements from their parent clubs. Thus, Don Mattingly settled for $1,375,000, nearly tripling his 1985 salary of $455,000; Dwight Gooden's salary jumped from $450,000 to $1,300,000; and Fernando Valenzuela settled for $1,833,000. After the dust settled over the latest contract wars, the average player salary surpassed the $400,000 mark, and the number of million-dollar-a-year players rose to fifty-eight. Topping the list of these plutocrats were Boston outfielder Jim Rice ($2,080,000) and outfielder George Foster of the Mets ($2,000,000).

Although failing to arrest the latest salary surge, the owners seemed to be taking united action to bar future breakthroughs. As evidence of such action, one could cite the cold-shoulder treatment players received in the latest re-entry draft, along with signs that owners were less likely to agree to inflated contracts in order to avoid arbitration. If so, owners had to proceed carefully lest they incur charges of collusion from a wary Players Association. Indeed, when the owners unilaterally elected to trim playing rosters to twenty-four men, an action that might save a club as much as $500,000 in salary payments, the Association screamed collusion. Although the owners and Commissioner Ueberroth insisted that the decision was voluntary, the decision was criticized for weakening all teams, especially National League clubs, where the lack of a designated-hitter rule required that managers make fuller use of their bench strength.

Adding more fuel to the smoldering relations between owners and players was Ueberroth's unilateral action in the drug controversy. In the wake of the Pittsburgh drug trials, the commissioner escalated his crusade against accused drug users. In the spring Ueberroth laid down his own punishment against the twenty-one players who were named as drug users in trial testimony. Of these, seven were suspended for a year but were allowed to play if they agreed to surrender 10 percent of their annual salaries and if they promised to engage in anti-drug campaigning. Four others were given half-year suspensions with lesser penalties, and all were required to submit to random drug testing for two years. Although the accused twenty-one players submitted to this punishment, the Players Association filed a class-action suit against the commissioner. Going beyond his edict, individual clubs adopted policies forcing players to submit to drug testing to prove their innocence, further widening the growing rift between players and owners. Indeed,

Opposite: In the fifth game of the 1986 American League championship series, Boston Red Sox center fielder Dave Henderson goes high over the fence in an attempt to grab California Angel Bobby Grich's long drive. (*Right*), Henderson appears to have made the catch, but the force of his arm striking the fence jarred the ball loose, causing it to go over for a home run. Henderson later made a dramatic game-saving home run in the ninth inning to keep Red Sox hopes alive. (Courtesy Jim Davis/*Boston Herald*)

Rich Gedman of the Boston Red Sox is out at second, tagged by New York Met second baseman Wally Backman, in the fourth game of the 1986 World Series. Making the call is umpire Dale Ford. (Courtesy Jim Davis/*Boston Herald*)

one club, the Pirates, filed a lawsuit against their former outfielder Dave Parker, charging that Parker's cocaine use affected his play during his 1979–83 contract years. In filing this civil suit, the Pirates sought to be freed from paying Parker $5.3 million in deferred contract payments.

For his part Commissioner Ueberroth announced on the eve of the 1986 season that baseball was now drug-free. Claiming the crisis was over because the players wanted tough action, Ueberroth conceded that a few incidents might yet crop up but argued that his edict was the positive step that ended the crisis.

Mercifully, such festering problems were thrust aside once the 1986 season began, although at the outset a spate of injuries that sidelined some thirty-three players challenged the wisdom of the twenty-four-man-roster decision. Among the hardest hit was the Dodger team, which lost the services of slugging outfielder Pedro Guerrero and infielder Bill Madlock. However, a surprising feature was the plenitude of rookies in the lineups of clubs. Some twenty-eight were opening-day starters, and forty-eight played in the first few days. Among the most promising of the young phenoms was a pair of American League sluggers. At Oakland, Jose Canseco, a twenty-three-year-old outfielder with only two years of minor league seasoning, established himself as a leading slugger. At California, Wally Joyner, a first baseman, led the majors with 17 homers in early June. Joyner's emergence dislodged veteran Rod Carew, who failed to land with another team and announced his retirement after an illustrious career. At Minnesota, outfielder Kirby Puckett now emerged as a formidable slugger and ranked among the league's leading hitters in June.

The 1986 season began on an upbeat note with record attendance marks set at opening-day contests. Thereafter, wide-open races in three of the divisions continued to attract fans, despite the fact that a family of five might have to shell out a hundred dollars at a single game. By early June, except for the world champion Kansas City Royals, perennial contenders in the weak American League West, other divisional winners of 1985 appeared likely to be dethroned. In the powerful American League East, the Toronto Blue Jays occupied the cellar in early June, while the Boston Red Sox, a .500 performer in 1985, enjoyed a 2¼-game lead. Landing Don Baylor from the Yankees provided inspiring leadership, while improved Red Sox pitching whetted appetites of long-suffering Boston fans. Pacing the Red Sox pitching staff was Roger Clemens, a twenty-three-year-old sophomore, who recovered from serious arm trouble to post a 9-0 record in the early going. Clemens's performance was highlighted by a record-breaking strikeout performance in which he fanned 20 Seattle Mariners on the night of April 29. But Boston was dogged by the formidable Yankees, whose latest pitching acquisition, ex–White Sox hurler Brit Burns, was lost to the club because of a chronic leg injury. Moreover, manager Earl Weaver had his Orioles back in contention, and for a brief spell the lowly Cleveland Indians gained the heights, a sortie that insured the Tribe of bettering its pitiful 1985 attendance mark.

In the National League East, the champion Cardinals suffered through a horrendous five-week hitting slump that buried the Birds in the division cellar, 14 games behind the streaking New York Mets. Winners of 33 of their first 45 games, the superbly balanced Mets boasted their best breakaway gait. A dominant pitching staff headed by precocious Dwight Gooden, plus a powerful batting attack, propelled the Mets to a six-game lead over the revamped Expos by early June. As the Mets romped in swaggering style, frustrated rivals took umbrage, turning encounters with the Mets into ineffective vendettas. Indeed, there seemed to be no stopping the Mets in the East. In the National League West, the division champion Dodgers lagged six games behind the Houston Astros, who battled the Braves, Giants, and Padres in a tight race during the early going.

In scaling the heights in their divisions, the Mets and the Astros went on to win by commanding margins. In the East the onrushing Mets won 108 games to top all major league teams. By September manager Dave Johnson's team boasted a 19-game lead, which they stretched to 21½ games by season's end. Behind the Mets trailed the Phillies, the only National League team to post a winning seasonal record over the New Yorkers. In third place roosted the forlorn defending-champion Cardinals, who were plagued by woeful batting. The Birds' .238 team batting average and measly totals of 58 homers and 601 runs scored stood as the worst offensive performance in the majors. On the face of it, it was a minor miracle that the Cards soared so high, but stout pitching and a major-league-high 262 stolen bases made overachievers of manager Herzog's crew.

In the West, meanwhile, the Houston Astros surmounted a poor preseasonal playing record and the gloomy forecasts of observers who predicted not only a losing season for the Texans but also that dwin-

During the sixth game of the 1986 World Series, Boston Red Sox shortstop Spike Owen stretches high for a throw that would have forced New York Met runner Ray Knight at second base, but the umpire ruled that the throw pulled Owen off the bag and Knight was safe. (Courtesy Jim Davis' *Boston Herald*)

dling attendance might soon force the team to quit the depressed Houston area. Indeed, in late June the Astros fell behind the surging Giants, but in July rookie manager Hal Lanier had his team back on top. By September the Astros held a 7-game lead, which they boosted to 10 by the end of seasonal hostilities. The Astros' 96 victories lapped the second-place Reds (a team that the Astros defeated in 14 of their 18 confrontations) by 10 games, and the third-place Giants by 13 games. As for the defending-champion Dodgers, they finished 23 games behind the leaders and barely escaped falling into the divisional cellar. With slugger Guerrero sidelined for most of the season and injuries striking down other key players, manager Lasorda's men collapsed. Steve Sax's lusty .332 batting and Fernando Valenzuela's 21 pitching victories were the only bright spots in a dismal Dodger year. Nevertheless, the team attracted more than three million paying fans.

While romping to one of the most one-sided victories since divisional play began in the majors, the Mets relied on overpowering pitching and hitting. Pitching keyed the team's success, as the well-armed Mets fielded a superb starting quartet in Bob Ojeda (18-5, 2.57 ERA), Ron Darling (15-8, 2.81), Dwight Gooden (17-6, 2.84), and Sid Fernandez (16-6, 3.52). Equally impressive relief pitching from veteran Jesse Orosco (21 saves, 2.33) and young Roger McDowell (22 saves, 3.02) enabled the Mets' pitching staff to post the best ERA (3.11) in the majors. Helping to shape this formidable pitching staff was the acquisition of Ojeda from the Red Sox, who received a promising young flinger, Cal Schiraldi, in return. Ojeda's presence compensated for a "falling off" in performance by Gooden, who slipped from a phenomenal rating to one of mere excellence.

The Mets led the league at bat with a .263 team effort and ranked third in homers with 148. Leading the attack was the infield trio of Keith Hernandez (.310-13-83), second baseman Wally Backman (.320), and third baseman Ray Knight (.298-11-76). Knight's sparkling effort followed a horrendous .218 batting performance in 1985. Additional power came from outfielders Len Dykstra (.295-8-45), Mookie Wilson (.289-9-45), and Daryl Strawberry (.259-27-93). While much booed by impatient Met fans, young Strawberry's power hitting showed signs of matching his great promise. Young Dykstra's rapid development prompted the release of veteran George Foster, another target of Shea Stadium boo-birds. Yet another power surge came from veteran catcher Gary Carter, whose .265 batting was enhanced by 24 homers and 105 RBIs. With solid depth at all positions, manager Johnson's team intimidated opponents, ignited several brawls, and won the hearts of hungry fans, who turned out 2,762,417 strong, to set a record annual attendance for a major league team in the Gotham area.

Such strength by the Mets overshadowed the Western champion Astros, who proved to be formidable rivals nonetheless. Pitching was the team's forte, and the Astros' 3.15 ERA ranked second to the Mets' record. Ex-Met Mike Scott's league-leading 2.22 ERA led the starters. Armed with his newly mastered split-finger fastball, Scott fanned a league-leading 304 batters. In 27 of 37 starts Scott held opponents to no more than two runs, and on the night the Astros clinched the Western title, Scott pitched a no-hitter. The right-hander's deceptively ordinary 18-10 record headed a starting corps that included Bob Knepper (17-12, 3.14), rookie Jim Deshaies (12-5, 3.25), and veteran Nolan Ryan (12-8, 3.34). Backing this crew were solid relievers Dave Smith (2.73, 33 saves) and Charley Kerfel (11-2, 2.59, 7 saves).

Offensively the Texans hit .255 with 125 homers and 163 stolen bases. Team leaders included outfielders Kevin Bass (.311-20-79) and veteran Jose Cruz (.278-10-72). First baseman Glenn Davis's 31 homers and 101 RBIs were the most by any Astro hitter since the days of Jim Wynn. Third baseman Denny Walling (.312-13-58) and second baseman Bill Doran (.276) added further strength. It was enough to power the Astros to victory in the West, but in the coming showdown with the Mets for the National League title, Astro hopes rested on their pitchers, whose late-season heroics were the talk of the majors.

As newcomers rose to power in the National League, so they rose in the American League race. Although the divisional races were a bit closer in the junior circuit, the same front-runner-take-all script summed up the outcomes. Not that fans were put off by the lack of close races in either league; on the contrary, fans showed in numbers great enough to set yet another attendance record.

In the East the Boston Red Sox took the lead in June and then fended off August assaults by the Yankees, Tigers, Blue Jays, and Orioles. On August 5 the Orioles, once again managed by Earl Weaver, moved to within 2½ games, but they slumped horribly thereafter, prompting Weaver's second retirement at the close of the campaign. On August 13 the Yankees closed to within 3½, but they then fell back, losing 13 of their next 21 games. Unstable pitching sank the Yankees and blighted the heroic efforts of reliever Dave Righetti, whose 46 saves established a new seasonal record, and first baseman Don Mattingly, whose brilliant hitting (.352, 31 homers, 113 RBIs, 53 doubles, and 117 runs scored) set a high standard in batting versatility and touted the young left-handed swinger as the best player in the game. As the Yankees swooned, the Tigers closed to within 5 games of the Red Sox, but they too slumped. As the decisive month of August ended, the reviving Blue Jays mounted a 9-game winning streak to close the gap to 3½ games, but then the Red Sox trumped this threat with an 11-game winning streak of their own. Ahead by 7 games in mid-September, manager John McNamara's men hung on to win by 5½ games over the second-place Yankees.

The American League Western Division race, meanwhile, saw the unheralded Texas Rangers move to the top and hold the heights through June. In July the California Angels took the lead from the stubborn Rangers, and they held it the rest of the way, winning by five games over manager Bobby Valentine's Texans. This turnabout in the West excluded the world champion Royals, perennial contenders and the favorites of most preseason forecasters. But the Royals could do no better than a third-place tie with the Oakland A's and finished 16 games off the pace. Despite young Bret Saberhagen's injury-ridden slump, Royal pitching (a 3.82 ERA) was the best in the American League, but the team's .252 batting almost touched bottom. George Brett's .290 batting led the team, but injuries kept the Royals' leader out of 38 games.

Feisty Met outfielder Len Dykstra is waved home by his third-base coach in the seventh inning of game seven of the 1986 World Series. The Mets' three-run rally in this inning powered the New Yorkers to the world title. (N.Y. Daily News Photo)

In the topsy-turvy American League East, where each of the previous five seasons saw a newcomer capture the title, Boston won for the first time since 1975. A combustive mix of pitching and batting powered the gritty Sox, whose hurlers notched a 3.93 ERA, third-best in the American League, where only four team staffs yielded fewer than four earned runs a game. Recovering from arm trouble, which limited his work in 1985, young Roger Clemens pitched masterfully. The big right-hander's 24-4 record was the best in the majors; his 2.48 ERA was topped only by Mike Scott of the Astros; and his 238 strikeouts ranked second among American hurlers. As the dependable stopper of Red Sox losing streaks, Clemens shone brightest among a corps of starters that included lefty Bruce Hurst (13-8, 2.99), the volatile Denny "Oil Can" Boyd (16-10, 3.78), and Al Nipper (10-12, 5.38). When help was needed, manager McNamara called on veterans Bob Stanley (4.37, 16 saves) and lefty Joe Sambito (2-0, 12 saves). Towards the end of the season, newcomers Steve Crawford and Cal Schiraldi (4-2, 1.41, 9 saves) arrived to bolster the bullpen. Obtained in the trade that sent Ojeda to the Mets, Schiraldi was recalled from the minors in July and quickly established himself as the team's leading "fireman."

More prodigious than the pitchers were the Sox hitters, whose .271 team batting matched that of the Yankees and stood second only to the surprising Indians, whose lusty .284 hitting led the majors. Leading the attack was third baseman Wade Boggs (.357-8-71), who won his third American League batting title. A dependable contact hitter, Boggs needed all his skills to fend off versatile Don Mattingly of the Yankees in the race for the batting title. With the divisional races virtually decided in September, the intense dual between these left-handed swingers added a badly needed touch of suspense. In the final week Boggs won, nosing out Mattingly .357 to .352.

An ideal leadoff hitter, Boggs also drew a league-leading 105 bases on balls. Behind him, second baseman Marty Barrett batted .286; thus the pair set the table for the quartet of heavy-hitting veterans that followed in the batting order. First baseman Bill Buckner (.267-18-102), outfielder Jim Rice (.324-20-110), DH Don Baylor (.238-31-94), and outfielder Dwight Evans (.259-26-97) took full advantage, driving in more than four hundred runs. For good measure, catcher Rich Gedman batted .258 with 65 RBIs, and outfielders Tony Armas and Dave Henderson combined for 26 homers and 105 RBIs. With dependables like these on hand, manager McNamara wisely used a set lineup and paid little heed to the measly 41 stolen bases notched by his team.

If McNamara's lineup was studded with aging vets like Rice, Evans, Baylor, and Buckner, the Red Sox looked like callow youths compared with the Western champion Angels. For openers, Angel manager Mauch was the dean of major league managers, but in twenty-five years of piloting big-league teams he had yet to win a league pennant. His dream now hinged on a clutch of aging vets and a few precocious youngsters. Mauch's oldsters amounted to a full lineup and included starters like catcher Bob Boone, infielders Doug DeCinces and Bobby Grich, outfielders Ruppert Jones and Brian Downing, and pitchers Don Sutton and Doug Corbett. For these Angels there could be few baseball tomorrows, a realization that goaded their present efforts.

Forty-one-year-old Don Sutton's 1986 performance assured his immortality. After a rocky start, the veteran right-hander became the nineteenth pitcher to win 300 games. Sutton finished with 15 victories and once again fanned more than a hundred batters, extending to 21 his record skein of consecutive seasons for accomplishing that feat. Another oldster, reliefer Doug Corbett, saved 10 games for the Angels, but otherwise Mauch relied on younger arms. Big Mike Witt (18-10, 2.84) was the ace of the staff, followed by young Kirk McCaskill (17-10, 3.36) and Pirate castoff John Candelaria, who overcame injuries to notch a 10-2 record. Between them Witt and McCaskill fanned 410 batters, and ailing relief ace Donnie Moore posted 21 saves.

Offensively the Angels batted a mediocre .255, but 167 homers powered the attack. Veterans Downing and DeCinces propelled 46 "dingers" and drove in 191 runs, and Reggie Jackson, playing his final season as an Angel, hit 18 homers and batted in 58 runs. But the team's best hitter was rookie first baseman Wally Joyner. After a herculean start, Joyner cooled off, but he still finished with a .290 average, 22 homers, and 100 RBIs. Two other youths, shortstop Dick Schofield, son of a former major leaguer, and outfielder Gary Pettis, drove in 115 runs. Overall the Angels' onslaught was good enough to win in the West, but it paled in comparison to that of the Red Sox swingers.

Nevertheless, when these rivals met in the seven-game American

Outfielder Dave Henderson of the Red Sox scores ahead of the throw to Met catcher Gary Carter in the second inning of the final game of the 1986 World Series. Boston's three-run rally in this inning gave the Sox a lead that failed to hold up. (N.Y. Daily News Photo)

League Championship Series, the Angels very nearly handed Mauch his first pennant. When hostilities began in Boston, Mike Witt outpitched Boston ace Roger Clemens as the Angels won 8-1. But this victory was soured by the loss of Joyner for the rest of the series due to a leg infection. The Red Sox rebounded to tie the series, but when action shifted to Anaheim, the home-based Angels won the next two games by scores of 5-3 and 4-3 to take a commanding three-games-to-one edge. Mauch's dream neared reality in the sixth game as the Angels carried a 5-2 lead into the ninth. In the sixth inning of this game, Red Sox outfielder Dave Henderson attempted a leaping catch of Bobby Grich's drive, but the ball hit Henderson's glove and bounced over the fence for a homer. But in the ninth Boston staged a last-ditch rally; Baylor's two-run homer chased starter Witt, and reliever Donnie Moore came on to face Henderson. With two outs and two strikes, Henderson, who seemed fated to be the goat of the series, hit a two-run homer to put the Red Sox ahead. Although the Angels rallied to tie the game, it was Henderson's fly ball in the eleventh inning that drove in the winning run in this memorable game. This bitter defeat crushed the Angels' dream. When action shifted back to Boston, the reprieved Red Sox won the next two games by decisive 10-4 and 8-1 scores to land the American League pennant.

Equally dramatic, meanwhile, was the Mets-Astros duel for the National League title. In the light of the Mets' elephantine romp over regular-season rivals, the Astros appeared as miscast pygmies. But Mike Scott won the opener at Houston by a 1-0 score, and after the Mets retaliated with two victories by 5-1 and 6-5 scores, Scott tied the match with a 3-1, three-hit pitching masterpiece. In the aftermath of Scott's latest win, the grousing Mets accused him of scuffing balls, but there was no gainsaying Scott's mastery. With the series tied, the Mets won the fifth game, a twelve-inning struggle, by 2-1. Then, as action shifted back to Houston, the rivals fought a marathon sixteen-inning battle, the longest in the history of postseasonal play. Nursing a 3-0 lead into the ninth, Astro starter Bob Knepper faltered, and the Mets rallied to tie. In the fourteenth inning the antagonists traded single runs, and in the sixteenth the Mets scored three runs that barely withstood a last-ditch rally by the Astros, who left the potential winning run on base. In losing their title bid, the stubborn Astros outhit the Mets and limited their rivals to a mere .189 average. The Astros also forced the Mets to rely on their bullpen in five of the six games, but the Met relievers met the challenge, fireman Jesse Orosco winning three of the games. Moreover, the Astros gained some compensation when Scott was voted MVP of the series. Although the Mets won in six games, their victory was a near thing and a humbling experience before their final test against the Red Sox in the upcoming World Series.

At least the slumping Mets would not have to face the slugging Red Sox designated hitter Don Baylor in all of the World Series games. This was due to a controversial decision by Commissioner Ueberroth aimed at settling the inter-league impasse over the DH rule. Earlier, Ueberroth had quixotically vowed to settle the dispute once and for all; to this end he had polled fans on the question of whether to scuttle or retain the rule. But when the returns showed an inconclusive standoff,

Met catcher Gary Carter agonizes over making an out in the final game of the 1986 World Series. Red Sox catcher Rich Gedman, also shown, fanned ten times in Series play. (N.Y. Daily News Photo)

When the Mets defeated the Red Sox 8–5 to clinch the 1986 World Series, pandemonium broke loose among Shea Stadium fans. A few even eluded police cordons to join Met players celebrating the final out. (N.Y. Daily News Photo)

Ueberroth ruled that in this year's World Series the DH rule would apply only to games played at the American League park. The decision naturally evoked critical gibes, including one that likened it to King Solomon's decision to cut the baby in half. Nevertheless, the ruling stood, and the furor over it inflamed the already feverish emotions that anticipated the impending clash.

Indeed, both Series contenders were starving for a world title. In their twenty-five-year history the Mets had won but one, but in Boston the famine had dragged on for nearly sixty-eight years. Not since 1918 had a Boston team won a World Series, although at that point in Red Sox history the club boasted a matchless 5-0 winning record in fall classics. But since 1918 Red Sox teams had appeared in three World Series, losing each time in seven games. No wonder Red Sox fans gnashed their teeth and muttered darkly about a curse hanging over their team.

Yet, when play began at Shea Stadium, the underdog Sox gave every indication of exorcising the spell. Despite the ruling that sidelined Baylor, or the leg injury that had first baseman Bill Buckner limping pitifully, the Red Sox won the first two games in the Mets' lair. Lefty Bruce Hurst outpitched Ron Darling in the opener, Boston winning 1-0 on a tainted run. The next night out, the Sox jumped on Dwight Gooden for eight hits and six runs, winning 9-3 and seizing a commanding lead in the Series.

When action shifted to Boston, where the next three games were

Four joyous Mets (left to right, Rick Aguilera, Bob Ojeda, Howard Johnson, and Kevin Elster) indulge in the traditional champagne celebration following the team's victory over the Red Sox in the 1986 World Series. (N.Y. Daily News Photo)

played, Red Sox euphoria dampened as the team's vulnerable second-line pitching failed. In games three and four the resilient Mets finally shook off their hitting slump and downed the Sox handily. In the first of these the Mets jumped on Oil Can Boyd for four first-inning runs, which were more than enough for pitcher Bob Ojeda to breeze to a 7-1 victory. The next night, Darling bested Al Nipper, the Mets winning 6-2; in this game the Mets erupted for three runs in the fourth, Carter's two-run homer being the big blow.

With the Series now tied at two games apiece, Sox manager McNamara again called on Hurst, who again fashioned a fine pitching effort; once more the Sox defeated Gooden, winning 4-2. Up now by three games to two, the Sox needed only one more win to take the Series, and in the sixth game, played at Shea Stadium, they very nearly turned the trick.

From the start, Boston ace Roger Clemens pitched masterfully, protecting a 2-0 lead until the fifth inning, when the Mets tied the game, one run scoring on a Boston error. The Mets returned the favor in the seventh, allowing the Red Sox to score an errant run and take a 3-2 lead. But in the eighth, after a blister forced Clemens to retire, Boston reliefer Cal Schiraldi yielded a game-tying run. The score was 3-3 when the tense game moved into extra innings. In the top of the tenth, the Red Sox scored two runs, the first on Dave Henderson's homer and the second on Marty Barrett's single, which scored Wade Boggs. Now all that was wanted was to retire the Mets—a tall order in the light of their reputation for last-ditch rallies. When Schiraldi got the first two outs, the Sox looked like sure winners. But the battling Mets lashed three consecutive singles to draw within one run at 5-4. At this point reliefer Bob Stanley took over and came within one strike of victory, something Schiraldi had done in his stint. But Stanley's wild pitch and a later error by Buckner allowed the Mets to score the winning run in a memorable 6-5 victory.

The dramatic Met comeback to tie the Series was the stuff of baseball legend. It dashed Boston's hopes, although a one-day rain delay allowed McNamara to pitch Hurst in the decisive game. Pitching on three days' rest, Hurst led 3-0 going into the sixth, when the Mets again rebounded, chasing Hurst with a three-run rally to tie the game. In the seventh, Ray Knight (the eventual Series MVP) homered to key another three-run assault, which settled matters. In winning the decisive seventh game 8-5, the Mets closed out the humdrum 1986 season with an electrifying victory. Their comeback matched the achievement of the Kansas City Royals, who, only a year before, became the first team to win a World Series after losing the first two games in their home park. The Mets' heroics drew record television audiences, including an estimated 90 million viewers for the last game, and in the aftermath of their victory the New Yorkers were treated to a record-breaking ticker-tape parade in Manhattan. And if the Red Sox fans still agonized over their team's continuing curse, such disappointments also were part of the latest demonstration of baseball's enduring hold on its adoring public.

EYEING THE FUTURE, DIMLY

As baseball moves towards the final decade of this century with live attendance and television audiences still increasing, the game's leaders are nevertheless well advised to ponder baseball's future without the aid of rose-colored glasses. They would be wise to heed Montaigne's advice—that men should never sit so high upon their stools that they forget that they rest upon their vulnerable rumps.

For there is danger in allowing present gains to obscure the problems that cloud the game's future. Certainly the drug-abuse problem demands forthright remedial action lest the game suffer some major scandal, such as games lost or thrown by drug abusers. As the 1986 season ended, a rising national clamor against drug abuse focused hostile attention on professional sports. For baseball, the revelations of the Pittsburgh drug trial still cast their pall of shame; the drug-related deaths of two prominent players in 1986 cast a similar pall over pro football and basketball. Such episodes keep warning flags flying, and baseball, in company with other prominent industries, faces the knotty problem of how to test for drug abuse without violating the civil rights of individuals. Thus, baseball's confrontation with the drug issue suggests that the problem is too pressing and complex to be dismissed by Commissioner Ueberroth's upbeat 1986 contention that his edicts had banished the problem.

Other major problems darkening baseball's prospects include soaring salaries; television's volatile presence; future expansion, with the accompanying problem of breakaway franchises; and festering disputes on the labor front, including a grievance filed by the players that alleges the existence of an owners' conspiracy to thwart the annual free-agent draft process. In all these problem areas, suspected greed is a common denominator, and players and owners are equally vulnerable to the charge. Greedy players, demanding ever-higher salaries, with some even refusing to sign autographs without being paid, pose a threat to fan support; so do greedy owners, some of whom exploit television advertisers, push for unfair tax advantages, and demand local subsidies under threats to move franchises. Such actions erode the game's credibility and cannot be solved by public-relations ploys. Rather, enlightened solutions to these and other problems of the game must come from a concerned meeting of minds representative of baseball's several constituencies, or else the possibility looms that government intervention might impose solutions. Moreover, the commissioner's role needs redefinition; in times like the present, some more creative posture than that of czar, or figurehead, or mouthpiece, is needed. As for Peter Ueberroth's avowed goal of reforming the post, opinion at the end of the 1986 season was divided over his leadership and his commitment to the task. Some, indeed, saw Ueberroth eyeing a political career, and were looking with renewed hopes to the newly elected National League president, A. Bartlett Giammati. As a former president of Yale University, perhaps this newcomer and avowed fan might become a force for inspired leadership.

Above all, baseball leaders would do well to consider their greatest asset: the devotion of the game's fans. Certainly the greatest challenge to baseball's continuing prosperity is to sustain such sturdy support. In order to keep the loyalty of fans amidst all the temptations of an affluent society, baseball leaders are challenged, as never before, to grow in wisdom and courage.

SOURCES

THE MAJOR SECONDARY SOURCES FOR THIS CHAPTER INCLUDE MY *American Baseball: From Gentleman's Sport to the Commissioner System* (1966, reprinted 1983) and *America Through Baseball* (1976); Ted Vincent, *Mudville's Revenge* (1981); Arthur Bartlett, *Baseball and Mr. Spalding* (1951); Wells Twombly, *200 Years of Sport in America: A Pageant of a Nation at Play* (1976); E. Phelps Brown and Margaret Browne, *A Century of Pay, 1860–1960* (1969); John A. Lucas and Ronald A. Smith, *The Saga of American Sport* (1978); and Peter Levine, *A. G. Spalding and the Rise of Baseball* (1985).

Among primary sources for this chapter, Albert G. Spalding, *America's National Game* (1911), and Francis C. Richter, *History and Records of Baseball* (1914), are basic. Others include Adrian C. Anson, *A Ball Player's Career* (1900); the *Proceedings of the National Association of Professional Base Ball Players* (1871); *DeWitt's Baseball Guide, 1872–77*; *Beadle's Dime Base Ball Player, 1871–77*; *Chadwick's Base Ball Manual, 1870–71*; and *Spalding's Official Base Ball Guide, 1877–80*. Also see such unpublished sources as Henry Chadwick's Scrapbooks, Harry Wright's Diary of a Baseball Manager, Wright's Note and Account Books, and Wright's Correspondence. The leading sporting weekly of this era was the *New York Clipper*.

CHAPTER 1:
IN THE BEGINNING
WERE THE PLAYERS

Major secondary sources for this chapter include my *American Baseball: From Gentleman's Sport to the Commissioner System* (1966, reprinted 1983) and *America Through Baseball* (1976); Ted Vincent, *Mudville's Revenge* (1981); Arthur Bartlett, *Baseball and Mr. Spalding* (1951); Lee Allen, *The National League Story* (1961); Harold Seymour, *Baseball, the Early Years* (1960); and Peter Levine, *A. G. Spalding and the Rise of Baseball* (1985).

Among primary sources are Albert G. Spalding, *America's National Game* (1911); Francis C. Richter, *A Brief History of Baseball* (1909); Adrian C. Anson, *A Ball Player's Career* (1900); Gustav Axelson, *"Commy": The Life Story of Charles A. Comiskey* (1919); N. Fred Pfeffer, *Scientific Baseball* (1889); Jacob Morse, *Sphere and Ash: History of Baseball* (1888); John M. Ward, *Base Ball: How to Become a Player* (1888); and Alfred H. Spink, *The National Game: A History of Baseball* (1910).

Among baseball guides and journals consulted are the *New York Clipper*, *The Sporting News*, *Sporting Life*, *Reach's Official Base Ball Guide*, *Spalding's Official Base Ball Guide*, and *Wright & Ditson's Base Ball Guide*. Records contained in these guides were official for the times; cautious supplementation can come from using the *Macmillan Baseball Encyclopedia*. Although the Macmillan book is more comprehensive than Hy Turkin and S. C. Thompson's *Official Encyclopedia of Baseball* (1956), the latter is far more faithful to the times.

Valuable unpublished sources in the New York Public Library's Spalding Collection include Henry Chadwick's Scrapbooks, Harry Wright's Diaries, Wright's Note and Account Books, and Wright's Correspondence.

CHAPTER 2:
THE GOLDEN 'EIGHTIES

Major secondary sources for this chapter include my *American Baseball: From Gentleman's Sport to the Commissioner System* (1966, reprinted 1983) and *America Through Baseball* (1976); Arthur Bartlett, *Baseball and Mr. Spalding* (1951); Lee Allen, *The National League Story* (1961); Harold Seymour, *Baseball, the Early Years* (1960); Lowell Reidenbaugh, *100 Years of National League Baseball* (1976); Fred Lieb, *The Baltimore Orioles* (1953); Ted Vincent, *Mudville's Revenge* (1981); Lee Lowenfish and Tony Lupien, *The Imperfect Diamond* (1980); John A. Lucas and Ronald A. Smith, *The Saga of American Sport* (1978); and Peter Levine, *A. G. Spalding and the Rise of Baseball* (1985).

Among the primary sources are Albert G. Spalding, *America's National Game* (1911); Adrian C. Anson, *A Ball Player's Career* (1900); Francis C. Richter, *A Brief History of Baseball* (1909); Alfred H. Spink, *The National Game* (1910); and John McGraw, *My Thirty Years in Baseball* (1923).

Among baseball guides and journals consulted are the *New York Clipper*; *The Sporting News*; *Sporting Life*; *Reach Guide*; *Spalding Guide*; *The Players National League Official*

CHAPTER 3:
THE WAYWARD
'NINETIES

Guide, 1890; Hy Turkin and S. C. Thompson's *Official Encyclopedia of Baseball* (1956); and *Sol White's Official Baseball Guide, 1907.*

Valuable unpublished sources in the New York Public Library's Spalding and Swales collections include Harry Wright's Note and Account Books and Correspondence.

Among official publications consulted is U.S. House of Representatives, *Organized Baseball,* Report No. 2002 to accompany H.R. 95, 82 Cong. 2 sess., 1952.

BENEATH THE MAJORS: THE PROFESSIONAL MINOR LEAGUES AND SEMI-PROS

Among many books available, the following are particularly useful: Richard E. Beverage, *The Angels: Los Angeles in the Pacific Coast League* (1981); Frank Dolson, *Beating the Bushes* (1982); Robert L. Finch et al., *The Story of Minor League Baseball* (1952); Pat Jordan, *A False Spring* (1975); Roger Kahn, *Good Enough to Dream* (1985); Bob Ryan, *Wait Till I Make the Show* (1974); Harold Seymour, *Baseball, the Golden Age* (1971); Society for American Baseball Research, *Minor League Baseball Stars,* I, II (1978, 1985); Hy Turkin and S. C. Thompson, *The Official Encyclopedia of Baseball* (1956); Robert Obojski, *Bush League: A History of Minor League Baseball* (1975); and Bill Heward, *Some Are Called Clowns: A Season with the Last of the Great Barnstorming Teams* (1974).

Among important articles are "The Tripartite Agreement," *Reach Guide* 1883; *Sporting Life,* Feb. 23, 1898.

CHAPTER 4: BASEBALL'S SILVER AGE

Major secondary sources for this chapter include my *American Baseball: From the Commissioners to Continental Expansion* (1970, reprinted 1983) and *America Through Baseball* (1976); Lee Allen, *The National League Story* (1961) and *The American League Story* (1962); Lowell Reidenbaugh, *100 Years of National League Baseball* (1976); Harold Seymour, *Baseball, the Golden Age* (1971); Eliot Asinof, *Eight Men Out: The Black Sox and the 1919 World Series* (1977); John D. McCallum, *Ty Cobb* (1975); James Kahn, *The Umpire Story* (1953); Richard Cohen et al., *The World Series* (1976); Steven A. Riess, *Touching Base: Professional Baseball and American Culture in the Progressive Era* (1980); G. H. Fleming, *The Unforgettable Season* (1981); Richard C. Crepeau, *Baseball: America's Diamond Mind, 1919–1941* (1980); and John W. Stayton, "Baseball Jurisprudence," *American Law Review,* May-June 1910.

Among the primary sources are Albert G. Spalding, *America's National Game* (1911); Lawrence S. Ritter, *The Glory of Their Times* (1966); John Holway, *Voices From the Great Black Baseball Leagues* (1975); John J. Evers and Hugh S. Fullerton, *Touching Second: The Science of Baseball* (1910); Gustav Axelson, *"Commy": The Life Story of Charles A. Comiskey* (1919); Grantland Rice, *The Tumult and the Shouting: My Life in Sports* (1954); Edward Barrow, *My 50 Years in Baseball* (1951); and Connie Mack, *My 66 Years in the Big Leagues* (1950).

Among baseball guides and journals consulted are *The Sporting News; Sporting Life; Baseball Magazine; Reach Guides; Spalding Guides;* Hy Turkin and S. C. Thompson, *Official Encyclopedia of Baseball;* and *Baseball Encyclopedia: The Official and Complete Record of Major League Baseball,* 1969 ed.

Official publications consulted include *The Federal Baseball Club of Baltimore, Inc. v. National League of Professional Base Ball Clubs and American League of Professional Base Ball Clubs;* 259 U.S. 200, 42 Supreme Court, 465; U.S. House of Representatives, *Organized Professional Team Sports,* Report No. 1720; 85 Cong., 2 sess., 1958; U.S. House of Representatives, *Organized Baseball,* Report No. 2002, 1952.

CHAPTER 5: THE BIG BANG ERA

Major secondary sources for this chapter include my *American Baseball: From the Commissioners to Continental Expansion* (1970, reprinted 1983); Lee Allen, *The National League Story* (1961) and *The American League Story* (1962); Harold Seymour, *Baseball, the Golden Age* (1971); Lowell Reidenbaugh, *100 Years of National League Baseball* (1976); Robert Peterson, *Only the Ball Was White* (1970); Ocania Chalk, *Pioneers of Black Sports* (1975); Marshall Smelser, *The Life That Ruth Built* (1975); Robert Creamer, *Babe, the Legend and the Life* (1974); James T. Farrell, *My Baseball Diary* (1957); Tom Meany, *Baseball's Greatest Teams* (1949); Sam Slote and Joe Cook, *It Sounds Impossible* (1963); J. G. Taylor Spink, *Judge Landis and Twenty Five Years of Baseball* (1947); Red

Barber, *The Broadcasters* (1970); and Richard C. Crepeau, *Baseball: America's Diamond Mind, 1919–1941* (1980).

Among the primary sources used are John Holway, *Voices From the Great Black Baseball Leagues* (1975); William Veeck and Ed Linn, *The Hustler's Handbook* (1965); Branch Rickey, *The American Diamond* (1965); Ed Barrow, *My 50 Years in Baseball* (1951); and Grantland Rice, *The Tumult and the Shouting* (1954).

Among baseball guides and journals consulted are *The Sporting News, Baseball Magazine, Reach Guide, Spalding Guide,* and *Baseball Encyclopedia,* 1969 ed.

Official publications include U.S. House of Representatives, *Organized Baseball,* 1952.

CHAPTER 6: SURMOUNTING DEPRESSION AND GLOBAL WAR

Major secondary sources include Richard C. Crepeau, *Baseball: America's Diamond Mind, 1919–1941* (1980); my *American Baseball: From the Commissioners to Continental Expansion* (1970, reprinted 1983); Lee Allen, *The National League Story* (1961), *The American League Story* (1962), and *The Hot Stove League* (1955); Lowell Reidenbaugh, *100 Years of National League Baseball* (1976); Robert Peterson, *Only the Ball Was White* (1970); Richard Cohen et al., *The World Series* (1976); James T. Farrell, *My Baseball Diary* (1957); Tom Meany, *Baseball's Greatest Teams* (1949); William B. Mead, *Even the Browns* (1978); Richard Goldstein, *Spartan Seasons: How Baseball Survived the Second World War* (1980); Paul Gallico, *Farewell to Sport* (1938); Arthur Mann, *Branch Rickey: American in Action* (1957); J. G. Taylor Spink, *Judge Landis and Twenty Five Years of Baseball* (1947); Robert Smith, *Baseball's Hall of Fame* (1965); Frank Graham, *The New York Giants* (1952) and *The New York Yankees* (1943); and E. Phelps Brown and Margaret Browne, *A Century of Pay, 1860–1960* (1969).

Among primary sources used are John Holway, *Voices From the Great Black Baseball Leagues* (1975); Bill Veeck and Ed Linn, *The Hustler's Handbook* (1965) and *Veeck as in Wreck* (1963); Branch Rickey, *The American Diamond* (1965); Ed Barrow, *My 50 Years in Baseball* (1951); Grantland Rice, *The Tumult and the Shouting* (1954); Leo Durocher and Ed Linn, *Nice Guys Finish Last* (1976); Leroy (Satchel) Paige and David Lipman, *Maybe I'll Pitch Forever* (1962); and Donald Honig, *Baseball When the Grass Was Real* (1976).

Among baseball guides and journals consulted are *The Sporting News; Baseball Magazine; Baseball Encyclopedia,* 1969 ed.; Hy Turkin and S. C. Thompson, *The Official Encyclopedia of Baseball; Reach Guides; Spalding Guides;* and *Spalding-Reach Official Baseball Guides.*

Official publications include U.S. House of Representatives, *Organized Baseball,* 1952; and *Organized Professional Team Sports,* 1958.

BEYOND THE PALE: THE BLACK MAJOR LEAGUES

Among many books available, the following are particularly useful: Richard Bardolph, *The Negro Vanguard* (1961); Janet Bruce, *The Kansas City Monarchs: Champions of Black Baseball* (1986); Ocania Chalk, *Pioneers of Black Sport* (1975); John Holway, *Voices From the Great Black Baseball Leagues* (1975); Effie Manley and Leon Hardwick, *Negro Baseball* (1976); Robert Peterson, *Only the Ball Was White* (1970); James A. Riley, *The All-Time All-Stars of Black Baseball* (1983); Donn Rogosin, *Invisible Men: Life in Baseball's Negro Leagues* (1985); Art Rust, Jr., *Get That Nigger Off the Field* (1976); Jules Tygiel, *Baseball's Great Experiment: Jackie Robinson and His Legacy* (1984); and Andrew Young, *Great Negro Baseball Stars and How They Made the Major Leagues* (1953).

Among useful articles are Robert Hoie, "All-Negro Minor League Team," *Baseball Research Journal,* (1979); John Holway, "Cuba's Black Diamond," *Baseball Research Journal,* 1981; Wm. J. Weiss, "First Negro in 20th Century OB," *Baseball Research Journal,* 1979; and Dick Clark and John Holway, "Charleston No. 1 Star of 1921 Negro League," *Baseball Research Journal,* 1985.

See Philip J. Lowry, *Green Cathedrals* (1986).

FROM FIELDS TO PARKS TO STADIUMS AND DOMES

CHAPTER 7:
POSTWAR PROSPERITY
AND PROGRESS

Major secondary sources for this chapter include my *American Baseball: From Postwar Expansion to the Electronic Age* (1983); Lee Allen, *The National League Story* (1961), *The American League Story* (1962), and *The Hot Stove League* (1955); Lowell Reidenbaugh, *100 Years of National League Baseball* (1976); Richard Cohen et al., *The World Series* (1976); Arthur Mann, *Baseball Confidential* (1951); Richard Bardolph, *The Negro Vanguard* (1961); Peter Golenbock, *Dynasty* (1975); Roger Kahn, *The Boys of Summer* (1973); Robert Obojski, *Bush League: A History of Minor League Baseball* (1975); Harold Parrott, *The Lords of Baseball* (1975); Joe Reichler, *30 Years of Baseball's Great Moments* (1974); Harold Rosenthal, *The Best 10 Years of Baseball* (1979); Bob Ryan, *Wait Till I Make the Show: Baseball in the Minor Leagues* (1974); Stan Woodward, *Sports Page* (1949); Paul Zimmerman, *The Los Angeles Dodgers* (1960); Jules Tygiel, *Baseball's Great Experiment: Jackie Robinson and His Legacy* (1984); Walter (Red) Barber, *The Year All Hell Broke Loose in Baseball* (1932); and Paul Gregory, *The Baseball Player: An Economic Study* (1956).

Among primary sources used are Bill Veeck and Ed Linn, *The Hustler's Handbook* (1965) and *Veeck as in Wreck* (1963); Branch Rickey, *The American Diamond* (1965); Leo Durocher and Ed Linn, *Nice Guys Finish Last* (1976); Ford C. Frick, *Games, Asterisks, and People: Memoirs of a Lucky Fan* (1973); Larry R. Gerlach, *The Men in Blue* (1980); Shirley Povich, *All These Mornings* (1969); Jackie Robinson with Al Duckett, *I Never Had It Made: An Autobiography* (1972); and Ted Williams with Tom Underwood, *My Turn at Bat: The Story of My Life* (1968).

Among baseball guides and journals consulted are *The Sporting News; Baseball Digest; Baseball Magazine; Sports Illustrated; Baseball Encyclopedia*, 1969 ed.; and *Official Baseball Register*, 1960.

Official publications include U.S. House of Representatives, *Organized Baseball*, 1952; *Organized Professional Team Sports*, 1958; *Telecasting of Professional Sports Contests*, House Report, No. 1087, 87th Congress, 1st sess., Aug. 1961.

Unpublished materials include Lee Allen, Notebooks (Hall of Fame Library, Cooperstown, New York); and A. B. Chandler, Unpublished Papers (University of Kentucky Library).

CHAPTER 8:
THE EXPANSIVE 'SIXTIES

Major sources for this chapter include my *American Baseball: From Postwar Expansion to the Electronic Age* (1983); Lowell Reidenbaugh, *100 Years of National League Baseball* (1976); Richard Cohen et al., *The World Series* (1976); Peter Golenbock, *Dynasty* (1975); Bob Ryan, *Wait Till I Make the Show* (1974); Paul Zimmerman, *The Los Angeles Dodgers* (1960); Lee Lowenfish and Tony Lupien, *The Imperfect Diamond* (1980); Walter Alston and Si Burick, *Alston and the Dodgers* (1966); Jim Brosnan, *Pennant Race* (1962); Ralph Andreano, *No Joy in Mudville* (1965); Red Barber, *The Broadcasters* (1970); Gordon Beard, *Birds on the Wing: The Story of the Baltimore Orioles* (1967); Leonard Koppett, *The Thinking Man's Guide to Baseball* (1967); Jack Mann, *The Decline and Fall of the New York Yankees* (1967); Bill Shannon and George Kalinsky, *The Ballparks* (1975); E. Phelps Brown and Margaret Browne, *A Century of Pay, 1860–1960* (1968); and Robert H. Salisbury, "Betrayed by Baseball," *Washington University Magazine*, Summer 1985.

Among other primary sources used are Leo Durocher and Ed Linn, *Nice Guys Finish Last* (1976); Ford Frick, *Games, Asterisks, and People* (1973); Larry Gerlach, *The Men in Blue* (1980); Jerome Holtzman, *No Cheering in the Pressbox* (1975); Donald Honig, *The Man in the Dugout* (1977); Mickey Mantle and Bob Smith, *Mickey Mantle: The Education of a Baseball Player* (1967); Joe Pepitone with Barry Steinback, *Joe, You Coulda Made Us Proud* (1976); Tony Oliva with Bob Fowler, *Tony O!* (1973); Brooks Robinson with Jack Tobin, *Third Base Is My Home* (1974); Shelby Whitfield, *Kiss It Goodbye* (1973); and Harold Parrott, *The Lords of Baseball* (1975).

Among baseball guides and journals consulted are *The Sporting News; Baseball Digest; Sports Illustrated; Baseball Encyclopedia*, 1969; and *Official Baseball Registers*.

Unpublished materials include Rudolf K. Haerle, "Member of the Team, But Uniquely Alone: A Sociological Analysis of the Professional Baseball Player," MS., 1974; Steven Riess, "Civic Financed Stadiums," paper read before meeting of the North American Society for Sports History, May 1980.

Secondary sources for this chapter include my *American Baseball: From Postwar Expansion to the Electronic Age* (1983); Lowell Reidenbaugh, *100 Years of National League Baseball* (1976); Richard Cohen et al., *The World Series* (1976); Lee Lowenfish and Tony Lupien, *The Imperfect Diamond* (1980); Roger Angell, *Five Seasons: A Baseball Companion* (1978) and *The Summer Game* (1972); Tom Clark, *Champagne and Baloney: The Rise and Fall of Finley's A's* (1976); Anton Graboni, *Guide to Baseball Literature* (1975); John Kuenster, ed., *From Cobb to Catfish* (1975); Jeanne Parr, *The Superwives* (1976); Lou Sahadi, *The Year of the Yankees* (1979); Russell Schneider, *Frank Robinson: The Making of a Manager* (1976); Bert Sugar, *"The Thrill of Victory": The Inside Story of ABC Sports* (1978); Kal Wagenheim, *Clemente* (1974); Maury Allen, *The Incredible Mets* (1969); Arnold Beisser, *The Madness in Sports* (1967); Joseph Durso, *Amazing: The Miracle of the Mets* (1970); Don Kowet, *The Rich Who Own Sports* (1977); James A. Michener, *Sports in America* (1976); Philip J. Lowry, *Green Cathedrals* (1986); and David N. Laband and Bernard F. Lentz, *The Roots of Success* (1985).

Among primary sources used are Larry Gerlach, *The Men in Blue* (1980); Jim Bouton with Len Shecter, *Ball Four* (1970) and *I'm Glad You Didn't Take It Personally* (1971); Curt Flood with Richard Carter, *The Way It Is* (1971); Bill Freehan with Steve Lilman and Dick Schaap, *Behind the Mask: An Inside Baseball Diary* (1976); Tom Gorman with Jerome Holtzman, *Three and Two* (1979); Lee Gutkind, *The Best Seat in Baseball, But You Have to Stand* (1975); Reggie Jackson with Bill Libby, *Reggie* (1975); Sparky Lyle and Peter Golenbock, *The Bronx Zoo* (1979); Denny McLain with Dave Diles, *Nobody's Perfect* (1975); Gaylord Perry, *Me and the Spitter* (1974); Bob Woolf, *Behind Closed Doors* (1976); and Fred Lieb, *Baseball As I Have Known It* (1977).

Among baseball guides and journals consulted are *The Sporting News; Baseball Digest; Sports Illustrated; Baseball Encyclopedia, 1976, 1982; Official Baseball Registers; Baseball; Baseball Bulletin; Baseball Quarterly; Baseball Research Journal; Journal of Sports History; Sport;* and *Baseball Dope Book, 1980.*

Official publications include *Basic Agreement Between the American League of Professional Baseball Clubs and the National League of Professional Baseball Clubs and Major League Baseball Players Association,* Effective Jan. 1, 1976.

Among the few available works, the following are especially useful: David Anderson, "All-Time College All-Stars," *Baseball Research Journal,* 1983; National Baseball Congress, *50 Years: The National Baseball Congress Tournament* (1985 publication); Ronald Smith, *History of Intercollegiate Athletics* (manuscript of forthcoming book); Hy Turkin and S. C. Thompson, *The Official Encyclopedia of Baseball* (1956); Harold H. Wolf, *The History of Intercollegiate Baseball* (Columbia University, 1962 Ed.D. Dissertation, available via University of Michigan Microfilms); John A. Lucas and Ronald A. Smith, *The Saga of American Sport* (1978); and Marque Winters, *Professional Sports: The Community College Connection* (1982).

Secondary sources for this chapter include my *American Baseball: From Postwar Expansion to the Electronic Age* (1983); Roger Angell, *Late Innings: A Baseball Companion* (1982); Tom Boswell, *How Life Imitates the World Series: An Inquiry into the Game* (1982); Reggie Jackson with Mike Lupica, *Reggie: The Autobiography* (1985); Kevin Kerrane, *Dollar Sign on the Muscle: The World of Baseball Scouting* (1984); Dick Schaap, *Steinbrenner* (1982); and Peter Ueberroth with R. Levin and A. Quinn, *Made in America* (1985).

Among baseball guides and journals consulted are *The Sporting News; Baseball Digest; Sports Illustrated; Official Baseball Registers;* and *Sport.*

For Marvin Miller's exit interview, see *New York Times,* Jan. 2, 1983, Feb. 12, 1983; and *Philadelphia Inquirer,* Jan. 16, 1983.

CHAPTER 9: THE SOARING 'SEVENTIES

BELOW THE SALT: COLLEGIATE BASEBALL AND OTHER AMATEUR FORMS

CHAPTER 10: AFTERWORD: THE ENIGMATIC 'EIGHTIES

PHOTO CREDITS

The photographs in this book are from individual collectors and institutional collections; all of these sources graciously permitted the reproduction of photographs used in this work. Photos are listed by page numbers and letters that indicate positions on the page—alphabetically arranged, reading first left to right, then top to bottom.

Individual Collectors

Mike Andersen: 106b, 169a, 179a, 227b
Author's collection: 20a, 24a, 25a, 42a, 44a, 55a, 60ac, 71bc, 73a, 80abcd, 81abc, 117a, 118a, 126a, 132a, 141a, 182b, 184a, 188b, 227a, 236c, 237a, 244a, 266ab, 267a, 286a, 317b, 319a, 365a, 366ab
George Brace: 116a, 130b, 133a, 134a, 135ab, 143a, 161a, 184b, 185a, 186a
Charles Burkhardt: 58a, 59a, 62a, 63a, 75a, 105b, 106a, 151a, 152b, 157a, 193a, 224a
Dennis Goldstein: 14a, 20b, 30a, 56a, 71a, 72a, 77a, 83a, 106c, 123a, 124a, 127b, 139a, 140b, 149a, 153a, 155b, 158a, 160a, 171a, 173ab, 177ab, 179b, 187a, 192a, 203a, 204a, 236a, 251a, 254b, 255a, 265a, 328a, 330a
John Lucas and Ron Smith: 13a, 16b, 32a, 64a, 65a, 68a, 327a, 328b
Eugene G. McGillicuddy, Jr.: 208a, 209a
Ray Medeiros: 97a
Ron Menchine: 92a, 93a
Gordon Miller: 122a, 130a, 140a, 253a, 262ab, 263ab
Mike Mumby: 99a, 100a, 131a, 152a, 154a, 155a, 170b, 178ab, 182a, 185b, 188a, 229b, 254a
Paul Roedig: 264a
Jim Rowe: 308b
Herman Seid: 144b, 170a, 172ab, 174a, 175a, 180a, 250a
Ron Smith: 48a, 79a, 90a, 91a, 95a, 96a, 98a, 142a, 197a, 315b, 329a
John Thorn: 26a, 27a, 31a, 37a, 46a, 47a, 52a, 53a, 60b, 84a, 89a, 114a, 115a, 125a, 126b, 143b, 156a, 181a, 191a, 195a, 204b, 205a, 223a, 224b, 232b, 237b, 241ab, 243a, 247b, 252ab, 281a, 305a, 312b, 321ab

Institutional Collections

A. G. Spalding & Bros.: 105a, 108ab
American Broadcasting Co.: 217a
Boston Herald: 369a, 371a, 372a, 373a, 374a, 375a
Boston Public Library: 43a, 49a, 70a, 76a, 119a, 120a, 136a
Detroit News: 150a
Harvard University Archives: 331b
Library of Congress: 79a, 90a, 91a, 94a, 95a, 129a, 145a, 331a, 332a
Little League Baseball: 333ab
National Baseball Library (Cooperstown, N.Y.): 14b, 16a, 19a, 21a, 22a, 41a, 45a, 66a, 105c, 107a, 121a, 127a, 128a, 132b, 138a, 144a, 147a, 148ab, 190a, 225a, 234a, 245a
Newman-Schmidt Studios, Pittsburgh, Pa.: 286b
New York Daily News: 352a, 368a, 378a, 379a, 380a, 381a, 382a
New York Historical Society: 50a, 51a, 53b
New York Public Library: 15a, 17a, 29a, 109a, 137a, 196a, 198a, 199a, 200a, 201a, 202a, 203b, 207a

New York Times: 226a
Office of the Baseball Commissioner: 258a
Pittsburgh Courier: 197a
Rawlings Sporting Goods Co.: 110abc
Smithsonian Institution: 146a
Temple University Libraries: 151b, 167a, 183a, 283a, 300a, 301a, 304a, 325a
The Sporting News: 118a, 318b
University of Miami: 334abc

Baseball Clubs

Atlanta Braves: 210a, 238a, 293a, 357b
Baltimore Orioles: 214a, 271abc, 292a, 308a, 358a
Boston Red Sox: 214b, 272a, 273a, 274a, 313a, 359a
California Angels: 214c, 316c, 360a, 367a
Chicago Cubs: 210b, 249a, 357a
Chicago White Sox: 141b, 215a, 344a, 345a
Cincinnati Reds: 210c, 288a, 290b, 291a, 349a
Cleveland Indians: 215b, 234b, 235a, 248b
Detroit Tigers: 215c, 273bcd, 303b, 347a, 348a
Houston Astros: 211a, 350a
Kansas City Royals: 101a, 216a, 351a, 364a
Los Angeles Dodgers: 211b, 238b, 239a, 242b, 243b, 249b, 257a, 259a, 260b, 279a,
    294a, 295a, 296ab, 297a, 298a, 302ab
Milwaukee Brewers: 216b, 269a, 270a, 278a, 307a, 361a
Montreal Royals: 211c
New York Mets: 212a, 285a, 318a, 320a, 362a
New York Yankees: 217b, 229a, 230a, 231a, 232a, 233a, 234c, 236b, 268a, 276a,
    292b, 314a, 315a, 316a, 322a, 340a, 358b, 365b
Oakland Athletics: 217a, 275a, 309a, 310a, 311a, 312a
Philadelphia Phillies: 212b, 240a, 277a, 305bc, 346a
Pittsburgh Pirates: 212c, 246a, 247a, 280a, 287a, 289a, 290a, 291b, 299a, 303a
St. Louis Cardinals: 213a, 353ab
San Diego Padres: 213b, 363a
San Francisco Giants: 213c, 241c, 242a, 248a, 260a, 261a, 354a
Seattle Mariners: 217c, 323a
Texas Rangers: 218a, 306a
Toronto Blue Jays: 218b

INDEX

PIRATES

Dodgers

SAN FRANCISCO
GIANTS

SOX
CHICAGO
WHITE SOX